THE LAST TIFFANY

Michael John Burlingham

THE LAST TIFFANY

A BIOGRAPHY OF

Dorothy Tiffany Burlingham

ATHENEUM NEW YORK 1989

Atheneum
Macmillan Publishing Company
866 Third Avenue, New York, N.Y. 10022
Collier Macmillan Canada, Inc.

Library of Congress Cataloging-in-Publication Data
Burlingham, Michael John.
The last Tiffany.
Bibliography: p.
Includes index.
1. Burlingham, Dorothy.
2. Women psychotherapists—United States—Biography.
I. Title.
RC339.52.B86B87   1989   616.89'14'0924   [B]88-34408
ISBN 0-689-11870-8

Macmillan books are available at special discounts for
bulk purchases for sales promotions, premiums, fund-raising,
or educational use. For details, contact:
Special Sales Director
Macmillan Publishing Company
866 Third Avenue
New York, N.Y. 10022

10 9 8 7 6 5 4 3 2 1

Printed in the United States of America

To my wife, Roseanne

Contents

Illustrations

Laurelton Hall. *Courtesy of the Tiffany Family Archives.*

Dorothy and Bob, 1915. Photograph by W. S. Ritch. *(Author's collection)*

Robert Burlingham with Mabbie and Bob. *Courtesy of Timothy Schmiderer.*

BETWEEN PAGES 268 AND 269

Dorothy in Vienna, 1925. Photograph by Franz Löwy. *Courtesy of Timothy Schmiderer.*

With "The Four." Photograph by Ingret Atelier. *Courtesy of Katrina Burlingham Valenstein.*

The Burlinghams at Semmering, 1928. *Courtesy of Timothy Schmiderer.*

Anna Freud. Photograph by Max Halberstadt. *(Author's collection)*

With the Freuds. *Courtesy of Timothy Schmiderer.*

Dorothy and Anna with Alfred de Forest. Photograph by Max Halberstadt. *Courtesy of W. Ernest Freud.*

Berchtesgaden, 1929. Photograph by Max Halberstadt. *Courtesy of W. Ernest Freud.*

Bob Burlingham. Photograph by Max Halberstadt. *Courtesy of Timothy Schmiderer.*

Mikey and Mabbie. Photograph by Max Halberstadt. *Courtesy of Timothy Schmiderer.*

Tinky. Photograph by Max Halberstadt. *Courtesy of Timothy Schmiderer.*

Robert Burlingham, 1927. Portrait by Erik H. Erikson. *(Author's collection)*

Charles Culp Burlingham, 1931. Photograph by Kaiden Kazanjian. *(Author's collection)*

At Black Point, 1933. *Courtesy of Timothy Schmiderer.*

Acknowledgments

No one was more helpful to my family research than Dorothy Burlingham herself. My interviews and correspondence with her were essential, and, at the conclusion of our second and final round of discussions in October of 1979, she presented me with a suitcase filled with Tiffany family memorabilia. Helpful, also, to my informational search was Grandmother's introduction to her niece, Louise Lusk Platt, whose unflagging love for and devotion to her grandfather had led her to preserve many Tiffany family letters, albums, and other documents which she kindly shared with me. Grandmother's nephew Rodman Gilder and niece Helena Gilder Miller were also generous with their Tiffany memorabilia, and their assistance is likewise greatly appreciated. Over the years I met many more individuals than is possible to name here to whom I am indebted for broadening my appreciation and understanding of the Tiffanys and their work. However, I would specifically like to thank Hugh F. McKean, who, together with his wife, Jeannette, have assembled the fine and extensive collection of Tiffany glass housed in the Morse Gallery of Art, Winter Park, Florida. And, for her many kindnesses and good-natured assistance over the years, I must also thank Lillian Nassau Palitz.

My cousin Timothy Schmiderer deepened my understanding of the Burlinghams in allowing me to mine the contents of what the family calls "C.C.B.'s trunk"—literally a steamer trunk loaded with Burlingham family memorabilia which Tim's mother, Mabbie, saved from annihilation in 1959, following her grandfather's death. And, for the memorabilia of Dorothy Burlingham herself, I am indebted to my aunt Tinky—Katrina Burlingham Valenstein.

For encouraging me to write this book, I am indebted to two friends, Robert Gottesman and Mark Epstein; to the former I am also grateful for his help with my book proposal and for mentioning the project to my editor at Atheneum, Susan Leon; to the latter for his editorial suggestions on the completed manuscript. Thanks, also, to Harvey Simmonds, a long-standing family friend, for skillfully editing my book proposal. For editorial help with the manuscript I am further indebted to my cousin Grace Warnecke, who blue-penciled the early chapters of several drafts, and to her father, George F. Kennan, who commented on the first two chapters of the first draft. Aunt Tinky faithfully read and reported on each draft as I completed it, considerably strengthening the final result, though, I must add, without agreeing with all that I had to say. Also, my wife, Roseanne, did me the necessary, taxing service of listening to virtually every word—and offering comments.

The profuse thanks which some writers reserve for their editors has, I confess, at times left me skeptical. But I no longer doubt, having experienced myself that gushing feeling of gratitude that comes with being helped to say better what one had wanted or intended to say. Susan Leon did this for me in the most firm and friendly spirit, and frequently under circumstance of no small pressure. I am fortunate indeed: my agent at William Morris, Michael V. Carlisle, to whom I was introduced by Grace Warnecke, has also been a thoroughly professional and loyal friend. And for the appearance of this book I am indebted to my cousin Dorothy Schmiderer Baker, who happily consented to do the design.

The notes reveal the names of those individuals who granted me one or more interviews, or whose correspondence furnished me with information, without which this book could not have been written. To them all a collective but heartfelt thanks. Finally, I would like to thank my mother, Rigmor S. Sheldrick, who taught me that the past held lessons which were important to learn.

M.J.B.

New York City
October 1988

Foreword

This is a biography of my paternal grandmother, Dorothy Burlingham, the last-born child of glass artist Louis Comfort Tiffany and the closest friend and colleague of Anna Freud, the daughter of Sigmund Freud. The impetus for this book was, however, the death of my father, Bob Burlingham, of a heart attack, in London, on January 25, 1970. At that time I was a senior in high school, and typically uninterested in my roots. My parents had divorced seven years earlier, and my mother had moved with us children from London to Princeton, New Jersey, where my mother's sister took us under her wing. After that I seldom saw my father, as he remained in England. I was nevertheless surprised at myself when his death left me emotionally unaffected. I remember actually trying to cry, thinking it would be better for me if I did. I loved my father deeply, but his psychological problems had often made him a remote figure, even in my childhood, and his death terminated a relationship marked as much by his absences, physical and otherwise, as his presence.

The years of college passed without much thought of him, but after graduation I began to feel the void in my life which my father had left. This expressed itself indirectly in a curiosity about my paternal ancestry. My interest gradually grew consuming and was, I now believe, a testament to the fine qualities in my father's character.

My father's paternal grandfather, Charles Culp Burlingham, was the first subject of my research. A New York–based admiralty lawyer, he had been a reformer behind the scenes both regionally and nationally for over sixty years. I simply went to the library and photocopied every mention of him that appeared in the *New York Times* between 1895 and 1959, the year of his death, at age one hundred.

Although I had majored in English composition in college, I then had no compelling subject to write about, and I impetuously decided to go to graduate school in filmmaking. I was accepted to the UCLA Department of Motion Pictures and, in that year of realizing that Hollywood was not for me, I researched and wrote a short documentary filmscript on my father's maternal grandfather, Louis Tiffany. Returning east in 1976, I expanded the script to forty-five pages and sent a copy to my grandmother in London. By this time my father's sister, whom we all called Mabbie, had met a tragic fate, and my correspondence with Grandmother had found a deeper level. To my surprise she liked my script and invited me to visit her in London, writing, "I realize that I am the last of the family who could give you information which might be of value to you."

She was nearly eighty-six years old, completely lucid, and more shadowy a figure to me than my father had been. Since Sigmund Freud's death in 1939, Grandmother had lived at 20 Maresfield Gardens with Anna Freud and together they had run the Hampstead Child Therapy Course and Clinic. As a child, however, her background and association with the Freuds had meant little to me. She was by nature reserved, and also greatly occupied with her work. After my years in London we saw little of one another, and my view of her was colored by resentments within the family. As a result, Grandmother was to me a somewhat frightening, though clearly important, person in our life, and this image of her remained with me until the summer of 1978, when I visited London for the specific purpose of conducting a series of formal interviews about her father. Somehow, in the historic atmosphere of the Sigmund Freud house, the idea of interviewing one's own grandmother seemed entirely appropriate.

It is sobering to realize that if not for my interest in her father, I might not have visited Grandmother before her death, and been left with my childish impression of her. I returned the following fall with my wife, Roseanne, for a second round of interviews. Again we talked about Louis Tiffany, but discussed the wider family as well, and gradually, without half realizing it, Grandmother's own life became the focus of our discussion. In retrospect this was inevitable since, I later realized, her personality and her life had fatefully linked the Tiffanys, Burlinghams, and Freuds. It was on the plane heading homeward that I decided to write this book, though it was another four years before I set pen to paper. Grandmother died a few weeks after my second visit—it seemed to us, after marshaling her last energies for our talks.

M.J.B.

New York City,
May 1988

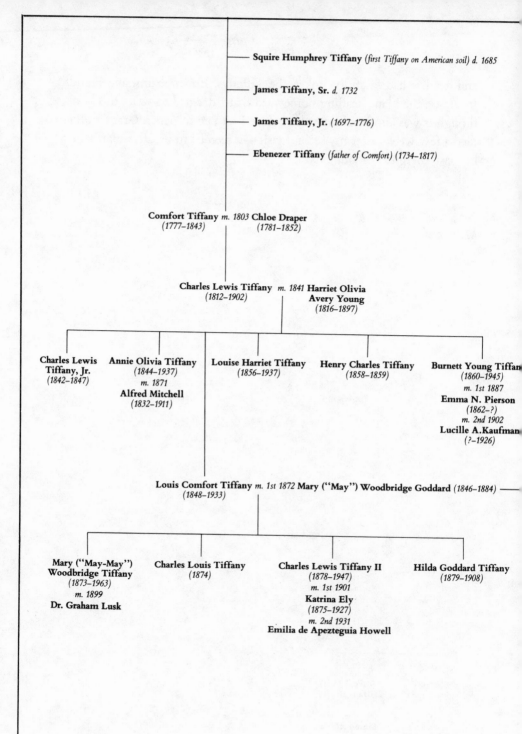

Squire Humphrey Tiffany *(first Tiffany on American soil) d. 1685*

James Tiffany, Sr. *d. 1732*

James Tiffany, Jr. *(1697–1776)*

Ebenezer Tiffany *(father of Comfort) (1734–1817)*

Comfort Tiffany *m. 1803* Chloe Draper
(1777–1843) *(1781–1852)*

Charles Lewis Tiffany *m. 1841* Harriet Olivia
(1812–1902) Avery Young
(1816–1897)

Charles Lewis
Tiffany, Jr.
(1842–1847)

Annie Olivia Tiffany
(1844–1937)
m. 1871
Alfred Mitchell
(1832–1911)

Louise Harriet Tiffany
(1856–1937)

Henry Charles Tiffany
(1858–1859)

Burnett Young Tiffany
(1860–1945)
m. 1st 1887
Emma N. Pierson
(1862–?)
m. 2nd 1902
Lucille A.Kaufman
(?–1926)

Louis Comfort Tiffany *m. 1st 1872* Mary (''May'') Woodbridge Goddard *(1846–1884)*
(1848–1933)

Mary (''May-May'')
Woodbridge Tiffany
(1873–1963)
m. 1899
Dr. Graham Lusk

Charles Louis Tiffany
(1874)

Charles Lewis Tiffany II
(1878–1947)
m. 1st 1901
Katrina Ely
(1875–1927)
m. 2nd 1931
Emilia de Apezteguia Howell

Hilda Goddard Tiffany
(1879–1908)

Charles Culp Burlingham *m. 1883* **Louisa Weed Lawrence**
(1858–1959)   *(1863–1937)*

Charles Burlingham
(1884–1979)
m. 1929
Cora Weir Carlin

Anne ("Nancy")
Hoe Burlingham
(1886–1974)

m. 2nd 1886 **Louise Wakeman Knox** *(1851–1904)*

Louise Comfort Tiffany
(1887–1974)
m. 1911
Rodman Gilder
(1877–1953)

Julia de Forest Tiffany
(1887–1973)
m. 1st 1910
Gurdon Satterstall Parker
m. 2nd 1929
Francis Minot Weld

Annie Olivia Tiffany
(1888–1892)

Dorothy Trimble Tiffany
(1891–1979)
m. 1914
Dr. Robert Burlingham
(1888–1938)

Robert ("Bob")
Burlingham, Jr.
(1915–1970)
m. 1st 1939
Rigmor Sørensen
m. 2nd 1964
Annette Müller

Mary ("Mabbie")
Tiffany Burlingham
(1917–1974)
m. 1938
Simon Schmiderer

Katrina ("Tinky")
Ely Burlingham
(1919–)
m. 1st 1943
Peter Heller
m. 2nd 1958
Dr. Arthur Valenstein

Michael ("Mikey")
Burlingham
(1921–)
m. 1st 1946
Sara Ruth Reid
m. 2nd 1978
Suzanne Bourg

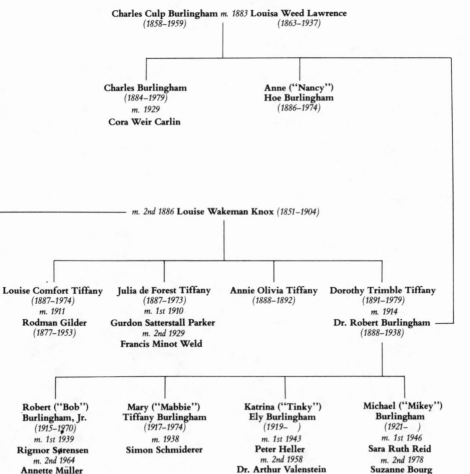

I

The Tiffany Imperative

Dorothy Trimble Tiffany was born to splendor in the Tiffany mansion in Manhattan. Outside the air was crisp with the change of season, and scented with falling leaves. The Clydesdales lathered as they dragged horsecars up the Avenue of the Gods, where, at the summit of Lenox Hill, beneath the soaring Roman brick edifice, the cock horse was unhitched and walked back down the hill.

Dorothy may have been born in the same attic sewing room where, twelve years later, her sisters were sent to be spared the awful sounds of their mother dying. Infrequently used for school and piano lessons as well as sewing, it was a dark, small room with a rickety table, a torn rug, plain chairs, and an upright Steinway. Nestled under the mansion's slate roof, removed from the living quarters by two flights of blue-carpeted stairs, the room could well absorb throes of death or birth.

On October 11, 1891, the groans sounding within the Tiffany mansion had, perhaps, a hopeful ring. At forty, Louise Knox Tiffany was bearing another child. For her husband, glass master Louis Comfort Tiffany, this was to be his seventh, and his last. His first marriage had produced two daughters but only one son, and Louise—Mama Lou—had borne him three more daughters. Papa Louis's elder sister, Annie, had a brace of girls, and was past childbearing. His younger sister, Louise, was a spinster, and Burnie, the youngest sibling, had recently hired a detective to obtain evidence for a divorce from his wife. The family thus saw it as fortunate that Burnie was childless. In short the Tiffanys had but one male heir, and they placed fervent hopes on a boy.

In fact, the entire prospect of perpetuating the Tiffany name rested on the thread of a boy who once had contracted a severe case of mumps, a disease which can induce sterility. Of Mama Lou's three girls, Louise Comfort, one of firstborn identical twins, would have had her father's name but for one letter. And, if this reflected the desire for a son back in 1887, what must have been Louis's expectations four years later, with a total of five daughters and but one son, in an era that equated femininity, among other things, with weakness? As it happened, the quirk of Dorothy's sex consigned her branch of the Tiffany family to extinction, while their chauvinism impacted on her in a separate way. This last-born Tiffany would also be the last Tiffany—in body and in spirit.

Whatever name had been chosen for a son was quickly discarded, and a lack of enthusiasm for naming another girl may be seen in the task falling to May-May, Papa Louis's eldest child. At eighteen May-May was like a second mother to her half-sisters, a warm and loving protectress. Her choice of the name Dorothy Trimble is intriguing because neither name had a family precedent. May-May (Mary) had been given the name of her mother, Mary Woodbridge Goddard; her brother, Charles, the name of his grandfather, and the youngest, Hilda Goddard, her mother's maiden name. Of Mama Lou's girls, Louise Comfort had the names of her mother and her great-grandfather, Julia de Forest the name of her mother's cousin, and Annie Olivia the name of her father's elder sister. Never had there been a Dorothy or a Trimble Tiffany. One explanation is that Dorothy resembled no one else in the family, or so it was said, and said so often that she never forgot it. Subliminally she was informed that she did not belong as did the others.

In many respects Dorothy did appear a Tiffany, small and olive skinned, with dark brown hair and thick dramatic eyebrows. An early photograph shows her happily dismembering a daisy, a trick her plant-loving papa would discourage. Her hair was fine, her features alert and responsive. But what the black and white print cannot show is that her eyes, large, expressive, and brilliant, were not blue like her father's and grandfather's, but brown. So perhaps it was her eyes; the character reflected in those eyes was different too.

In May-May's choice of names, also, is something of the emotions of a young society girl. Trimble is straightforward enough; from the inscription in a book in Hilda's library we know that Mrs. Trimble was a family friend. But the derivation of the name Dorothy is decidedly romantic. It was the name given the heroine of a novel called *Benefits Forgot,* by (Charles) Wolcott Balestier. Though not serialized until December 1892 in the *Century* magazine, the day's leading literary forum, May-May had probably read the manuscript by the time of Dorothy's birth, since it had been completed two years earlier and she was intimate with Wolcott's sister Josephine Balestier, a fellow student at the Brearley School. Without forcing significance on the matter, May-May might also have admired or identified with the fictional Dorothy's quiet determination, which caused her to utter lines like, "You don't understand, Papa . . . I shall never marry Mr. Deed."

More interesting, perhaps, is the Tiffanys' connection to the social and artistic worlds in which Dorothy's name was spawned. Josephine Balestier had left New York after graduation to join her brother in London, where he, as representative of the American publisher Lovell & Company, could offer introductions to the cream of British society. At her age the prospect was especially thrilling, and she shared all of it with May-May. Fascinating missives arrived at 7 East 72nd Street from Chale on the Isle of Wight and Cavendish Square in London. In one rapturous passage Josephine gushed, "I find invitations for every day this week. Grand finale—theatre with W. and Henry James Sat. Eve. Hurrah!"

According to Edmund Gosse, the British critic, James was Wolcott Balestier's "closest and most valued friend" in England; Rudyard Kipling was soon to marry Wolcott's other sister, Carrie. James prefaced Wolcott's *The Average Woman,* and Kipling coauthored *The Naulahka: A Story of West and East* with his brother-in-law. Through Wolcott, Josephine also met the pre-Raphaelite painter Dante Gabriel Rossetti and Hamo Thornycroft, whom she rashly declared "the greatest living sculptor." This web of artistic and literary relationships crossed the Tiffanys at least twice more. Mama Lou's cousin Lockwood de Forest had met the Kiplings in 1882 while establishing an export business in Ahmadabad; also, the editor in chief of the *Century* was Richard Watson Gilder, Papa Louis's good friend. Victorian society was a small and exclusive club.

If Dorothy's name reflected May-May's and Josephine's effervescent response to their luminary world, that world was shrouded less than two months after her birth. On December 6, in Dresden on business, Wolcott died of typhus. Three weeks later Josephine wrote on mourning paper,

"My life is broken. Wolcott and I one; without him I am blind and dumb and crippled." Later, she managed to add, "I am so pleased about the little one's—the *littlest* one's—name. Dorothy Trimble Tiffany is beautiful. Wolcott was very proud of 'Dorothy.' "

At this point there is little reason to proceed further with Dorothy, whose import begins with her reaction *to* her family. Physically unlike her siblings, in later years she would act out a separatist role. At its end, her personal history would reflect, as would none of her siblings', her generation's wrenching lurch into the twentieth century. To appreciate this, however, we should know the family from which she sprang, the character of her grandfather and his influence on her father, and her father's character and his influence on her. The manner in which the Tiffanys influenced Dorothy is the subject of later chapters; but what is important to understand now is that the motivational force behind the family's achievements was probably the single most decisive factor in Dorothy's development.

That motivational force was, in a phrase, the Tiffany imperative: a dynamic tension in her progenitors, usually the eldest male, stoked by the obligation to honor the father, on the one hand, and the urge to surpass him, on the other. Dorothy's grandfather had risen to it; her great-grandfather had also; with the decade her father would soar higher than either of them.

The means by which the Tiffanys realized their ambition seems to have been an uncanny knack for divining the mood, taste, and fashion of the times. This gift had made Dorothy's grandfather, Charles Lewis Tiffany, "King of Diamonds," as it was making her father "Rebel in Glass." Her father's early work in glass had coincided with a dramatic increase in demand for church windows. Twenty years later, as America entered the so-called stained-glass decades, Louis Comfort Tiffany was a glass master. In this way he came to symbolize his age, as had his father the gaslight era before him.

We leave Dorothy, then, in her infancy, surrounded by her mother, sisters, cousins, aunts, nursemaids, and nannies. Her physical needs were admirably met, and yet, somehow, she was a lonely, unhappy child. We will return to Dorothy later, in her first and formative decade, a decade that coincided with the Tiffanys' greatest influence.

B y 1891, Charles Lewis Tiffany was approaching his eightieth birthday, and was still the undisputed leader of his family and business. He walked to work each morning—twenty-three blocks from Murray Hill to Union Square. Erect as a soldier, the collar of his double-breasted Chesterfield edged in velvet, he crossed 15th Street and turned rapidly into his store. The year before, the *Mail and Express* had suggested his name as a Republican mayoral candidate, noting that he had never needed glasses and was as active as a man of fifty. He made a courtly, dignified impression in his formal high silk hat, his mustache and beard bristling hard and white, his hair soft and also white. Closer, the knit of his brow and set of his upper lip revealed a determined man who knew what was rightfully his. The Blizzard of 1888, with its drifts up to ten feet, had not prevented this New Englander from opening up shop.

His achievement was large. In one broad stroke, Charles had walked out of a Connecticut village, plunged into the maelstrom of New York, forged America's foremost jewelry and silver house, amassed a personal fortune, and made his surname synonymous with the best. His "shop," of course, was Tiffany & Company, the crux and crucible of the family's power.

In 1870, when Charles had removed Tiffany & Company to Union Square's southwest corner at Broadway and 15th Street, it became the first business establishment in what had been a residential area. Then somewhat north of the mercantile center, the handsome five-story cast-iron building he erected was regarded as perhaps the most advanced in New York. One of the city's first fireproof buildings, its elevator, rest room, and modern safe deposit system were all pioneering features. A score of years later, it lay midway along what was known as the ladies' mile of grand Broadway emporiums, wrapped in the aura of a national institution. But where once its brownish green façade had been warmed by gaslight, it was now brilliantly lit by the dazzling rays of electric bulbs. The *Globe* described it as "standing as isolated among the buildings, as a simple Quaker girl [among] the bizarre and stylish girls of these times."

If so, it was a girl who knew the power of Washington Irving's "almighty dollar." Annually Charles sold over $6,000,000 worth of diamonds alone. To put that figure in perspective, a nine-carat "pure white" diamond which sold for $2,000 then would today fetch over $70,000. And the business of other gems—emeralds, sapphires, rubies, pearls—as well as "fancy goods" and silver, generated many millions more. Charles's clientele was drawn from the wealthiest and most influential families in America: the Astors, Whitneys, Belmonts, Havemeyers, Rockefellers, Vanderbilts, Goulds, and Morgans. Due to Charles Tiffany more than any other single jeweler, three American women—Mrs. John Jacob Astor, Mrs. Clarence Mackay, and Mrs. Leland Stanford—were reputed each to own more diamonds than any of the crowned heads of Europe except Queen Victoria. In fact, through his London and Paris branches, Charles catered to these same crowned heads, as evidenced by the number of his royal appointments.

But the unique position of the House of Tiffany is best appreciated in relation to the city it served. In the previous half century, due to successive, massive waves of immigration, the number of New Yorkers jumped nearly tenfold, to just under 2,000,000, a figure that would rise dramatically with the incorporation of the Bronx, Brooklyn, Queens, and Staten Island as boroughs of New York City. And with these numbers came the irrepressible vitality to build and rebuild. In a finger snap the provincial village in which Charles Tiffany had founded his store became an international lodestone, a world-class metropolis in the vanguard of the industrial and technological changes sweeping the Western world. Two achievements of the "elegant eighties," the Brooklyn Bridge and the Statue of Liberty, became national symbols. But few of the city's landmarks could endure, and each generation of New Yorkers knew a different city than their predecessor. Where the more expansive parameters of Paris spawned but one Baron Haussmann and one radical reconstruction, in Manhattan the overwhelming ratio of people to available space made urban renewal ceaseless, like the molting of skins.

For decades Tiffany & Company had been playing a sort of Broadway leapfrog with its chief jewelry and silversmith rival, Ball, Black & Company. Tiffany's 1870 Union Square building had instantly eclipsed Ball, Black's 1860 white marble shop on Spring Street, which had eclipsed the 1853 Tiffany's between Spring and Prince, which had in turn eclipsed the old Ball, Black's still further south. And as the city had spilled northward, it had built upward. Small buildings had been swallowed by tall buildings, swallowed by still taller buildings. When an old abolitionist church had been razed to make way for Tiffany's on Union Square, wood had bowed to cast iron and the roof line had risen from thirty-five to ninety feet. The use of steel in floors and exterior walls was revamping old structural formulas, making the height of a building no longer exclusively reliant upon the area of its base and thickness of its walls. Manhattan stood on the threshold of the skyscraper era. The tinkle of horsecars was yielding to the gear grinding of electrified trams, the rumble of subways, and roar of the first handmade, imported motorcars. The new media— typewriter, telephone, snapshot and motion picture camera—would shape the very ideas they expressed. The modern age would arrive over-night, bringing its inventors and investors unprecedented profits.

No single image expressed this transitional phase in American history more conspicuously than the eruption, like toadstools on a lawn, of behemoth neo-Renaissance châteaus. The mansions themselves were no more fit for survival than the era in which they were built; within another half century they too would vanish. Yet their image, if fleeting, was colorful and compelling. And if Tiffany & Company was the crucible of the family's power, the Tiffany mansion at 27 East 72nd Street was its most vivid symbol.

Guidebooks invariably identified it as the Charles L. Tiffany mansion, since it was Charles who had footed the $100,000 construction bill. This monument to Charles Tiffany's business acumen bore, however, the character of his imaginative son: wealth had bred art. From the sidewalk it fairly soared 113 feet from huge, rough-cut blocks of mustard brown-stone over patterns of yellow and brown brick to the spine of its steeply pitched roof. From the third-floor loggia one could see south to the gilded nude figure of the huntress Diana, housed, amidst recent public outcry, on the spire of Madison Square Garden. To the east one could see the masts of ships plying the river; to the west the treetop panorama of Central Park. The perch atop Lenox Hill made a strategic redoubt; indeed, the palazzo walls were thick and high enough to withstand a battering ram, while behind the massive Syrian entrance arch a filigree barrier rolled up and down like a medieval portcullis. At the mansion's southeast corner a Jules Verne-like turret provided a 270-degree prospect. Lacking nothing but an alligator-infested moat, it commanded the head of Madison Avenue with the authority of a German landgrave's castle.

Within were three palatial apartments. Louis had designed the lower floors to his father's simple taste. But though we know he approved, found it "very imposing and elegant," in the eleventh hour Charles had decided against moving from Murray Hill. Lenox Hill was far removed from Union Square, after all, and the opulence may also have been too much for him. The Bavarian-born financier Henry Villard leased the space instead after the bankruptcy of his Northern Pacific Railroad and receivership of his yet-to-be-completed Villard Houses.

Above the Villards lived Charles's elder daughter, Annie Mitchell, with her husband, Alfred, and their teenage daughters Alfreda and Charly, and above them, Louis, Lou, and their brood occupied the top two floors. The lower floor was marked by broad, open spaces, but, in an era of insimplicity, the studio was a teeming "decorative jungle." This fairyland stage set of weird, dreamlike malapropisms had all the bravura that had made Louis Tiffany the leading exponent of the American Aesthetic Movement. A magpie's nest of incongruous design elements, it was also masterfully rhythmic, sweeping, and original. "Arabian Nights in New York," declared Alma Mahler Werfel.

One entered the boundless hall through a vestibule lined with East Indian weapons and Hindustani wood carvings. At night no ceiling was visible; the inky expanse was punctuated by electrically backlit stained-glass windows which glowed like enchanted flowers. Hundreds of vessels of bronze, clay, and glass fell vinelike from the firmament, suspended on bronze chains cast with bells, deities, elephants, and peacocks; mosque lamps pierced deep shadows, iridescent amphoras glinted in the firelight. Persian carpets, potted palms, wicker chairs, and copper vats were scattered on the floor, and the iron superstructure was molded throughout to give the impression of a gigantic cavern. At the center, a massive dark-blue tree trunk swollen by four giant bulbs seemed to fly into infinity, each bulb ablaze with flames of a different hue. This was a molded brick and plaster chimney rising from a cluster of four hooded hearths, each facing one of the cardinal directions. At the north end, a Byzantine archway flanked by tiered mosaicked columns led to a trickling marble fountain and Middle Eastern niche. The walls surrounding were faced with veined marble and iridescent dragon tiles, and hung in places with architectural fragments scripted in Arabic; above the vestibule, atop a row of highly polished marble columns, a worn stone ledge led to the carved teakwood facade of an Ahmadabad house; nearby a teakwood couch swung from cire perdue chains. Behind a profusion of Oriental vases, tiles, and ceramics keyed to Japanese "cinnabar red," lay an organ loft and stentorian pipes. Lunette windows were set in the gables, and the wooden beams above were stenciled with aphorisms such as PLAIN LIVING AND HIGH THINKING, this the philosophy of the elder Tiffany.

On November 30, 1891, the studio that had also been the scene of *Paasch-Feests,* oyster roasts, Orientals, and other entertainments was set for the golden anniversary of Charles and Harriet Tiffany. Even Burnie, the family black sheep, was present. At thirty-one, the youngest of their children, Burnie had gotten drunk in a bordello one night in 1887 and proceeded with Emma N. Pierson to a justice of the peace to be married. Charles's investigations had revealed that Emma was "not bad of the kind but . . . of the very worst kind." Firing Burnie from his $600-a-year clerical post at Tiffany & Company, Charles sent him abroad to begin a four-year exile in Russia, Europe, and Africa. Evidently the evening's celebration had warranted his return and reinstatement, at $750 a year, as a Tiffany & Company clerk. In attendance, then, were all four children, one grandson, and eight granddaughters—including the seven-week-old Dorothy. After dinner friends and employees joined the family in showering Charles and Harriet with gold: gold medals, gold "loving cups," and gilded testimonial books. Louis's present, a mosaic portrait of his father as the honorable counselor Joseph of Arimathea, was especially appropriate.

In a genealogical study that Charles commissioned toward the end of his life, his ancestral line was traced, somehow, to the reaches of ancient Greece, where the name had been Theophania. Theophania was also the Greek festival of the epiphany held in midwinter to honor Apollo, the sun god. The family was named for the festival, according to one account, because they sold epiphany silk, a fine quality colorful silk reserved for special occasions. In pre-Christian times, a branch of the family had migrated to Gaul, settling in Brittany. There they had stuck to the same trade and been called Tiffiny, as the silk they sold was called tiffin. After the Norman invasion the family emigrated to Yorkshire, where the name was anglicized to its present spelling. Eventually offshoots of the Yorkshire Tiffanys made their way south to Richmondshire, near London, which was to become the point of departure for Squire Humphrey Tiffany, the first Tiffany to land on American soil and Charles's great-great-great-grandfather. From ancient times, therefore, the Tiffanys had been businessmen with an eye for quality merchandise. They were generally of medium to small height, dark-haired, dark-complexioned, with bright blue eyes quickly changing with mood.

Squire Humphrey and his wife, Elizabeth, were first recorded on the ledgers of the Plymouth Colony of Massachusetts Bay in 1660. Presumably they had arrived from England shortly before that date. If so, like their *Mayflower* predecessors, they may well have been fleeing Anglican persecution, for Oliver Cromwell had died in 1658 and his Puritan Roundheads were in rout. On the other hand, if Squire Humphrey had arrived in America during Cromwell's rule, it is also possible, even probable, that he was fleeing the economic chaos that the politically inept soldier had wrought. The title of squire indicated a man of good birth and independent means—one therefore not employed in any trade or profession—with a coat of arms granted by the College of Heralds. The Tiffany escutcheon pictured a knight garlanded with oak leaves, his visored helmet surmounted by the head of a greyhound biting a stag's foot. A chevron and three lions were emblazoned on his breastplate above the motto *Patria Fidelis*. A huntsman and patriot; in short, Squire Humphrey was a gentleman. But whether he escaped England to protect his faith, his pocketbook, or both, is not known.

He did not stay in Plymouth long, moving within three years to the area of Massachusetts then known as Rehoboth. He settled there for good, raising a family along strict Puritan lines. The squire met his end in the summer of 1685 on the road from Swansea to Boston; surprised by a severe thunderstorm, he was struck by lightning and "into eternity did go."

Ninety-two uneventful years later, following the outbreak of the Revolutionary War, a boy named Comfort was born to the Tiffanys. Comfort was Squire Humphrey's great-great-grandson, and the father of Charles. Like his father and grandfather before him, the first world Comfort knew was the Tiffany farmhouse in Attleboro, a town within the old territory of Rehoboth. But Comfort was ambitious, enterprising, and independent-minded. In 1803 he married Chloe Draper, daughter of a local tanner. When Comfort's father died five years later leaving him a modest inheritance, he decided to invest in a cotton-manufacturing company. They moved, by rutted dirt roads, to Danielson, in northwestern Connecticut's Wyndham County, a glorious country of rolling hills, deep lakes, thick forest, lush soil, and rushing rivers. There Comfort became a cofounder and partner in the Danielson Manufacturing Company. As one of the first cotton manufacturers in Connecticut, he took a calculated risk with his inheritance, showing a spirit not seen in the family since Squire Humphrey.

Although Danielson was little more than thirty miles west of Attleboro, Comfort's move proved crucial to the as yet unborn Charles. Comfort chose Danielson in large part because the power generated by the waterfalls of the upper Shetucket Valley peaked at the confluence of the Quinebaug and Five Mile rivers, where, on the eastern bank, the village of Danielson was nestled. It was this power that drove the mill. Also, the Quinebaug flowed south from Danielson to Norwich, where there was direct steamboat passage through Long Island Sound to New York, providing Comfort and his partners with both an outlet in the big city marketplace and a base for the export of their cotton goods. In this way the Tiffany axis shifted from Boston to New York, the most rapidly expanding city in the United States. By the time Charles was born on February 15, 1812, Comfort's company was on its way to becoming one of the largest manufacturing plants in New England.

Charles had two elder sisters, a younger sister, and a younger brother. But he was the eldest male and consistently acted the part. He attended the local schoolhouse, then the nearby Plainfield Academy, a private secondary school run by a Yale graduate.

At this point Comfort made a decision that changed Charles's destiny. After twenty years in the cotton business, having reaped a handsome return on his investment, Comfort sold his interest in the Danielson Manufacturing Company and bought the water rights on the opposite (western) side of the Quinebaug. Charles and his partners founded a competitor firm, the Brooklyn Manufacturing Company, and built a mill. At the same time Comfort purchased a nearby country store, took fifteen-year-old Charles out of school, and put him in charge.

It was typically shrewd. Among Charles's first customers were the local half-breed Indians Comfort had hired to spring a low dam across the Quinebaug, dig the canal to carry water to the breast wheel, and build the mill itself. Comfort could now partially pay them in barter—corn, rum, and molasses—from the Tiffany store. And later, when the mill was operating, the mill workers naturally shopped at the store and Charles received a percentage of the weekly paychecks his father had just issued, making a double profit for the Tiffanys.

Charles set to his tasks, rapidly learning the necessary skills, stocking shelves, working the counter, balancing the books. Once business had developed sufficiently to hire help, Charles journeyed by the Norwich & Worcester Railroad to the Norwich ferry and from there to Manhattan's bustling South Street seaport to purchase goods not available in Wyndham County. Before long business had swelled to a point where Comfort could build a larger store. With the new store running smoothly, Charles resumed his studies in nearby Brooklyn, Connecticut.

He graduated two years later and returned to the store, all together spending seven years building the foundation for his later endeavors. It was here that he developed the firm courtesy he never failed to show his customers, the integrity that backed his sales, the small marks of character that are useful in a backwater town where the clientele is limited and must be patiently courted. He impressed people then as he did later as a punctual, industrious, economical, and confident individual. His few recreations included fishing the bountiful Quinebaug and pursuing the affections of his childhood sweetheart and neighbor, Harriet Young. Beneath the cool reserve Harriet saw another side of Charles, a playful warmth and twinkling eye that few others observed.

Comfort meanwhile, around 1830, had bought out his partners and renamed the firm C. Tiffany & Son. But Charles decided that "the future of the cotton industry in Connecticut offered nothing to satisfy his ambition." The great abolitionist crusade had begun, also, and with it the first stirrings of conflict with the cotton-producing states. Most important, perhaps, at the store he had developed a taste for his own command.

He was quick to use a favorable wind. Harriet's brother John Burnett had recently taken a job in a New York stationery and dry goods establishment. Charles had often visited the city on business and was drawn to its vitality. He discussed with John the possibility of combining his experience at the store and mill with John's knowledge of dry goods. They agreed that the range of merchandise in dry goods would give them latitude to establish a market.

This was the era of Jacksonian democracy. Economically, President Jackson's tenure had been marked by strife between conservatives and speculators, deflationary and inflationary interests, with alternating periods of euphoria and panic. For several years the economy had boomed due to the president's war on the monopolistic Bank of America. But Old Hickory's Specie Circular of 1836, demanding silver or gold only for government-held western lands, had halted the fevered speculation. Storm clouds were gathering, and Charles and John could hardly have been encouraged, especially since they needed the financial backing of their parents. And sure enough, though John's father was a well-to-do Wyndham County judge, legislator, and competing mill owner, he no doubt felt that the risks outweighed the gains, for they got not a penny from him. Comfort, however, had gambled successfully with his future almost thirty years earlier. His seed money had been inherited somewhat late in life, however, and he knew that Charles, at twenty-five, already had the experience and savvy to negotiate the shoals.

So he agreed to loan Charles and John $500 apiece, a figure close to $50,000 in today's dollars. Despite John's greater years, Charles's authoritative manner would ensure his dominance of the firm, and, reasoned Comfort, increase its chances of success. If they failed, Charles could always return to C. Tiffany & Son.

It was a perilous time. New York had not recovered from the Great Fire of 1835, when rows of volunteer firemen had manned long wooden bars, hand-pumping water in seesaw fashion only to have their hoses freeze in subzero weather. The fire had raged unchecked for four days, razing the business district and causing millions of dollars in damage. Despite the picturesque firemarks or plaques affixed to the buildings of insurants, most companies refused to compensate the victims. By the following year the bank war had further unsettled the economy. As 1837 commenced businesses were bankrupting like firecrackers. Thousands were unemployed; inflation had almost doubled the price of flour, and people were hungry. One evening an angry mob looted flour warehouses at Coenties Slip and Washington Street—the prelude to wider misery. In May stock and commodity prices broke. On May 10 the banks of New York suspended specie payment. On the following day Philip Hone wrote in his famous diary, "All is still as death."

What followed was the worst depression the city, or country, had ever known, and shock was felt worldwide—an irony not lost on many in that fiftieth anniversary year of the U.S. Constitution.

Suddenly the prospect of opening a shop in New York seemed akin to hoisting sail in gale-force winds: the ship would either move rapidly or sink like a stone. Charles and John sat on the chain fence surrounding City Hall Park and debated anew. Although neither knew just how bad the depression would be, they did know that their clientele had been reduced overnight. But Charles reasoned that one class of people who would never be kept from the fashionable shops was the well-to-do Brahmins; and their best chance therefore lay in so-called "fancy dry goods." If they could find a suitable location, Tiffany & Young might weather the depression and establish a neat trade in the process.

Their youthful confidence was bolstered by the national confidence stemming from phenomenal natural resources, unlimited space, and explosive growth. Since the Revolution the population of New York alone had swelled seventeenfold to over 200,000. In just the two weeks before the crash, 5,000 immigrants had poured onto its wharves. The completion of the Erie Canal (Mayor De Witt Clinton's "ditch") in 1825 had caused a good deal of the city's nascent gigantism, as it ran from Lake Erie to the Hudson River and south from Troy, connecting the farm produce of the entire Great Lakes region with the New York market. And Charles was amply familiar with the locus of this mercantile activity: the South Street seaport.

Striding beneath the bowsprits of the packets and clippers nosing the buildings across the docks, Charles went looking for merchandise. Though short, he held himself straight, and his high beaver hat made him seem taller still. He dressed correctly in vest, gates-ajar stiff collar, and swallowtail coat. His boots were heeled and polished, his hair groomed, and his bright blue eyes sparkled against a dark complexion. Thick black brows combined with a certain sharpness of feature (inherited from his mother) lent him the air of one to be reckoned with: upon closer inspection his upper lip appeared to subdue the lower. Only an under-the-chin beard and village-spun manners labeled Charles a newcomer. But he knew exactly what he was looking for. At that time quality meant imported, and it was upon choice foreign novelties that his eye fell in the summer of 1837.

The city, in the early 1800s, was poised on the brink between charm and bedlam, the line between culture and chaos as finely drawn as the side of the street on which one happened to be walking. Gotham could be genteel. Family servants met at dawn at hand pumps (one every four blocks) to draw the day's water, and, if the mistress was discriminating, took an extra trip to the "tea-water" pump. Gas sconces had replaced whale-oil lamps in some homes, and many streets were lit by gas. Freestanding homes, like those of Brahmins Henry Brevoort, Samuel Ward, Hendrick Remsen, and a few dozen others, were of exceedingly fine quality, and rarely over four stories. The well-to-do could live in a row, as they did at the Colonnades and on Washington Square North. Beyond that was rolling countryside, dotted on the one hand by wasteland and shantytowns, but on the other by fine farms and suburbs such as Gramercy Park and Union Place (soon to be Union Square, the northernmost reach of Broadway). Further north, affluent New Yorkers had summer seats in Westchester County; to the east, in Jamaica, Queens, old Dutch farmers stubbornly refused to acknowledge the existence of any "new people."

Steamboats chugged down the Hudson, rounded the Battery, steamed up the East River and crossed back to the Hudson—with complete disregard for wind direction. More satisfactory still were the *Sirius* and *Great Western,* the first steamships to have made the Atlantic crossing. Public street transportation was invariably a noisy affair: either the chattering of wooden wheels over cobbles (buggies, open-sided accommodation stages, closed omnibuses), or the whoosh and clang of steam-powered locomotion (the New York & Harlem Railroad plied Fourth Avenue from Prince Street to the Village of Yorkville). From Castle Garden to Canal Street pushcart vendors hawked bluepoint and saddle rock oysters, while "Hot Corn Girls" sold the legacy of the Manhattan Indians. The great Fulton Fish Market, Washington Market, and Merchants Exchange were bazaars offering everything from bluefish cheeks to dried venison.

These images coexisted on easy terms with the city's underbelly. Garbage was eaten, not collected—by foraging pigs, goats, and oxen. Sewage was pumped into the rivers and the streets were choked with offal. To the east and west lay the rough-and-tumble waterfronts, home to the homeless—hoboes, squatters, tramps, bums. Not far off Broadway, to the east, near the intersection of what is now Baxter and Worth, lay the squalor of the Five Points, a notorious slum where roving gangs of unemployed immigrants (like the Plug Uglies) enjoyed nothing so much as robbing, beating, or even murdering a shopper gone astray. The firefighters were volunteers, and police nonexistent. "Bravest" and "finest" were terms for the future; if conditions turned riotous the mayor called out the militia.

Charles and John, meanwhile, scouted locations for their shop. Low rents were not hard to find, but they could hardly open in a district where the better customers hesitated to shop; and few shopped off Broadway or above Canal. In fact, most shopped entirely within the fashionable and safe parameters of the recently rebuilt business district on Broadway near

Cortlandt Street, where the rent ranged from $3,000 to $5,000 per year. With only $1,000 investment capital, Charles and John had a hard time and very nearly gave up the enterprise.

Eventually, however, they found an old-fashioned four-story, two-dwelling building at 259 Broadway—the city's backbone. It was on the southwestern corner of Warren Street, opposite the coolly elegant City Hall, but seven long blocks north of Cortlandt Street. The space was narrow and deep, sandwiched between A. T. Stewart's dry-goods store to the south and Madame Scheltema's dressmaking shop, which occupied the corner lot. A. T. Stewart's rise in business had been meteoric, and his decision to relocate that far north gave Charles confidence. The other inducement was the rent, $600 a year.

And so Tiffany & Young opened for business on September 18, 1837. All day long, Charles and John watched the hoop-skirted, balloon-sleeved society ladies disappear into the store one door south of their own, and with quickly mounting hopes, observed some pass by Stewart's and promenade the fifteen feet across their own storefront, clutching their dresses off the sidewalk and dipping their plumed hats, only to plunge into Madame Scheltema's, the modiste. Three days later, Charles sat at his desk, dipped his quill into ink and entered a total of $4.98 in sales in his small green cashbook. The following evening he added $2.17. Nevertheless, by week's end, after paying advertising costs, and themselves $10 apiece, the partners were thirty cents in the black.

Charles had taken great care in the arrangement of the goods, and, as hoped, it was not long before ladies noticed the Tiffany & Young display. The window was "something like a picture," they were heard to exclaim. Word got around that "the very show of goods is a work of art." Oriental goods had become the height of fashion after the *Empress of China* had inaugurated direct trade between New York and Canton (in 1784), and Charles had sought out ships from the Far East, striking up a banter with their captains. He had discovered that many of them supplemented their incomes by selling personal stocks of merchandise more attractive than the standard stuff; and by sheer persistence Charles managed to acquire eye-catching items at no cash outlay by convincing the skippers to let him sell them on consignment. Through this and other inventive means, Charles and John had completed a competitive stock, primarily of stationery, but also including Japanese fans, Chinese umbrellas and lacquered furniture, papier-mâché and terra-cotta wares, porcelain vases, walking canes, and an assortment of items referred to as gimcracks.

Charles was evidently possessed of both aesthetic and business sense. Customers discovered that the merchandise was both well made and reasonably priced. Though cash on hand often dipped to alarmingly low levels, by strict living and word-of-mouth publicity the partners survived their first and most difficult year. Then, one morning, as Charles arrived to open up shop, he saw something that must have brought a smile to his lips. The old apple seller who habitually posted herself in front of A. T. Stewart's was this morning standing in front of Tiffany & Young. That was progress!

On Christmas Day 1838, Charles logged $236.90 in sales in his green book, and on New Year's Day (when New Yorkers then exchanged presents), he recorded $675. The partners would have been wiped out that very night, however, had they not brought home the day's take, as the store was broken into and $4,000 worth of goods (four times the original investment and the equivalent of perhaps $400,000 today) was stolen.

T alking to reporters some fifty years later, Charles pulled from his desk a sheet of writing paper from the original stock. The men observed that it was a large sheet, finely textured, and, though somewhat yellowed with age, the folds showed no signs of tearing. His demonstration showed that his intention from the start had been to give the public the best quality goods; according to "An Appreciation" of Charles Tiffany by Annabel A. Groan, that, along with "the finest quality service that could be secured," was his business principle. His ideal was "absolute undeviating honesty, even in the smallest detail of the business."

Catering to the carriage trade was a time-consuming business, and Charles, John, and one errand boy saw to the chores themselves. Time passed quickly, Charles continually percolating inventive stratagems to secure different merchandise. If he heard that a choice shipment was due to arrive in Boston, he hurried north. If there was no cash on hand, he scratched around. And if just two objects cost the entire borrowed amount, and he believed he could sell them, he did not hesitate to incur the risk. His taste rarely failed his confidence.

Although necessity had initially gotten Charles into the business of
luxury goods, a few years later, with the worst of the depression over,
he was clearly in his element. He quickly refined his knack for choosing
and displaying quality goods into a more sophisticated skill for selling
the public the very product which seemed to reflect its aspirations at a
given moment. Tiffany & Young began tapping into the American
dream, adding, for example, a line of costume jewelry from Hanau,
Germany, which Charles believed New Yorkers might buy to symbolize
their renewed prosperity. There was something naive in this addition to
the stock (Charles recalled it as "cheap, garish and badly made"): costume
jewelry, after all, rings of wide-eyed, fairy-tale romance, the adolescent
girl playacting with glass diamonds, rehearsing for the lady she dreams
of becoming. But here also was ingenuity. America was that adolescent
girl, preening, posturing, vainglorious, the bud about to blossom. Americans wanted symbols of their money, and Charles had measured their
pulse. Each evening as he saw to his books the Hanau baubles sparkled
rainbows under the gas jets. Destiny winked at him.

Tiffany & Young was in fact stuffed with such an assortment of
gimcracks that they rented an additional forty-five feet across Warren
Street to display it all. At the same time Charles made two policy changes,
each helping to forge Tiffany & Young's reputation. He marked every
object in his store with a price tag, ending the undignified, widely
practiced custom of bargaining over goods. And, having observed that
many New York shops cloaked their ads in the mantle of "French-made,"
regardless of the place of manufacture, he decided to invest in an overseas
representative and separate the wheat from the chaff. A third partner, J.
L. Ellis, contributed the capital to send John abroad on an annual buying
trip. Interest in the Hanau paste had convinced Charles that he could do
even better, and, no sooner had John arrived in Paris than he discovered
Palais Royale, a higher-quality, higher-priced line. Tiffany, Young &
Ellis informed its customers that Palais Royale was not so-called Parisian,
but *made to order in Paris under the supervision of the only store in America
with a representative abroad.* The new line moved even faster than the
Hanau paste.

Four years after founding Tiffany & Young, Charles was sufficiently
established to approach one of Connecticut's most prominent citizens to
ask for the hand of his daughter in marriage. The gentleman he approached was, in addition to being a judge and cotton mill owner, a

former president of the Connecticut Senate and a former U.S. congressman; his wife was a *Mayflower* descendant six times over. But Ebenezer and Anna Young were friends; their son was Charles's partner, and their daughter, his childhood sweetheart.

On November 30, 1841, Charles and Harriet Olivia Avery Young were married. Knowing her husband so well, it could not have surprised Harriet when, despite Charles's flourishing income and her (presumably) substantial dowry, he took her to 124 Chambers Street, an unfashionable area of cheap rents by the Hudson River. Charles, she knew, admired economy. There amidst the fishy odors drifting north from the Washington Market, the kindly, doe-eyed brunette ran an efficient, pennywise household, adding a note of congenialty and domestic security to their life. Unfortunately, this exhausts our knowledge of Harriet, a conventionally retiring and private Victorian lady.

Charles and Harriet's home was only a short distance from the store, which was by this time retailing some of the most tasteful and costly wares in New York. One Tiffany, Young & Ellis ad featured Chinese tea caddies, silver and gold filigree vases, carved ivory chessmen, paintings, Dresden china, Bohemian glass, Berlin iron and bronze work, and French porcelain. Other ads, including Tiffany, Young & Ellis's first catalog, released in 1845, trumpeted an emporium of articles "of taste and utility," useful as well as fancy, suitable for gifts, "for sale at fixed prices for cash only"—and virtually all imported. From England, France, Germany, Italy, and China arrived extracts, perfumes, pomades, toiletries, sealing wax, dog and horse whips, art engravings, cutlery, silver and vermeil tea and coffee services, cigar boxes, writing cases for traveling, cuspidors, belts, brushes, combs, clothing, clocks, sugar plums and bonbons! Nor was jewelry overlooked.

Tiffany, Young & Ellis have determined to pay special attention . . . so that they will receive by French steamer and packet a limited number of every new style of bracelets, hairpins, dress combs, head ornaments, chatelaines, scarf pins, brooches and shawl pins, in gold and imitation.

"Gold" meant gold-plated. An ad explained that

since jewelry has been so much an article of "fashion" and liable to so frequent changes of taste, it is not surprising that it has extensively super-

ceded the more expensive manufacture of solid gold, and is now very
generally approved by people of rank, wealth and fashion, both in Europe
and in this country.

Indeed, the jewelry department had grown to the point that Charles had
recently hired an expert in the field, Thomas Crane Banks.

In 1846 Tiffany, Young & Ellis made headlines by opening a branch
at 760 Broadway between 8th and 9th streets, startling the business
community with a move so far north and pioneering what soon became
known as the "uptown movement." The following year, the two downtown shops consolidated one block north of Warren Street, at 271 Broadway. Situated on the southwest corner of Chambers, catercorner from A.
T. Stewart's new Marble Dry Goods Palace and opposite the grand Irving
House hotel, it was a strategic and prestigious location.

Thus far, Charles had built his reputation on the skill of foreign
manufacturers, artisans, and craftsmen; his ads, like those of his competitors, reflected small confidence in American products—for example: Tiffany, Young & Ellis "have always for sale the largest, richest and best
collections of elegant articles of taste and utility, to be found on this side
of the Atlantic." That American-made was inferior to European-made
had been taken for granted as an order of nature. However, within a year
of opening the new shop, the expanded quarters enabled Charles for the
first time to hire his own designers and begin the manufacture of jewelry
and silver. This change led to the acquisition of real gemstones, both to
sell loose and to set in both custom and ready-made designs.

Over the winter of 1847–48 John Young and Thomas Banks left New
York for Paris to acquire a new stock of novelties and jewels. Charles
remained in New York as usual to run the store and may not have paid
special attention to John's departure—124 Chambers Street was focused
on a family matter, the birth of Harriet's third child. Their first, Charles
Lewis, Jr., had died the previous year at age six. Their second born had
been a girl, Annie Olivia, now four; and they prayed for a boy. Three
days after Charles's thirty-sixth birthday, on February 18, Louis Comfort
was born. The boy brought his parents relief, happiness, and tremendous
luck. Four days later commenced the event which, more than any other,
catapulted Tiffany, Young & Ellis's emporium for imported gimcracks
into a world-class jewelry house.

Charles did not get wind of it until the morning of March 24 when he grabbed an extra put out by the weekly *Sun*. The steamer *Cambria* brought the first news of a revolution which had broken out in France on February 22 (over a month before!). As Charles discovered, through a stroke of blind luck John had arrived in Paris to find Louis Philippe's regime crumbling, the aristocracy fleeing before the mob, and the price of gems down by 50 percent. John had done what anyone would have done under the circumstances—abandoned his schedule for novelties and invested the entire capital on loose precious stones. The full story was told upon his return by the firm's diamond ledger. It flatly and meticulously recorded the acquisition of a fortune in emeralds, turquoises, opals, pearls, rubies, and, most of all, diamonds—hundreds and hundreds of diamonds. If John thus inadvertently helped scores of royalists escape with their heads, in the uproar he also acquired a few of the French crown jewels.

So long as Americans danced the polka to show sympathy with the revolutionaries, Charles did not feel compelled to return to France the hated symbols of monarchy (among them, Marie Antoinette's diamond-studded stomacher). Rather he broke them into their dazzling components and quietly sold them along with other gems set in Tiffany, Young & Ellis designs. The new owners were a rough-hewn, if cash rich, fraternity of tobacco-spitting industrialists, clipper ship moguls, railroad magnates, and textile tycoons. With the gold rush 'Frisco forty-niners checked into hotels like the Gerard House opposite Grand Central Station and alternately appalled and pleased with their matted whiskers and gold dust. Charles immediately discontinued the sale of costume jewelry and led his ads with the single word "DIAMONDS" at the top in capital letters. Overnight Tiffany, Young & Ellis was transformed into one of New York's top diamond merchants. The press corps, with whom over the years Charles had developed a cordial relationship, with dry humor now crowned Charles "King of Diamonds."

The diamond had of course always been the symbol of the wealthiest strata of American society, and it would continue to be the weapon of choice through the society wars described by Edith Wharton, though never again would it shine as magically as it did under the flickering hues of gaslight. But with industrial and technological progress had come the emergence of an American middle class and a broader affluence, which Charles had tapped in his progression from paste to gold plate to jewels.

It was a far cry from selling corn, rum, and molasses at the country store, but Comfort had not lived to see it. After his death four years earlier Chloe had moved to Brooklyn, New York, to live with her sister-in-law, Eliza Tiffany Morse. Chloe therefore saw what Comfort had not, and it must have filled her with satisfaction. Their son had risen to the Tiffany imperative, honoring and yet surpassing his father.

Charles had acquired his parents' puritan values. Thrift, industry, moderation, piety—he had it all. And everything that his father had been, he also was. He had Comfort's independent, ambitious, enterprising spirit; he too had broken away from childhood moorings, set off on his own, and started his own business. But in Charles these qualities were magnified. Instead of shifting from one village to another, Charles had plunged into New York. Beyond enterprise Charles had shown daring. And as to ambition, even his mother, who lived four years more, did not see the full measure of the leap her son would make.

II

Diamond of the First Water

Charles spent the next two decades working himself to the bone, driven to capitalize on his windfall and create a legacy for young Louis. He continued to upgrade his standards, serve his customers well, and put no limit on what he hoped to achieve. By the end of the Civil War, he had turned his shop into an arbiter of taste, the first American institution of its kind capable of challenging the European masters at the great, international expositions.

Within two years of the diamond coup Charles was able to establish a Paris office by taking Gideon F. T. Reed as a partner. The branch was invaluable for the edge it gave the company on the import market (few, if any, competitors had such offices at the time), and the establishment at 79, rue de Richelieu instantly and relentlessly capitalized on foreign market fluctuations, just as Charles had done during the 1848 Revolution. His early experience at the mill evidently paid off. *The Arts of the Tiffanys*, written by Gertrude Speenburgh in 1956, quotes Charles's secretary George F. Heydt as noting that Charles at an early age had "learned to cope with the fluctuating cotton market . . . [and this was] . . . excellent experience, extremely valuable in his subsequent career as merchant and craftsman."

Charles's influence at the store increased with the departure of John Young. John's and Harriet's father, Ebenezer Young, died in August of 1850, and, after coming into his inheritance, John decided to retire. He was officially listed with the firm for several years more, but by 1851 had moved back to Connecticut, settling in Norwich. John and his wife, Lydia, had twice lived in the same building with the Tiffanys, first at 124 Chambers Street, then at 57 Warren Street. The Tiffanys' firstborn son had been born at 238 East Broadway—an earlier address of the Youngs'. The Youngs and Tiffanys had been close-knit, and they visited often after John's retirement.

Charles was younger and more ambitious than his brother-in-law, however, and had no intention of retiring. Each day served up a new lesson, and in this period he was learning the art of public relations from a professional. One of the more curious aspects of Charles's career is his emulation of Phineas Taylor Barnum, whose success in business was, after all, founded on the premise that one could not lose money underestimating the taste of the American people. Perhaps their respective accomplishments merely indicate the diversity of American taste, though time has made caricatures of them both. Charles was neither so staid nor Barnum so vulgar as their legends would have us believe. Barnum did have a flair for capturing the public's attention that Charles admired; each was a product of small-town Connecticut; each was shrewd; and each in his own way was something of a creative genius.

By the early fifties they were acquaintances, if not friends. Barnum shopped at Charles's store, and Charles could not have missed Barnum's American Museum five blocks to the south. It was the large marble building with the brass band blaring from the balcony, and strewn with banners and freak show posters heralding the likes of the Giant Baby, Armless Man, Highland Mammoth Boys, and Major Littlefinger. Charles could also see the long lines queuing at the corner of Broadway and Anne Street. He knew why Barnum was one of the richest men in New York. But Barnum appealed to a nobler side of human nature as well, with his legitimate museum, art gallery, lecture series, waxworks, and sponsorship of the likes of diva Jenny Lind (whose sparkling voice was reportedly matched by the purity of her moral fiber). And it was on Lind's American tour that Charles learned from Barnum, a former public relations man for the New York Zoological Institute, the benefits to be had *by association* with someone, or something, in the public eye.

Jenny Lind was to the mid-nineteenth century what Adelina Patti would be to the Gilded Age, and she had yet to be heard on American shores. She was major news for weeks before her arrival, and front page news for weeks afterwards. Huge crowds flocked after her, at night mobbing the Irving House hotel where she stayed. A treacle of adulation followed her every incident and word, all of which Barnum had carefully choreographed. Soon she made her way across the street to Tiffany, Young & Ellis, where the Prince of Humbug introduced her to the King of Diamonds. Lind ordered a special tankard for the captain of the ship that had brought her over, and Charles in turn presented her with one of the firm's first historically important pieces of silver. The design and execution represented the state of the silversmith art: a mermaid rising from a foaming sea formed the handle; Triton's tail, the finial of the lid; and a rainbow which had appeared on the recent voyage over arced across the tankard itself. Lind was so thrilled that she ordered several replicas.

Charles analyzed the publicity the firm received through this commission, and made it the prototype for a long series of public relations plums. He realized that trophies, cups, medals, presentation pieces, and other articles of commemorative silver were usually commissioned to reward excellence of one kind or another, their sale reflecting prestige on the maker as did no other product. The more illustrious the recipient, the greater the attendant—and free—publicity. Illustrated weeklies like *Harper's* and *Frank Leslie's* regularly featured these awards, reproducing the presentation pieces themselves in woodblock prints, and often crediting the maker. Knowing this, Charles resolved to make the best silver in New York.

The firm's first salaried silver designer was Gustave Herter (the founder of the Herter Brothers interior decorating concern, and future competitor of young Louis Comfort—presently learning to talk). Charles initially retained a number of craftsmen free-lance, but before long he recognized the superior talent of John C. Moore and, in 1851, signed him to an exclusive contract. This was both aesthetically and tactically prescient because, in obtaining Moore, Charles simultaneously deprived the competition of his services. And after Herter left the firm, Moore passed the business along to his son, Edward Chandler Moore, ultimately to be regarded as the finest silversmith in America.

Charles did not stop at hiring the best silversmith; he instructed Moore to upgrade their silver to the British sterling standard. At that time American silver varied widely in purity, due in part to the practice of using ore from old Spanish and Mexican coins. A customer buying

American therefore had little way of knowing how much silver he was getting for his money, and thus most preferred British sterling, guaranteed at 925 parts fine out of 1,000. The combination of the new silver standard, Moore's artistry, and an 1844 protective tariff of 30 percent on imports eventually made it possible for Tiffany, Young & Ellis to rival British quality and undersell it at the same time. Not surprisingly "the fetish idols of free trade" became Charles's grindstone and he a member of the American Protective Tariff League. The competition was subsequently forced to match the Tiffany sterling standard (which eventually became written into U.S. law), strengthening the overall quality of American silver. And within four years of hiring Moore, Charles's firm had replaced Ball, Black & Company as the leading silversmith in New York.

Over the years the firm was commissioned to make silver presentation pieces for political cartoonist Thomas Nast, poet William Cullen Bryant, soprano Lillian Russell, British Prime Minister William Ewart Gladstone, Statue of Liberty sculptor Frédéric-Auguste Bartholdi, and others who captured the public imagination. The firm would continue this demonstratively successful public relations practice even after the founder's death. In 1904 Mayor George MacClellan turned Tiffany's silver controller handle to start the first subway in New York. Today Tiffany's makes the Super Bowl, or Vince Lombardi, trophy.

Before long Charles was pursuing publicity as aggressively as P. T. Barnum himself. He saw one opportunity when Barnum began trumpeting a purported rivalry between his midgets General Tom Thumb and Commodore Nutt for the hand of tiny Lavinia Warren. (The announcement of Lavinia's engagement to Tom was made, naturally, at the height of public interest.) Charles received no order, but nevertheless made a miniature silver filigree horse and carriage which he gave the couple after displaying it for several weeks in his windows. On another occasion one of Barnum's elephants ran amok and trampled a number of people to death. After the public weal had been restored following the animal's capture and execution, Charles bought the mammoth carcass, stuffed it, and displayed it in his showcase window, promising to reduce it into wallets, belts, and like memorabilia in the near future. Sure enough, the "killer elephant" goods were a huge success.

With this marriage of unabashed theatrics and high standards Charles created Tiffany & Company. J. L. Ellis soon joined John Young in retirement, and, in the spring of 1853, Charles moved his business thirteen blocks uptown to 550 Broadway, between Spring and Prince streets. The five-story Gothic structure he erected there was described by one writer as "chaste." On May 1, 1853, Charles gazed at his new building and thought perhaps of his father. It had taken Comfort over a quarter of a century to buy out his partners. With his father's help, Charles had built the House of Tiffany in less than sixteen years.

It was then that Charles commissioned his friend Henry F. Metzler to create a company symbol. Because Metzler was a carver of ship figureheads the nine-foot wooden Atlas that he produced was touted on a Tiffany & Company plaque as having "plowed the waves of the sea." But this Atlas with whom Charles evidently identified was bowed not under the weight of the world, but rather by an enormous working clock mounted in a Gothic arch above the entrance. The symbolism of the clock face was unmistakable. Time is limited and therefore burdensome; and punctuality is respect for the time of others.

For this reason, among others, Charles had developed the reputation as an exacting boss as the number of his employees had increased. He hired male clerks only and preferred native-born Americans. He was a judge of talent and character, and was swift to whip raw recruits into a competent, correct cadre, spotless in dark suits and gleaming stiff white collars, immaculately groomed, courteous, and honest. Charles set the standard.

The sight of him standing in the doorway invariably made the clerks pull themselves a little straighter. His Draper sharpness of feature had broadened and settled with age, and the under-the-chin whiskers had prospered into a full beard and mustache. But no one mistook the blaze in his eyes, nor doubted the iron fist beneath the velvet glove. Charles Lewis Tiffany was a disciplinarian, cool and hard as a hickory stick. He cared for his boys, of course, and they loved him back. He was fair, even generous, with his salaries and employment benefits, just in his treatment of the men, and quick to recognize talent, and many of his employees worked for Tiffany twenty-five years, fifty years, and more, rising with the firm and creating an esprit de corps—like diamond expert George

McClure, and Charles T. Cook, the delivery boy who succeeded Charles as president.

The scope and quality of Tiffany & Company's silverware rapidly improved, and its jewelry designs began to set the style across America. The house did phenomenal business while the mid-century popularity of the Oriental pearl lasted, the well-known photograph of Mrs. George Gould wearing her million-dollar rope of Tiffany pearls becoming a classic definition of wealth. The discovery of American freshwater pearls in the early 1850s then opened up another avenue of business. Charles was there from the beginning, buying a perfect pink pearl weighing over one hundred grams from a New Jersey farmer for a trifle, and selling it to Empress Eugénie for a fortune.

Charles's publicity skills continued to serve him well, to the point even of being able to attach the company's name to an event which had nothing to do with the jewelry business, though everything to do with the aspirations and pride of Americans: the connection of the transatlantic cable. In an era which had seen the western frontier pushed back by railroads, the invention of the rotary printing press give birth to the daily paper, and the time of the Atlantic crossing drastically reduced by steam-ships, no single feat galvanized public enthusiasm so much as the laying of Cyrus W. Field's Atlantic cable, which promised news from abroad instantaneously. In the summer of 1858 Field's steam frigate *Niagara* was off the coast of Ireland laying the last miles of cable. Charles, in Europe on business, paid Field a visit and struck a deal to acquire the leftover cable—twenty miles of the stuff—and a letter signed by Field stating

Of course, any quantity of cable can be manufactured in England, and many specimens have been circulated in this country, but to few if any of these, attaches the peculiar value which the cable purchased by you possesses, from the fact that they were part and parcel of the cable which is now actually laid.

In mid-August, soon after the world's first message was telegraphed across the Atlantic, a Tiffany & Company ad appeared in the *New York Times,* printing Field's letter and announcing that it was selling (at 50¢ apiece) four-inch pieces of cable fastened with brass ferules, accompanied by facsimiles of Field's letter of authenticity. The House also offered cable paperweights; cable cane, umbrella, and whip handles; cable seals; cable watch charms; cable bracelets; cable festoons; and, "for ornamenting parlors and offices," cable coils. The following week a picture of the Telegraphic Jubilee crowd marching past Tiffany & Company in *Frank Leslie's Illustrated Weekly* made it appear as if the new marvel of modern technology were somehow Tiffany's achievement. It was Charles's greatest public relations coup; and, when the cable went on sale, his shop was besieged once again, and this time, "policemen were required to maintain order."

By the 1860s the allure of the Tiffany name automatically generated publicity so that Charles did not have to seek it out as he had in the forties and fifties. The patronage of the ultrarich was the apex of the clientele pyramid which Charles had established. The public insisted on knowing where society figures bought their spectacular jewels, and the attendant publicity in turn attracted the *haut bourgeois* and celebrity classes which, in turn, drew a broader base of shoppers to the store. And to each social and economic stratum Charles catered with everything from former crown jewels to gimcracks. One admirer called the House of Tiffany "a social work of art."

Charles and Harriet were themselves sought out at society functions, including the Academy of Music soiree for Prince Albert Edward, Queen Victoria's young and eligible son and successor, the biggest ball of that era. Charles and Harriet attended the dinner-dance with the crest of New York society, supped on *Consommé de volaille, Pâtés de gibier à la moderne, Salades de homard à la russe, Macédoines de fruits,* and other delicacies served by Delmonico's, and danced quadrilles, lancers, galops, polkas, and waltzes until early morning.

Financier Pliny Fisk's description of Charles as "a very quiet, very dignified gentleman" does not sound like a person who is socially at ease, however. As Annie Tiffany would observe in her diary, "It is not [Papa's] natural make to be cordial . . . People, I suppose, think him stiff . . ." He found social functions time-consuming and perhaps painful, and remained aloof as much as he politely could. The Tiffanys were intensely private, and the degree to which Charles publicized his business was matched by the pains he took to keep his personal affairs and those of his family out of the public eye.

It was not for the purpose, then, of making a social gesture when Charles Tiffany moved his family for the fourth and final time in 1860, but to obtain larger quarters. That year Harriet gave birth to Burnett, named in honor of her brother John Burnett, Charles's first partner. Louise had been born in 1856 and Henry had lived less than a year; of six born, four survived. Although the new home at 255 Madison Avenue was located on the western slope of Murray Hill—"the synonym of fashion"—it was a severely plain row house, four stories high, three windows wide. A Corinthian portico was its only architectural flourish.

In the same year Charles bought a summer seat from his former partner J. L. Ellis. For years the Tiffanys had rented cottages on the Pequot, a strip of oceanfront opposite Groton, Connecticut, which sloped from the mouth of the Thames River, where the fishing and sailing were good. The new place had similar advantages but a closer proximity to Manhattan. Near the village of Irvington-on-Hudson, the estate comprised the northern reach of an old Dutch farm, its sixty-five acres bounded by the eastern shore of the Hudson River and the Albany Post Road. The house lay on the crest of a hill overlooking a wide expanse of lawn which rolled down to the sparkling Tappan Zee—so named by the Dutch because the river at that point seemed as wide as an ocean. An avenue of elms that began near the Irvington train station to the south cut horizontally across the lawn and swept up to the house. Practically hidden by wisteria, it was a rambling wooden home built by farmer Barent Dutcher in 1775, and now as homey as a well-worn slipper. Charles loved the place deeply and christened it Tiffany Hall, delighted that his was one home on the Yonkers-to-Scarborough "millionaire's row" which did not look like that of a millionaire.

It was at this juncture that the long-festering economic and political power struggle between North and South came to a head, and the southern states began to secede. Few Americans were unaffected by the raw and visceral Civil War. For Tiffany & Company, advertisements for fine jewelry, precious stones, watches, silverware, bronzes, clocks, rich porcelains, and other "articles of art and luxury" suddenly seemed superfluous. Then with the bombardment of Fort Sumter in April 1861 business virtually died, and the House was facing a serious threat to its existence.

Yet Charles's opposition to slavery was vehement, and, like his fellow Unionists, he could not forget Harpers Ferry, nor "Bully" Brooks crippling Charles Sumner in the Senate chamber with a gutta-percha cane.

Charles had seen the Compromise of 1850 create a stampede of fugitive slaves to Canada, and runaways seized, shackled, and shipped back south. He had read New York's Democratic papers equate Northern "wage slavery" with Southern race slavery, and despised this and other notions calculated to stir up secessionist sentiment among the city's huge immigrant population. He had chafed under three consecutive presidents, one New York governor, and one New York mayor with Southern sympathies (Mayor Fernando Wood, who owned the inflammatory *Daily News,* had proposed the city secede), watched Stephen A. Douglas's "popular sovereignty" lead to war in Kansas and the Supreme Court rule in the Dred Scott decision that the Constitution did not apply to blacks.

So if Tiffany & Company might otherwise have seemed out of touch, its founder was not. He was quick to join the antisecessionist Republican Party, to cofound the Union League Club and huddle at League headquarters with men like City College Professor Wolcott Gibbs and landscape architect Frederick Law Olmstead. And before long Charles lit upon the logical way to aid the Union cause and revitalize his business in one fell swoop. Tiffany & Company would get into the armaments business.

Charles was not the only retailer to have this idea, naturally, but through his Paris branch he was one of the fastest to act upon it. From the French army, he obtained a complete line of uniforms, weapons, tents, ambulances, and "campaign conveniences"—corps badges, epaulets, gold braid, and medals. He submitted a list of these to the U.S. Army quartermaster at City Hall, and rented an additional storefront at 552 Broadway, almost doubling his capacity. Within eight months he had turned his jewelry and silver house into a military depot. By the war's end, the House had won a reputation for filling enormous orders at top speed. The sale of six hundred silver officer's swords produced by the silver shop had meanwhile put Tiffany & Company back in the spotlight along with Union aspirations, and Charles had earned another fortune.

One brush with violence occurred shortly after Gettysburg when a conscription office opened on the corner of 46th Street and Sixth Avenue. During the next two days the *Daily News* used a $300 service exemption clause to stir up the city's immigrant population, pillorying those who could afford the exemption and those who had "caused" the war. On July 13, 1863, the so-called draft riots broke out. A mob of fifty thousand, described by diarist George Templeton Strong as "Celtic," raged through

the streets for three days, looting, beating, and hanging blacks and aboli-
tionists. Governor Horatio Seymour and Mayor Wood were slow to
respond, and Charles and his boys were forced to shutter the windows
and pass out rifles and grenades. The police arrived just as the human
tornado was heading up Broadway toward Tiffany & Company. For
Charles luck and pluck seemed to go hand in hand.

As it was upon his eldest son's shoulders that Charles's hopes for
passing down his legacy lay, the Civil War years posed a double
threat to the future of Tiffany & Company. It is fitting that Louis
Comfort Tiffany's birth coincided with the 1848 Revolution, as he was
revolutionary in spirit. By the advent of the Civil War, as young Louis
came of age, no one knew this better than his father. One may in fact
view Louis's complex evolution within the framework of Charles's struggle to make of him a businessman, and Louis's determination to realize
a different destiny. Charles may have identified with Atlas, but making
a businessman of Louis Comfort Tiffany was a labor fit for Hercules.

Louis was a small, wiry, round-faced boy, with reddish brown hair and
thick dark brows. Like his father and grandfather, he had blue eyes that
sparkled against a dark complexion, and he too was ambitious, enterprising, and independent—qualities that had led Comfort and Charles to set
off on their own tracks. From them he acquired inexhaustible energy and
a prodigious capacity for work. But unlike either Comfort or Charles,
Louis was a born artist: sensitive, proud, imaginative, and headstrong.
Louis had also been born to great wealth in a country which had become
unhinged from its Puritan moorings. Comfort and Charles were products
of the first Industrial Revolution, the age of textiles, steam, and iron.
Louis grew up in the age of steel, chemicals, electricity, and oil, and the
accumulation of wealth in his lifetime was on an entirely different order.
Yet as *New York Times* art and literary editor Charles de Kay wrote in
1914, "Louis Comfort Tiffany was born with a golden spoon in his
mouth, but the spoon was immediately tucked away and he was seldom
permitted to remember its existence." Louis, in fact, never for a moment
forgot that golden spoon, but de Kay's words spoke to a fundamental
schism between Louis's generation and his forebears'. He was a child of

enormous wealth; he had leisure time, something that no Tiffany had known. And for Louis, that was tinder to fantasy.

His great boyhood influence was of course Tiffany & Company, a world of craftsmanship, quality, taste, beauty, and materialism. The colorful gems and gleaming gold and silver objets d'art in his father's showcases were as natural to Louis as the air he breathed. At a tender age he could distinguish brass from copper, gold from platinum, garnet from ruby, and appreciated the ways in which these materials responded to the artisan's touch. He knew the subtleties of chased silver, cloisonné enamel, quarter-sawn oak, letter press printing, and faceted gemstones. He saw the craftsman's skill and effort, the decorum of the clerk, the prices fetched.

But profit did not seem to interest the boy. His mind reeled with color, whether a carnelian or a six-carat "pigeon blood" ruby made no difference. Fueled by exotic fictions like Washington Irving's *The Alhambra* and James Fenimore Cooper's *Leatherstocking Tales,* his imagination ran wild. In the 1850s illustrated weeklies often featured African, Middle Eastern, and Oriental locales, and Louis seemed all too capable of imagining himself as somewhere, or someone, else. By the fifties New York itself was a spectacle of amusements that had not existed to distract Charles at a similar age. Niblo's Garden was a stone's throw from Tiffany & Company—a combination garden, café, theater, and social center. Henri Franconi opened his two-acre Hippodrome when Louis was five. Fronting Fifth Avenue and 23rd Street, it treated New Yorkers to the fare of a Roman circus: javelin and lance sports, monkeys astride ponies, ostriches chasing horses. The New York Crystal Palace opened in the same year, an immense iron and glass replica of the Hyde Park, London, Crystal Palace, site of the first great international exhibition. Nearby, on the site of the present New York Public Library, was the fantastic Egyptian-style Croton reservoir, a popular Sunday promenade.

At the time Manhattan was still built close to the ground, making conspicuous any structure over five stories. Thus from the doorway of Louis's first home at 57 Warren Street he could see the masts of tall ships to the west and the cupola of City Hall to the east; from the corner were visible the spires of Trinity Church and St. Paul's. On 10th Street, where the family moved when Louis was four and where they were to reside for the next eight years, the steeples of St. Mark's-in-the-Bouwerie and Grace Church were dominant. Further uptown the Latting Observatory and shot towers (for manufacturing bullets) projected dramatically against the low-slung horizon. Possessed in later years of a drive to erect towers of many sorts, all of them dramatic, the skyline of New York probably did impact on him. The seed of another motif may have been planted with a fad for octagonal homes which began in America in the year of Louis's birth; and the first sight of the Islamic architecture so influential in his artistic development may not have been abroad at all, but instead near Bridgeport, Connecticut, where Barnum had built his wildly theatrical mansion Iranastan. Erected in 1848, it remained a tourist attraction until it burned down in 1857, exactly one hundred years before Louis's own Persian-influenced Laurelton Hall was consumed by flames.

As Louis's artistic appreciation grew, so did his irreverence for the dollar, and Charles took this for insurrection. Charles had battled to establish the Tiffany hallmarks of quality and worth, while Louis grew up secure enough in these values to see beyond them. He saw that his father leaned toward the financial side of the art and commerce equation, that the intrinsic value of precious materials tended to subordinate artistic expression. And besides, though money was the object for Charles, to Louis frugality must have seemed the most tangible and paradoxical product of his father's labors. The struggle began, Charles meeting Louis with the full force of his disciplinarian personality, bending him like a sapling in the wind. In Charles's view the boy was careless, forgetful, and dreamy—in a word, spoiled. He seemed especially galled by Louis's handwriting and spelling.

In actuality, the boy's hand was not as bad as Charles made out. We know that Charles was never satisfied with his own handwriting—he thought it "stiff" and "cramped"—yet a graphologist characterized his copperplate script as "good and bold," and it was used for years as the model for the store's correspondence. In all likelihood, such peevish criticism masked an inner conflict. It was surely not coincidental that Charles used the same word—"stiff"—to criticize his own handwriting that Annie used to describe his personality.

Nonetheless, Charles remained relentless in his standards and drive for self-improvement, and he expected the same of his son. At the age of nine Louis had written, "I went to the sircus with Emile, I had a very nice time." Five years later, after a stint at the Flushing Academy on Long

Island and a succession of private tutors, Louis still could not spell to his father's satisfaction. Charles felt that the time had come to act decisively. The Civil War had commenced, and his solicitor Daniel Kingsland was sending his boy—Louis's circus companion, Emile—to the Eagleswood Military Academy. Louis would go too. In a sense, the move was typical of the same shrewd logic that had moved Charles to answer both patriotic duty and economic necessity by transforming Tiffany & Company into a military depot. Sending Louis to Eagleswood was both a means of dealing with his son and a patriot's sacrifice to the Union cause. With a little luck, Charles must have hoped, Louis would be spared the battle-field and would choose to join him at Tiffany & Company, rid of his careless habits, ready to learn the trade and eventually to take over the helm.

Thus on November 7, 1862, fourteen-year-old Louis Comfort Tiffany arrived at the school via Philadelphia and the Camden and Amboy Railroad. It snowed that day and the boy absentmindedly left his easel at the depot: though only twenty miles from Battery Park as the crow flies, Eagleswood was an infinite emotional distance from home. He awoke to reveille, slept after taps, and spent the hours between 6:00 A.M. and 8:30 P.M. never far from misery. He suffered the usual humiliations of the plebe; outranked, outflanked, and out of step, his every move was dictated by bugle blasts and flourishes of the snare drum. The academy was modeled after West Point, the cadets "organized into a battalion of five companies and . . . thoroughly instructed and exercised in Battalion drill." Everything had its place, gloves in one corner of the closet, umbrella in another, and overcoat on a nail in the back; it was therefore not long before young Louis received several marks—"not for bad behavior," he assured Annie, "but for forgetfulness." He wrote brave letters to his parents, but to Annie confessed, "I don't sleep as nicely as I did at home for the beds are just like boards so I am pretty tired." And again, "On Friday evenings we all have a letter to write which is rather difficult because I am such a miserable speller and when they examine them they are so full of mistakes that I feel quite ashamed of myself." He was also deeply homesick, missed his horse at Irvington, and shared with one boy, Eddy, a profound dislike for military life.

Two weeks after his son's arrival Charles wrote him these words of encouragement:

I was much pleased to see very great improvement in your hand writing, particularly in the forepart of the letter, before you got in a hurry . . . Cultivate a bold free hand & never allow yourself to write in too great haste.

Then he turned to the point, suggesting not only the worldview which had forged his own identity, but also a vital dimension to his filial relationship with Louis.

I feel confident that the two weeks you have been at [Eagleswood] has not been time wasted. I am not disappointed to hear that the discipline of your school is at first somewhat irksome—but do you not think yourself that in the end you will like it, & that it will be for your future good. A pleasant home and the care of too indulgent parents are not the best calculated to bring out and strengthen the highest qualities of a young man. A diamond, though of the *"first water,"* without hard grinding & polishing, would always remain without lustre.

The phrase "diamond of the first water" had a twofold meaning in the Gaslight Era. It indicated to the trade a diamond of the purest color and most expensive grade, and was also employed as an epithet for the best. (Jenny Lind, for example, was called "a diamond of the first water.") Thus the tacit parallel between the product that Charles sold and the ordeal to which he was subjecting Louis reveals a fundamentally positive view of his elder son, one which, for all his sniping, was surely communicated to Louis in a thousand other ways, and helped forge his unshakable belief in himself. Whatever criticisms Charles leveled at Louis, he also imparted the belief that his flaws were superficial, not structural, and this was a truly precious gift. No doubt it was easier to believe, before Freud, that at the human core lay not a welter of selfish, murderous drives, but a diamond in the rough. And what a quintessentially Victorian way to say "Buck up!" The "care of too indulgent parents" was probably a euphemism for Harriet, since Charles was hardly soft. Continuing in a teasing vein, he added,

The weather here is getting very cold and the shop windows in Broadway begin to display great assortments of skates, without doubt by the time of your vacation, skating in Central Park will be *fine*—*but perhaps* you will be *unwilling* to *leave* [Eagleswood] & prefer spending your vacation there, if so, I can send you a pair of Broadway skates from here.

He closed with the promise of a box of cakes and fruit. Louis had to be consoled by this, and by the fact that it soon would be Christmas.

But after this same Christmas furlough, Louis had nothing to look forward to but hard grinding and polishing. And then he discovered that his friend Eddy was leaving the academy, and that was the last straw. On January 14 the child marshaled his courage and poured out his heart to Papa.

> I have written to Mama and you a good many times, but they were such homesick ones that I tore them up, but I can not stand it any longer for to tell you the truth. I have tryed & tryed to be a man but tears will come and I know I can not help it. Dear Father won't you take me away from this school for I cannot learn my lessons, already the teachers are beginning to scold me for not learning them, but I do try. I feel so sick, so miserably homesick. Eddy is going to leave on the first of February and I know I cannot stand it longer. Some boys have left on Christmas. Oh! Papa if you only knew how badly I felt you would not refuse me for you put me here to learn and not to be miserable. I think that I can leave without being dismissed but I have said enough. Eddy is going for certainty and I can not stand it here alone for I do not care anything for anybody else . . . The boys are not nice and I think that most all [are] going in July . . . P.S. Papa don't think any less of me for this letter. I have given it a fair trial and am satisfied that I cannot be happy or learn as much as anywhere else. I will study all the time and mama can hear me or I will go to school any where you like but I promise you that I will study no matter where it is as long as it is not here.

Charles was not swayed by this appeal, however, and Louis remained at Eagleswood for three long years, years which he would recall negatively even in middle age. But he did settle down, and became one of the few cadets to receive no demerits for the 1862–63 year (a "mark" evidently differed from a demerit in being erasable). Eagleswood in fact may have proved far more congenial to Louis's talents and temperament than the unhappy schoolboy would then have admitted. In one letter he mentioned having gotten a "good mark for speaking," and in 1864 he won two of the academy's top prizes, for mathematics and drawing. Gradually his round cheeks gave way to a firm jaw, and petulance tempered into intense willfulness. In his blue dress Union Army uniform, the cap, boots, breeches, and jacket with rows of brightly polished brass buttons, with lambent eyes and hair curling darkly over his ears, he appeared self-possessed and handsome.

Drawing, it seems, had been Louis's first talent. At age nine he had written of winning a prize "for drawing well." We know, also, that Louis had attempted to bring his easel to Eagleswood, and that, one week after his arrival, he had professed natural philosophy—the study of nature—to be his favorite subject. At Eagleswood map making and the sketching of land and troop configurations were course requirements (following the West Point model). But Eagleswood also offered electives in drawing and painting. About C. W. King, the instructor for "Figure, Landscape, and Mechanical Drawing and Painting," nothing is known; but in 1863 the well-known landscape painter George Inness was lured to the military academy by the promise of a house in exchange for one of his paintings. At Eagleswood Inness served, informally at least, as an artist-in-residence, and Louis did not forget his "inspiring quality."

Whatever the aesthestic influence at Eagleswood on Louis, authority did not subdue him; rather, it spun him in a chrysalis. By his fifteenth birthday he had developed a studied indifference to the business world, an imperious confidence in his own taste, and the determination to become an artist without rival. His handwriting assumed a novel elegance, his signature ended with a flourish, and from the shell of a cadet misfit, Louis Comfort Tiffany the tastemaker began to emerge. It was fitting that his name was pronounced like that of Louis Quatorze, the Sun King, because he intended to act the part of the Tiffany scion. He would now correct his elder sister. "I agree with you when you say it is most time for me to make another visit home, although I would rather have the word *quite* put in the place of *most.*" He also felt moved to reveal to Annie the glories of nature. "I think Autumn is the most beautiful season in the year and I am sure that no person cannot help admiring the foliage."

One month after Grant accepted Lee's surrender at Appomattox, Louis prepared to take his final exams. His mind, however, was already roaming the fields at Irvington. He wrote his mother, "When do you expect to go to Irvington? I hope you will go soon for as soon as school closes I want to go to work sketching." And to Annie he wrote, "How does your dog do? I hope he will not desert you before I have time to paint him." Louis graduated in July 1865 and boarded the first northbound steamer at Perth Amboy. If Charles had genuinely hoped to mold Louis as his successor at Tiffany & Company, he had miscalculated. The Eagleswood Military Academy had just graduated a corporal whose chief pursuit would be beauty and greatest passion, flowers.

III

Along the Hudson River

Louis awoke at dawn each day that summer and disappeared along the banks of the Hudson River to return at dusk with burrs in his socks, his hair rumpled, his fingers flecked with paint, looking—his father may have thought—as if he had just been chased by the Headless Hessian Horseman of Sleepy Hollow. A painting of two calla lilies, signed and dated 1865, could be Louis's earliest extant work. Already he was able to capture nuances of color and texture, and the extravagance of the flower's shape. One lily towers over the other, revealing a continuing preoccupation with height, rank, and stature (like all Tiffanys, Louis was physically small, only five feet six at full growth).

He was also busy that summer making connections, demonstrating an early grasp of the artist's need for self-promotion. Since his father knew few painters and was not especially social, making contacts at Irvington was difficult. Annie, now twenty-one, had just graduated from Mrs. Hoffman's two-year finishing school, leaving her with a higher level of education than her brother (who by this time had an abiding prejudice against formal education of any kind). Together, brother and sister decided to stage a big house party at summer's end for neighbors, family, and their friends. After a trip downriver to Yonkers for a group photograph, the youngsters spent the weekend riding the bridle paths, playing croquet, and rowing the Tappan Zee. On Saturday evening they held a dance, on Sunday morning piled into a four-in-hand and went to church. Among them was Emile Kingsland, who punctuated the festivities by reading aloud from *Nicholas Nickleby,* "whenever there was time." Annie called him "one of the kindest, most obliging fellows I ever knew."

Lieutenant Kingsland had graduated from Eagleswood the year before Louis, and he knew Harry Gray, a math professor (and lieutenant colonel) in Louis's first year. Gray was the son of Henry Peters Gray, a leading portrait and history painter, known as a colorist. Emile wrote Louis from New York on October 2, "You're a nice boy to keep a promise. Where are those two pieces of music you were going to find me, the 'Waterfall Gallop' and 'Promotional Waltz.' Where is your head?" But he added what Louis had hoped to hear. "I have seen Harry G——— and spoken to his father who says he will be happy to see you." Gray was a prominent member of the National Academy of Design and the Century Club, the two art organizations of importance in mid-century New York, and he was in a position to further Louis's career. The result of their meeting is not known, but shortly thereafter Louis was able to persuade Charles to send him and Annie on a tour of the art capitals of the world. After graduation, Louis had evidently declared his intention of becoming an artist, and Charles, recognizing the futility of opposing his decision, had given him his full support. This, of course, was helpful, if not essential, to an artist in an era when expensive peregrinations were the norm.

Blessing their "darling Papa," Louis and Annie departed on November 1 aboard the paddle steamer *Scotia,* chaperoned by their aunt Lydia Young, widow of Charles's first partner. They returned on March 21, 1866, by the *Persia* after touring England, Ireland, France, Italy, and Sicily. The trip redoubled Louis's appreciation for art while initiating a lifetime love of travel. The pencil sketches and watercolors within the covers of his small sketchbook confirmed his talent, sensitivity to light and color, and love of flowers. And he spent that summer much as he had the last, painting in the fields at Irvington and along the banks of the Hudson River.

Charles's purchase of the old Barent Dutcher farm was perhaps as fateful for Louis as Comfort's move to Danielson had been for Charles. For seven successive years now the Tiffanys had summered by the effluence which Henry Hudson had named "the Great River in the Mountains." The Hudson had been a boon to the Indians, Dutch, and British in turn, and for Americans had been especially provident after construction of the Erie Canal. It had helped to make New York City the commercial hub of the United States, graced the long valley through which it flowed, and given rise to the first distinctly American school of art. The pantheists who painted the river valley's "Divine Architecture" and "Sublime Subject" were such zealots they were dubbed "Hudson River Painters."

Louis grew up in the most formative decade of the Hudson River school, and was still a boy when its undisputed champion, Frederic Edwin Church, became the first painter to achieve worldwide recognition for American fine art. Church's reputation was based largely on two canvases, *Niagara* and *Heart of the Andes,* the twin apotheoses of the school's botanically accurate, sweepingly majestic style. From the great French academician Jean-Léon Gérôme came the verdict, *"Ça commence là-bas."*

At home Church's popularity was such that when he and his wife appeared in public crowds often burst into spontaneous applause. His atelier in the Studio Building at 51–55 West 10th Street was a virtual national landmark. Surely, in the spring of 1859 when *Heart of the Andes* had gone on display there, young Louis Comfort had been among the twenty thousand to pay a quarter to stand before the masterpiece. Lit by flickering gas jets, framed by black crepe curtains, it was, according to *Littell's Living Age,* an unforgettable sight, a five-by-eight-foot window to another world, "a complete condensation of South America—its gigantic vegetation, its splendid Flora, its sapphire waters, its verdant pampas and its colossal mountains." If by some chance Louis had missed it there, he might have seen it at the spring 1864 Metropolitan Sanitary Fair, a benefit for Civil War casualties (where a pair of Tiffany & Company commemorative swords were awarded General Grant and Admiral Farragut). Or he might have seen it three years later at the 1867 International Exposition in Paris (where Tiffany & Company became the first American silversmith to win a medal from a foreign jury). Church was the legend of Louis's boyhood. What young American artist would not have hoped to follow in his glorious footsteps?

The coordinates of Louis's own "most formative decade" crossed, therefore, at precisely this physical, spatial, and historical juncture to nurture his innate interests and abilities. "Nature is always right"; "Nature is always beautiful"; Louis subscribed to both maxims. As a boy how often had he heard of the manifest destiny of Americans "to overspread and to possess the whole of the continent which Providence has given us for the development of the great experiment of liberty"? The nationalistic fervor sweeping the land had also taken hold of artists, limners of the

American landscape in particular. Fidelity to nature, the hallmark of the Hudson River school, was charged with the intensity of a creed. To study and reveal nature was thought to be a higher calling, one which exercised a moral effect on artist and patron alike. And for Louis, nature would remain always his most important source of inspiration, guiding him through a labyrinth of media as if by Ariadne's thread.

The starting point for artists in New York was then enrollment in the "antique class" of the all-powerful National Academy of Design. The academy's respect for tradition was emphasized by the building in which it was housed—a replica of the Doge's Palazzo in Venice. Louis, a mustache newly grown upon his face, found himself within its marble and brownstone walls on November 5, 1866, drawing from plaster casts of Greek and Roman statuary. The academy set a tortoise pace for the *nouveau,* however, convinced that "until the student knows his letters he can not read." Only by demonstrating proficiency at each level did he progress from antique to "life" charcoal drawing, and thence to oil and color. Color was considered secondary to form, and draftsmanship more fundamental than either composition or color. But Louis was impatient, the ordeal of Eagleswood having left him with hair-trigger sensitivity to dogmatism of any kind. He was quick to rebel against the ascendancy of form and the formists. It was not long before he had wangled his way back into the studio of his former mentor George Inness, whom Louis would recall as a colorist.

A second-generation Hudson River painter, Inness was one of the enduring talents of nineteenth-century American art. His Barbizon-inspired style subordinating detail to mood achieved a monochromatic, often ocher atmosphere of still melancholy, even in an upbeat theme such as the postwar harvest in *Peace and Plenty* (1865). Louis was relieved to be inspired rather than taught by Inness in any formal sense. He observed the bearded, bespectacled master, painted his own pictures, bristled— probably—at Inness's occasional criticisms, and listened intently to heated exchanges between Inness and fellow painters William Page and James Steele MacKaye. Inness "set high ideals before the student," Louis recalled. Devoted to the mystical notions of Emanuel Swedenborg, he strove to capture the spirituality that Swedenborg taught was embodied in nature. Inness believed that "the true use of art is, first, to cultivate the artist's own spiritual nature and, secondly, to enter as a factor in general civilization." And, most importantly, "The true artistic impulse is divine." All this Louis took to heart.

Louis was also frequenting the studio of Samuel Colman at the same time. If Inness sharpened his color sense and idealism, Samuel Colman brightened his palette and broadened his view of art. Colman was the son of New York publisher of prints and fine arts bookseller William Colman, who had opened one of the first art galleries in New York, exhibiting among others Thomas Cole, leader of the Hudson River school. After Cole's death Asher B. Durand had become the school's principal painter, and Samuel Colman had studied under him. Though sixteen years older than Louis, Colman became his friend and traveling partner, linking Louis's fine and decorative art interests. Due no doubt to Colman's galvanizing influence, Louis's very first entry in an academy exhibition was a watercolor called *Afternoon*. (In 1866 Colman had become a cofounder and first president of the American Water Color Society, promoting the "secondary" medium in the face of academic disapproval.) So when Louis found himself within the academy palazzo once again in the spring of 1867, it was, typically, to challenge the status quo. The work was displayed, as usual, in stacks from the top of the wall to the bottom, the Hanging Committee "skiing" inferior work to the more remote positions. But evidently they had seen something in *Afternoon* because it was "hung on the line"—that is, at eye level. At nineteen Louis also won his first notice, a favorable one.

Inness believed that the best way to learn art was "the Paris way," and in early 1868, Louis once again left New York. He lodged in Tiffany & Company's branch office at 79, rue de Richelieu and painted in the Passy atelier of Léon Charles Adrien Bailly. One wonders why Louis bypassed the prestigious Ecole des Beaux-Arts, but, as the young American painter J. Alden Weir wrote his father, the drawing instructor at West Point, "the old students act toward the nouveaux . . . as the cadets to the plebes." Louis had been hazed at Eagleswood, and simply did not care to be stripped and painted Prussian blue or caput mortuum—as happened to some Americans. Louis did "study hard under Bailly, a thorough teacher of drawing who . . . took particular pains with the young American." In May Louis exhibited a still life at the Palais des Champs Elysées. If "the Paris way" meant struggling with draftsmanship once again, Louis compensated at the theater and opera. Sporting wide-striped ties and velvet collars, he cut a dashing figure below the footlights, adoring his Divine Sarah Bernhardt. At the salons he was impressed enough by Orientalist Léon Adolphe August Belly to visit his studio. Venturing south of the capital, Louis made a gouache of the buttressed bulk of the Blois cathedral—"the finest château in France," he later declared.

He returned to New York in 1869, taking a studio (which he maintained through 1878) in the YMCA on 23rd Street, opposite the Academy. Still very much the Hudson Valley painter, he titled one canvas *Along the Hudson River.* A view upstream, it framed an impressionistic panorama of shifting water and light, as a schooner's sails made the most of a calm day. Another landscape, *View of the Hudson,* was acquired by Thomas B. Clarke, a small coup since Clarke was the foremost collector of American art at that time.

A third landscape is interesting from a psychological point of view. In *Clouds: A Study of the Hudson,* Louis painted a steep incline with four earth-bound firs reaching toward the heavens. In descending order down the slope, the trees were all of equal height except for the second. The second tree Louis painted twice as thick and twice as tall as the others. Four was of course the number of the Tiffany siblings, and he was the second-born. The configuration of trees which attracted his notice was therefore an objective correlative to the preeminent position he was assuming in the family.

The Tiffany scion was certainly hurtling rapidly down the track. At twenty-two he became the youngest member ever elected to the Century Club, and the following year became an Associate Academician. The very character traits which Charles Tiffany had once thought liabilities in a businessman had subtly turned to Louis's advantage, metamorphosing into creative tools.

Having abandoned his hopes of Louis's filling his shoes at Tiffany & Company three years earlier, in 1868 Charles signed what must have been bittersweet papers of incorporation. The House of Tiffany would thrive, but not as a family business. But Charles also saw mutual advantages to Louis's being an artist. His success would enhance the reputation of Charles's "school of art taste" and "teacher of art progress," and add luster to his image as art patron. Charles became a trustee of the Metropolitan Museum of Art and the Museum of Natural History, a founder of the New York Society of Fine Arts, and a fellow of the Geographical Society and of the National Academy of Design. Naturally his presence in these organizations was helpful to Louis, and over the years his father's finances, reputation, clout, and connections advanced Louis's career immeasurably.

I t was just then, with the cogs whirring smoothly, that Louis jumped the tracks and established himself as an Orientalist. Oddly enough, Frederic E. Church may have indirectly helped spark Louis's interest in Orientalism. Returning from Beirut and Damascus in 1869 infatuated with Syrian architecture, Church built a Moorish mansion called Olana near the spot where Henry Hudson had wintered his fleet 260 years before. Louis would have known of Church's Orientalist fervor at an early date through landscape painter Lockwood de Forest, younger brother of Louis's boyhood friend Robert de Forest, a cousin of Mrs. Church. Then, too, Louis had seen Orientalist canvases at various Parisian salons during his last stay, as well as observed a Moorish influence in Samuel Colman, who had traveled in southern Spain in the early sixties and painted works like *Hill of the Alhambra, Granada.* This fascination of Western artists with Eastern subject matter had roots in Napoleonic imperialism and the occupation of Egypt by France in 1798. By Victoria's time some painters were employing the odalisque-in-the-oda theme to legitimize the unconscionably erotic. Of course there were Westerners who painted the Muslim world with real reverence; but in any case, by 1870 Orientalism was very much in the air, and like Charles, Louis was quick to use a favorable wind. In 1837, that wind had blown toward New York. Now it blew to North Africa. By May 5 Louis was in Tangier.

He had begun his travels in Italy and then made his way to Egypt, and from there west across the continent. It was as Mark Twain had described it in *Innocents Abroad,* his 1867 account of his trip to Morocco: "The pictures used to seem exaggerations—they seemed too weird and fanciful for reality. But behold, they were not wild enough. They have not told half the story." Louis, too, felt the fabric of his own technological, Victorian society—the conceptions, mores, forms, inhibitions, and inventions—ripped away by an Eastern culture virtually unchanged since the sixteenth century. He experienced an epiphany in the most literal sense: it came to him—a divine manifestation—in a blinding flash. Overwhelmed by the hot ashy light and vibrant color of the tropics, Louis discovered his spiritual nature as a colorist. His intuitive attraction to color—and to colorists like Gray and Inness—had been questioned by the academics. But, he would recall:

> When first I had a chance to travel in the East and to paint where the people and the buildings also are clad in beautiful hues, the preëminence of color in the world was brought forcibly to my attention.

He crossed the Strait of Gibraltar to Algeciras, and traveled to Seville, San Roque, and Granada, all the while making quick sketches and water-colors and buying photographs to serve as the basis for finished studio paintings.

> I returned to New York wondering why we made so little use of our eyes, why we refrained so obstinately from taking advantage of color in our architecture and our clothing when Nature indicates its mastership, when, by its use under the rules of taste, we can extend our innocent pleasure and have more happiness in life, at the same time adding to the happiness of our neighbor.

The revelation of color's "sovereign importance" was the verso side of Louis's discovery of nature, and it fused his artistic identity. Years later he gleefully recalled enraging "the 'legitimate' water colorists or sticklers for 'wash' by using body color freely." But nature itself was on the colorist's side. As he observed,

> It is curious, is it not, that line and form disappear at a short distance, while color remains visible at a much longer? . . . Color and movement, not form, are our earliest impressions when babies. Insects are attracted by color (not form) when in search of food. For that very reason flowers develop color, because they must have the visits of insects to reproduce their kind. And if the plant has flowers that require a visit from a moth or night-flying beetle, why, then it produces—not a pink or blue blossom, which would not "carry" in the dark, but white or pale-yellow petals that call the favoring insect out of the night sky.

Within five years Louis was well on his way to becoming an important American painter, and one of the first to achieve a lasting reputation for Eastern scenes. In 1872 his large canvas *On the Way Between Old and New*

Cairo was given the "post of honor" in the Academy's South Gallery. And *Bazaar in Cairo,* a large watercolor, was said to have "received more praise than any other work in this collection." Louis was invited to show at major exhibitions, where his paintings sold for $500 to $1,000. He was the talk of the town; one paper rhapsodized that he was "beyond question taking the lead of the young men and is consequently in great danger of being spoiled by flattery." At the 1876 Philadelphia Centennial Exposition the judges accepted eleven of his works—eight of them Middle Eastern scenes. And the following year painter Wyatt Eaton wrote J. Alden Weir in Paris in an effort to convince him to return home. "I believe there is no reason why we should not go on progressively here as well as abroad—Swain Gifford, Thompson, Homer Martin, Winslow Homer, Tiffany, Inness and some others are going ahead splendidly."

Recently, the academy's Hanging Committee had been skiing old work and hanging new on the line, delighting the younger, more progressive wing of members and critics, but angering the long-dominant conservatives. The latter responded by instituting a "seven-foot ruling," which guaranteed each one of them seven feet of wall space at annual exhibitions. When the young sculptor Augustus Saint-Gaudens had a plaster figure study rejected on grounds of lack of space, he and some others walked. Among them were George Inness, Albert Pinkham Ryder, John La Farge, Thomas Eakins, John Singer Sargent, and James Abbott McNeill Whistler—in short, many of those who left a mark on American art. In 1877 Louis became a cofounder and first treasurer of this Society of American Artists. In March 1878 he participated in the landmark Kurtz Gallery exhibition, which shattered the National Academy's aesthetic stranglehold. New York *Tribune* critic Clarence Cook wrote, "This exhibition means revolution." And it did.

By this time Louis had been married for almost six years. Charles and Harriet, before their betrothal in 1841, had first been neighbors, playmates, and childhood sweethearts, and their marriage had solidified a relationship between families who had thoroughly understood one another's values and expectations. Louis and his future bride had also met at a young age under similarly old-fashioned circumstances. As children Louis and his siblings had frequently visited their uncle John and aunt Lydia Young in Norwich, Connecticut—sixty-five miles down the Quinebaug and Shetucket rivers from Danielson. Even after John's death the Young home at 73 Washington Street had remained the locus for a lively group of young cousins and friends. It was on one such visit to Norwich that Louis had penned the fateful words, "I have a very nice time here. I am getting acquainted with two or three girls, their names are Lilly Perkins, May Goddard and Ella Morton . . ."

Since that time May (Mary Woodbridge) Goddard had become Annie Tiffany's bosom friend. She was the youngest of four children born to Mary Woodbridge Perkins Goddard and Levi Hart Goddard, a prosperous businessman. May had lived a year in the Salem countryside before moving to a house in Norwich just a few blocks from the Youngs. There they had taken in May's elder orphaned cousins, the Mitchells. The children of the Tiffany, Goddard, and Mitchell families had spent many cold winter evenings playing games like ring toss and parlor croquet; together they had summered at the Pequot outside New London, swimming, sailing, and fishing the Thames River.

Then, when the Goddard and Mitchell boys went to war, May was left at home to worry. She kept a notebook in which she logged the authors she had read (Dickens, Trollope, Thackeray, Beecher, Charlotte Brontë, Macaulay), and beautifully transcribed poems which held special meaning for her, revealing a struggle between her strong religious and patriotic feelings and her fear of death—among them, "The Reveille," "Waiting for Our Soldiers," "Mortally Wounded," and " 'Buried with His Niggers.' " This last was about Robert Gould Shaw, the young white officer who had led the first black volunteer regiment in the Civil War, and died with them while storming a fort outside Charleston. The bodies of the Union dead had been desecrated and buried in a common grave, and the regiment had become a cause célèbre; Augustus Saint-Gaudens would make their memorial, which still stands on Boston Commons.

Alfred Goddard had not come back either. Killed in his first battle, he had been given a hero's funeral in Norwich. But Harry Goddard and Alfred Mitchell had returned, and May's postwar entries had turned to themes of nature, maternity, and love. By the time she had descended with a Norwich contingent on Tiffany Hall in the summer of 1865, she had grown beautiful. Annie had declared her "the loveliest girl I ever knew . . . Besides being the prettiest, she is the best girl I ever knew." Yet according to May, until an autumn day in 1871, neither she nor Louis knew there was anything more between them than "the love of a brother and sister."

Their romance probably began in January 1870, when May came to New York to visit Annie. To pass the time they formed a "Thought Exchange Society," with Charles acting as its president, Harriet the vice-president, and Annie the motioner. Louis (the artist) and May (the secretary) must have huddled together over the tiny book in which they recorded the Society's activities. May had actually come to promote the bid of her shy cousin, Alfred Mitchell, for Annie's hand, but appearances were against him. Though a major in the 13th Connecticut Regiment during the Civil War, he had squandered an inheritance, drifted through the whaling, ship chandlery, mining, and writing professions, and was keenly sensitive to his appearance as a treasure hunter. But with May, who had grown up with him, readily testifying to his "spotless purity," Charles eventually gave his consent.

It was just six months after the pair's April wedding that Louis and May fell in love, and May wrote her brother Harry:

> I am so very very happy . . . Louis says he is in love with me and I believe him, and so—well he has asked me to be his wife and I have promised that I will be . . . it all happened one day about three weeks ago, and . . . seemed so strange and funny . . . I thought perhaps there was some mistake about it so I did not dare tell anybody about it and I told Louis to go away and stay away two months at least and let me think a little, but somehow it did not take quite so long to think it out and he could not wait and I could not wait . . . I am so happy and so sure that Louis loves me and that I love Louis that we are both very ridiculous, and I am afraid will be just about as silly as Alf and Annie have been . . .

One of Louis's landscapes provides a moving testament to their courtship in Norwich. Placing his easel on a grassy knoll, Louis painted the pastoral splendor of George D. Fuller's country store. May presumably watched, skirts spread over a picnic blanket, hair chignoned as usual, her lips like Cupid's bow, her kind eyes admiring the genius of which she was convinced. She too loved nature and eagerly shared her beloved "inland city" and its surroundings with Louis. Later, a trotter whisked them through the rolling country and shaded lanes of nearby Salem, past May's pre-Revolutionary ancestral homes. The Goddards were also from gentry stock, with long roots in rural Connecticut, and the Tiffanys were assured that May, though two years older than Louis, would prove a conventionally excellent Victorian wife, selfless in her devotion to family, hearth, and home. They were married in the Goddard home on May 15, 1872.

May's sister Julia G. Piatt would later describe May's marriage to Louis as "nearly twelve years of rare happiness on earth," adding that "the only drawback she ever had—was her ill health," a reference to a constitutional frailty in May which loomed ever larger with the years. Even so, Julia wrote, "she would not have exchanged her lot for any on earth."

It seems that May was worn down by the combination of childbirth and incessant travel. She became pregnant within three months of settling into the Tiffany home at 255 Madison Avenue and, on April 3, 1873, gave birth to Mary Woodbridge Tiffany, whom they called May-May. The birth left May tired and thin, and her recovery was slow. Yet she became pregnant again within the year and left for Europe soon afterward. Louis's Islamic tableaux had brought great success and, having exhausted his source material, he was anxious to be painting from life once again. The plan was to link up with Samuel Colman and his wife in France and travel to Algeria after the baby was born—an annual or biennial trip having become vital to Louis's artistic progress.

They arrived in London in the spring of 1874 and made a quiet crossing to France. After meeting the Colmans in Paris they took adjoining suites in the Hotel de France et Bath, on the rue St.-Honoré (near the Louvre). One morning after Louis and Samuel had left for the academy, May wrote Annie a long, cheerful letter, a good part of it devoted to reassuring her sister-in-law (and herself) that the French cuisine was helping to restore her weight. "I have just finished a delightful lunch or déjeuner of chocolate, bread & butter & scrambled egg," she began. Louis had also tempted her with crepes and asparagus with a special sauce, and had brought her pretty flower pots filled with sweet strawberries, each as long as her little finger. Their suite, she wrote, had "sun in the morning, good attendance & very nice table." In the parlor between their suites Samuel had shown off his new sketches, "and they were beautiful—the watercolors particularly." Samuel had found the French exhibition "remarkably poor" that year, in contrast probably to the vibrating light, broken brushwork, and flattened perspective seen in the landmark impressionist exhibition at Nadars Gallery. May observed that much had changed since

Louis's last visit to France. He lamented the partial destruction of a column and statue of Napoleon in the Place Vendôme by a Republican mob during the Commune. "But [it] is being rebuilt," May added hastily. She made no other mention of the effects of the Franco-Prussian War and the abrupt transition from Second Empire to Third Republic.

And why not? It was May's first trip abroad and she and Louis were deeply in love. One "warm & lovely" day they strolled through the Tuileries; in London she had bought stockings in silk, lisle thread, and balbriggan in beautiful shades to match her traveling dresses. And in Paris she found "lovely little traveling dresses for baby [May-May] of batiste for 10 francs—prettily embroidered." But May also wrote that her hands were so thin that her engagement ring kept slipping off her finger. And she mentioned an acquaintance who had "lost her child & was alarmingly ill for a long time . . ." Despite her optimism, May must have had doubts—and possibly prophecy—about her health and pregnancy and travels (they planned to tour Brittany before settling on the French Riviera to have the baby). Yet May could not admit to Annie, nor to herself probably, that she would have felt more secure at home in New York.

By October they were settled midway between Monaco and the Italian border in Menton's Hôtel d'Italy, the snow-capped Maritime Alps at their backs, before them the azure Mediterranean. Here May got two months of precious rest, and Mrs. Goddard arrived by Thanksgiving with May's cousin Lilly Perkins, and May's old nurse, to help May through the last month. Since Annie's birthday fell on Thanksgiving that year and she was expecting her first child, they arranged a meal in May's room with a blazing fire and champagne toasts, and, in order to be together in mind and spirit if not in person, dined at the same time as the Mitchells at home.

On December 9, with his father in attendance, Charles Louis Tiffany was born and pronounced by the obstetrician, a Dr. Marriot, a "very large fine" and "remarkably strong" child. To the family's relief his assessment of May was equally sanguine. Wrote May, "I did not think I could love another child as we do Baby May but I am not afraid now! This dear little fellow seems just as necessary to us as our little girl and Louis is quite as proud of him as I am." But she added:

Tomorrow when the Dr. comes the important question of wet nurses is to be decided. As I had only a few drops of milk my little boy has had nothing but cow's milk from the first & as the milk in Menton is not remarkably good—the cows being fed on what they can get—we are a little afraid to risk for him the changes of milk in these countries.

That same day the baby got diarrhea and the doctor saw at once that nothing could save him. Louis had already suspected Dr. Marriot's competence when he saw him "finishing May on too fast," and he had switched to a Dr. Bennet, "one of the finest medical men in Europe, especially for ladies." Evidently it was Dr. Bennet who had alerted them to the local (of course unpasteurized) milk. But too late. By a weird twist of fate Annie gave birth to a girl on the same day that little Charles died of dehydration, December 29. They buried him two weeks later in Menton's fortresslike *cimétière,* situated on a hill overlooking the harbor.

Dr. Bennet told them that the baby must have been born sickly (not a surprising conclusion, given May's health and after so much travel) and would not have survived regardless of the bad milk, but May did not believe him. She bore up stoically, saying to Louis that if one child had to die she was glad it was theirs "as Annie has none." She wrote Annie, "God has taken away his precious gift and He knows why. Poor Louis— it seemed as if he *could* not lose his boy. He loved him more than I had thought a man could love a little helpless baby of three weeks."

But May was devastated (she dated her letter 1876 instead of 1875!), and her health failed again. The doctor insisted that she lie still in bed for two weeks before he made a thorough examination. Louis wrote his parents on January 3, "all of last winter [Dr. Bennet thought] there was something wrong and that it was not simply weakness, but that there was a decided cause and if it was not cured she would only get up worse than before." Despite this sobering diagnosis Louis added, "We shall go to Algiers as soon as May is well." By the tenth, due to May's condition, this plan seemed less certain. Annie tactfully suggested that they go elsewhere (no doubt thinking of more healthful spots). But missing the point Louis replied:

I do not think our health will allow it. I did want so much to go to India or Persia but it is not the place for either of us and is also bad for baby May so that I shall have to give up my hopes in that direction, but I still have hopes that I shall be able to obtain subjects which I can make original.

If they did indeed return to New York, they were back—in Algeria—by December for the winter season. Unbeknownst to them, May's "decided cause" was probably the first stage of tuberculosis, diagnosed only in the twelfth and final year of her "rare happiness on earth."

Barring this depressing incident, there is indeed no reason to doubt May's happiness in marriage. But her happiness was conditioned by the prevailing expectations for marriage and female acquiescence. Louis wanted her to accompany him on his travels and May was eager to do his bidding. But she was not constitutionally fit for the voracious enthusiasm and breakneck speed with which he traveled, and this should have been evident before Menton, if not from the outset. Thus, with Louis, the Tiffany imperative began to assume a solipsistic aspect. The baby's death and May's collapse was a warning which, in his single-minded pursuit of beauty, Louis did not heed.

IV

The Cultured Despot

Among Louis's more useful traits as an artist were his restless curiosity, a seismographic sensitivity to change, and a chameleonlike adaptability to the cultural climate. In an earlier, more constant age these qualities might have distracted him from his purpose, diluted and siphoned his energies. But in an era of increasingly rapid change they served to keep him abreast of the latest developments and made him thoroughly a creature of his times. The rampant capitalization and industrialization of the first half of the nineteenth century had brought fabulous riches to relatively few while establishing a broadly based middle class. The leap in technology and productivity was of course accompanied by a host of ills: materialism, exploitation of labor, pollution, and a decline in the aesthetic environment. The result was a widespread critique of culture, which, in England, took the shape of a reform movement.

From this grew the British Aesthetic Movement (and its American counterpart), which cross-fertilized the decorative and fine arts. This aim was joined to the larger social and moral ends of the reform movement, so that it became commonplace to speak of these decorative art objects as "missionaries to convert the philistine." The idea was to reach into the home and remake it artistically, ennobling and inspiring people on an everyday level, and help, thereby, to create a better society.

Of the many spokesmen for the British Aesthetic Movement, John Ruskin and William Morris were most persuasive. Ruskin, the art critic and advocate of the pre-Raphaelites, shared with Morris, the leader of the Arts and Crafts Movement, a contempt for the uniformity and shoddiness of machine-made goods. Morris coined the phrase "fine arts workman" and commanded, "Have nothing in your home that you do not know to be useful or believe to be beautiful." Ruskin extolled the virtues of the medieval craftsman and vilified Victorian standards. But while Ruskin crusaded for truth to nature in art, Morris applied himself to its marketability.

In America the catalyst for these ideas was the 1876 international Philadelphia Centennial Exposition. It stimulated a wave of creativity and led to the founding of many new clubs, groups, exhibitions, publications, and organizations. In 1877, in New York alone, the Society of American Artists, the Tile Club, and the New York Etching Club came into being. Also that year, inspired by the exhibit of the Royal School of Needlework, South Kensington, London, Candace Wheeler founded a New York Society of Decorative Artists. Devoting it to "all items of feminine manufacture," Wheeler aimed to unite the craft ethos of William Morris with the needs of "indigent gentlewomen." Her extraordinary Board of Managers included Mrs. John Jacob Astor, Mrs. Cyrus W. Field, Mrs. Hamilton Fish, August Belmont, Joseph Hodges Choate, and William Cullen Bryant. And, with these connections, sister societies were quickly established in other major cities.

Textile art was one medium now being taken seriously by fine artists. Samuel Colman, a connoisseur and collector of Oriental textiles, knew Wheeler from the "blue teas" given by Julia Ward Howe in Newport. At these teas (where guests could speak of anything they pleased so long as it related to the theme of blue) Wheeler, Colman, and John La Farge had somehow managed to discuss textiles at some length. Through this connection Colman, Louis Tiffany, and Lockwood de Forest joined Wheeler's Board of Managers, and on Wednesday evenings the latter two taught a course on unglazed pottery.

With the emergence of an Aesthetic Movement in America the decorative arts were effectively legitimized, breeching the sacrosanct wall between them and the fine arts. It was as if Louis's longest suit of cards had suddenly been declared trumps. His turn to the fine arts had, he admitted later in a monograph on his career, been made in a spirit of "reaction against the commercial element" in his father's business. But in seven years of painting he had blown off enough steam to see that the fine arts were not necessarily pure nor the mercantile world corrupt, and that the applied arts fold in which he had been nurtured was grounded in a venerable tradition. With adolescent revolt tempering into artistic iconoclasm, he began to appreciate and draw upon this background.

Louis had been particularly influenced by Edward C. Moore, his father's chief designer and silversmith. Moore avidly collected Islamic pottery and metal and glass objects (today part of the collection in the Metropolitan Museum) and helped to introduce a "Saracenic" style in American industrial art. Louis was no doubt already under Moore's influence in 1875 when he had written Annie, "I am trying now to study into the Saracens history and in their old life. There will be plenty of field for me [in Algeria] which has never been touched before and yet which embraces the finest architecture & ornaments in existence." Islamic prohibitions against representational art had spawned an unsurpassed decorative art tradition—geometrically complex arabesques, striking color combinations, superb craftsmanship—to which Louis's travels had given him considerable exposure.

Another influence on Louis was Annie's brother-in-law Donald G. Mitchell, best-selling author of *Reveries of a Bachelor* and coeditor with Harriet Beecher Stowe of the decorative arts magazine *Hearth and Home.* As chairman of the decorative arts judges at the Centennial he had predicted that "to those living in cities whose rear windows look upon neglected or dingy areas or courts . . . the equipment of a window with rich designs would be a perpetual delight." Examples of the painter's sensibility turned to decorative arts were everywhere—Frederic Church's Olana, James McNeill Whistler's Peacock and Primrose Rooms, and La Farge's Trinity Church, hailed as "the finest specimen of a decorated interior to be found on this continent." It would have been surprising had Louis not wanted to try his hand.

Louis got that opportunity after January 7, 1878, when May bore a son named Charles Lewis Tiffany II. With Louis's sister Louise and brother Burnie also living under the patriarchal roof, Louis's family of four needed to make other arrangements, giving him the chance to decorate his own apartment. While taking temporary quarters at 68 Madison Avenue, Louis began to design a showplace penthouse at the Bella Apartment House at 48 East 26th Street, near the northeast corner of Madison Square, dubbed by O. Henry "the flye-eye of New York." At the "pupil" of this most fashionable part of the city were a placid green park, with its flowering gardens, statuary, fountains, nannies, and prams. Carriages rattled around the Square—the pivot from which one "would see the world"—passing the striped awnings and wrought iron fence of Delmonico's, the grand Fifth Avenue Hotel, the old steepled Madison Square Presbyterian Church, aristocratic brownstone mansions, and Gilmore's Garden (soon to be renamed Madison Square Garden).

Louis's first effort at interior design was widely praised. *Artistic Houses* included the Bella in its "Series of Interior Views of a Number of the Most Beautiful and Celebrated Homes in the United States." Donald Mitchell wrote ten articles about the Bella which appeared in the periodical *Our Continent,* progressing from room to room, issue after issue, like a baroque soap opera. Mitchell put his finger on the essence of Tiffany's style when he wrote that Louis had "welded the decorative arts of the east and west into one harmonious whole." Employing a filching, ransacking eclecticism, Louis had assimilated motifs of mixed parentage and made them original through their new context. Though he had never studied interior design his work epitomized the new Aesthetic Movement.

He juxtaposed an elevator with a medieval lobby and India-red walls, in the dining room crossed a wooden colonial mantel, blue Japanese textiles, and a painting of a turkey and pumpkins. The library walls he faced with Chinese matting divided in the manner of Japanese *kamoi;* by filling one section with a Colman seascape he advanced the textiles to the level of fine art while treating the painting decoratively. In the parlor he hung an Irvington-on-Hudson scene on pink Japanese wallpaper, and scattered mica on the ceiling to reflect the light of a mosque lamp. At night the flame of a gas torch flickered over a rack of Moorish weapons and bits of glass, studs, and ornamental nails embedded in the ax-cut beams of the lobby. The hall contained one of his first stained-glass windows, of crude amethyst glass leaded into a serpentine shape. True to Donald Mitchell's prediction at the Centennial, the "rich design" obscured a neglected, dingy area—the shaftway.

If Louis needed further encouragement to make a career in industrial art, he got it from the example of Tiffany & Company. At Philadelphia the firm had won its first gold medal and *Harper's Weekly* had written that its exhibit, featuring a thirty-carat yellow Brunswick diamond and a necklace of twenty-seven rare Golconda diamonds, "attracted more attention than any other object at the Centennial, if we except the great Corliss engine"—the very symbol of American industry. Tiffany &

Company's jewels were therefore second in fascination only to the technology which had financed them. Two years later at the Paris Exposition Universelle Tiffany & Company won a gold medal for jewelry and the *grand prix* for silverware, and Charles was created a Chevalier of the Legion of Honor of France. British designer Christopher Dresser wrote that Tiffany & Company now occupied "the proud position of being the first silversmith of the world."

It was natural that Louis conclude:

> As to those who cling to the view that art lies only in hands of painters and sculptors, their patrons are tending to become relatively fewer as time goes on. No profession is more overcrowded. Clients do not keep on increasing; it is rather the other way around.

Unlike William Morris, Louis had no socialistic tendencies and, one day in the spring of 1879, he resigned from the Society of Decorative Arts, exclaiming to Candace Wheeler:

> There is no real bottom to it. You can't educate people without educational machinery, and there is so much discussion about things of which there is really no question. My wife says she cannot afford to have me stirred up each Wednesday, but I have been thinking a great deal about decorative work, and I am going into it as a profession. I believe there is more to it than in painting pictures . . . Colman and de Forest and I are going to make a combination for interior decoration of all sorts. I shall work out some ideas I have in glass. De Forest is going to India to look up carved woods, and Colman will look after color and textiles. You had better join us. It is the real thing, you know; a business, not a philanthropy or any amateur educational scheme. We are going after the money there is in art, but art is there, after all.

They rented an old four-story building two blocks north of the Academy palazzo and Louis's old YMCA studio, on the corner of 25th Street and Fourth Avenue—a horsecar route—with windows on both sides. Lockwood de Forest did not get to India until January 1881, and it is uncertain what role he played in the first two years of the firm's existence. His definition of art as "any work well done" and fine art as "anything exceptionally well done" must have amused and pleased his colleagues, however, and when he returned in the summer of 1882 he established an import business on the second floor, supplying intricately carved teakwood screens, handmade textiles, and "lost wax" bronze chains. Candace Wheeler had meanwhile claimed the third floor for her embroidery and needlework department and Louis the brilliantly lit top loft.

Wheeler was there with him one day as he stared at the jumble of shapes which the gables made in the low-set white ceiling, and she heard him murmur, "I think . . . I shall paint it a light black." The odd distinction—light black, as opposed to the more familiar dark gray— evidently impressed her as the expression of a sophisticated sensibility. She recalled it years later, adding that "Mr. Tiffany was certainly a very inspiring and suggestive associate in art, and he had the recklessness of genius when it came to ways and means."

The array of like-minded talent was matched by their connections to château millionaires, making the ascent of Louis C. Tiffany & Associated Artists one of the swiftest in the history of the interior decorating business. Their commissions included the Fifth Avenue mansions of pharmaceutical dealer George Kemp, financiers Ogden Goelet and Cornelius Vanderbilt II, art collector and first president of the Metropolitan Museum John Taylor Johnston, and former Secretary of State Hamilton Fish; also the Veterans Room of the Seventh Regiment Armory, the Union League's main hall and staircase, the drop curtain for the Madison Square Theatre, and the Hartford home of Samuel Clemens (Mark Twain). These commissions brought the Associated Artists handsome fees and the reputation as the most artistic—and unorthodox—decorators in America. Their last important commission, in the winter of 1882, the redecoration of several of the public rooms of the White House, including the East Room, State Dining Room, and Red and Blue Parlors, signaled their preeminence in the field. *Artistic Interiors* observed that "the beauty and artistic value of Mssr. Tiffany's decorations are best appreciated by those guests who knew how the White House used to look." That comment, and the bill which Louis submitted in August of 1883, must be considered classics of the trade. He wrote, "We beg to hand you herewith our bill for decoratings etc in Executive Mansion—being the balance of work done per agreement. If convenient to you we should be very glad to receive a check for the amount, as at this time we are in need of money."

It is interesting to try to track the connections which resulted in these commissions. Louis's military training was no doubt helpful in securing and executing the prestigious Armory commission, which, since Kemp was an influential member, surely led to the decoration of his Fifth Avenue mansion. Louis's Eagleswood years also led to the Madison Square Theatre job, as James Steele MacKaye, author of the phenomenally successful *Hazel Kirke,* the inaugural play, had then been a painter, and one of Inness's protégés. John Taylor Johnston happened to be Robert de Forest's father-in-law. And Samuel Clemens Louis probably knew from the highbrow receptions of Mrs. Helena de Kay Gilder, the granddaughter of poet Joseph Rodman Drake and a founder of the Society of American Artists. Charles Tiffany, a founding member of the Union League Club, may have brought this commission and that of Hamilton Fish, the club president. And it seems likely that he also brought the commission to do the White House. Earlier that year he had been a guest at a lavish dinner given by President Chester Alan Arthur (who was, like Charles, a devoted salmon fisherman). In February of 1882 he had written his children:

I had a delightful trip to Washington. I went in company with eight other Gentlemen, self-appointed committee, ostensibly to present to the President thirty-six oyster forks, a present from thirty-six gentlemen—but really to have a good time, & we had it. I returned feeling like a boy. A full description of the oyster forks (they were beautiful, every gentleman's name was beautifully etched on his fork) and why the present took the shape of forks, as well as a complete account of the good time we had, how President Arthur gave us the most delicious & elegant dinner in the "White House," and how he had the good taste to give your papa the seat of honor at the dinner &—I will give you when I see you; today I haven't time.

While few businesses are instantly successful, thrive for a few heady years, and dissolve abruptly at the pinnacle of success, Louis C. Tiffany & Associated Artists did exactly this. Candace Wheeler would recall that in 1883 "the wave of popular decorative arts [had] broken over us and receded." A new generation of Beaux-Arts–trained artists had in fact begun to remake America along classical lines, and the freewheeling originality of the Aesthetic Movement was being replaced by "scientific eclecticism," which was, essentially, a return to the specific historical models of the Renaissance. As Parisian art dealer and founder of art nouveau, Siegfried Bing, observed almost certainly about the salon of Cornelius Vanderbilt II:

> A name synonymous throughout the world with enormous wealth had commissioned Tiffany to design the decor and furnishings of a formal sitting room to be based upon the artist's ideas. The expenses came to over one hundred thousand dollars. But after the housewarming, when it had been apparent that the break with the consecrated rules had horrified the visitors, the whole installation was promptly demolished and replaced by a decor pure Louis XVI.

But there were more pressing reasons for the breakup. "I think Mr. Tiffany was rather glad to be rid of us all," Candace Wheeler admitted in her memoirs. Samuel Colman had been first to exit the firm, apparently to oversee the construction and decoration of his own home in Newport. And according to Lockwood de Forest, "Soon after my return from India [in the summer of 1882] it became apparent that the organization of the Associated Artists as constituted would not work. A reorganization was important but we failed to agree as to how it should be done and broke up. Mrs. Wheeler took out all her department and I did mine with the India business. Mr. Tiffany and I divided the stock on hand."

No doubt the necessary change was a restructuring of control along more egalitarian lines. Tiffany money had evidently bankrolled the firm, giving Louis the right to name recognition and leadership over his colleagues. Why else would they have submitted to anonymity, particularly Colman, his former teacher, who was sixteen years older than Louis and a highly regarded artist in his own right? Wheeler was also his senior (by twenty-one years), and de Forest was a talented landscapist. They must have tired of being "Mssr. Tiffany's" Associated Artists.

But Louis had scuttled the enterprise rather than relinquish his command, and the men he invited to join his new firm did so with no illusions of parity. They were the painter, illustrator, and diplomat D. Maitland Armstrong (nephew of Hamilton Fish) and Donald Mitchell's son William Pringle Mitchell. May wrote Annie that Louis "does not intend [to] & does not have more but less worry since dropping Mrs. W. & Mr. de F.," adding, "Mr. Armstrong works as much as ever but has no control over affairs & Pringle is much more satisfactory without . . . Mrs. W."

In addressing the problem of theatrical decoration, British aesthete Oscar Wilde once wrote that "the facts of art are diverse, but the essence of artistic effect is unity. Monarchy, Anarchy, and Republicanism may contend for the government of nations; but a theatre should be in the power of a cultured despot." Louis had met Wilde—velvet suit, knickerbockers, scarlet tie, and all—on his 1882 American tour, and Wilde had praised the "master hand" responsible for the drop curtain at the Madison Square Theatre—the first Associated Artists commission. From the very inception of the firm, then, Louis seems to have patterned himself on this cultured despot—for whom "there may be a division of labor but . . . no division of mind."

Having cultivated his spiritual nature Louis was set to enter as a factor in general civilization. His pursuit of beauty, as a painter, had been solitary, but his missionary work in industrial design would involve many others. His seizure and retention of control at the outset was therefore crucial in that, ultimately, it allowed him unrestricted creativity in the making of handmade art objects, and the productive capacity to reach and sway a relatively wide swath of humanity.

Sadly, the breakup of the Associated Artists had yet another cause, harbingered in the spring of 1879, when May had said she could no longer afford to have Louis stirred up at the Decorative Arts Society. In August May had given birth to a second daughter, Hilda Goddard Tiffany, and Samuel Colman had written his partner, "I congratulate you, and your wife, for the accession to your happiness, by the arrival of another little girl. I hope she will be so sweet, and charming, as little May. I hope your wife still continues to improve, and that she will soon be quite strong again." But the birth took its toll, as did the high-pressure interior decoration business. A photograph taken by Napoleon Sarony the following year shows May perched on a "carved stone wall" beside Louis and the three children, looking beautiful but hard pressed, as if locked in a struggle against overwhelming odds. By the winter of 1882–83 her health was failing fast, and Louis realized, finally, that he had to cut back. The Associated Artists disbanded shortly thereafter.

Directly after completing work on the White House Louis took his family to St. Augustine, Florida. But May's "decided cause" had returned with a vengeance and before long she could not walk half a mile without being "laid up and coughing badly." With the doctors recommending the purified, cooled air of the Adirondacks, Louis took her to Blue Mountain

Lake (Edward Livingston Trudeau's tubercular sanitorium at Saranac Lake not being established until 1885). It was here, in August, that May had written of Louis's intent to have "less worry" by dropping the Associated Artists. But May did not improve and Charles Tiffany had to summon Annie home from Europe.

> I have not read what [your] Mama has written you *all along,* but presume she has kept you informed of all family affairs, but I fear she has not given you quite a correct, or what we today consider a truthful idea of the state of May. A consultation of doctors at the Prospect House, Adirondacks, decides that she must be removed next week. She will be brought to our house at Irvington where she of course will have the best of nursing & can have the attentions of Dr. Lusk, who I believe is expected home from Europe very soon. May has failed very much since she was at our house & went to the Adirondacks. I fear you may never see her again if you do not return this fall. I think I am not alone in this opinion. Louis is very much depressed.

On September 14 May arrived at Irvington with Louis and her sister Julia Piatt. Her doctors had been using morphine as a stimulant to appetite, and she arrived heavily sedated, unaware of the seriousness of her condition. At Irvington she was treated by the family physician, William T. Lusk, a gynecologist, and one of the first to perform cesarean sections successfully. He took her off narcotics and sustained her with enemas of beef stock absorbed directly through the bloodstream. By September 23 she was feeling better and wrote Annie, "It took our faithful Dr. Lusk to cure me after all & ever since he came home (a week ago) and ordered [an] entire change of treatment I have been improving." Louis stayed at her side continually, sometimes painting flowers—red, pink, and cream peonies on one occasion—as if to capture the essence of their life so that May might live. Julia Piatt wrote her cousin Kate Trott, "Louis—his care and patience and tenderness—it is beyond anything I ever saw—or hoped for—it seems as if May must live—but only God knows."

But soon even May must have known she was doomed. After a ghastly winter of sputum and hemorrhages she died on January 22, 1884, with her husband and sister at her side—"an angel now," wrote Julia.

This impending personal tragedy notwithstanding, the years between 1878 to 1883, for Louis, marked a sharp increase in the number of his artistic endeavors. The inspiration of nature and his single-minded absorption in art had a snowballing effect on his productivity, it seemed. When he turned to interior decoration he did not stop painting. In 1878 he exhibited two canvases at the Paris Exposition Universelle and toured Brittany with Samuel Colman. Throughout the following four years of the Associated Artists' existence, he did not travel abroad, vacationing instead with his family at Irvington in summer, and in Florida for at least part of two winters, producing a body of domestic landscapes and family groups. Naturally, decorative work consumed a large share of his energies during this period; and, by the winter of 1881–82, Louis was also helping Stanford White design the Lenox Hill mansion at 27 East 72nd Street. Construction was under way by the fall of 1883.

The full extent of Louis's immersion in art, however, can be measured by the fact that this discussion has yet to consider his work in glass. It stemmed of course from wider interests in the decorative arts but, by 1883, had largely consumed them. As the Boston *Herald* noted, "The great aesthetic wave, which has carried taste and beauty into the adornment of the modern home, has borne colored glass upon its crest." And, as usual, Louis was at the crest.

His earliest efforts seem to have predated his decorative work. He claimed to have begun work in glass in 1872, at age twenty-four, and given the intensity of color in glass, this is a logical date, as it closely follows his color revelation of two years earlier. But not until 1878 did he produce a documented work in glass, years in which he was still making strides as a painter, so it is safe to assume that this early work was probably limited to experiments, probably with decorative tiles. Louis did not leave a record of his earliest motivations and intentions; like his father, he was neither a conversationalist nor monologist. He spoke with great effort, usually to the accompaniment of helpful gestures. When excited he was likely to begin hopping up and down; when angry he could explode. Nor was he much given to literary pursuits, a shame since the one journal he did keep (on a trip through Brittany in 1907) is vividly written. By contrast, the monograph on his career, *The Art*

Work of Louis C. Tiffany, ghost written by Charles de Kay, is dated by frequent fits of bombastic prose. Seven short articles penned by Louis between 1893 and 1917 fill the gap somewhat, but raise as many questions as they answer. And for a Victorian he wrote precious few letters.

Of the first three years we know little, therefore, except that Louis conducted the experiments in his YMCA studio until "there was some kind of explosion," and "mother put a stop to it." Realizing he could proceed no further without expert assistance, in 1875 he turned to the Thills Glasshouse in Williamsburg, Brooklyn.

From the ferry he could see the Gothic towers of the Brooklyn Bridge under construction and the piers below Brooklyn Heights, where merchants cultivated gardens on warehouse roofs below their brownstone homes. Nearby Williamsburg was then a fashionable resort district, though Thills was in no way remarkable. It was one of twenty large glasshouses in America producing some of the worst stained glass ever made: windows composed of large pieces of anemic glass in limited colors and uniform thicknesses, designed, executed, and painted upon by different individuals, none of them necessarily artists. The use of brown enamels to achieve all representational details further compromised the glass, muddying the color and dimming the transmission of light. The mid-nineteenth century American product represented the nadir of the art.

Louis would probably never have considered glass had it not been for an interest in medieval glaziery and the revival of the art form in Europe in the 1860s. While restoring the great Gothic cathedrals of France, architect Eugène Emmanuel Viollet-le-Duc had discovered and published lost techniques of the medieval glazier, fueling claims of aesthetes on both sides of the Atlantic that medieval glass was the finest ever. And, following his trip to North Africa, when Louis had stood on the cool stone floors of Chartres, Notre Dame, and Sainte-Chapelle, he had been instantly persuaded. Like the boy transfixed on tiptoe by the microcosmic world of his father's rubies, emeralds, and sapphires, the man had stood in shafts of light gazing at these majestic windows as their celestial colors streamed down upon him.

Louis's relationship with materialism was obviously complex. He had rebelled, albeit—in retrospect—briefly, against "the commercial element" of his father's business, before going after the money himself. But Louis had not thrown idealism to the winds. Instead, by accepting a materialistic framework for his artistry, he had drawn a finer line between his father and himself. His discovery of glass expressed this most profoundly. Anyone who has seen the great rose windows of Chartres has, intuitively or otherwise, understood the relationship between glass and jewels. Designed to refract light prismatically, and placed to raise heads beatifically, they resemble nothing so much as magnificent, celestial jewels.

Louis would certainly have been intrigued by the myth of medieval glaziers grinding sapphires to make blue glass. But for him the point was otherwise. Glass is little more than silica—liquid sand in effect frozen at a high temperature—and as such inherently worthless. Rather, the value of glass is entirely dependent upon its transformation into an object of beauty. In this symbiotic scheme of things spiritualism is primary and materialism subordinate to an almost alchemical transmutation. Value results when beauty is attained; spiritualism creates materialism; artistry produces merchandise. For Louis the balance was perfect. He was in business, but for art's sake.

He discovered that medieval glass was distinguished from the refined, standardized, machine-made product by a few basic qualities. Like the cheap claret bottle or common preserve jar, it was full of iron oxides, bubbles, and other impurities which refracted a brilliant dancing light. The glass varied considerably in thickness and therefore in intensity of color, adding to the play of light while lending itself naturally to modeling and contour effects in its subject matter. The colors of medieval glass were especially pure and deep and the windows constructed of many small pieces. It was the artful juxtapostion of color in the design aided by natural decay in the glass and a pulsing light which brought these great windows to life.

The art began its long decline in the Renaissance when the artist supplanted the craftsman. The primitive, abstract figures painted on medieval glass seemed crude, perhaps, in comparison with the finely detailed, realistic renderings on Renaissance glass. But in relying on his virtuosity with the brush, the Renaissance artist denigrated the glass itself, beginning the long slide which resulted in what became known as the "pure enamel style" of the mid-nineteenth century. And while the revivalist efforts of William Morris and the pre-Raphaelites had certainly improved the quality of British glass, the field was still largely unexplored in America, and, as Louis divined, ripe for a renaissance.

At Thills he witnessed the plight of the American glassmaker firsthand.

Because the quality of American glass was so poor, American artisans were forced to buy British glass, though not before the cream had been skimmed by London firms (such as Clayton & Bell; Heaton, Butler and Bayne; and Henry Holiday). And windows made of these glass seconds were then usually passed over by the American episcopacy which, like the mother Church of England, preferred the finished British product. Victim of both prejudice and a lack of initiative, there was no easy solution for the American glassmaker.

This state of affairs determined Louis from the outset to improve the standard of American glass beyond that of the British. Unlike the pre-Raphaelites, who turned their painterly skills to designing windows for others to execute, Louis intended to involve himself in every aspect of the art, starting with the manufacture of the glass itself. He believed that the only way to eliminate the use of enamels and begin painting with glass rather than on it was to be both artist and artisan, to design and execute the work.

From this kernel of intent burgeoned the aesthetic which revolutionized the field. The idea was again to make glass the communicator, medium, and message. Each representational detail formerly applied with the brush was, in so far as possible, to be rendered within the fabric of the glass itself. Already at Thills Louis was at work on inventions to minimize the use of enamels not only for draperies (the stuff of saints and madonnas) but for flesh tones. But one cannot properly discuss the early glass of Louis Comfort Tiffany without also mentioning the efforts of John La Farge. Together, or rather independently, they cofounded the American School of Stained Glass.

La Farge was thirteen years older than Louis. The son of a French Catholic immigrant, he was elected to membership in the Century Club in the same year that he married the great-granddaughter of Benjamin Franklin. Dissimilar with regard to age and background, La Farge's and Louis's artistry was nevertheless marked by striking parallels. La Farge had also started out as a painter and a colorist and had become highly successful while falling under the influence of the British Aesthetic Movement, interesting himself in the arts of the East (Japan particularly), the decorative arts, and stained glass. The professional practice of interior decoration had also led him to specialize in glass and, eventually, also to seek the assistance of the Thills Glasshouse in Williamsburg.

Like Louis, too, La Farge had been inspired by medieval craft, French

churches, and the pre-Raphaelites, and he was equally bent upon revital-
izing the art of stained glass. The late 1870s found the two men working
at Thills by day and most likely huddling together at the Century Club
in the evening. Wrote Siegfried Bing, "The most inspiring spirit of
emulation existed between these two spirited artists, each encouraging
and assisting the efforts of the other."

The emulation was mutual and synchronous, and resulted in many of
the technical and aesthetic advances characteristic of the American School
of Stained Glass. Acting upon a shared body of inspiration and intent,
they lit upon many of the same ideas at the same time. Unfortunately,
this serendipitous confirmation of each man's sensibility soon dissolved
into a bitter dispute. The issue at stake was nothing less than the opalescent
or "American" glass that lent the school its name, appraised recently by
a curator of American decorative art at the Metropolitan Museum of Art
in New York as "one of the greatest contributions to the stained glass
repertoire since the Middle Ages."

La Farge recalled that he began to think of ways to make windows
with a soft pearly light in the winter of 1876–77 while painting murals
for Boston's Trinity Church. Inspired by the beautiful light cast on
Byzantine frescoes by thin sheets of mother of pearl, alabaster, and onyx,
he made an analogous window of glass. But in resorting to enamels he
violated the integrity of the glass, and so continued to ponder the problem. Eventually he happened upon an imitation porcelain used in util-
itarian glassware. This semitranslucent "opal" glass had the creamy
iridescence of the mineral for which it was named, and La Farge soon
realized that an opal window might serve a dual function, transmitting
a subdued light by day, while reflecting like a mosaic at night. He had
begun experimenting by the latter part of 1877, cutting ends from opal
bottles and sides from opal boxes and inserting them alongside "antique"
glass in his window for banker William Watts Sherman when, he recalled, "Mr. Lewis [*sic*] Tiffany . . . came to see me."

Louis first combined antique and opalescent glass in the year following
the visit to which La Farge referred, in a window of St. Mark made for
the Islip Episcopal Church on Long Island. La Farge never claimed to
have invented opalescent glass, but on many occasions to have first
recognized its possibilities for windows and to have first acted on it. But
Louis disagreed, writing in an 1893 issue of *The Forum* that opalescent
glass had in fact been used before in windows, though "not to any great

extent." He made no claims for himself, but did not give La Farge credit either.

A key difference in their earliest work with opalescent glass may explain the misunderstanding. By late 1877 both men were electrified by the potential of opalescent glass and rushing to manufacture it. But while La Farge approached makers of commercial opal glass in Sandwich, Massachusetts, and was turned down on account of the small size of his order, in 1878 Louis built his own glasshouse.

Three years at Thills had acquainted Louis with "the prejudice and mental habits of glassmakers" bound to traditional methods. Impatient and frustrated, in 1878 he formed Louis C. Tiffany & Company, and hired as foreman Andrea Boldini, who "represented himself" as having worked under the famous Venetian glassmaster Dr. Antonio Salviati. The delicacy of Louis's phrasing may have been due to the fact that this and a second Tiffany glasshouse burned to the ground within two years while under Boldini's supervision. Nevertheless with Boldini's help Louis appears to have been manufacturing opalescent glass in 1878.

La Farge did not begin to manufacture opalescent glass until after the spring of 1879. His *Watts Sherman* window, made earlier, a vision of painted flowers growing through a trellis, contained pieces of commercial opal glass which, being cut from bottles and boxes, were relatively small. Consequently, in all six panels of the window, the opal glass is confined to a number of small white blossoms. *St. Mark* is not known to exist, but a black and white photograph of the window shows that the glass bore little resemblance to that used in La Farge's blossoms; indeed, all of it appears to have been made to order, presumably by Boldini. The ingredients of opal glass were hardly secret, having been known to commercial glassmakers, La Farge acknowledged, for "an indefinite period." It was relatively simple to create an insoluble white precipitate in the glass formula by adding chemicals such as tin peroxide, stannic acid, antimonic acid, silver chloride, lime phosphate, and bone ash. By regulating the amount of additives, one could control the degree of opacity. Thus, if La Farge had been first to use opal glass and had alerted Louis to its possibilities, Louis was probably first in its manufacture.

In the spring of 1879 La Farge sued Louis, claiming that he had appropriated his ideas, but either dropped the case or settled out of court. Then in November of 1879 La Farge filed a patent for opalescent windows, granted in February of 1880. These circumstances lay the groundwork for the story that La Farge told art critic Russell Sturgis in 1904, six years before his death. La Farge maintained that in 1880 he had twice been approached by Charles Tiffany (acting as broker for his son, who was ill and about to depart on a "recuperative" trip abroad), once to propose a partnership with Louis, to which La Farge agreed, and again to ask that Louis be allowed to use the opalescent process while the details of the partnership were being settled. However, according to La Farge, on Louis's return "the negotiations went to pieces," supposedly leaving Louis in possession of the formula.

Since Louis had already definitely begun manufacturing opalescent glass, perhaps La Farge meant that he had waived the rights afforded by the patent in return for the promise of partnership. It is difficult to know what the circumstances were since Louis left no comparable account and La Farge's version is clearly biased. Twenty-four years elapsed between the events and their telling, years in which Louis parlayed opalescence into far greater commercial and popular success than did La Farge. By 1904 the prodigious output and sharp promotion of Tiffany glass had created a monopolistic juggernaut, and at fifty-six Louis was hitting his stride. La Farge on the other hand was sixty-nine and near the end of his tether. Finding himself playing Salieri to Louis's Mozart, he confessed bitterly to Sturgis, "I wish I were 'Tiff,' all except the genealogy & personality, which is Israelite & Jebusite."

The proposed partnership seems to have been key from La Farge's point of view. In fact he recalled the matter as having been "considered as settled." When asked by Sturgis why the negotiations went to pieces La Farge would give no explanation but implied that he had been deliberately tricked. That La Farge would divulge the formula or waive the patent (whichever the case may be), without having discussed the matter with Louis directly or having worked out the details, shows the importance of the partnership to La Farge. Not being wealthy, having turned to glass in order to make money, he probably viewed partnership with Louis as a means of rising above his financial constraints and developing his ideas to their fullest potential. Louis, on the other hand, may have hoped to use the opalescent process without the encumbrance of patent restrictions while collaborating with a great talent. Here is where damage may have been done. The guess is that the partnership turned out to be the one recently offered the Associated Artists; that is, an unequal one. The humiliation of such an offer would certainly explain La Farge's anger and his reluctance, a quarter of a century later, to elaborate on the details. For Louis's part, one may assume he acted out of arrogance, not deceit. He would not have reached the top of his profession had he not believed himself to be the best. John La Farge had a similar feeling, so a collison was inevitable.

In any event, the two men could not be separated, it seemed. In 1880, after the second of Louis's glasshouses had burned, he turned to the Heidt Glasshouse in Brooklyn—where La Farge was also working. Their advances were discussed jointly in the January 1881 *Scribner's Monthly* under the title "American Progress in the Manufacture of Stained Glass."

> The use of glass of varying thicknesses is not new, but in the new method of work this is carried out in a manner that is entirely novel, and gives effects never before attained. The hot glass, while at a red heat, is rolled with corrugated rollers, punched and pressed by various roughened tools, or is squeezed and pressed up into corrugations by lateral pressure, or is stamped by dies . . . Next to this comes a revival and modification of the old Venetian method of imbedding bits of colored glass in sheets of clear glass. This is done by scattering filaments and irregular bits of colored glass on the table on which plate glass is made, and then pouring the hot glass (either white or colored) over the table and rolling it in the usual manner to press the colored threads or pieces into the sheet . . . Lastly comes the most original feature of all, and this is the use of solid masses and lumps of glass pressed hot into moulds, giving a great number of facets like a cut stone, or by taking blocks of glass and roughly chipping them into numerous small faces. These, when seen in the window, have all the effects of the most brilliant gems, changing their shade of color with every changing angle of vision.

Appropriately enough, the use of glass jewels seems to have been pioneered by Louis (in *St. Mark*). Louis may also have been first to insert translucent beach pebbles in a window. The plating of glass sheets, one directly behind the other to modify tone and color, had been demonstrated at the Philadelphia Centennial and was subsequently used, and patented in different forms, by both men. Clearly the flow of ideas was not unilateral, nor was it restricted to technique.

La Farge, for example, reflected in his *Watts Sherman* window the elegant style and subdued colors of the pre-Raphaelites, among whom he had lived briefly. Two years later, in 1879, Louis adopted the same motif of organic forms winding in and around a grille in his *Eggplants* and *Squash* windows. The illusion of three-dimensionality on a flat surface is similar, but the treatment is entirely different. The colors are brilliant, the contours naturalistic and achieved without any paint. In La Farge's *Peonies Blown in the Wind* (made at Heidt in 1880) the paint is gone, the colors are vivid, and the flowers more lifelike. But an elaborate ornamental border surrounds the inner panel. In the same year Louis (now also at Heidt) made a number of ornamental windows for the Seventh Regiment Armory, and another window for his Bella penthouse that was abstract, or possibly symbolist. There had very likely never been an abstract or symbolist stained-glass window before, and certainly not one so brilliantly colored, primitive, or childlike.

The fact that stained glass was for many artists prohibitively expensive must have been a factor in Louis's choice of the medium. Calculated or not, it put him at a great advantage. The elimination of enamels, simple by definition, demanded ceaseless scientific and aesthetic experimentation, and this was costly. In the case of a new glass to portray draperies, it took Louis a full decade to achieve satisfying results. In 1917 he wrote, "How many years have I toiled to make drapery glass? My chemist and furnace men for a long time insisted it was impossible, claiming that the metallic oxides would not combine, and that was the trouble for many years. The mix would disintegrate. New styles of firing ovens had to be built, new methods [devised] for annealing the glass." As to flesh tones, Louis did not make a figural window in which he claimed to have entirely eliminated surface enamels until 1912. Thus, in contrast with some other technical advances, the advent of opalescence came with blissful ease.

In October of 1880 Louis countered La Farge's opalescent patent with three applications of his own, granted in February 1881. One was a variation of the plating method described in La Farge's patent; the others were original. One referred to an iridescent metallic luster on decorative glass tiles and mosaic, the other to the application of this luster to opalescent window glass. In windows, the iridescence enhanced the mosaic effect of opalescent glass at night while allowing the transmission of light by day. Later, when adapted to crystal, this luster became famous under the name Favrile.

By 1883 glass had become Louis's primary focus, and seemed almost to reflect the paradoxes of his personality. Headstrong yet capably led, fluid yet a solid, fragile yet possessed of great tensile strength, it raised him up and slung him down again. One day his master, the next day his slave, it enraged and enraptured him. Ultimately it defined his identity: as an artist, scientist, and merchant; industrialist, medievalist and Renaissance man.

A s Louis gradually found himself becoming a leading exponent of the American Aesthetic Movement, he also found himself at this time apart from his former associates, feuding with his erstwhile collaborator, and worse still, a widower. Six days after May's death Julia Piatt wrote her cousin about Louis, "It would break your heart to see him." His desolation prompted Julia, principal of the Utica Female Seminary, to take temporary charge of her sister's children, May-May, Charles, and Hilda, who was not yet five. According to the line taken by Robert Koch in *Rebel in Glass,* grief led Louis to indulge for a short while in "fast and fancy living." Moving in theatrical circles together with playwright James Steele MacKaye and architect Stanford White, he "enjoyed the enthusiastic admiration of his contemporaries" and "young ladies in the chorus" alike. Such blatantly compensatory behavior would be consistent with one overwhelmed with remorse. The prolonged agony of watching May's brave descent into death certainly wounded Louis emotionally. Had he not been traumatized, his behavior, years hence, when the disease resurfaced in one of his daughters, would otherwise be inexplicable.

A commission to renovate the Madison Square mansion of Leonard Jerome (Charles's friend and grandfather of Winston Churchill) represented the first of several new ventures calculated to get Louis back on track. The intensity of his competitive spirit resulted in a second, highly coveted decorative assignment, and a financial scrape. It began when Louis's friend Steele MacKaye announced plans to build an art theater—the first of its kind—to be based upon the aesthetic standards advanced by Oscar Wilde. Like bees to honey, the project drew both Louis and La Farge. And though La Farge and MacKaye entered into preliminary discussions, Louis was not to be denied. By January 1885, he had wrested the job from his dollar-conscious rival by offering to decorate the theater for a percentage of the profits.

Completed at top speed, the Lyceum was the first theater to be lit entirely by electricity. The gallery sconces, personally installed by Thomas Edison, represented Louis's earliest electric lighting fixtures. The New York *Morning Journal* described them as smoldering "like fire in monster emeralds," and echoed Wilde in praising the "master hand" responsible for the decoration, which it adjudged "ultra-aesthetic." Unfortunately, MacKaye's inaugural play, *Dakolar*, flopped, and the Lyceum closed four months after opening.

It was just this kind of botched business that led Charles Tiffany to tease young May-May about that "dreadfully careless Papa of yours." Charles may well have advised Louis how next to proceed, for his moves were masterful. After taking a lien on the property and suing, he bought the theater at auction for $21,000. Of that amount the New York Supreme Court awarded him all but $167.74 as a settlement, in effect giving him the Lyceum for the price of decorating it. Then, after putting it back on its feet, Louis sold the theater to entrepreneur Daniel Frohman, increasing his profit in a manner that Comfort Tiffany would have admired.

Louis was also busy that year with the Lenox Hill mansion, "an endless job to complete," it seemed to Charles. Louis's apartment, the first to be occupied, was ready in time for Charles's seventy-fourth birthday on February 15, 1886. For this occasion Louis staged a full-dress surprise party in his studio, attended by members of the firm as well as the family. Before dinner, which lasted from seven to midnight, May-May, Charles, and Hilda entered in costume to recite a dialogue in German—and, wrote Charles, "were *much applauded.*"

Edmund Gosse, the influential British critic, wrote that "the Tiffany house . . . is the one that pleased me most in America." He thought it "the most beautiful modern domestic building I have almost ever seen." This must have been music to Louis's ears, since the sketch that he had handed Stanford White had lent the mansion its fundamental character. But it must have been sad, also, to have watched the place rise virtually in proportion to May's decline, and then to have occupied it alone. Louis's widower status may well have played a part in Charles's reluctance to move from 255 Madison Avenue. He would not have wanted to witness any fast or fancy living. Curious among the mansion's features were the moralizing proverbs stenciled on the beams in the gables—like, A LIFE RETIRED IS WELL INSPIRED; HOPE MAKES A GOOD BREAKFAST BUT A BAD SUPPER; ALWAYS READY; GOOD FOLKS ARE SCARCE, TAKE CARE OF ME; KEEP

GOOD COMPANY AND YOU SHALL NEVER WANT. These, of course, were just the kind of pithy sayings upon which Charles pivoted his affairs, and their presence was clearly intended as a sort of insurance of conscience among the wildly theatrical and exotic trappings of Louis's lair.

After an appropriate interval, it would have been entirely characteristic of "the honorable counselor" to have begun discreetly shaking a few family trees in an effort to provide his son and grandchildren with the stabilizing influence of a wife and mother. Louis's second wife was thus culled from the same safe province as his first, and was likewise the product of a family intrigue. As May Goddard had once worked to promote her cousin's bid for Annie's hand, so did Julia Brasher de Forest, the spinster sister of Lockwood, Robert, and Henry, discreetly labor to procure a Tiffany family entrée for Miss Louise Wakeman Knox. The circumstances of Louis's and Louise's first meeting are not known, but their feelings for one another were rapidly kindled in the romantic atmosphere of Julia's machinations.

Like May and Alfred, Julia and Louise were cousins once removed. Julia's father, Henry Grant de Forest, and Louise's maternal grandmother, Jane de Forest Wakeman, were brother and sister. The de Forests were Huguenots, French Protestants who had landed on American shores thirty-seven years before Squire Humphrey Tiffany. The original Lockwood, the father of Henry and Jane, had arrived in New York in 1817 to found the shipping firm of de Forest & Son, and had made a fortune. Intermarriage with the Johnston, Weeks, and Kemble families had consolidated the de Forests' position (the Kembles were related to the DuPonts, the Johnstons were a shipping power, and the Weekses were distinguished by Robert D. Weeks, first president of the New York Stock Exchange).

Louise Knox (or Lou, as she was called) was also calculated to impress the Tiffanys by virtue of her paternal ancestry. In an age that revered its clergymen, Lou was descended from four successive generations of clerics, three of them Dutch Reformers, the oldest denomination in New York, and the most severe. John Mason, her great-great-grandfather, had been the first English-speaking pastor of the New Dutch Church on Nassau Street, and later chaplain at West Point during the Revolutionary War. Lou's great-grandfather, John M. Mason, and her grandfather, John Knox, had also established their reputations in New York. But her father, James Hall Mason Knox, had strayed to Pennsylvania and the (Tiffanys') Presbyterian fold. With these forebears Lou's values could rightly be assumed.

Unlike May, Lou was neither beautiful nor delicate. She was attractive, with long chestnut hair, bright eyes, and expressive features, but her strength of character was more apparent. She was also constitutionally fit; she loved skating in Central Park and swimming at Southampton, where her Wakeman grandparents had kept a cottage. A civic conscience was evident in her philanthropic work with the New York Infirmary for Women and Children, and her generous disposition was evident in the nickname friends applied to her home: "The Knox Chop House." And unlike May who, for all her sweetness and devotion, was entirely conventional, Lou was of an independent frame of mind, born in part, perhaps, of an unhappy childhood.

Her mother, Mrs. Louise Wakeman Knox, had died when Lou was two; thus she was raised in Presbyterian rectories by a rigid father and a stepmother, Helen Ritchie Thompson, who reserved all her affection for her own children with Dr. Knox. The daughter of Chief Justice Oswald Thompson of the Pennsylvania Supreme Court, her heartlessness had left Lou with deep psychic scars. Lou did not remain long in her father's house. Instead she moved to New York and lived with her maternal grandfather, Burr Wakeman, at 19 West 36th Street. Upon his death in 1879, and receiving an inheritance, Lou, still unmarried, bought a house at 39 West 33rd Street and lived there by herself, listing her name in the city directory. All of this, to be sure, was in defiance of the vicious pressures brought to bear on a single woman by Victorian society.

Lou had borne her notoriety with good will, however, creating a life for herself shared by few daughters of the cloth. Her friends were artists and intellectuals, their steady procession through her house no doubt contributing to her reputation. A scrapbook assembled by Julia de Forest provides details: Lou had known one artist particularly well, a William Alexander, who had kept a studio at the Chelsea Hotel. In the company of friends, she had posed for him, skated with him, taken the ferry to Manhattan Beach with him, dressed in costume and reveled with him; once, at a costume party, she had become Dickens's late-to-marry Dolly Varden in *Barnaby Rudge:* "a pretty, laughing girl, dimpled and fresh, and healthful—the very impersonation of good humor and blooming beauty." After her grandfather's death, Lou had lived in Southampton for a year before selling his town house and traveling abroad with a girl friend. It was then that Alexander had drawn her home, calling it "the

Knox Chop House," and showing it padlocked and closed to her circle
of friends. He had corresponded with her as late as 1881, sending greetings
from the Rocky Mountains to the Alps. But the relationship appears to
have ended, painfully, after her return. Pictures taken in 1883 show a
weight upon her, a sadness seeping from her like an emanating vapor. At
thirty-two her marital prospects were dim.

Three years later, thanks to Julia de Forest, Lou found herself engaged
to Louis Comfort Tiffany. Julia had expressed her support of Lou repeatedly, but never so forcefully as in the following cri de coeur to Annie
Mitchell, who, out of loyalty to May, had found it difficult to imagine
a second Mrs. Tiffany. Wrote Julia:

> I knew that Lou dreaded seeing you & I knew that it wasn't as easy for
> Lou to express what she feels as it used to be years ago before she had so
> much sorrow . . . I know what a brave true strength of character she has
> to meet troubles & anxieties, & what is perhaps harder to meet, the petty
> wear & tear of life. I don't say this to praise Lou, it comes from the very
> depths of my heart. I have been with her when she has gone down with
> those she loved into the shadow of death. I have been with her when she
> thought I was so ill that she would have to part with me and we were
> alone in a country where she had no one to help her bear the anxiety. I
> have been with her when she has been harassed & worried with other
> peoples cares & her own, when she has passed through very painful
> experiences, & very petty prolonged nagging experiences too. We are
> none of us perfect, & I know that Lou is not, but where she gives her love
> she gives it without stint and is singularly honest & true in her power of
> recognizing her own failings & weaknesses, & inexpressibly tender with
> the weaknesses & failings of those whom she loves.

On June 15, 1886, Louis and Lou began a two-week pleasure trip along
the Pennsylvania and Lehigh Canals, accompanied by Julia de Forest,
Robert and Emily Johnston de Forest, publisher Henry Holt and his
daughter, and a Mr. Walter C. Tuckerman. Emulating the artistic high
jinks of the Tile Club, they set out from Bristol, Pennsylvania, in a gravel
scow refitted with a salon, cabins, promenade deck, and a plentifully
stocked galley. They headed for Mauch Chunk, Pennsylvania, a popular
resort town in anthracite coal country, and made a deliberate three knots
per day under the locomotive power of two donkeys, Molly and Polly.
Festooned with flowers, Chinese lanterns, and a striped black-and-yellow

canvas awning, the *Molly Polly Chunker* was promptly taken for a traveling circus.

Their jaunt was chronicled by the elfinlike Henry Holt in the form of a ship's log. The activities of the Artist and the Charge merited particular attention, especially when they succeeded in eluding the Chaperons. Near Tullytown he noted, wryly, that the

> . . . moon and clouds, and great pines, and pools full of sunset, and pollard willows, and strolls in soft grass, are *not* the objects of this expedition. Its object is primarily PHOTOGRAPHY. So all of those slighter things were forsaken, and the Artist and the Charge of the chaperones tied themselves together in a little bag which they called a developing-tent, and amused themselves till midnight, "handling plates," they told us. But nevertheless the Royal High Chaperon [Emily de Forest] first thing next day, ordered a developing tent that would hold her too.

On the following evening

> began what they call "development" again. But this time the closet was large enough to hold the Royal High Chaperon, as well as the two occupants of the night before, so the "development" did not last so long.

On June 21st and again on June 30th they passed through Easton, Pennsylvania, where Lou's father was serving as interim president of Lafayette College. Louis may then have asked Dr. Knox for his blessing, because the engagement was announced soon afterwards. The same party then headed to an Adirondack camp for another week of merriment.

On November 9, Henry Holt added to the log of the *Molly Polly Chunker:*

> The power of any stream is developed by judiciously checking its course. The stream of Love is no exception. The Chaperons knew all this, and regulated their Charge accordingly. Their wisdom was justified in the end.
>
> On this auspicious day, all the company of the MOLLY POLLY CHUNKER assisting, the Artist and the Charge were married, "and lived happily ever after."

Dr. Knox performed the ceremony on a cool clear day at the Brick Presbyterian Church on Fifth Avenue. Lockwood de Forest had decorated the balustrades flanking the pulpit with yellow, palm, and white chrysanthemums. Lou wore a Knox heirloom of soft cream satin, a veil of silk lace embroidered with chrysanthemums designed by Julia de Forest, and a corsage of white chrysanthemums selected by Louis, the inner leaves blushing faint pink. A necklace of diamonds fastened by flat silver links (from Louis) and a little diamond pin (from Annie) sparkled as Lou entered the church with Henry de Forest. "Lou smiled as she came up [the aisle]," wrote Julia de Forest, "& then when she saw Louis her face grew sweetly solemn." The couple stood as Dr. Knox pronounced them man and wife, then kneeled to receive the benediction. "Louis looked very pale when he came into the church," Julia wrote, "but as they walked down the aisle together they both looked perfectly radiant."

They spent their first night together in Julia de Forest's Cold Spring Harbor farmhouse. The following morning Louis wrote his sister Annie, who had not attended the ceremony:

Here we are *very, very* happy in the little house at Cold Spring. Others will tell you about the wedding for I don't know anything about it except that I am married & all went well. The children are coming to spend Sunday here. It is a beautiful day & Lou & I have been out sketching. I did not realize how lonely I have been & how much I needed Lou. I can't explain to you my happiness & Lou's loveliness. I wish you could have been with us. Julia really married us, for she did everything.

Two days later Julia found them both looking "supremely happy." The children arrived the following day to a snowstorm and freezing temperatures, but went to church regardless. Seeing them "all together & so happy" was sweet to Julia. For Louis, having his three children mothered again must have been very wonderful. Lou knew what a loving stepmother could mean, having been mistreated herself. Her tenderness and devotion indeed proved boundless, and was later acknowledged by May-May, who named her only daughter after her.

After Christmas the family, nannies and servants in tow, set out west, for a belated honeymoon, camping in the newly established Yellowstone National Park and traveling with a pack train of horses. When they started home from Monterey, California, in the spring of 1887, Lou's belly was already swelling with twins.

At thirty-nine, Louis Comfort Tiffany was between the wiry physique of youth and the more prosperous distribution of middle age. His brown hair still curled as it had on the corporal, though it was shorter on the sides and brushed behind the ears, and the caterpillar mustache had flourished into ram's horns and a full beard. Now fully the aesthete, his tie was invariably secured with a stickpin, his vest pocket always properly fobbed, and he wore his wedding ring on the pinkie of his left hand, along with what in photographs appears to be a star sapphire.

Almost three years had elapsed between May's death and his marriage to Lou when, in December of 1886, he incorporated the Tiffany Glass Company, for "the manufacture of glass and other materials and the use and adaption of the same to decorative and other artistic works of all kinds." Now, as master of his own glass company, and with his domestic life resecured and his emotional life resettled, he turned his energies primarily to the making of colored leaded windows (as stained glass is more accurately called). In the six years that Louis operated under the Tiffany Glass Company name, his incessant experimentation and reckless expenditure of capital stretched the technical vocabulary of glass to new limits, achieving the fluent, mature style for which his windows are famous.

His entry into the field of glass had, through fateful prescience, coincided with an epic religious revival in America, reactive to a perceived decline in spiritual values in the late nineteenth century. In 1875, the year that Louis had turned to Thills, over four thousand new churches were under construction in America. And naturally this spurt in church building created a concomitant demand for memorial windows. But the problem, as one glassmaker put it, was that "nine out of ten priests are prejudiced against American [glass] houses." Louis had removed legitimate objections by improving upon the British import, only to have his experimentation raise new issues. The very nature of glass as a translucent medium, it seems, was denied by the introduction of opalescence. The prominent church architect Ralph Adams Cram vocalized the opposition; he thought "Hoffman Bible pictures done in opalescent glass . . . abominable." And the new, profuse style of the American School of Stained Glass, he wrote, "was based on entirely new principles wholly at variance both with those that held during the great five hundred years of the Middle Ages and," he thundered, "with the whole ethos of Christian art."

In time, though, Louis was able to deal successfully with archconservatives within the church through either the intervention of well-placed friends, circumvention, or a combination of both. His cousin Charles C. Tiffany (grandson of Comfort's brother James) was senior examining chaplain to Henry Codman Potter, the Episcopal bishop of New York. Through Reverend Tiffany, later Archdeacon Tiffany, Louis had a direct line to the apex of the episcopacy, the wealthiest and most socially prominent denomination in New York. No doubt, at the right time and place, favorable words were spoken in Louis's behalf. Helpful also was the considerable influence of the Reverend Dr. Knox in the Presbyterian and Reformed Protestant Dutch Churches. Congregationalists within the Presbyterian Church ordered especially large numbers of Tiffany windows.

But more important to Louis's success than any highly placed individual was the phenomenal popularity of stained glass, starting in the seventies and continuing until World War I. The lush textural extravagance and gentle beauty of leaded, colored glass became the epitome of fashion. Blossoms, feathers, wings, flowers, fish and fruit—in fact, the Sublime Subject and Divine Architecture—resurfaced in industrialized urban spaces, on mantels and walls, in windows, skylights, overdoors and transoms, in railroad cars and stations, in steamships and terminals, in homes, apartment and municipal buildings, and, most of all, in churches.

Ecclesiastical windows traditionally generated the greater share of the glassmaker's business, and Louis's business was no exception. The selection of windows might have been left to the absolute control of the church, thereby negating popular trends, if not for the fact that memorial windows were generally donated by relatives of the deceased, whose wishes had to be taken into account. Consequently, Louis was sometimes able to sidestep even the most intransigent church officials, providing that the laity was sufficiently fashionable, ambitious, or simply appreciative of his windows.

Louis's iconoclasm was not restricted to technical innovations, i.e., traditional subjects done in opalescent glass. In pioneering the ecclesiastical landscape window, he became the first to make church windows without figural or allegorical content. Many of his windows—and eventually they numbered in thousands and stretched from coast to coast—had absolutely no connection to the scriptures whatsoever. Pantheistic rather than monotheistic, they echoed the concerns of the Hudson River school and Louis's early work as a painter.

In the summer of 1889 Louis and Lou went to Paris for the Exposition Universelle. As they would often do in the coming years, they left Julia de Forest in charge of the six children, who now included twins Louise (called Comfort) and Julia and the one-year-old Annie Olivia. On August 22 Louis wrote them all from Paris:

> We neither of us are well. [We] both have colds & I have been very busy buying things for the Tiffany Glass Company . . . this buying of religious objects to sell is not so much fun . . . We shall be glad to get back to you all. I never felt so homesick for my children. I long to be with you all & to have Comfort and Julia take my hand & show me the lilies.

At the exposition, symbolized by the 984-foot tower of Gustave Eiffel, Tiffany & Company won another *grand prix* for silverware, a gold medal for jewelry, a gold for its exhibit of North American gemstones, and thirteen other medals. Louis had evidently not thought to exhibit his glass, but discovered to his great surprise that La Farge had, demonstrating to a European audience for the first time the repertoire of the American School of Stained Glass. His initiative had brought him a medal of the first class and the decoration of the Chevalier of the Legion of Honor of France. While Louis had single-mindedly, and perhaps myopically, been gaining the advantages at home, La Farge had quietly slipped around his back and won international acclaim. With mounting disbelief Louis read the jury's citation of La Farge, and La Farge alone, as "the great innovator, the inventor of opaline glass [who] has created in all its detail an art unknown before, an entirely new industry, and in a country without traditions he will begin one. . . . " All of this resulted from the exhibition of a single representative work, the *Watson* window, based on "the Sealing of the Twelve Tribes." Louis had been outsmarted, and surely knew it.

Conceding defeat, Louis focused on the upcoming World's Columbian

Exhibition in Chicago, conceived as a definitive statement on American culture on the quadricentennial of Columbus's discovery of America. Intent on a showdown with La Farge, he called for a special gallery devoted to stained glass, and when denied it wrote, "This is . . . to be regretted as in new art, such as this, exhibitions are of great use; the artist comes face to face with his fellow artists, and patrons are better able to judge the merits of the work of each." Arranging, instead, to use space reserved for Tiffany & Company in the Manufacturers and Liberal Arts Building, Louis set out to prove that he was the foremost glassmaker in America.

Enthusiasm for the Columbian Exhibition was intense, as was the competition. Augustus Saint-Gaudens, visiting Chicago in the planning stages, exclaimed, "Do you realize that this is the greatest meeting of artists since the fifteenth century!" At a cost of $15 million a windswept wasteland outside Chicago was transformed into a White City—so-called because the buildings grouped in the Court of Honor were painted a dazzling alabaster white. To Richard Watson Gilder, then supreme arbiter of American arts, the sight of the court at night lit with the full force of incandescence, was "something not of this world." It was, in fact, the dream of a new generation of Beaux-Arts–trained architects, sculptors, and muralists for a better society. Of Greek and Roman and Renaissance derivation, it was "scientifically eclectic" in that specific historical sources were evident: the tomb of Mausolus at Halicarnassus, the Arch of Septimius Severus in Rome, the Florence Cathedral. Fantastic in combination, the rotundas, towers, arches, concourses, colonnades, canals, and heroic figures were all made of a stuccolike mixture called "staff," which, like the set of a Cecil B. De Mille epic, would soon crumble to dust.

Between May 1 and October 31, 1893, the vision was contemplated by some 27 million people. And not everyone was enthralled with stately classicism. One of those opposed was Lockwood de Forest, who exhibited a Carved Teak Room. He wrote that "looking down on the people of the East . . . was no doubt started by the Greeks, who thought they had the highest civilization and called every other people barbarians. Perhaps the worship we have been taught of Greek art and literature has rendered us blind to what art in its fullest sense really means." More direct was architect Louis Sullivan, who wrote, "The damage wrought by the World's Fair will last for half a century from its date if not longer."

Louis was likewise swimming against the current, but he had been careful to place his contribution within the overall context of this emerging American renaissance. He insisted, however, that the White City was based upon an art historical fallacy. "A very false idea of classic art grew up during the Renaissance," he later wrote, "an idea that it was cold from lack of color." And this was a stroke of genius, allowing Louis to proceed legitimately with his own inclination while, in effect, transforming the White City into a backdrop for his exhibit, a neo–Byzantine chapel.

His plans had been sufficiently ambitious to involve the reorganization of his business as the Tiffany Glass and Decorating Company, and the purchase of the two buildings adjacent to 333 Fourth Avenue. He too had looked to classical culture, but had chosen that period in history when its capital was Constantinople, and Roman culture, Christianity, and the East had all melded together. The American tour of Sarah Bernhardt as Justinian's empress in Victorien Sardou's *Theodora* had touched off a vogue for the neo–Byzantine, which had made Louis think of Constantinople's "sacred fortress" Ravenna, and mosaic, which he called "the parent of stained glass."

The altar, stairs, lecturn, candlesticks, baptismal font, retable, tabernacle, ciborium, and reredos were all faced with shimmering, glittering opalescent and iridescent bits of mosaic, some as small as a quarter of an inch square. A million pieces of glass were used in the reredos alone to portray facing peacocks and a scrolling Eucharist. The effect was intensified by marble, mother of pearl, mussel and abalone shell, quartz pebbles, copper beads, onyx and alabaster, all worked in with the glass. Yet the heart-stopping color, exoticism, and unconventional materials were balanced by the austere Romanesque design, combining in brilliant, mysterious grandeur.

Divided between a flanking silver and opal Light Room, and a green-keyed Dark Room, were the windows themselves, twelve of the finest quality, ranging in subject from *Jesus Blessing St. John* to *Feeding the Flamingoes.* The latter Louis called "more realistic, more elaborate, and showing more clearly the possibilities of American glass than any window in our exhibit." Designed by Louis in 1885, the window portrays a languorous maiden feeding peacocks in a setting borrowed from Louis's

Lenox Hill studio. The window's virtuosity lies less in the design, however, than in its vitreous translation, beginning with the silky opalescent
drapery glass in the maiden's robes. Mottled glass, confetti glass, plated,
layered, and acid-etched glass all made their appearance. Stained glass had
not been known to shift colors within a single piece, yet a goldfish
swirling in a bowl of turquoise water was evoked by a single disc of thick,
rippled glass.

Louis made his views explicit in "American Art Supreme in Colored
Glass," published in an 1893 number of *The Forum*. He claimed "the
introduction of new and original ideas . . . equal in merit to the best that
has been done," and declared "the best American colored windows
. . . superior to the best medieval windows." This *"bizarre manifeste,"* as
one French critic termed it, served its controversial purpose. John La
Farge immediately jumped into print to defend form and tradition while
the director of Berlin's *Gemäldegalerie,* Wilhelm von Bode, allowed that
some Tiffany windows were indeed "of a perfection which allows them
to be placed alongside the product of antiquity or the Middle Ages."

The chapel rapidly became one of the most popular and critically
acclaimed exhibits at the exhibition, its opalescent windows reported to
have attracted more attention than any other single product of American
industrial art. Yet, despite this success, Louis had not yet risen to the
Tiffany imperative. By the October closing he had won an astounding
fifty-four medals, but Tiffany & Company, for the quality of its work-
manship, materials, and designs, had won fifty-six. Together, with their
double-barreled vision, father and son had certainly emerged as the leaders
in the field of industrial arts. Wrote British critic Cecelia Waern, "It
would be almost absurd to expect a serious 'return to simplicity' in the
land of mushroom fortunes, 'social strugglers,' stimulating sun and air,
enervating steam heat, and many other factors." But Louis put it best in
Harper's Bazaar: "We are an extravagant people, leading extravagant
lives."

I f the chapel was a testament to the keenness of Louis's competitive
spirit, it would lead to the international acclaim the glassmaker
desired, though not for another seven years and not primarily for
stained-glass windows.

At the 1889 Paris Exposition Universelle, Louis had seen the hand-blown glass vases exhibited by Emile Gallé, and been struck by his application of naturalistic designs to three-dimensional forms. Two years later he met Arthur J. Nash, a British glass sales representative and former manager of the Edward Webb Glasshouse in the Stourbridge district in England. In February of the following year he and Nash established a furnace in an old laundry and cleaning establishment in the Corona section of Queens, and began glass-blowing experiments. The partnership was, surprisingly enough, an equal one, with Louis the art director and Nash the plant manager. But a conflict surfaced almost immediately, Louis rejecting practically the entire first year's production, and repeating "Too much Stourbridge" (the name of the new company and Nash's old district). When the building burned nine months later, wiping out Nash, Louis seized control of the company, built a new factory, and renamed it the Corona Furnaces. Restricted by Nash's traditional approach no longer, Louis attempted to make free-blown flower-form vases, and reproduce his iridescent patina in red lead crystal. The earliest of these experiments were conducted simultaneously with the exhibition of the chapel in Chicago, but not until 1895 did Louis succeed in striking "the Tiffany colors," the hallmark of Favrile glass.

The diversity, scope, and originality of Louis's artistry seem to have been pivotal to the decision of Siegfried Bing to promote him abroad. Bing was the product of a well-to-do family of German-Jewish merchants, importers and exporters of glass and porcelain. In Paris, Bing had begun importing Japanese art, particularly wood-block prints, catering to the craze for japonaiserie which had swept the West in the 1870s. Louis probably met Bing through Edward C. Moore, who, as Tiffany & Company's chief silversmith and art director, had pioneered the Anglo-Japanesque style in American industrial art. Louis had since extensively patronized Bing's shop at 19, rue Chauchat, assembling an early collection of Japanese arms and armor.

In February 1894, Bing arrived in New York to write a report on the state of American art for Henri Roujon, the director of the Beaux-Arts. Bing was also looking for a glassmaker to demonstrate abroad the qualities which he believed had made America progressive as a nation, namely its freedom from tradition and its technical ingenuity. La Farge had evidently met Bing with an elaborate account of his development of opalescent glass. But considering the recent achievements in Chicago, it is not surprising that Bing's report praised Tiffany as "the first name which comes to mind" in the field of American industrial art. By April 1894 Louis had removed the chapel to his 333 Fourth Avenue showrooms where Bing could see it for himself, as he could the magnificent interiors Louis had recently designed for the Henry O. Havermeyers on Fifth Avenue. In his report Bing hailed Louis's windows, mosaic, and blown glass, adding:

> While glass was the object of his particular passion, Tiffany was also commissioned to design complete interior installations. In town houses, theatres, gathering places of all kinds, chapels large and small, his work is characterized everywhere by the close and homogeneous accord among all decorative elements, whatever their size, between furniture and the most ordinary everyday objects.
>
> Tiffany saw only one means of effecting this perfect union between the various branches of industry: the establishment of a large factory, a vast central workshop that would consolidate under one roof an army of craftsmen representing every relevant technique: glassmakers and stone setters, silversmiths, embroiderers and weavers, casemakers and carvers, jewelers, cabinetmakers—all working to give shape to the carefully planned concepts of a group of directing artists, themselves united by a common current of ideas.

Bing also credited La Farge in his report, but probably never considered him seriously for his ulterior purpose. "Alas," La Farge once wrote, "my work is only for transparency picture work. It wouldn't do for paper weights or anything like a cup or bottle. It would be like making a sonnet into a water-paper basket or a jack-hammer." This was precisely the prejudice which Bing and Roujon hoped to cure in the French, whose decorative-arts consciousness lagged far behind that of the British and Belgians. Also, Farge had recently argued against Louis's dismissal of "mere form" and tradition in *The Forum,* further distancing himself from Bing's position.

Bing returned to Paris with the exclusive European distribution rights to Tiffany glass. The following year he opened his Salon d'Art Nouveau, albeit to an unreceptive Parisian audience, but proceeded to promote his concepts and his artists so tirelessly and, at times, shamelessly, that the pavilion Art Nouveau Bing was the sensation of the 1900 Paris Exposition. At the Exposition Favrile glass won the *grand prix* and Louis was created a Chevalier of the Legion of Honor of France. By then he was established as the foremost American exponent of the new decorative style, and his glass was being hailed worldwide. At fifty-two he had reached the top.

V

The Kubla Khan, Mama Lou, and Me-Too

Dorothy Trimble Tiffany's birth, on October 11, 1891, preceded the establishment of the Corona glass factory by just four months, and the subsequent burst of fevered creativity, which ended in fin de siècle Paris, marked the point for her father's ascendancy over his father. Dorothy's formative years were, therefore, the ones of her family's greatest prestige and power. Certainly the imperative that drove Charles and Louis was as much a factor in her development as the opulence and fame it engendered.

Being the eighth granddaughter of nine grandchildren was, to be sure, no signal honor. Dorothy must have sensed even then on some level her family's disappointment in another girl, and the incapacity to refocus its aspirations on the eight healthy females. The driving ambition of her father, grandfather, and great-grandfather would not be instilled in her. It was not her fate to carry the family imperative to a higher level or to perpetuate the Tiffany name, but instead, as a female and last-born child, to grapple with the human repercussions of single-minded ambition from the vantage point of the twentieth century. Of all the siblings, Dorothy alone would escape the patriarchal order that had spawned and bound them, and remake her life along entirely new lines.

If her early life had a drawback, it was a lack of purpose. She had no inkling of destiny, no directional sense. She did not seek her fate, but was driven to it at a great cost to herself and to others around her. The Western world was changing at a revolutionary rate, and her life was a vehicle for these colliding values. The Tiffanys had the means to insulate themselves from change, but hardly the spirit. Dorothy would plunge into the current of her times as deeply as had her father and grandfather. But as a female, with no charted course, her genius had to be survival.

Specific details of Dorothy's childhood are few and far between. On January 2, 1892, Josephine Balestier wrote her close friend, May-May, the baby's half-sister, "I am so sorry & so anxious about the Dear Daughter Dorothy. Do send me a word to say that she is entirely well again. Rud [Rudyard Kipling, her sister's fiancé] also was grieved to hear she had been ill." This was not a serious illness, but within five months little Annie Olivia, born in the year following the twins, contracted scarlet fever and died on April 24. Dorothy was six months old at the time. Through psychological reconstruction, Dorothy came to believe that Annie's death dealt her a trauma, as her mother grew depressed and her nanny took to comparing her, detrimentally, to "marvellous Annie."

Her mother's depression was probably less of a factor than her nanny's brutal favoritism. Like many affluent Victorian women, Mama Lou believed that the mother's role properly began after the child had attained a certain level of maturity, and became crucial during the passage through adolescence. A young child's needs were thought to be more bodily than spiritual and therefore capably met by a trained nurse or nanny. Consequently, in just those years that are now recognized as all important to personality development, the child was at the mercy of a hired professional. Despite Dorothy's every apparent advantage, it was her bad fortune to be raised by a nanny who was devoted to the memory of her late sister.

For three and half years Annie had been the youngest, and most special, sibling, an effervescent sprite with honeyed hair and dramatic eyes. Dorothy had evidently not matched her charms, since, after her birth, Annie had remained the family's doted-upon favorite. Dorothy did not take her place even after her death, was held hostage to her memory and, sensing her mother's despair, perhaps felt guilty over Annie's fate. Having already disappointed the family with her sex, Dorothy grew up feeling inferior, and in great need of improvement. When this lack of self-worth began to manifest itself in her posture, her father slapped her into an iron posture-corrective brace.

Annie had been the sibling closest to Dorothy in age, so her death also deprived Dorothy of a playmate, leaving Comfort and Julia as her closest contemporaries. But they were four years older than she and, like most identical twins, primarily bonded one to the other. They looked, dressed, acted, and frequently thought alike, the exclusivity of their relationship symbolized by the charming Windsor chair which Louis designed especially for them; three it could not accommodate. Stunning beauties and talented singers, they did everything first, did it together and, Dorothy thought, did it best. She, on the other hand, did not like her looks (and never would), and refused to sing along with them. She was the lonely one, the outsider, and, as she felt it, "the Ugly Duckling." Her desperate cries to be included with them earned her the nickname Me-Too. Anxious to catch up with her elder siblings, Dorothy greeted each birthday enthusiastically. In October of 1897 Julia wrote her aunt Annie, "Dorothy is six and she is very glad."

Dorothy saw her life as "divided" between city and country. The city of course meant the Lenox Hill mansion and the unorthodox workings of her father's mind. The breakfast room, located in one of two gables facing 72nd Street, and brightly lit by flower-and-vine motif stained-glass windows, featured a white enamel tabletop supported by two sawhorses—an idea evidently pioneered by Louis in 1886. Now in the collection of the Chicago Art Institute, it is described as unprecedented in American cabinetwork. Also in this room, protruding from the north wall like the stylized breasts of African sculpture, were the ends of two barrels—one studded with ornamental nails, the other faced with mosaic—which swung open on hinges, one to reveal a wine cooler, the other a silverware safe; a most ordinary arrangement, it must have seemed to Dorothy. Tutored at home until age eleven, Dorothy's formal education began amidst these fantastic surroundings.

The clip-clop of horsecars plying Madison Avenue had yielded to the gear grinding of electrified trams, and the Lenox farmhouse opposite 27 East 72nd Street to the mansion of William B. Cutting, heir to the Fulton steamship fortune. R. Fulton Cutting built a second mansion five blocks south of his brother's, and the Rhinelander sugar trust financed châteaus on the northeast and southeast corners of 72nd Street. William Lemuel Skidmore (coal), Henry Gurdon Marquand (railroads), and Dr. Christian Herter (son of Herter Brothers' founder) also moved to the hill. By the mid-nineties, 72nd Street was no longer way out in "the Dakotas"; hence the growing importance to the family of country life.

For years they had summered at Irvington-on-Hudson, occupying one of two stately fieldstone and slate houses, built by Louis's father, flanking the approach to Tiffany Hall from the Old Post Road. But after marrying Lou Knox, Louis had become enamored of Cold Spring Harbor on Long Island's north shore, the harbor of Cooper's Leatherstocking Tales, where the de Forests had their summer seats. In 1889, he had designed and built a white shingle neocolonial house overlooking the harbor called the Briars. An hour by train from Manhattan and ten minutes more by trotter, it was skirted by wild dogwood, laurel, and forsythia. Louis had cleared the land and begun his gardens by Dorothy's birth, continuing to make improvements throughout her childhood, building a fountained pool for lilies and bog plants in front of the house, and ringing it with a boxwood circus. Later he built a tower with a working windmill, and wrapped a veranda around the house to a wooden deck in back, where the family took in the view through the conifers to the sparkling Sound below. Beneath the deck, Louis fashioned of logs a curious mine-shaftlike back entrance to the house, guarded by a bronze dragon.

Despite these additions, the Briars's interior remained simple and comfortable, the home that Mama Lou and Dorothy loved best. Certainly Dorothy's happiest memories were here—feeling the warmth of her mother's eye upon her as she rode her horse around the boxwood circus; rising at dawn to find her papa inspecting his dew-soaked flowers, taking his hand and being part of his happiness.

She knew that sharing his precious flowers was a special token of his affection. In the spring he sometimes drove the girls in a buggy twelve miles to the Hicksville plains and, in a field of blue bird's-foot violets, set them loose with little baskets and trowels, their smocked dresses like splashes of white against the blue colorfield, their cries of discovery like a carillon of bells. Exhausted, their baskets full, they returned to show him proudly the prize specimens, those with white centers and feathery leaves, which they later transplanted to "run riot in a lovely secluded woodland" near the Briars. Louis commuted to work in the summer, Dorothy recalled, and

> Immediately on reaching the house . . . would set out to inspect the garden. He knew every plant and flower and spent much time directing the planting. To watch the flowers grow from bud to full bloom was his greatest pleasure.

It struck Dorothy—much later—that her father was "passionately in love with flowers."

Sometimes she painted with him, or clammed on the beach below the house for his breakfast, searching at low tide for little spouts of water streaming off the wet sand. The next morning, a napkin tucked under his chin, his plate heaped with her harvest, he seemed contented. He loved dogs, she recalled, "and they greeted him excitedly and never left his side." One of his favorites was a mutt called Funny, so named because he could not run in greeting since, as a puppy, his front legs had been crippled by rickets; unable to move, he "grinned" instead.

Dogs and flowers: the fond associations of a little girl to her father. Yet the man remained a mystery to her and the task of deciphering her papa may have been more nettlesome than most. His reticence multiplied the enigma, and bringing him out was not easy. Later, Dorothy would diplomatically write, in a biographical sketch, that "a complex character such as my father's inevitably appears in different lights when seen from different points of view." Privately she spoke of his "autocratic" ways.

Her memories are, tellingly, ones in which she fitted into his artistic tableaux. He enjoyed his daughters in an idyllic way. He was not one to play games with them, but he would gladly paint or photograph them dressed as Indian, Arab, or Grecian maidens. Abroad one summer he admired a young girl "about fifteen" playing with a top,

> balancing and whirling it on a piece of cord attached to two bamboo sticks, one held in each hand—and then tossing it high in the air—Most lovely attitudes as she looked up with rapt expression and arms outstretched—to catch it as it fell. Slim, graceful, child's figure. Never saw anything more beautiful. Shall certainly buy a set of these tops and have my children learn to play with them. Can't understand why cinematographers don't get sets of these pictures for exhibition. Think I will buy a cinematograph . . . and photograph my children playing top.

Believing, as Louis did, in the spiritual grace of good taste, the aesthetics of his own home environment naturally fell under intense scrutiny. At home, particularly, it was important that life dovetail with art. And this meant no respite for or refuge from his artistic temperament. His personality might be compared to a certain stretch of road in Brittany between Morlaix and Quimper, where, he wrote, one "kept coming to the top of the world and then drove down into the valley again." Elsewhere in the same journal he wrote of "an enchanted world in the sky—indescribably lovely and grand and beautiful," and of returning to "the world of everyday." Taken together these descriptions read like a chart to his life and artistic visions.

The struggle to exalt life to the plane of imagination resulted, predictably, in alternating passages of rapture and rage. Said glassman Jimmy Stewart, recalling Louis's delight on the day of striking the Tiffany colors, "I can see him prancing around and dancing around there yet, and pulling his belt up and so forth, yeah." But he, Louis, just as quickly raged at a worker who accidentally dropped a cigar butt into a batch of glaze. On the home front, enthusiasm and affection were also inevitably replaced by annoyance and anger, and vice versa. Damage to a plant, any plant, accidentally or otherwise, was considered a crime. Carelessness was also a criminal act in the Tiffany household. But the greatest crime, Dorothy recalled, was unpunctuality. Woe betide the girl who delayed Papa—especially at mealtime. Under strict orders to be in their chairs before the dining hour, the girls were once severely rebuked for arriving as the hour was tolling.

Knowing that Papa was at the height of his creative powers could hardly have cushioned Dorothy from the aftershocks of his aesthetic choreography. Artistic license repeatedly clashed with discipline, gentle beauty with the overbearing ways of a domestic tyrant. The combination was confusing, to say the least. Dorothy thought that "his ideas ran away with him," that he was "crazy."

Recounting these feelings late in life, Dorothy was asked if her father was considered crazy at the time. "Crazy is not the right word," she answered. "He was eccentric. I think many people thought he was eccentric." Asked if he was considered eccentric even at the height of his fame and influence, she replied, "I think some people did. But that's the point, I think. Any of these ideas that other people had didn't touch him. I don't think he was influenced by them in the slightest."

His paradoxes certainly sharpened Dorothy to the workings of the creative spirit, though it was a long time before she could write of him. "Originality—what he has seen he plays with—like a dream he is unafraid of trying things—even if odd. There is a drive to catch his ideas—to follow through an idea. It is what genius is made of, facts and creativity."

Ultimately, Dorothy's view of her father was shaped in relation to her mother, who represented a different, even opposite, set of values. Dorothy recalled her as "rather stern . . . but very lovely too." She proved a loyal wife and devoted mother, dedicated to philanthropic and charitable causes. It was probably due to Dorothy's self-image that, while Comfort and Julia each thought herself her mother's favorite, Dorothy was sure she was not. Yet the twins may have gotten more attention because they were older, and Dorothy had yet to "attain." Mama Lou was devoted to all her children and stepchildren. Given her druthers, she would have remained with them even in summertime, yet because Louis liked to travel in her company, she went with him.

It would seem that Mama Lou had left behind the vestiges of her liberated past. Actually, the degree to which Louis had been aware of his fiancée's feminism is an open question. A sequence of portraits might, however, indicate a dawning recognition on his part of her true character. The first, *A Corner of My Studio,* painted shortly after their wedding, was fraught with sexual symbolism. Framed in a sweeping vertical format, Lou sits with undraped shoulders by the womblike hearth of the Lenox Hill studio as tongues of orange flame shoot up the dark priapic bole. Two years and three children later, Louis again painted Lou in the studio, reclining on a divan in a dress with a concealing ruffled throat, beside a stack of books, reading.

An 1899 photographic portrait of Lou captured this intellectual side— Lou proudly refusing to doff her pince-nez spectacles, leaning an elbow on six artfully stacked books. Eighty years later Dorothy could remember every detail of her mother's library haunt: the green double-desk, the well-stocked shelves, the green leather couch curved to fit the turret on the northwestern corner of Madison Avenue and 72nd Street, the cascade of opalescent magnolia petals in the bay window, the glint of firelight on the Japanese sword guards peppering the hearth. Lou's acquisitive curiosity was reflected by the legend on her bookplate: *Moveo et Propitior,* which appears below the image of an eagle and translates literally as "I Move and Am Appeased."

By 1890 both Lou and Julia de Forest had become trustees of the New York Infirmary for Women and Children, and it was to this cause, primarily, that Lou devoted her extracurricular energies. She could frequently be found slogging through dense scientific treatises relating to Infirmary cases, which included mental disorders such as hysteria, "hystero-epilepsia," and neurasthenia. Astoundingly, one winter, provoked by these conditions, Lou read Freud's *Interpretation of Dreams*, or rather Julia de Forest did, translating it aloud to Lou from the German, a fact recalled by Dorothy, who had evidently sat at their feet. Since the winter in question can be dated to within four years of the landmark 1899 publication, under the title *Die Traumdeutung*, their reading it amounted to something of an intellectual odyssey.

The Infirmary was located in a picturesque four-story mansard-roofed building at 5 Livingston Place on Stuyvesant Square. There, on the northern fringe of the Lower East Side, Lou encountered a world at odds with Lenox Hill and Cold Spring Harbor, a world that her husband, for instance, did not care to explore. She discovered, groaning under the weight of unrestricted immigration, individual wards and national colonies that exceeded the population of many major American cities. It was reported as early as 1882 in *New York by Gaslight* by James D. McCabe, Jr., that more individuals were sardined into the Seventh Ward of Manhattan than lived in all of Hartford, Connecticut, more in the Eleventh Ward than in Richmond, Virginia, and more in the Seventeenth Ward than in Providence, Rhode Island. Little Italy, the Jewish quarter, Chinatown and the Fourth and Tenth Wards were similarly choked. An aggregate of five hundred people inhabited each acre of the Lower East Side, as opposed to sixty-two people elsewhere in Greater New York. Under the worst conditions, over seven hundred human beings occupied a single fetid five-story tenement. In winter, apartments had little heat, air, or light. In summer, vapors from open toilets in cellars rose through alleyways to windows thrown open to escape the heat of cooking stoves. Virulent disease was an ever-present fact of life.

Poverty, in this so-called Gilded Age, was far more conspicuous than wealth. Eleven of the twelve million families in the United States subsisted on an average annual income of $380, of which $100 could go to the rent of a room in one of these same tenements. No wonder an enraged citizenry drove the socialite Bradley-Martins out of town when, in the middle of a recession, they gave the most lavish costume ball ever seen in New York. But such was the result of a free-enterprise system internally unregulated on the federal level. The country was ruled by trusts, monopolies, and big business at the expense of most everyone else. Protective tariffs, once the stimulant to fledgling industry, had by the Gilded Age become the industrialist's windfall. And, in 1894, when congressional Democrats enacted a two percent tax on incomes over $4,000, Joseph Hodges Choate, dean of the New York bar, convinced the U.S. Supreme Court that the tax represented "a communist march on private property." Robber baron William H. Vanderbilt expressed himself succinctly on the subject of private obligation to public welfare. "The public be damned!" he snarled.

The desperate plight of the poor had given rise to a nascent social conscience, however. The populist revolt had swept from the Great Plains to the plutocratic East with the message that "the makers of clothes are underfed; the makers of food are underclad." In New York, Jacob Riis's photographs had revealed exactly *How the Other Half Lives,* and a Progressive movement had taken hold. As a result, the eighties and nineties saw monopolistic enterprise under attack for the first time, housing reform and social welfare programs begun, the first settlement houses established, the worst slums destroyed, and the first model tenements built.

Tenements were the special target of reformers for a variety of reasons, many of them practical. Most frightening was the threat of a city-wide pestilence such as cholera or yellow fever, smallpox, diphtheria, consumption, or typhus. Of prime importance, therefore, among the functions of the New York Infirmary for Women and Children was its Tenement House Service, which was, in effect, a charitable out-practice. The physicians were followed by sanitary visitors who, armed with sponges, disinfectants, soaps, clean linen, and pamphlets in several languages, taught the rudiments of hygiene. This Out-Practice has recently been called "the first establishment of a medical social service." A dispensary at 128 Second Avenue was also run along charitable lines, as was the Infirmary itself. A Fresh Air Fund sent mothers and their children to the country, and a Tribune Fund helped to pay funeral expenses.

Lou's role at the Infirmary was primarily fiduciary. On one occasion, in staging a Chrysanthemum Festival in the Lenox Hill studio, she raised $2,800 to pay back an Infirmary loan. Lou was closer to the workings of the Infirmary than the average trustee, however, due to Julia de Forest, who seemed to be on every committee, was herself assistant treasurer and a close friend of the Infirmary's resident physician. Together, Lou and Julia had mobilized the support of Annie Mitchell; Henry de Forest; Mrs. Lockwood de Forest; Robert de Forest's father-in-law, John Taylor

Johnston; and at least one nonfamily member, Mrs. Henry Villard. With this supporting cast, Julia and Lou wielded considerable influence.

The involvement of society women in medical charities was nothing new, of course. Victorian men were typically pleased to have their wives assume their social conscience, while remaining confident in their superior status as breadwinners. What distinguished Lou's efforts, and perhaps led Dorothy to later call her mother "a liberated woman," was the Infirmary's unconventional charter. Not only did it exclusively serve women and children, but, more important, it was also staffed entirely by women, from sanitary visitors, to nurses, to doctors. It had its own Nursing School (founded in 1885) and Medical College (founded in 1868). The training is said to have surpassed that of many men's medical colleges.

The Infirmary, College and Nursing School had all been founded by Dr. Elizabeth Blackwell, the first female physician accredited in the United States. Her motivation in becoming a doctor seems, interestingly enough, to have stemmed more from the challenge facing a woman than any Nightingaleian notions. Despite being "disgusted" by the idea of treating bodily diseases, she had resolved to become a doctor when a friend dying of a gynecological ailment had confessed that she would have been spared the worst of her suffering had she been treated by a female physician. Astounded "at the arrogance of the male sect [*sic*]," Blackwell founded a matriarchal society of women professionals.

Four decades later the Infirmary trustees continued to run Blackwell's microcosmic society, and under the aegis and noses of their wealthy husbands. Blackwell's original intent was reflected in the 1889 *Annual Report,* which stated, "The Committee feels assured from their experience, that the women who come to the Dispensary find their treatment more acceptable, being administered by physicians of their own sex." As the product of an elitist, male-dominated medical establishment, Blackwell may not be unanimously embraced by later-day feminists. But her matriarchy-within-a-patriarchy, autonomous from and ideologically opposed to the system which funded and endorsed it, was nevertheless for the time a triumph of female ingenuity.

Lou was effective at the Infirmary precisely because she kept her professional and domestic interests separate. She lived one moment providing for a tenement mother and her children, the next spending enough at Delmonico's and the Metropolitan Opera to feed that family for a year, but was rewarded by her relationships as a wife and mother on one hand, and by her philanthropic feminism on the other. If the daughter of a Presbyterian minister at times sat within the wife of a sybaritic artist and judged her critically, it was a price she had to pay. For sixteen years she maintained this balance, nurturing her husband, her children, and herself.

In 1899 when Lou had family portraits taken, she chose Gertrude Käsebier, the Photo-Secessionist highly regarded for her unconventional treatment of mothers and children. Käsebier captured eight-year-old Dorothy in a pose no etiquette book would have advised, sitting sideways in a ladderback chair, though facing the camera, her chin pressed against the head of a remarkably lifelike doll.

The family photographer, however, was Julia de Forest. A serious amateur, she made a remarkable record of Mama Lou's children from birth to maturity, her thoroughness and sensitivity reflecting scientific and aesthetic intent. She had traveled abroad extensively with Robert, Henry, and Lockwood collecting art reproductions, and in 1881 published *A Short History of Art*. Asked later if her father had directed Julia in the taking of these photographs, as was his custom, Dorothy exclaimed, "Oh no! She was very much her own person." Working with highly detailed glass plate negatives and a gushing light, she approached the ethereal moods of girlhood from a naturalistic perspective. (Julia de Forest's energy, it seemed, was indefatigable: she also embroidered many of the exquisite linen, Egyptian cotton, and Dacca muslin dresses worn in these portraits.)

Two years after the Käsebier study, Julia took another portrait, memorable because Dorothy, with the aid of a box, was made to stand at an equal height with her sisters. Wearing identical skirts and white blouses tied loosely at the neck, Comfort and Julia glared at the slight to their seniority, while Dorothy, in a dark dress and equally serious mood, asserted her newfound status. The pageboy hair pictured by Käsebier had grown long enough for a pompadour, and the following fall Dorothy joined the twins at the Brearley School on West 44th Street, proudly walking the thirty-block distance, three little Gibson girls in black lace-up boots, ankle-length skirts, flannel shirtwaists, jabots, inflexible collars, and tailored jackets, struggling to keep pace with Papa.

At nine, Dorothy went to Paris for the Exposition Universelle and there saw the glass that had brought the widest fame to her patronymic. She saw the full range of Favrile: the floriforms like three-dimensional flowers, blown in all stages of development from bud to wilting blossom;

Cypriot vases resembling the crumpled amphoras excavated at Cyprus in the 1870s, their surfaces alternately pocked, nacreous, and irisdescent; lava vases bulging with thick flows of golden luster glass; twisting and soaring gooseneck vases; vases emulating the color, iridescence, and intricacy of peacock feathers; vases clear on the outside, iridescent within, and embedded with millefiori flowers. As one of the master blowers put it, "Every piece was something out of this world . . . when we had it all finished, it was beautiful, it surely was beautiful. That's the only thing I can term it as, beautiful."

After the Exposition Julia de Forest escorted the children to Norway, possibly because Jens Thiis, director of the Nordenfjeldske Kunstindustrimuseum, had begun collecting Tiffany glass. Years later, Dorothy recalled sitting on the back of a donkey-drawn cart with her sisters somewhere in Norway, dangling her legs at the untwining road.

One could certainly imagine, at this juncture, a pair of influences less promising for a young girl than Papa Louis and Mama Lou. They were different influences, to be sure, but, due to Mama Lou's determined efforts, complementary. Her scientific philanthropy tempered his chauvinistic artistry, and his inventiveness leavened her sobriety. The fantastic extravagance on Lenox Hill was met by the simplicity of the Briars, the Tiffany Studios countered by the New York Infirmary, and the prerogatives of men challenged by the rights of women. Dorothy, the youngest Tiffany, and a female, was in turn balanced by her grandfather, the patriarch.

In 1900, at the respective ages of nine and eighty-eight, separated by nearly eight decades, they represented the poles of a family at the height of its glory; he, born in the second term of James Madison's presidency, she, in the first term of Grover Cleveland's. Yet Dorothy did not recall her grandfather as kindly as one might expect. The formal Sunday dinners at 255 Madison Avenue were to be tediously endured, on her best behavior, in a state of high alert, while under the minute examination of ancestral portraits. Later Dorothy would say that, "My grandfather would do anything to make money." But this comment was largely reflective of Dorothy's own radically reorganized values, and may also have been less responsive to her grandfather's life than his death—the event which seemed to throw the delicate familial balance unrecoverably out of whack.

Harriet Tiffany had died in 1897, and Charles, continuing to rule his business and family with a firm hand, had promptly turned thirty-seven-year-old Burnie and forty-year-old Louise out of his house, leading one to conclude that the black sheep and his spinster sister had, all these years, been hiding behind Mama's skirts. They moved, ominously, to the glittering Waldorf-Astoria, "a terrible place for Burnie," thought Louis.

At the 1900 Paris Exposition Universelle, Tiffany & Company's million-dollar gem exhibit assembled for J.P. Morgan won the *grand prix,* capping Charles's illustrious career. Before escaping that summer with a few friends to Maine, the eighty-eight-year-old Republican told the New York *Tribune* that he was prepared to "whoop it up" for McKinley, because, "we want a man with power." As to the candidacy of William Jennings Bryan, and the Free-Silverites, he opined, "My business would be very seriously disturbed. At present it is doing very well and I want it to stay so."

Leaving the Poland Spring House one afternoon not long after for a solitary stroll, Charles got lost and struggled for hours through the brambles, scrub pines, blackberry bushes, and thistles of Androscoggin County, using the sun as a guide. Trembling and bleeding, his clothes filthy and torn, he finally stumbled across the United Community of Shakers at Sabbathday Lake, and requested a glass of water of the village eldress. Sister Aurelia, taking him for a tramp, brushed off his clothes and his explanations, and sat him down to lunch. "It is a dreadful thing to be out of work, sir, but thee should thank God thee has thy strength and health," she said.

When he returned to New York Charles had a field day with this story, recalling for reporters the pasteboard box Sister Aurelia had handed him as he left, containing three ham sandwiches, four doughnuts, two slices of apple pie, and a jar of grape jelly. The eldress herself revealed the sequel: a liveried footman delivered to her door a $300 Tiffany & Company silver service, with the signed note, "In return for the kindness you showed me after my encounter with the blackberry brambles last week."

Back at Tiffany Hall one fall evening in the following year, Charles reached to put a log on the fire in the library and fell, injuring his hip. He declined precipitously after that and, in the dead of winter, the great

William Merritt Chase was rushed in to do his portrait. Charles was still able to sign a copy of *The Tiffanys of America* for the New-York Historical Society in a fairly strong hand on January 18, 1902, but the celebrations planned for his ninetieth birthday on February 15 had to be canceled. He died in the morning three days later, of pneumonia, with his children at his side.

His death was reported around the world in papers ranging from the *Danielson Transcript* to the *Vienne Freie Presse,* and B. Altman, Lord & Taylor, W. & J. Sloane, and sixteen other stores closed during the hours of the funeral service. He was buried from the Madison Square Presbyterian Church by Dr. Charles H. Parkhurst, the firebrand preacher who had warmed his heart with unrelenting attacks on the "lying, perjured, rum-soaked and libidinous" politicians of Tammany Hall. The organist played his favorite hymn, "Lead Kindly Light," and he found his resting place on the crest of a small hill in Brooklyn's Greenwood Cemetery, sharing a plain granite headstone with his Connecticut sweetheart.

The estate amounted to $12 million, exclusive of realty, to which the four children had rights of first refusal. Considering the $20 million dollars left in the same year by diamond mogul Cecil Rhodes, the extent of Charles's philanthrophies becomes apparent, as does the discretion with which it was administered. Twelve million was a Croesian fortune, nevertheless, the equivalent of $120 million untaxed dollars today.

By bizarre fluke, the day of Charles's death, February 18, 1902, was Louis's fifty-fourth birthday. As his daughter Comfort would later write in a poem, "Then came the rush of wealth!"

As augured by the coincidence of death and birthdays, the money was a mixed blessing. Its unsettling effect, through the provisions of the will, was particularly visible in Burnie. Charles had divided his estate into eight parts, three-eighth shares going to Annie and Louis, coexecutors of the estate together with attorney Charles E. Miller and Tiffany & Company's president-successor, Charles T. Cook. With primogeniture, not sex, appearing to be the determining factor, Louise and Burnie each received an eighth share, with Burnie's $1.5 million placed in a trust administered by the executors. Charles's final word to his reprobate son was the annual stipend available to Burnie through the fund—a mere $3,000. The bequest raised eyebrows in the press, but, as Burnie had the track record of a drinker and gambler, was quite understandable. Canny to the end, while punishing Burnie for past transgressions, Charles also gave him an incentive to mend his ways, as the executors had the power to increase the stipend.

But Burnie was definitely addlepated. As a boy he had, for some reason, been privately tutored in Norwich, and Louis had bullied him unmercifully at home. He seemed oddly content playing Falstaff to his Hotspur brother, marrying the prostitute Emma N. Pierson less than four months after Louis had married Lou. Though Charles's executors relented and increased Burnie's annual income to a comfortable $25,000, the $4.5 million which Louis received outright seems to have goaded Burnie anew. At the Madison Square Garden Women's Exposition he chanced upon Mrs. Lucille Kaufman, working the Hyde Exploration Expedition booth in the guise of an Indian princess. They were married, on April 25, 1902, two months after his father's death and just four hours after Lucille had secured a divorce from Mr. Kaufman. The executors discovered, subsequently, that it was Lucille who had prodded Burnie into applying for the greater figure, promising to marry him if he were successful. They immediately reduced his allowance by $7,000.

Burnie dragged the family name into the tabloids with some consistency over the next years, first contesting the provisions of his trust fund, then arguing that Louis's $665,000 purchase price for the Lenox Hill mansion was a deflated figure. The Tiffany name surfaced again as Burnie was pursued by fourteen creditors; he finally declared bankruptcy in 1904, from which he emerged officially eight years later. Among the disclaimers he was forced to make under oath were that he had "not touched a drop of intoxicating liquor in nine years," and, that he had not, one day at Irvington, clenched his fist and threatened his father. Apparently a servant had eavesdropped on a family conversation and later repeated something to his sister Louise that had made her cry, and Burnie, demanding that the servant be fired, had gone too far.

Whatever Burnie's problem, he never rose higher than a $750-a-year clerk at his father's store. His marriages to a prostitute and a scheming divorcee, which closely followed the second marriage of his brother and death of his father, respectively, and were perhaps, therefore, perversely directed at them, also did not reflect a particularly nice light on his view of women, particularly his mother. Once banished by his father, and effectually excommunicated by the family, Burnie eventually banished himself and Lucille to Santa Barbara, where they were spared further humiliation.

If Burnie and Louis shared anything, it was a flair for the dramatic, that thunderous roll of the kettle drum, though Burnie's was usually an inverted percussive blast. Louis, too, was unsettled by his father's death and release from his iron chancellorism, but his reaction took a characteristically different form. The sapling which Charles had bent before the wind in the mid-nineteenth century, came whipping back in the aughts of the twentieth.

The Victorian age was ended; with Edward VII ascended to the British throne, Louis could finally begin that prodigious spending spree, that sustained wave of creative profligacy for which he had been thirsting. He could finally realize his dream of omnipotence. This fantasy was most obvious in 1913, when he appeared at his Costume Fête at the Time of Cleopatra in the guise of an Egyptian potentate. But it—his incarnation as a self-styled pasha—really began in 1902. From that point, his restaurants were four star, his railroad cars private, his hotel and liner suites imperial. And it was toward the end of this spree, after the equivalent of $40 million dollars had been spent, that his son wrote, "Grandpa would turn over in his grave if he knew how Papa had handled the money he left him!" Louis was a lot smarter than his brother, and a whole lot more talented, but like Burnie, he too got his Oedipal revenge.

Despite his wholehearted endorsement of business, Louis's attitude toward moneymaking had remained ambivalent even during Charles's lifetime. By all rights Louis should have made a fortune off his flourishing glass trade, but the Tiffany Glass Company, for one, never once showed a profit. Receipts in 1891, for example, amounted to $450,833.74, but expenditures were $454,633.34. Unlike his father, Louis put quality above profit, running his business in effect as a mission, one which taught the gospel of good taste at cost. Louis's readiness to spend the capital that his father had reverently earned was about as hostile and contemptuous a gesture as he could have made.

The imperative which sent Louis soaring and Burnie plummeting was clearly a volatile one. It would have been surprising, with Charles gone, if the balance which Mama Lou had diligently constructed had not been affected. The first gust of shifting wind hit Lou as Louis began to buy up the lands adjacent to the Briars. When finished he owned a 580-acre Gold Coast fiefdom bounded, to the south, by the road connecting the towns of Oyster Bay and Cold Spring Harbor and, to the north, by Long Island Sound. The finest prospect over Cold Spring Harbor lay half a mile west of the Briars along Ridge Road on a slope overlooking a natural cove; but Louis could not obtain the site. For years it had been the setting of public picnic grounds and an old-fashioned hotel called Laurelton Hall, but the owner, Dr. Oliver L. Jones, of an old Cold Spring Harbor family, refused to sell to the cosmopolitan multimillionaire. Eventually, however, the property passed into other hands and Louis seized it, for a considerably "advanced" price. Razing the hotel, he began to plan his masterwork, a synthesis nonpareil of the fine, decorative, and industrial arts, a showplace and legacy. "In Xanadu did Kubla Khan/A stately pleasure-dome decree."

This turn of events was a blow to Lou, as the Briars was her sanctuary from the Lenox Hill/Stuyvesant Square conflict. The Briars expressed Lou's sense of propriety and humane scale, whereas, to her, the Lenox Hill mansion was an unapologetic statement on wealth and imagination—as would be the new dwelling. It was clear, to Dorothy in particular, that Mama Lou wanted to remain in her beloved Briars.

This followed on the heels of another, greater crisis. Lou had managed to keep her domestic and ideological identities in check by keeping them separate, but as her daughters matured her aspirations for them spilled, uncontrollably, into the parlor. It was over the issue of education that Lou's commitment to the rights of women came into open conflict with Louis's value system.

The twenty years of revolutionary experiment following the Civil War had seen the establishment of four great American women's colleges, Vassar, Wellesley, Smith, and Bryn Mawr. By the year of Dorothy's birth there were over two hundred women's colleges in America, and over two hundred more that were coeducational. *The Forum* inquired, "Why train a girl specifically to be a wife and mother when no great need is felt for training a boy to be a husband and father? In education, as a public matter, the two sexes meet on common ground. The differences can be attended to privately." These ideas were still very much in the vanguard at the turn of the century. Most Brearley "Beavers" saw their future as a seamless progression from debutancy to engagement, marriage, and maternity. They sang: "When I see the college crammers/ Studying Greek and Latin grammar/ Gee whiz! I'm glad I'm free/ No college course for me!"

Progress had been made since 1873 when Dr. Edward H. Clarke had announced that women were constitutionally weak and therefore in themselves an obstacle to their higher education. Yet a former Wellesley president observed that " . . . the public mind is [still] uncertain . . . liable to panic, and . . . doubtful whether, after all, it is not better for a girl to be a goose."

Dorothy, in her first year at Brearley, had done reasonably well in English, history, and science, excelled at math, and switched to French after three months of German. In the upper forms, Julia wanted to go into medicine, and Comfort was inclining to art and literature; both had their sights set on Bryn Mawr. Mama Lou was adamant that they be allowed to go, and on this issue she made a stand. Comfort later recalled in a short story her mother insisting to her father, "Girls need an education as well as boys. Besides, how do you know that [Julia] won't be a doctor someday?"

"Well I never," Louis had said, flushing. "A woman doctor! What foolishness! But that's your idea. I've given in on many points—on this one I insist! No daughter of mine will become a doctor!" A war began; battle after battle, Louis's voice rising in anger at his wife's intransigence.

Louis's attitude was curious, considering his collaboration years before with Candace Wheeler and subsequent employment of women in his glass companies. There were fifty in the Women's Glass Department of the Tiffany Studios, executing all but the largest memorial windows. In 1904 Clara Driscoll, designer of the dragonfly lamp, was one of the highest paid women workers in the United States. Clearly Louis was not opposed to the concept of working women. Nor was he opposed, in principle, to higher education. His son Charles Lewis II had just graduated from Yale with high honors, and joined Tiffany & Company. Comfort rationalized that "Papa was an artist. He had had very little formal education. He did not understand why girls needed more than school." His reservations may in part have stemmed from the belief that women in society do not work for a living. But more to the point, probably, was the fear that his daughters would intellectually surpass—and abandon—him.

The threat to the Briars and to Lou's dreams for the future may have weakened her physical resistance. By the summer of 1903 she was resting long hours on the tan library couch at the Briars. Propped up by orange cushions, the air full with the scent of chrysanthemums, she listened to the staccato beat of the hammers half a mile down Ridge Road. Louis returned each evening with handfuls of the small wild flowers that he knew Lou loved dearly, but, not knowing her preference, Dorothy wondered why he brought such small tokens of his affection.

Lou was dying—of bowel cancer—by the time they returned to Lenox Hill. She was able to rest under the influence of morphine, but when it wore off she lay awake groaning. And this was how Dorothy mostly remembered her, as "very sickly." "It was terrible. Oh, it was a horrible ending . . . It was ghastly. We all, my father included, were moved up to the top floor so [as] not to hear her groaning. To this day I can hear her groaning."

Each morning the girls met their spinster aunt, Louise, Louis's younger sister, and asked when they could see their mother, and each morning Louise replied, "Tomorrow." Comfort recalled Louise in "The Sewing Room," a short story about Mama Lou's death. "Though she never lived with us, she managed our family with a firm sweetness. She knew what was right for us and what was wrong. In the midst of turmoil she would say with a smile, Everything is going to be fine." When they asked how their mother was faring, Louise would reply, in her lilting voice, "about the same." They were never told the truth; but they knew.

Comfort's story recalled her mother as "self-sufficient, a tower of strength, the source of understanding." She had taught the girls to keep their emotions under control, "while Papa's sudden tempers and harsh voice kept us terrified at his lack of control." The prospect of losing Mama Lou's stability must have frightened them all.

Finally, after an operation, they were allowed to see her. She seemed much better, holding Dorothy's hand and telling her of the times they would have together when she was fully recovered, the special mother-daughter talks marking her "attainment." Then she relapsed.

Comfort wrote of her last visit:

> One day, as I was passing Mamma's room, Aunt Bessie [Louise] came out of it, and asked me, "Do you want to see your mother now?"
>
> "Oh, may I?" I asked hopefully.
>
> Aunt Bessie did not answer, but she opened the door and I followed her into the room. We walked slowly to her bed. There a woman lay on her back with closed eyes. She was snoring, her mouth wide open. I gazed at her with utter horror. Could this be my mother? I thought back to the last time I had seen her. Then she had had her usual radiant expression. Now her face was pasty, flattened—nothing about it reminded me of my mother.
>
> "Don't you want to kiss her?" asked Aunt Bessie, nudging me toward

the figure on the bed. I pulled back. "No, no, I might wake her," I whispered.

"You won't—the doctor has given her morphine," said Aunt Bessie, trying gently to push me forward; but I was rooted to the spot. My eyes never left that unfamiliar face. I was trembling. How could I kiss this stranger?

"Kiss her!" Aunt Bessie insisted.

I wanted to shout, Leave me alone. I wanted to strike Aunt Bessie, to push her away. More than any time in my life, I longed to sob in my mother's arms. I was overwhelmed by the realization that this never could be.

The next morning Louis broke the news to the girls.

"Your mother died last night," he said. "You must know I need you now. It is very hard for me." I was sure Aunt Bessie had prompted him.

He wanted our pity but all I could feel was a dumb fury against him. What had he ever done for Mamma? I remembered how often his voice was angry when he talked to her. I felt he had never loved her. How could I pity him now?

We finally kissed him in a perfunctory way. We did not say a word. His unpleasant job was done. He left us with a tired shrug of his shoulders. Suddenly I felt a choked feeling. Poor Papa, I thought. Perhaps he misses Mamma too.

For twelve-year-old Dorothy the unforgettable part was her mother's suffering. Later she confided to an uncomprehending friend something to the effect that "I'm glad my mother's dead because she isn't groaning anymore." Attempts to shield her from the illness may have propelled her to even darker psychological depths than her sisters, who were old enough to see through their aunt's well-intended deceits. Misinterpreting her father's gift of wild flowers indicated doubt in her mind of her father's love for her mother; lacking concrete information, doubt could easily have transposed him into the agent of her death. Papa did not love Mama; therefore Mama died.

Lou's death did seem to affect Dorothy the most profoundly. The sixteen-year-old twins had at least known something of their mother, though, ironically, not so much as May-May, Charles, and Hilda. In "The Sewing Room," Hilda explains to Comfort:

"I think when she decided to marry Papa she vowed to herself that she would make up to us older ones all we had suffered. And she did."

"She loved [Julia] and me too," I said.

"Of course—you were her very own. But she knew what it was to be a stepchild. She showered on us all the love we had missed."

In the spring of 1904 Dorothy was denied the maternal attentions promised since birth just as her spirit was ripening to receive them. That is why the memory of her mother groaning remained with her to the day of her own death, like a thread on which one had better not pull, lest it unravel. If the Tiffany imperative was the single most influential condition of Dorothy's childhood, Mama Lou's agonizing end gave her destiny its final shape. It wounded her, tarnished her view of her father, and set her on a lifelong search for the spirit and values, if not the living breathing presence, of her mother.

VI

Dorothy

ou died on May 8, and a few months later the family moved to
Laurelton Hall—for the profusion of laurel, Louis decided to keep
the name. But there was no trace of the resort hotel and public picnic
grounds. The painter had stepped bodily into his canvas: the Kubla Khan
and his pleasure-dome were one.

Since all that remains of Louis's masterwork are a few scattered ruins,
it is hard to imagine the exquisite beauty and extraordinary originality
of this dwelling. Louis declared "the fundamental idea" to be Persian.
One visitor remembered it as "a cross between a Moorish temple, an
Italian villa and a Pennsylvania barn"; another as mingling "the perfume
of the Orient with the horse sense of America." Of cream-colored stucco
with a molded turquoise-green copper roof, it was a blend of Islamic,
Mission-Moorish, and art nouveau elements. A long asymmetrical structure, possessing the awkward elegance of an Edwardian ocean liner or
Pullman railroad coach, it stretched 280 feet westward, descending in
eight levels from porte cochere to stables. It contained museum-quality
Chinese and American Indian rooms, a three-story octagonal inner court,
a living room lit by Louis's favorite stained-glass windows, and a dining
room featuring a table for each of the day's meals. Breakfast was served
at the table facing the Sound (to keep the rising sun from their eyes).
A hearty meal, in those days, it often consisted of waffles, fishballs or
steamers, and large red baked apples, well-cored and filled with cream so
thick it stood one's spoon upright. The cream and the apples came from

the adobe farm across Laurel Hollow Road which Louis had designed to look like a Moroccan village, populating it with Clydesdales, Herefords, Rhode Island and Buff Orphington chickens, doves, and a flock of pheasants which sometimes strayed down the hill issuing shrill communiqués.

A team of thirty-five gardeners maintained the land, two greenhouses, and two conservatories, at a high professional standard of horticulture. Tropical cordyline trees, cacti, banana trees, date palms, and Oriental evergreens sprouted suddenly, in pots, along Long Island's north shore. A mile-long blue gravel drive wound past rhododendrons, honeysuckle, and laurel, by fields of daffodils, through woods flourishing with dark masses of red cedar and the lighter green of deciduous trees, and along a hundred yard alley of espaliered apple trees. Crossing Laurel Hollow Road it passed a thatched gazebo below the mansion and ponds edged with marsh marigold, joe-pye weed, Japanese iris, boneset, wild rice, forget-me-nots, goldenrods, and day lilies, past carefully tended beds of tulips, azaleas, and pink phlox. From the mansion's northern face, a fountained terrace bordered with petunias descended in tiers toward the Sound, ending in a twenty-foot hanging garden supported on black locust trunks. From the purple and white wisteria planted over dead chestnut trees in the woods to the window boxes full of mesembryantheum, every detail was supervised by Louis, who directed his gardeners with as much enthusiasm as his glassmen. It was said by the day's outstanding architects that "Mr. Tiffany never reached greater heights than in the landscape planning and gardening scheme of this estate." Even the ceramic capitals of the loggia depicted blooming flowers, wine-colored Oriental poppies, East India lotus, saucer magnolias, and peonies, accurate to the details of the buds.

A pair of turquoise Fu lions guarded the loggia at the southern side, and a dozen polar bears snarled on the orange and black mosaic floor within. Cypress-tree designs stenciled on the walls of the inner court were copied from the seraglio of Istanbul's Topkapi Palace, the placement of the loggia's limestone columns inspired by the Red Fort at Delhi; an Islamic prayer niche adapted for the display of Favrile glass actually faced Mecca. Mosque lamps burned in tiered arches colonnading the court; an indoor fountain trickled beneath a silvery-blue glass dome. The water (for this and nine exterior fountains) came from a forty-thousand-gallon hillside tank. It rose in a blown-glass amphora and dropped to a marble pool ringed with quartz crystals and exotic potted plants, brimmed into a canal flanked by roses, geraniums, hydrangeas, and chrysanthemums and vanished underground at the seaward entrance.

After dinner the girls followed Papa into the court where he ensconced himself on a green velvet divan (immediately dubbed "the throne") to savor his cigar and cognac, and harbor breezes sweetened by petunias, boxwood, and wood smoke. Dorothy recalled him playing different colored lights on the amphora (of glass so thin it periodically cracked, shivered, and exploded) until he lit one evening on the idea of passing a spotlight through a revolving filter to change the color imperceptibly, from coral to crimson, lavender to emerald, as one of the German romantics rumbled through the pipes of a player organ.

When Louis discovered that a huge furnace and smokestack were required to heat his leviathan, he handed grounds superintendant Mr. Terwilliger a wash drawing of a minaret.

"Can you do this?" he asked.

Terwilliger looked at the drawing. "How big will it be?"

"Sixty feet," said Louis.

Terwilliger whistled. "We can do it," he said, "but have you any idea what it will cost?"

Smiling gently, Louis replied, "I don't want to know."

The work at Laurelton Hall was not completed until 1908, but when fully decorated was estimated to have cost $2 million.

The Afterword to the 1914 monograph on Louis's career, pointed out that Louis, "while . . . under the stress of business *plus* creative art . . . was so far from neglecting home life . . . that he found time to plan and carefully carry out no less than four homes in succession." In other words, he had designed the Bella, Lenox Hill mansion, Briars, and Laurelton Hall with the satisfaction of the entire family in mind. And indeed, at Laurelton Hall, he had not forgotten his daughters, building a squash court, tennis courts, and a bowling alley. The box stables at the western end were for their horses, and the twenty-foot mahogany sail-boat, *Waterbaby,* was for their sailing pleasure. To create a wider stretch

of beach he built a seawall and breakwater, and he refurbished an old ferry
into a changing room, a cork-lined tunnel ensuring privacy en route.

If Laurelton Hall was Louis's greatest pleasure, for Dorothy, as for the
twins, it was no Xanadu. For them, a terser parallel might be found in
the Mogul tomb that Shah Jehan built for his wife, Mumtaz Mahal. It
seems incredible that, once again, Louis had found himself raising a
monument to his wife's decline. A museum, treasury, showcase, waxworks, and tomb—Laurelton Hall was all of these things to Mama Lou's
daughters; but it was never a home. Comfort expressed the barrenness of
this Taj Mahal in her poem "Daffodils":

> Garden with gravel path hedged by boxwood,
> children walk up and down sedately, talk in whispers,
> admire from a distance but do not touch—
> red peonies in one section,
> blue irises stand stiffly in another,
> fragrant roses in restricted places.
> Blooms, blooms everywhere,
> but not a flower to be loved.

Louis was stricken by Lou's death, and his misery was reflected in his
increasingly autocratic behavior. The ulterior subject of the stanza was
the taboo on picking flowers, even wild flowers, which grew in great
abundance around Laurelton Hall. His insistence on punctuality also grew
more oppressive. Soaring above the residence was a clock tower with
Westminster chimes—the analogue to Tiffany & Company's Atlas; and
on no part of the grounds could these chimes not be heard. In the drawing
room were three more clocks, telling the month, day, and hour.

Laurelton Hall certainly contributed to Louis's reputation as an eccentric. There was the mansion itself, so unlike anything ever built, and in
the darkness of the clock tower's spiraling staircase, Louis had lined the
wall with suits of Japanese armor and had installed blinking lights in the
visors—or so said the children who tore down the stairs, shrieking, at the
whirring of the gears. Visitors arriving by car were greeted by the sight
of a totem pole surmounted by a whale. Then there were Louis's white
summer suits, which he changed, if soiled, up to three times a day. The
legend grew from these kernels of fact, and Louis was easily placed, in

a white kaftan, atop the minaret, muezzinlike summoning the faithful to prayer.

But weirdest of all, to Dorothy's mind, was a mural-sized painting called *The Opium Fiend's Dream* which hung in the smoking room, testifying to the more decadent aspects of a Mogul empire. It portrayed a prostrate addict, his cushioned head surrounded by the nightmarish apparitions summoned by the opium: a prince astride a bejeweled elephant, a great trunked and winged beast, serpents and skulls, rogues hacking ruffians, heads impaled on spears, horrible monsters, and the life cycle of an Oriental prostitute, from girlhood through lewd, pouting maturity to old age. Dorothy could not take her eyes off these "dreadful creatures and abnormal humans in grotesque positions, sadistically mutilated, dripping blood and vividly colored." Visitors were aghast at Louis's readiness to display this vision to his thirteen-year-old daughter, even if intended as a warning, and eventually he took his easel and transformed a plume of smoke from the hookah into a billowing cloud, "dimming the horrors."

The problem with Laurelton Hall lay in the circumstances surrounding its inception. Mama Lou, Comfort, Julia, Dorothy—none of them had wanted it. The local folk deprived of their picnic ground had not wanted it either and, as a result, Louis found himself at odds with them on more than one occasion. The Town of Oyster Bay had disputed Louis's claim to riparian rights, hoping to thwart his plan to enlarge his private sand beach, but the court had ruled in his favor, and Louis had reclaimed five underwater acres with a seawall and breakwater. The Town of Oyster Bay continued the fight, however, and finally got a reversal in the appellate court. The jubilant townsfolk, envisioning a triumphant return to their old picnic grounds, decided to build thirty-five public bathhouses directly below Laurelton Hall. But they had not reckoned well enough, because Louis, rather than see his Xanadu overrun by townspeople, simply "torpedoed" the breakwater, flooding the beach.

With the sudden influx of wealth, Louis's senses seemed to swell in a crescendo of sublimated sexuality: textures, colors, scents, shapes, and symbols. Victorians well understood the link between sexuality and money; to climax was "to spend." Dorothy understood little of what was happening on a conscious level, but instinctually she understood it all, understood that her grandfather's death had loosened her father's restraint, and her mother had become upset; understood that his inhibitions had loosened as his discipline had sharpened; that he had never been so carried away, and that the alien environment at Laurelton Hall would not have been to her mother's liking. Mama Lou, it seems, had tended to the ascetic, Papa Louis to the epicurean, and, in the absence of Lou's checks and balances, while letting loose artistically, he was tightening the family's regimen. Dorothy shrank from it all, from Papa and his patriarchal confusion.

In December of 1904 Louis made the single largest philanthropic contribution of his life, a $300,000 bequest to the Infirmary for Women and Children. But if guilt fueled his generosity, the gesture did not ease his mind and, for the first time in his life, Louis turned to drink. This period was recalled in another of Comfort's stories, which concluded, "Every night was the same, only some nights were worse than the others." After dinner, the girls usually sat with their father until he retired, but now, long after they had gone to bed, they could hear him smashing around downstairs, ranting at housekeeper Mary Ferguson. Like the staged effects of a Gothic play, yells, crashes, bangs, and slammed doors filtered eerily upstairs as they lay awake shivering, "terrified at something beyond our understanding."

Before long Dorothy had to hide his drinking from her friends, though this was not always possible. Once, at a house party in New York, he sat so heavily in his chair that it collapsed, heaping him on the floor. This sodden period, and one some years later, instilled in Dorothy a lifelong fear and horror of alcohol.

The full extent of the tragedy which had befallen them became evident when the twins were denied the opportunity to go to college. Although permitted to audit some courses at Barnard, Julia's lack of formal medical education crippled an otherwise brilliant microbiology career, and Comfort's literary and artistic efforts likewise lacked sophistication and polish (later she went back to Barnard and graduated Phi Beta Kappa). The effect on Dorothy was less immediate, though her conception of the future was limited by knowing she would not be allowed to go to college.

The girls were not, however, left without feminine support and guidance. Their care was ensured by their half-sisters, particularly by May-May, who assumed Mama Lou's place on the Infirmary Board of Directors and the maternal role in the family. Married in 1899 to Dr. Graham Lusk, son of the family physician, May-May was the one who "dared the most" with Papa, and hence the likely candidate to intervene in their behalf. Hilda, at twenty-five, was the youngest of May's children, and, while unmarried and living at home, could minister to her half-sisters on a daily basis. In 1901 their brother Charles Lewis II had married the spirited Katrina Ely, a Bryn Mawr graduate, who was able to give Dorothy more disinterested advice than either May-May or Hilda.

Then, of course, there were Dorothy's aunts. But Louise was phobic and sickly. Electrical baths had not cured her heart disease, nor had her father cured her vertigo by once whisking her aloft in a hot air balloon; and she may not have provided Dorothy with much useful counsel. A prodigious knitter, one can almost hear her interrupt her humming to intone "a stitch in time saves nine." She had inherited Charles's Madison Avenue town house but, due to an unreasoning fear of burglars, never lived there. She nevertheless maintained the place exactly as it always had been, continuing to have his paper, the New York *Tribune,* delivered to the door each morning, and paying a watchman to retrieve it a few hours later. Annie Mitchell was surely a better example. At finishing school, she had received the equivalent of a two-year college education in solid studies, not the more common ornamental branches, and she held her brother's talents in an elder sister's disregard. Their father had supposedly lamented her being a girl because she, apparently, was the one with a head for business. Dorothy liked Annie, but the Mitchells were little in evidence, having moved in 1891 to Sunflower Lodge, a refurbished fisherman's cottage on the Pequot outside New London.

The greatest influence on Dorothy in the aftermath of her mother's death was probably Julia de Forest. A spinster by choice, she lived in the 121 East 35th Street home of her brother Henry Wheeler de Forest, an attorney for powerful railroad interests. Julia's commitment to the Infirmary, and perhaps also to its underlying principles, was greater than Lou's had been. Her true partner-in-life appears to have been the former resident physician of the Infirmary, Dr. Eleanor Kilham, who was also unmarried. A Phi Beta Kappa graduate of the Wheaton Seminary, a graduate of the Infirmary Medical College, and a former professor there, she had received postdoctorate degrees from the universities of Zurich and Vienna, and would be decorated in Paris after World War I with the *médaille d'honneur* and the *médaille de reconnaissance d'honneur,* for her work with the American Committee for French Wounded. After retiring from the Infirmary Dr. Kilham lived with Julia in the de Forest home on 35th Street, the two spinsters echoing the Infirmary's matriarchal bias with their Boston marriage. This intellectual partnership very likely served Dorothy with a model recreated in adulthood. She knew, later, that she had been "searching for something for myself, I'm sure, without knowing it, even as a child."

In the summer following Lou's death, it was probably Julia who arranged for the children to stay with her brother Robert and his wife, Emily, at Fir Tops, their Dark Harbor, Maine, estate. Her tactic spared the children of having to accompany Papa, in his present condition, to the 1904 St. Louis Exposition. Julia had been a close witness to Mama Lou's marriage, and seemed to have taken an increasingly dim view of Papa Louis. Once she wrote Dr. Graham Lusk:

> Ideas penetrate slowly to Mr. Tiffany's mind, new ideas; that are not in the decorative line. I can just see his absorption in getting ahead & his indifference to your interests. I sometimes think he cannot be sympathetic, only appreciative when things are completed.

Julia made a great effort to keep Lou's spirit alive for the girls, to guide them according to what Lou would have wanted for them. Emily de Forest wrote May-May of "the beautiful way [the children] all seem to live with the thought ever present (although seldom expressed) of what Aunt Lou would most like them to do." Julia's key concern in the summer of 1904 seems to have been the transfer of Lou's maternal responsibilities to May-May. In a philosophic mood she wrote:

> You must not worry about any of them, it is because we all have to grow that God takes people home to another world to wait there to see what He does to develop those whom they loved. If our generation did not pass on the younger ones would always be children.

On another occasion she expressed her pleasure to May-May and Graham over the way they were providing for the children's spiritual welfare. Her characterization of Katrina Tiffany might reveal the sober, moralizing side of her own nature, as Katrina was young and full of spirit, once endorsing a line of furniture with the then scandalous suggestion: "I sleep on Simmonds Beds." But sexual expression does not seem to have been part of Julia de Forest's feminism. Wrote Julia to May-May:

I have looked with great happiness at the way in which Papa has been turning to you & Graham and appreciating you both more & more, and trying to bring your influence into the children's lives as the influence Mama would wish for them. I do not deprecate Katrina, nor what she does for them in many ways, but you & Graham are giving them the spiritual things which Mama wanted so much for them. I use the word not in the sense merely of the things we associate with going to church, but in the sense of the search for truth, & the aspirations for usefulness & the love of others, the things that are *not* making merry & eating & drinking & pleasure seeking. Katrina's childlessness has turned her thoughts more in that direction than one likes to see just now, & I hope by & by her life will swing back a little the other way.

Upholding Mama Lou's standards without directly crossing the Kubla Khan was a task which required great ingenuity on the part of Julia de Forest, who admittedly had "done a good deal of living in complicated families." One of her methods was revealed again in a letter to May-May, in which she mentioned having read to Comfort, Julia, and Dorothy Nathaniel Hawthorne's "The Snow Image," a short story included in *Twice-told Tales*. Subtitled "A Childish Miracle," it begins with a comparative description of the parents of Violet and Peony Lindsey, beginning with their father:

> With a heart about as tender as other people's, he had a head as hard and impenetrable, and therefore, perhaps, as empty, as one of the iron pots which it was his business to sell. The mother's character, on the other hand, had a strain of poetry in it, a trait of unworldly beauty,—a delicate and dewy flower.

The tale unfolds and Peony and Violet make of snow a figure in their own image, which comes to life and plays delightful games with them. Even Mrs. Lindsey is forced to conclude that this charmed snow image is beyond the realm of her experience. But when Mr. Lindsey returns from work, being the hard head that he is, he mistakes their friend for a real girl, and insists that she step into the parlor and warm herself by the potbelly.

> But, after all, there is no teaching anything to wise men of good Mr. Lindsey's stamp. They know everything,—O, to be sure!—everything

that has been, and everything that is, and everything that, by any future possibility, can be. And should some phenomenon of nature or providence transcend their system, they will not recognize it, even if it comes to pass under their very nose.

"Wife," said Mr. Lindsey, after a fit of silence, "see what a quantity of snow the children have brought in on their feet! It has made quite a puddle here before the stove. Pray tell Dora to bring some towels and sop it up!"

Here were caricatures, from Julia's perspective, of Papa Louis and Mama Lou, and in Mr. Lindsey's incomprehension of the snow image, a metaphor for Mama Lou's decline and death. These were powerful ideas to plant in the heads of young girls.

In June 1905 Comfort and Julia graduated from Brearley to begin the progression from debutancy to motherhood which their father had more or less decreed. Julia de Forest was powerless to oppose this, but in the rocky academic year following Dorothy's mother's death, Julia saw an opportunity. Her plan, a flanking action, was for Dorothy to go away to boarding school beginning that fall, and in so doing minimize Papa Louis's influence on her. Julia must have persisted, because Dorothy was not at first enthused at the idea of leaving home. Eventually, however, she convinced Dorothy of its soundness and, so as not to appear the instigator, had Dorothy propose the plan herself. But, being lonely and dependent on his daughters, Louis refused, telling Dorothy of his experiences at Eagleswood. It took some doing, but he finally relented and, in September, Julia de Forest notched a triumph for Mama Lou as Dorothy began her first term at St. Timothy's, a top-drawer school for girls in Catonsville, Maryland. This proved to be the first step in Dorothy's fateful disengagement from her family. No longer "Me-Too" in relation to the twins, she started down the road to a different destiny.

The shock of separation was excruciating, however. "It was horrible," she recalled. "I hated it the whole time I was there"—though, she admitted, "I would have been unhappy anywhere. My mother had died . . . and it may have been the best for all I know. From Aunt Julia's point of view it was the best, but I think she made a mistake." Tense, fearful, and painfully shy, she went through agony when called upon in class, saying "something preposterous or nothing at all." Realizing that she had made a terrible mistake, she begged her father to allow her to return home. But he refused, and she spent "five miserable years" in boarding school.

Her willful then suppliant behavior must have reminded Louis of himself at her age, because after tacking one way, he abruptly veered back in the direction his father had taken with him. It was as if the voice which had warned her against boarding school had been that of the recalcitrant Cadet Tiffany, and the voice which insisted she remain that of his iron-fisted father. She had made her decision, he told her, and she must stick to it. Unfortunately, he imparted no hope that the hard grinding and polishing would make of her a diamond of the first water. Instead, at a distance, he remained coolly authoritarian. When she wrote for his permission to drink tea and coffee, he replied with "a four-page letter saying no in every possible way." They were not good for her health, he told her.

Thus, like an animal stepping into a trap, did Dorothy Trimble Tiffany gain entrée to this Edwardian girls school, whose motto, *Vérité sans peur,* set the moral tone. Morning prayer was required at St. Timothy's, French alone spoken before lunch and German and English thereafter—the German later proving enormously helpful. Maids wearing starched uniforms and organdy caps fixed their beds, and waitresses served them lamb chops, steak, and "Kossuth cakes." Dorothy studied diligently and played hard, despite her misery. She vied for Miss Sally's "Tidy Prize," recalled objects on her shelf from memory, played sonatas on the piano, and sewed at lenten tea. For charitable organizations she polished shoes, shampooed hair, and sold chances. She joined the Theta Taus and played on varsity soccer and basketball teams, and, in doing all that was calculated to make of one a superior young lady, earned the reputation of "a good scholar and athlete."

She was photographed in the fall of 1909, a silver trophy in one hand, a leather basketball in the other, having captained her team, the Spiders, to victory over the Brownies. Dark brows flashing, brown eyes blazing, an anxious tooth catching her sensual lower lip, this was not the child who had posed so sweetly for Gertrude Käsebier ten years earlier. No longer diffuse with contentment, she had the sharp, smoldering looks of a Gypsy. Living like a Gypsy had, in fact, always been her fantasy, she declared many years later in a letter to her son. Curious, quick-gestured, and expressive, her magnetism was already evident. Instantly one sees the intensity which made her team captain.

One episode that had surely contributed to her state of mind had begun when Louis departed for Brittany in the summer of 1907. This was the trip on which he kept a journal, and we know he boarded the SS *Amerika* on July 18 and, after his children had left the ship, departed for Cherbourg with three long-standing employees. He read on the journey a biography of Louis Pasteur, remarking that he was finding it more and more interesting. He had reason to be interested in the man who had validated the germ theory of disease. Perhaps he was reminded of his firstborn son, Charles Louis, whose death might have been prevented by the use of pasteurized milk, and his thoughts may have inevitably led to May, and her battle with tuberculosis. Upon his return to the piers of Hoboken on September 14, he wrote that "the weather was of course sizzling—but the trials of the custom house were soon over. My three children were there to meet me with the Auto, and we made a quick voyage to Cold Spring Harbor."

The three children were, presumably, Comfort, Julia, and Dorothy. But Hilda was also living under her father's roof, so by all rights there should have been four. The most like her mother in many ways, Hilda was also beautiful and slight, and her frailty a constant source of concern to the family. In all probability she had contracted the disease which had killed her mother before Louis had left for Brittany. The removed, academic interest in Pasteur and silence on the subject of Hilda's condition were completely in character. He had been burned three times now, and as Comfort pointed out, "he was afraid of illness."

Dorothy remembered Hilda as "a very beautiful person," adding, "she had so many people in love with her, but was in love with one special one [who] wasn't in love with her. That was the real tragedy." By the fall of 1907, she was probably already under Dr. Trudeau's care at his Saranac Lake sanitorium. In Comfort's story "A Pleasure Trip," Dr. Trudeau called by telephone in January 1908 to say that Hilda had about three months to live. Shortly thereafter Louis decided to take a sail up the Nile, despite the fact that the khamsins, desert sandstorms, would begin in March. The prospect of losing Hilda, after May and Lou, was obviously beyond his capacity to endure.

Against their will the twins were made to accompany their father to Egypt. In their absence Dorothy saw Hilda twice. The first time she was in a foul mood, and was told by one family member to not "go again because you don't do Hilda any good." But Dorothy insisted on returning soon, "because I wanted not to leave the feeling with Hilda that I was grumpy." Meanwhile the Kubla Khan was marshaling the desperately unhappy twins up the Nile on the dahabeah *Nepthis,* of Cook's Nile Steamer Services. He had planned to go beyond Aswan but, as he wrote May-May on February 12, "we would have to hurry & I wanted to sketch on our way back." With this the *Nepthis* turned and began a slow passage downriver, with Louis frequently interrupting its progress, jumping ashore to make watercolors.

He made no mention to the twins of Hilda but to May-May wrote, "I am so troubled that Hilda does not improve more." He would seem to have been resigned to her death because, on this trip, for the first time, he painted the great tomb monuments at Giza, Karnac, and Luxor. The watercolors remain, charged with ethereal beauty, testaments to a father's inability to stand by his daughter in her most terrifying hour.

Miraculously, when they returned at the onset of summer, Hilda was still alive. Yet even then, in the face of the twins' near hysterical entreaties, Louis found excuses to delay the trip to Saranac Lake. He simply could not stand to see Hilda's suffering face. Just moments before they finally did arrive in Saranac, on September 14, 1908, she died.

This ordeal was less traumatic for Dorothy than for the twins, who never forgave their father, as Comfort put it, for "sacrificing [Hilda] for his pleasure." Comfort and Julia talked about it to such a great extent that Dorothy came to accept their account, further prejudicing her view of her father. In "A Pleasure Trip" Comfort wrote, "He brought on [Hilda's] illness by this thoughtlessness of her health. He made her take trips when she was not up to them. He drank too. He knew she was frail. After all her mother died of T.B."

Back at school the following year Dorothy led the Spiders to victory and, had events taken their normal course, her five-year ordeal would at least have been rewarded by a diploma in the spring of 1910. But, "My father, in the last term of the last year said I needn't go back. And I didn't. And I was unhappy about it because I wanted to finish . . ."

From this recollection it appears that Louis had not actually forbade her to return to St. Timothy's, but merely given her the choice of going or remaining with him. With May-May married, Hilda gone, and the twins of a marriageable age, Louis was probably more lonely than ever, and concerned that if Dorothy did graduate from high school, she might start campaigning for college, and he would be left absolutely alone on

Lenox Hill. Perhaps he knew she would not refuse his scrap of "sympathy." Indeed, filial relations were so strained, and she so fearful, that she did not insist on returning . . . "I didn't dare."

Back at Cold Spring Harbor she played tennis, sailed *Waterbaby,* and rode her mare Fiddlesticks. From chauffeur Jimmy Ryan she learned how to drive, crunching the blue gravel under the wheels of her father's handmade yellow Crane. She painted and, encouraged by her father, photographed, using the first popularly available color process, the Lumière Autochrome Screen plate, developing images composed of minute, pointillistlike dots in a darkroom at Laurelton Hall.

All of this sounds pleasant, and even enviable, but not from Dorothy's point of view. Of the entire four years between leaving St. Timothy's and the time of her marriage, she stated laconically, "It was a fruitless time. I came out."

The loneliness gripping Louis made even his daughters' nuptials a contest of wills. He opposed each young woman's choice in turn. He had cited Dr. Lusk's hearing difficulties as a potential obstacle to May-May's happiness, had faulted Julia's fiancé, the handsome, roguish architect Gurdon Satterstall Parker, and also Comfort's, the Harvard-educated editor and historian Rodman Gilder, son of Richard Watson and Helena de Kay Gilder. Eventually he came around, however, and renovated his mansion's northeastern wing into showplace apartments, so that, if he could not have his daughters to himself at 27 East 72nd Street, he could at least keep them around the corner at 898 Madison Avenue.

Dorothy came out between Julia's and Comfort's weddings. The following morning, January 21, 1911, the *New York Times* announced, DEBUTANTE AND HER SISTERS RECEIVE GUESTS, CHIEFLY THIS WINTER'S BUDS. The dinner dance, held at home, was described as "small and informal"—the way Mama Lou would have wanted it. Seventy-five guests filled the L-shaped green marble ballroom, dancing to Van Baar's orchestra. At the stroke of midnight a buffet supper was served. Among the eligible bachelors were many social register names—Butler, Perry, Bodman, Stokes, Boulton, Hadden, McDonald, Hinkley, Atterbury, and Kissel—but no earth moved under Dorothy's feet that night.

The loss of his daughters was traumatic for Louis, and he fell seriously ill in 1910, the year of Julia's marriage, with a kidney ailment, related probably to his second bout with the bottle. As fate would have it, three young nurses came to his aid, their number equaling the daughters he was in the process of losing; and, once recovered, Louis asked each to stay on with him at Lenox Hill. Sarah Eileen Hanley, an adventurous redhead, accepted his offer. As Dorothy recalled, "She stayed with him until his death doing everything for his comfort and delighting him with her simple, vivacious and engaging ways."

Louis dedicated her copy of *The Art Work of Louis Tiffany*, "To Patsy Hanley who has been like a devoted daughter for many years." But, as she was only in her twenties, and attractive, Patsy was more to him than a daughter. Dorothy wrote that "he wished to marry her, but she refused thinking that his children would resent it." The family did not condone the arrangement, but they accepted it. As one descendant put it, "Patsy got him off booze, and on her."

She was from Sligo, in northwestern Ireland, the sister of a former mayor of that town, and though he tried Louis was not able to modify her brogue. Devout in her Catholicism, at least until she met Louis, and then again after his death, she revered him with almost religious intensity, called him "Padre." When asked on her deathbed what he had been like she replied passionately, "He was a god on earth." He had long since abandoned the ceremonies of the church, but she accepted him without reservation and he responded by welcoming her to the fold of his class and culture. Unlike Lou, Patsy was uneducated and nonintellectual, and this suited Louis fine. He once painted her as *Madonna Enthroned*.

Eccentric, equivocally moral, high-handed: Louis was perceived to be all these things during Dorothy's bud to blossom years. The story of his drunken collapse after Mama Lou's death was, in fact, one preserved by her future in-laws and repeated seven decades later. Another memory was turned to a rhetorical question. "What do you think of a man who brings his mistress into the same house as his daughters?" Such selectivity is also indicative of the morality of Dorothy's family-to-be.

Only shards of biographic material remain with which to reconstruct Dorothy's courtship and marriage, so if Robert Burlingham had precursors, none are known. The Burlingham brothers, Charles and Robert, were guests at Comfort's and Julia's house parties as early as 1910, and Robert may have been Dorothy's one, constant suitor. The brothers were a study in contrast. Charles was seven years older than Dorothy. A matter-of-fact, mustachioed lawyer, his passions ran to railroads and Gilbert and Sullivan. He could, when invited, reel off statistics on most every train running in America, or plunk out wry verses like, "He pulled a pistol from his holster/ Which he'd raised from a Colt." He had matriculated through Harvard College and Law School in just five years and, after a brief period at the august firm of Cravath, Henderson and de Bersdorff, had joined his father's admiralty law firm, where he remained.

But it was Robert who courted Dorothy. Not quite four years older than she, he had been bred a gentleman and spoke the King's English. Taller, slimmer and more emotional than his brother, he attracted Dorothy by his gentleness and blazing charm. His love of the outdoors was reflected in a well-conditioned physique, and the future surgeon was seemingly evident in his capable hands and penetrating eyes behind oval wire-rim glasses. He had graduated from Harvard (with T.S. Eliot) in the Class of 1910, and when Dorothy met him was enrolled in the Columbia University College of Physicians and Surgeons. Most important, his values were allied closely to "those spiritual things" so dear to Mama Lou.

The direct descendant of five *Mayflower* Pilgrims, including religious elder William Brewster, Robert had been taught that one's duties are more important than one's rights, that public service must balance personal ambition. His grandfather, Aaron Hale Burlingham, had been born in 1822 on a no-account forty-acre farm near Lake Erie, and as a boy had been virtually sold into slavery by his debt-ridden father. Upon reaching maturity Aaron had, in his own words, become "the first young man who had broken away from the narrow and unpromising limitations of that backwoods neighborhood with a determination to get a college education." He had ridden the Erie Canal at a cent a mile from Rochester to Utica and, seven years later, graduated a Baptist minister from the Hamilton Theological Seminary. As if to prove that duties came before rights, Aaron had given his son, Charles Culp Burlingham, the Christian name of his father, who had indentured him to help pay off his debts. C.C.B., as the son was known, had continued the ascent which Aaron had begun, transferring from St. Louis's Washington University to Harvard, converting in Boston to the Episcopal faith under the influence of evangelist Phillips Brooks, and marrying into the formidable Lawrence family. Louisa Weed Lawrence, Robert's mother, was the granddaughter of millionaire printing-press magnate Richard March Hoe, inventor of the "Lightning" or revolving cylinder press which had made possible the daily newspaper.

In 1876 C.C.B. had arrived in snobbish, class-conscious Cambridge a self-proclaimed "Baptist pup," and three years later had graduated, Phi Beta Kappa, "one of the most looked-up to and loved" men in his class. At Cambridge he had also undergone an ethical crisis to which Annie Hoe, the aunt of his future wife, was privy. "Annie," he had written, "there are some things which I cannot understand, one of them is, how to reconcile my duty to myself to my duty to my fellow men." This quandary resulted in a lifelong juggling act, a career at the bar balanced by another, "messing about in public and quasi-public business." Indeed, at no time was the duality between his profession and avocation more evident than during Robert and Dorothy's courtship. At the time the lawyer was succeeding in winning considerable relief from liability for his client, the White Star Line, following the *Titanic* disaster, while also tirelessly working on behalf of mayoral reform candidate John Purroy Mitchell. (By a curious coincidence, Louis had been booked aboard the ship, but had canceled his reservations after learning that the dining service was "that awful table d'hote.") If, in his legal capacity, C.C.B. denied fair reparation to those victimized by the White Star Line's failure to provide the *Titanic* with enough lifeboats, he compensated for it by helping the Fusion Party throw a torch into the Tammany wigwam. For C.C.B. God was the final arbiter in the reconciliation of his double-duty ethic—he got down on his knees and prayed every day of his life, toward its end noting that his favorite passage from the Psalms was "Watchman, tell us of the Night," and his favorite hymn St. Bernard's "The World is very evil; the Times are waxing late ..." Dorothy may have observed a personal symbolism in the fact that the Burlinghams' church, St. George's, faced the Infirmary for Women and Children across Stuyvesant Square.

Robert's reconciliation of duties was more conventional than his father's. He aimed to be a doctor, and Dorothy thought this the most attractive of ambitions. The handsome Ivy Leaguer seemed a respectable catch, though, predictably, not to the Kubla Khan.

Dorothy recalled that "there was a collision of personalities ... it was horrible." The nature of their dispute is unknown, but Louis threw Robert out of his house, and forbade Dorothy to see or otherwise communicate with him for a year. Robert sensibly decided to vanish from the scene, and spent the year in a surgical internship at Ancon Hospital in the disease-infested Canal Zone. The Panama Canal, beacon of American technology, was a year from completion.

Considering the respective values of Dorothy's family and that of her suitor, there was nothing surprising about the two men's clash. After President Theodore Roosevelt had begun his assault against "the malefactors of great wealth," the Tiffanys had cursed the Republicans for having tried to bury T.R. in the vice-presidency. But the Burlinghams had applauded the miscalculation which, upon William McKinley's assassination, had sent Roosevelt to the nation's highest office. While Louis was seething at his famous Oyster Bay neighbor for bringing black servants to his Sagamore Hill estate, and, therefore, to Oyster Bay, C.C.B. was furthering the cause of equal opportunity. In 1904 Roosevelt had ordered Charles F. McKim, then restoring the White House along its original neoclassical lines, to "smash into little pieces" the Tiffany opalescent screen. In the same period T.R. and C.C.B. were putting their heads together over the matter of civil service reform. And at a time when Louis was pleased to report "no jews" aboard the *Bremen* on a transatlantic crossing, C.C.B. was advancing the career of Justice Benjamin Nathan Cardozo. The autodidact and inheritor of wealth did not jibe with the self-made Ivy Leaguer in any way. Both men adored the theater, but C.C.B.'s heroine, the consummate British Shakespearean actress Ellen Terry, was to Louis's idol Sarah Bernhardt what tea is to champagne. There was more. On C.C.B.'s desk was a plaster replica of Terry's hand, while Louis's mail was set into the palm of Italy's Queen Elena. The Kubla Khan's ideal was that of benevolent tyrant, C.C.B.'s emerging reputation that of a modern-day Earl of Warwick of American jurisprudence, a "setter up and puller down of kings." The Kubla Khan was center stage; the kingmaker at home in the wings, nudging the qualified, independent jurist onto the bench. The Burlinghams' brownstone, on the "slummish" eastern slope of Murray Hill, and their Black Point, Connecticut, cottage, were also far cries from the Tiffany mansion and Laurelton Hall. Devoutly religious, absolute in their morality, abiding by the law to the letter, teetotaling and, above all, liberal Democratic, the Burlinghams represented a virtual insurrection against Louis's regime. This was no doubt Dorothy's intent.

These values aside, Dorothy's and Robert's other common denominator appears to have been their respective battles for autonomy in the face of domineering fathers. Their struggles were waged in disadvantaged times, however, as the climate of Edwardian America was not yet the frenzied, defiant one which followed the war. Dorothy's revolt had been largely subterranean. Though she had not gone to college or even graduated from boarding school, she had managed to keep Mama Lou's spirit alive, and she hoped to sustain it through her choice of spouse and their life together. Robert's revolt was as subtle. Despite the fact that his father and brother were both prominent lawyers and his parents were united in their suspicion of doctors, he had resolved to be a doctor himself. His class and family did limit his career options extremely, though they might also have condoned the clerical profession. Unfortunately for Robert, it seems from the existing correspondence that his life had been, and continued to be, an uphill battle to "equal the case" of his family. The lofty double-duty goals and narrow field of choice imposed upon him may have left him with a greater sense of inadequacy than accomplishment. At age six he had expressed anxiety to his father that a letter he had written him was not long enough. A few years later to his father he had begun, "I hope this will be a nice letter. I never can write nice letters." Virtually every facet of his life was similarly measured in terms of achievement and failure, right and wrong, moral and immoral.

The ethic which drove the family was inadvertently described by the Reverend Aaron Hale Burlingham in a letter to the editor penned while steaming to Europe in 1892 on the SS *Veendam*. Aaron had compared the time of an Atlantic crossing by a slow Dutch ship like the *Veendam* (ten days burning five hundred tons of coal), with the American Greyhound Craft class ship (which made the crossing in five or six days while burning two thousand tons of coal). In the Greyhound Craft, Aaron had noted approvingly, "every nerve of the machinery is kept strained to highest possible tension every inch of the passage," showing "American aggressiveness." The Burlinghams' double-duty ethic was, it seems, like that Greyhound Craft, the demands of personal ambition plus social conscience being far greater than either the one or the other.

Perhaps Robert empathized with Dorothy's plight because he was so completely under the influence of his own father. He may have seen himself as her savior, and seen in this a brilliant opportunity to rise to his family's expectations: he could help Dorothy Tiffany while helping himself.

The lovers' year-long enforced separation had begun. Dorothy spent this final year under her father's town and country roofs in what may have seemed like a round of endless and sometimes fantastical social obligations. On Shrove Tuesday, February 4, 1913, she found herself dressed as an attendant maid to the Queen of the Nile, played by actress Hedwig Reicher, for the occasion of the now famous Egyptian Fête at the Time of Cleopatra. Sealed papyrus scrolls had been hand-delivered to the Four Hundred, announcing in hieroglyphs and English that guests were to come either as Egyptians, nomad tribesmen, Greeks, Persians, Ethiopians, Romans, Syrians, East Indians, or Arabs. Costumes had been made to pass inspection for authenticity by a committee composed of "acknowledged authorities on costume art." Museums had been "ransacked for ideas," and "authoritative books on the life of Cleopatra's age . . . taken down from their shelves and . . . broadcast over town." Charles L. Tiffany II, Dr. Graham Lusk, Gurdon Parker, and Rodman Gilder were dressed as Roman lictors and, equipped with fasces, the symbol of Roman authority, were directing traffic. Robert de Forest, then president of the Metropolitan Museum of Art, and his wife, Emily Johnston, were the maharaja and maharani of Punjab; their grandchildren, the Stewarts, were lotus blossom scatterers; Katrina Tiffany was Osiris, Comfort Gilder Isis; Julia Parker and May-May Lusk were, like Dorothy, attendants to Cleopatra. And Louis was of course hosting the Tiffany Studios affair (at the 345 Madison Avenue address) in the guise of an Egyptian potentate.

The fête pivoted on a pantomine, designed by Egyptologist Joseph Lindon Smith, depicting a romantic encounter between Cleopatra and Marc Antony. By 10 P.M. considerably more than the Four Hundred were assembled and were sitting in the Rug Room, according to place of national origin, before the ramparts to Cleopatra's palace. The Havermeyer, Macy, Fisk, Roosevelt, and Rockefeller families were all represented. John D. Rockefeller was a Persian prince; his wife, Minerva; the educator Horace B. Mann, a Roman senator. Albert and Henry Herter were Egyptian noblemen; Theodore Steinway, a Roman soldier. The president of the National Academy of Design, John White Alexander, played a mummy later miraculously brought to life by a fakir; artists Luis Mura, Herbert Adams, and Childe Hassam had come, respectively, as a statue, an Assyrian rug merchant, and Rembrandt's Noble Slav. Tiffany & Company gemologist George F. Kunz was an Egyptian warrior, Loyal (son of "Damn the Torpedoes") Farragut came as a Hindu, and Cass Gilbert and Thomas Hastings, architects respectively of the Woolworth Building and the New York Public Library, as Persian merchants.

The pantomime began with "four colossal Ethiopians" bearing Cleopatra's palanquin to center stage, where a beaded, baubled, bangled, and mortally embarrassed Dorothy was obliged to refresh the great queen with an enormous peacock feather fan. After "an Egyptian [song] dating back to the time of the pharaohs" and dances copied from frescoes in Egyptian tombs, Marc Antony (the actor Pedro de Cordoba) presented Cleopatra with a slave who executed a sensual faunlike dance. Next, dancer Ruth St. Denis was unrolled from a rug to dance half-nude in a way that young and impressionable Dorothy Stewart had never seen before, "so free and all over the place."

After making their obeisance to Cleopatra the guests dined on an eight-course dinner catered by Delmonico's. Enough cases of St. Marceau Brut 1906 were imbibed to fuel the riproaring after-dinner turkey trot—a dance considered so risqué that, on at least one occasion, it provided grounds for dismissal from college.

As themes of sexuality and slavery gave way to whirling, inebriated revelry, it probably did not occur to Dorothy, or anyone else, that behind the historical pageantry and celebration of cultural opposites—West and East, Antony and Cleopatra—lay a highly personal allusion to Louis's newfound happiness with Patsy. Dorothy did know that her mother would not have enjoyed the entertainment, and to her dying day Dorothy shuddered to recall it, once suggesting that the commemorative album of photographs be burned.

Following the fête, Dorothy was again spirited by her papa from the world of everyday—to Granada, Spain, and the Moorish palace of the Alhambra. Careening from fantasy to fantasy, she found herself on May 15, 1914, in a white, green, and gold toga serving roast suckling pig, duckling, frog legs, turtle, and peacock on silver salvers to one hundred and fifty "men of genius" who had come to Laurelton Hall "to inspect the spring flowers."

In the four-year hiatus between St. Timothy's and marriage, the one event which Dorothy did not, from the distance of over half a century, deem fruitless was the inception of a small intellectual salon which she cofounded in 1913 with her best friend, Dell Carrère. The daughter of architect John Merven Carrère, Dell shared Dorothy's impatience with idle distractions, her seriousness of purpose, and her enthusiasm for philosophies and pragmatic programs. Their membership included Katrina Tiffany's father Theodore M. Ely, a vice-president of the Pennsylvania Railroad, and Charles Gould, a lawyer, author, and friend of Papa Louis's. Presumably they met at the Tiffany mansion and the Carrère residence at 471 Park Avenue, where the young, female cofounders led their older, male colleagues in this collective broadening, self-improving enterprise. Though the salon was quickly ended by marriage, war, and Dell's death in childbirth, in this brief partnership lay the seed of Dorothy's future.

Louis had promised that, after the passage of a year, if Dorothy and Robert still found themselves in love, they could see one another again. And, when Robert returned from Central America, the couple discovered to their delight that their feelings for one another had not changed. She remained impressed with his fineness of spirit, noble ambitions, and "lovely smile," and he was enthralled with her. But Louis had said nothing of marriage and, when Robert asked for her hand, Louis refused to give them his blessing. At the onset of summer, therefore, in desperation, Dorothy visited the Lusks' Adirondack retreat, Camp Comfort. And, at the sprawling eight-building, fourteen-acre camp overlooking Upper St. Regis Lake, she laid the situation before her half-sister. May-May evidently understood the root of her father's opposition and was prepared to make a sacrifice in Dorothy's behalf, because it was announced shortly thereafter that the Lusks were selling their Manhattan town house to take (we may assume reluctantly) the third floor of the Lenox Hill mansion. And Dorothy was to marry Dr. Robert Burlingham.

Dorothy's obstacle-laden courtship had, by this time, won her a pair of young female admirers. Twelve-year-old Louise Lusk, her niece, thought Dorothy "a delight," while to Clarinda (Chloe) Garrison, a teenage neighbor of the Burlinghams at Black Point, Dorothy was "a heroine," and the way she and Robert had "stayed true" was simply "too romantic!"

The papers on September 14, 1914, were full of the short advances and grudging retreats along the Western Front. The Tiffanys' yellow Crane, its sideboards bright with flowers, glided into the parking lot of St. John's Episcopal Church at Cold Spring Harbor, crunching to a halt before the beautiful wooden chapel. A gaggle of geese started up from the tree-skirted lake, turned in a great, wheeling arc, and landed on the other side. The leaves were beginning to turn to the autumnal colors so loved by the bride's father. With an orchid boutonniere fastened to the lapel of his swallow-tailed coat, the portly, graying Louis led Dorothy through the nave toward a chancel lit in the kaleidoscopic colors of his stained-glass windows.

The service was small and simple at Dorothy's request. No previous announcement had been made in the papers and the fifty guests did not fill the pews of the small chapel. Dorothy wore her mother's wedding dress, the gown of soft cream satin draped over her shoulders with rare lace, her veil of the same lace held in place by a coronet of orange blossoms. She stood beneath the arching stucco ceiling, her face quiet and lovely, a bouquet of orange blossoms and roses in her small hands. With Charles Burlingham standing beside his flushed and beaming brother, Louise Lusk, the flower girl and Dorothy's one attendant, adjusted the court train. Then the Reverend W. E. McCord did his job.

VII

Mother Love

M r. and Mrs. Robert Burlingham did not settle in the Tiffany mansion at 27 East 72nd Street, as had the Lusks, nor did they join the Gilders and Parkers around the corner at 898 Madison Avenue. Had they desired, room would have been found for them somewhere in the cavernous compound. But the passage from maidenhood to wifehood had swept away the last vestiges of Dorothy's tagalong identity. Instead of following her sister's dutiful example, Dorothy and Robert moved into the Osborne Apartments on the northwest corner of 57th Street and Seventh Avenue, within short walking distance of Roosevelt Hospital, where Robert had begun his surgical internship. Not intending to spend her weekends at Laurelton Hall, either, Dorothy gave her mare to Louise Lusk.

The Osborne was a large, elegant brownstone with an elaborately mosaicked foyer, though Dorothy's and Robert's apartment was modest; their bedroom, noted Chloe Garrison, still following their romance with an eagle eye, was scarcely larger than the double bed it contained. Innocently inquiring "who crawls over whom," she elicited furious blushes, and within two months of the wedding, Dorothy was pregnant.

Content, for the time being, with the vicarious satisfactions of Robert's medical explorations, Dorothy, now twenty-three and standing on the brink of motherhood, took that role very seriously indeed. An early photograph of the couple shows them standing before the white clapboards and flowering trellises of the Burlinghams' oceanfront cottage.

The picture had probably been snapped in the summer of their engagement, since Dorothy appears to be slipping a ring on her finger to
Robert's beaming approval. Other photographs confirm this visit to have
been a joyous one. Captured, demurely clutching the hem of her ankle-
length skirt, mimicking the crouched position Robert had assumed to
take her picture, Dorothy's smile was radiant, her eyes brilliantly dark.
She grins in a third picture while stepping on Charles Burlingham's foot.
In playful togs—Oxford shoes, a long skirt buttoned up the front, a
flappy cardigan, button-down collar, a tie tucked in her shirt, her waist-
length hair wrapped with a braid—she was having fun at last. However
these snapshots are not the fond keepsakes of lineal descendants secure in
values unruffled by dramatic change. A paragraph in the July 11, 1914,
New York Times revealed that Robert had become ill

> about a month ago when he went to stay with his parents at Black Point,
> their country place at Crescent Beach, Connecticut. Miss Tiffany, whose
> engagement to the doctor was known to her immediate relatives and
> intimate friends, went to the Burlingham home about a week ago, and
> is still there. Dr. Burlingham is now recovering.

Dorothy would say later that Robert had suffered a nervous breakdown before their marriage, but she had not known of it then, although,
she said, she would have married him regardless. It is possible that this
illness, significant enough to have been mentioned in the papers, was that
breakdown, misrepresented to Dorothy, perhaps, when she arrived in
the third week. It could not, however, have escaped her that Robert's
"machinery was strained to highest possible tension," since, according
to Chloe Garrison, he was "uptight" and "twitchy," "even to the casual
eye."

Conceivably, Dorothy was less the victim of circumstance, and more
the orchestrator of her fate, than one might suppose. Perhaps she married
Robert in a state of unconscious precognition of the fact that he was not
to be her future, but instead the springboard to it. She did say that she
would have married him regardless, though probably meaning that she
had made up her mind not to be denied under any condition. At any rate,
Dorothy knew only approximately ten months of untroubled marital life
before jumping from the frying pan into the fire.

Chloe Garrison recalls Dorothy and Robert in July of the following year paying a quick visit to Black Point, a secluded beauty spot on the Connecticut coast midway between Old Saybrook and New London. The summer community of Old Black Point was private and exclusive; the image of blazing sun and salty surf, ice tea, wicker furniture and shadowed porches, gnarled trees, manicured hedges, croquet and weathered wooden beach huts, each with the name of a prominent family over the door. In 1907, when the elder Burlinghams had bought their cottage, they had done so appreciative of the fact that the Point was invariably cooler than the mainland. Dorothy and Robert were no doubt glad to escape the city's sweltering heat; by July she was heavy with child and had spent most of the summer in their tiny apartment while Robert had bent to his labors at Roosevelt Hospital. Why then did they arrive at Black Point entirely without luggage, clothing, or provisions of any kind? Their unpreparedness made an impression; almost seventy years later Chloe Garrison Binger recalls loaning Dorothy some of her smocks. The suggestion, certainly, is that their marriage had hit a turbulent pocket.

Back in the city Robert Burlingham, Jr., kept Dorothy waiting three weeks past the expected date before delivering himself into the world on August 29. A beautiful, bright-eyed, chubby-cheeked infant, Bob seemed well worth the wait. Mother and child were soon photographed by W. S. Ritch, Dorothy wearing a tea gown of Oriental jacquard silk, her hair parted in the middle, rolled along the sides and pinned in back. The white-robed, dark-haired baby in her arms was alert and happy, but did not remain so for long. At six months he developed eczema so severe that Dorothy had to coat his entire body with a thick tar salve to keep him from scratching himself. This, it seems, was symptomatic of a wider allergic condition: suddenly, he could not stomach breast milk or cow's milk, but only goat's milk. Then he stopped eating entirely and had to be force-fed, growing woefully thin.

Dorothy could not, even then, have imagined the joy or heartbreak that this child would cause her, or that he would shape her destiny as decisively as she would shape his. Bob was so sensitive that she would learn to gauge changes in her own mood by his behavior. His reaction to her mood shifts actually preceded her awareness of any change; he was a living dowsing rod for her emotional state and her marriage. Later she would write that Bob was from infancy "very loving, very affectionate, & could not stand separation from those he loved." But at the time, as seriously as she took her maternal role, she had no conception of how deeply she and Robert were affecting their son.

Dorothy's life began to fall apart in earnest in September 1916. The disintegration may have begun earlier; the sequence of events is not clear today. The pieces of the puzzle are few, the gaps as numerous as they are misleading, and the relationships complex. But we do know that Dorothy's son, father-in-law, and husband all became sick within a short time of one another, three generations at a stroke.

At summer's end 1916, anxious to be resettled in New York, Dorothy and Robert left Bob in Black Point with his grandparents. It was then that the infant had his first severe asthmatic reaction, growing blue in the face, coughing and gasping for air. When Dorothy rushed back to him he clung desperately to her. Dorothy and Robert were naturally upset, but the family's fine Park Avenue physician advised that Bob merely needed time to adjust to his parents' habits and schedules, and not to be alarmed.

In the same year C.C.B suffered a nervous collapse, his second. The first had come less than a month after he had argued the first case heard in the newly formed U.S. Circuit Court of Appeals, on October 27, 1891. The dizzy spells, unpredictable faints, and upset stomachs which he experienced had been caused, he believed, more by "under care . . . than over work." Laid up for ten months he had learned "never to eat when tired and to rest either before or after dinner." His second collapse lasted approximately six months and was precipitated by the war, which transformed "the close preserve" of the admiralty bar into a booming international business. The pressures of the *Titanic* case had supposedly come close to causing a collapse, and two years later, in spite of past experience, "I worked so hard, or so unwisely, that I worked myself out." Again he fell prone to unpredictable faints and an upset stomach.

C.C.B. and his wife, Louie, naturally assumed that Robert's breakdown was also a case of overwork and undercare. Dorothy herself later attributed it to the pressures of medical school. C.C.B's and Robert's breakdowns were not similar, however; it was C.C.B.'s last attack, but Robert's were to reoccur chronically for the rest of his life. His may also have been triggered by stress, but the symptoms—a rising euphoria followed by a crashing depression—were different. Unlike C.C.B., who in moderating his habits learned to control his nerves, Robert's manic-depressive psychosis was, at that time, uncontrollable.

The chronology of their respective illnesses is unknown, and one can only guess who fell ill first. Since Dorothy blamed the pressures of medical school on Robert's breakdown, it must have occurred before his internship ended in the spring of 1916, and this would place it ahead of Bob's first asthma attack. Given Bob's ultrasensitivity and the severity of his attack, it would seem likely that he was reacting to the emotional state induced in his mother by his father's breakdown. Perhaps that is why he was left in Black Point while they returned, alone, to New York.

There is some evidence to suggest that Robert's breakdown may in turn have been set off his father's collapse, or by the pressures which precipitated it. It was surely not by happenstance that at the very moment that Robert's grandfather had been steaming for Europe on the *Veendam,* impatiently praising the faster Greyhound Craft, his father had lain ill, victim of his first nervous breakdown. The drive to "keep strained to highest possible tension every nerve of the machinery every inch of the passage" was deeply ingrained in the family, and the pressures building in C.C.B. no doubt increased the pressures within Robert, and indirectly on the infant Bob in turn.

Dorothy later pointed to Robert's emotional ties to his father, variously described as being "like a cricket," and "a pea in a griddle." At Harvard C.C.B. had grown a mustache to cover a curled upper lip, and likewise disguised a deeply emotional, even fanatic, nature with gaiety and wit. Even when discouraged or anguished, he let show only his guiding light. During the Korean War, he sent one grandson to fight in the greatest of apparent humors but, when the young man returned a few minutes later to retrieve his umbrella, he found C.C.B., then in his nineties, collapsed against the wall, sobbing his heart out. Robert was also very emotional, but as gentle as his father was domineering, and, as a result, highly susceptible to his influence. The speculation is, therefore, that C.C.B. set off Robert, and Robert, through his effect on Dorothy, set off Bob. Like a string of firecrackers, off they went, bang, bang, bang!

If Dorothy had not yet realized the extent of Robert's dependence upon his parents, it would dawn on her soon enough, and with finality. Far from achieving real independence, in marrying Robert she had merely shifted spheres of influence, traded one paternal authority for another.

C.C.B.'s courage, mental agility, and irrepressible drive did create an intimidating impression, and Robert's mother was a power in her own right (Dorothy was told she was the driving force behind C.C.B.). He himself insisted on many occasions, "I was just a Baptist pup until I met Louie Lawrence." To her son Charles, as surely to Robert, she was "a great and noble lady." Her sartorial style was once descrribed as "a pyramid of cloth from the top of her head to her toes." She swathed herself in swirling layers of black and white cloth, often wearing a black flowerpot hat and shawl, white silk blouse, long black skirt and black flapping coat. After losing her sight in one eye she wore a patch and became known at Black Point as "the Pirate." She was known to walk into a room rapidly and leave, with a tap-tapping of her cane, as abruptly as she had entered. The cane was evidence of a mysterious malady, possibly Milroy's disease, a form of lymphedema, which she shrouded by skirts and never mentioned. Family and friends appreciated that behind her idiosyncratic façade was a high-minded spirit. Moral and intellectual, her bedside bible was *War and Peace.*

Louie had been raised in Murray Hill and Irvington-on-Hudson, the third of six children born to Adeline Elizabeth Hoe and investment banker De Witt Clinton Lawrence. She had been educated in New York's finest private girls' school of that time, Miss Anna C. Brackett's, where she had befriended May Minturn (Mrs. Henry Dwight Sedgewick), her sister Edith (Mrs. Isaac Newton Phelps Stokes), and their cousin Carlotta Russell-Lowell, all nieces of Colonel Robert Gould Shaw. Louie and C.C.B. had subsequently made friends of Colonel Shaw's mother and sisters and, after C.C.B.'s first collapse, it was the Shaws, Minturns, and Russell-Lowells who had rescued them financially.

At May Minturn's suggestion, Louie had taken C.C.B. to Philadelphia for a consultation with an associate of the renowned neurologist Silas Weir Mitchell, who "wasn't greatly interested" in the case but who nevertheless prescribed the "rest cure" for which Mitchell was famous. Louie, however, had already decided that the best thing for her husband would be to get him as far from doctors as possible, a decision for which C.C.B. always praised her.

C.C.B.'s law firm had not then been "distinguished for its generosity," and his income had virtually ceased the day he stopped working. Just six months after the death of Mrs. Lawrence, in 1882, Louie's father had disgraced the family by "walking off with the French widow down the block," and since then C.C.B. had been supporting Louie's younger sisters, Grace and Edith, in addition to his own three children. De Witt had evidently also run off with the family money, throwing C.C.B. and Louie entirely on their own resources. One day Colonel Shaw's sister, Mrs. Robert B. Minturn, wife of the shipping magnate, had handed Louie a check for $1,600 (one year's rent) and her son, Bob, gave them another $1,000. This had enabled Louie to leave the children with C.C.B.'s elder brother, Albert Starr, and spirit her husband first to Old Point Comfort, Virginia, then to Morristown, New Jersey, next to Keene Valley in the Adirondacks, and finally to Cornish, New Hampshire—where C.C.B. had finally recovered.

What had worked in 1891–92 Louie naturally assumed would work again in 1916. Assuming once again the role of self-appointed healer, she put her husband on another rigorous travel regimen. The album of photographs and postcards from this trip, to Bermuda, indicates that they visited Saltus Bay, Chiappa's Bay, His Majesty's Dockyard, and the Eagle's Nest Hotel; also the Fairyland Waters, Harrington Sound, Somerset Island, and St. David's Island, and scores of old houses, churches, and gardens in between. And it is possible that Robert went on this same recuperative trip. Photographs show only his parents and sister, Nancy, but who took them? Not Charles, who was holding down the fort at his father's law firm. It is possible that Dorothy, in a state of shock, numbly let her mother-in-law take command of Robert's recovery, also.

Recover, of course, he eventually did, and after graduating from Roosevelt Hospital Robert was invited by the College of Physicians and Surgeons to teach medicine, and to become an assistant in clinical pathology. If these responsibilities, in addition to entering into his own private surgical practice, were not in and of themselves enough to "strain his machinery," he also agreed to serve as an assistant physician at the Volunteer Hospital.

Once again, it seemed, C.C.B., Robert, and Bob were all perfectly fine, and Dorothy did not object when Louie suggested that Robert move his family to Murray Hill. One would not want to repeat Dorothy's experience, and Louie's idea was to post a watch on Robert and Bob. They moved to 129 East 38th Street, directly across the street from the Burlinghams' brownstone at No. 140, where Louie literally had a window on their world. For Dorothy, this proved to be the mistake of her marriage.

The memory would always burn in Dorothy of being invited to tea one afternoon at No. 140 and, upon arriving, encountering a small group

Comfort Tiffany in 1827

The family store, Danielson, Connecticut

Charles and Harriet,
in the early 1850s

Annie and Louis Tiffany,
at about the same period

Louis at Eagleswood
Military Academy

Louis as a young painter,
about 1867

Louis and May with their children *(from left to right)*
Hilda, Charles, and May-May, in the early 1880s

Louise Wakeman Knox

Louis dressed as a fisherman *(top right)* and painting Lou *(below)* on Old Pennsylvania Canal trip, at the time of their 1886 engagement

Louis in 1887

Julia de Forest and Louise Tiffany

Louis and Lou, 1898

Mama Lou and
Dorothy

"Me-Too," with twins
Julia and Comfort

Harriet and Charles Tiffany
on their Golden Anniversary,
November 30, 1891

Louis Comfort Tiffany,
standing beside one
of his stained-glass
windows

The Charles Lewis Tiffany mansion at 27 East 72nd Street

Dorothy with her father

Mama Lou, 1899

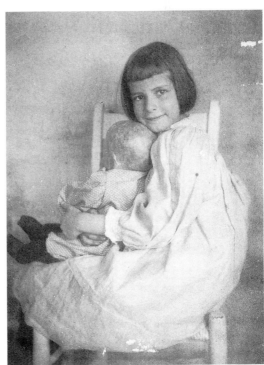

Dorothy at age eight

At Cold Spring Harbor

The Briars

Dorothy, Comfort, and Julia

As captain of The Spiders, 1909

(Left) Dorothy at Black Point, 1914; *(right)* with Robert Burlingham during their courtship

"The Kubla Khan"

At Peacock Feast, May 15, 1914

Laurelton Hall

Dorothy and Bob, 1915

Robert Burlingham with
Mabbie and Bob, 1919

of paintings upon which the daughter of Louis Comfort Tiffany was expected to discourse, if not insightfully, then at least knowledgeably. Rather than the expected cozy tête-à-tête over tea and crumpets, Dorothy felt herself coolly put to the test, and flunked, by her mother-in-law. For if Dorothy did not know her stuff, Louie certainly did.

The Lawrences, as one in-law put it, "were rich & married rich & have lots of famous relatives; a formidable family in every way." They trace their American heritage back to a Captain Samuel Lawrence of the Revolutionary Army and claim connection through the captain's daughter-in-law, Hannah Bouton, to French royalty. Louie's father and uncle, De Witt and Cyrus, had each married a daughter of printing press manufacturer Colonel Richard March Hoe, and the Hoes—daughters by the Colonel's second wife—had in turn twice married Harpers, of the Harper Brothers publishing empire, one of the largest in the world. In girlhood Louie had been taken by her grandparents on their annual pilgrimage to London, Paris, and Florence and had frequently visited Brightside, the colonel's magnificent seventy-eight-acre estate north of Manhattan at Hunt's Point. On occasion, Louie had also accompanied the colonel downtown—a trip of three miles across Hunt's Point by trotter, and down the East River by ferry—to the Hoe works, which sprawled two square blocks fronting Grand, Broome, Columbia, and Sheriff streets.

With their fortunes, the colonel and his brother Robert, a partner in the Hoe firm, had each assembled renowned art collections. Louie's grandfather had been a bibliophile, his collection of the printing and allied arts crowned by a Guttenberg Bible; her great-uncle had collected everything from Rembrandts to Kang Hsi vases. Uncle Cyrus had carried on the tradition, assembling distinguished collections of paintings, including Monet, Corot, Daumier, and Cassatt, and fine Chinese porcelain and Shaker furniture. Aunt Emily Hoe Lawrence had been painted by Mary Cassatt. Other of Louie's aunts were musical. Annie Hoe Platt and Mary Hoe Harper had been trained as pianists by Clara Schumann; Fanny Hoe Harper had a beautiful soprano voice. Annie Hoe Platt had been a regular at the Choral Society which had met in the marble town house of John Taylor Johnston; Annie had also attended the highbrow receptions given by artist Helena de Kay Gilder and, escorted by C.C.B., had mingled with Walt Whitman, Mark Twain, William Dean Howells, Stanford White, and others. Through Joe Evans, the hunchback, midget painter, and popular president of the Art Students League, Louie had come to know many of the great artists of the day herself.

So perhaps there was an element of competitiveness in the test which she sprang on Dorothy; perhaps, between the lines, an implicit slight to the eccentricity of Dorothy's patronymic; perhaps the first intimation that her failures as a wife and mother had precipitated the problems of her husband and son. Something stung Dorothy enough to recall the afternoon more than half a century later. Perhaps her marriage was in trouble; surely there must have been more to Robert's collapse than the pressures of medical school. With her problematic filial relationship, it would not be surprising if Dorothy were having a tough time fitting the role of Robert's wife. In any case, under the circumstances, Dorothy was not about to explain to her mother-in-law the complex, private reasons for her lack of interest in contemporary art. Instead she patiently viewed the Burlinghams' portrait of Annie Hoe Platt by Abbott Henderson Thayer, Joe Evans's landscapes—both the rainy-day and sunny-day ones—and whatever else Louie had hung for her benefit, and extemporized as best she could.

Louie does seem to have been an overinvolved mother and an interfering mother-in-law, and no doubt with the best intentions and highest principles. Of her children, Charles got along best in the role of dutiful eldest son, being constitutionally fit for his father's lengthy shadow and downtown office. Whenever C.C.B. became overexcited, Charles simply switched off. In the midst of crisis, he was fond of saying, "A hundred years from now it won't make any difference." His birth in June of 1884 was later fondly associated in C.C.B.'s mind with a Fourth of July display of rockets which had burst through the mist outside their windows a month later. Anne Hoe Burlingham, the middle sibling, had been born in 1886 and named for Louie's favorite aunt, who had died the following year in childbirth. At an early date Louie had removed her high-strung daughter, whom they called Nancy, from Brearley, educating her at home, and since then she had scarcely been allowed on a date, much less held a man's hand; at thirty she was the painfully shy Jane Austen spinster who stays home to play Bach for father. Louie likewise sought to protect Robert, thinking him too fragile to have become a doctor, or even to have married; and this attitude certainly could not have encouraged his independence. His birth was forever associated in her mind with the Blizzard of '88, which had struck a week afterward.

Louie thought she knew what was best for her son and grandson, and with them living across the street she was in a position to air her views. It was not long, therefore, before she and Dorothy had clashed, and, predictably, over the issue of nannies. Dorothy knew only what her mother had practiced on her: assigning the young child to the supervision of a good nanny or nursemaid until time came for the mother to address the finer task of character formation and good breeding. The mother's first crucial duty, in both Dorothy's and Louie's view, was in selecting the right person for the job. Given Dorothy's bitter memory of psychological mistreatment at the hands of her own nanny, she must have been especially sensitive to the issue.

In another day and time, Dorothy might have related Bob's asthma attack to separation anxiety. But, accepting her doctor's counsel, instead of giving him the security he desperately needed, she continued to leave him with surrogates. She would regret this "wrong handling" of him for the rest of her life. Bob's asthmatic reactions occurred each and every time she left him, the infant crying, coughing, clinging, gasping for breath. Dorothy always made a point of calling home and was invariably assured that Bob had quieted down. She had reason to believe that she was doing the right thing.

Here the nanny story diverges into opposite points of view. According to C.C.B., he returned from work one evening to hear Bob screaming frantically and, upon investigating, discovered that his nanny had locked him in a closet. How long this had been going on is uncertain, but perhaps after each painful parting, this was how the nanny had silenced him, with a purgatorial threat, on one hand, and a baffle for his cries, on the other. On this occasion, however, from across the street and through the doors, windows, and walls of the apartment, C.C.B. had heard Bob shrieking; and he, or Louie, fired the nanny on the spot. Dorothy, for her part, recounting it in later life, made no mention of the closet incident; she said only that she never forgave Louie for firing the only nanny she really trusted. C.C.B. maintained that Dorothy subsequently gave the nanny a letter of reference, and this he found hard to forgive.

Barring the possibility that Dorothy and C.C.B. were speaking about two different nannies, each fired by Louie, and, for the sake of argument, assuming the sequence of events most damning to Dorothy's character, perhaps the wrong handling which she regretted to her dying day did include putting her trust in a sadistic nanny. The damning tag is her letter of reference; but this can be interpreted in a number of ways. The least plausible is that Dorothy endorsed the nanny's sadistic treatment of Bob, that she knew of it all along, and later invented the concerned telephone calls and the nanny's reassurances; a more plausible version is that the telephone calls were as real as her ignorance of what was going on, and that Dorothy refused to believe her mother-in-law's account, suspecting her of fabricating the incident in order to undermine her authority. Dorothy may then have recommended this nanny for future employment even after being told that she had locked Bob in a closet. This would have been the act of a willful and confused person, and Dorothy was both. Like her father, she fiercely resented interference in her life and could have written the reference as an act of defiance. Whatever happened on that day, relations between 129 and 140 East 38th Street were severely strained.

Today it appears that Bob's ailments were physically and emotionally rooted, his asthma linked to anxieties and a delicate constitution (a situation that sister Mary Tiffany—"Mabbie"—Burlingham's birth on May 1 could not have alleviated. Dorothy later conceded that her confinement and separation from Bob made "everything so much worse" for him). But in 1917 no one knew what his problem was. The day's primitive psychological consciousness was reflected in the then preeminent authority on child care, behaviorist John Broadus Watson, who advocated minimal affectionate display toward one's children. Both Dorothy and Louie had strong and apparently contradictory views on the subject of raising children, though, unfortunately, these are not known. The only clue to their respective beliefs is to be found in Louie's scrapbook, into which she carefully pasted clippings from newspaper health columns. Her main source appears to have been Dr. J. Jastrow, a professor of psychology at the University of Wisconsin. In one *Saturday Evening Post* article entitled "Mother Love," Jastrow claimed that both Dr. Watson and Sigmund Freud questioned the subject's value. Though Watson and Freud were agreed on little else, he noted, "Freud makes central in his system the family romance in which the too strong attachment of daughter to father or son to mother gives rise to complexes and neurotic troubles, and in which sex relations play the leading part," while "Watson pronounces all mother love as damaging and looks forward to the day when children will be brought up (unparented) more or less officially and objectively." Louie evidently approved of Jastrow's caricatures of Watson and Freud as well as his conclusion that both their views were without warrant. Of Dorothy's approach, all that remains is a neatly systematized page on which she conscientiously tracked her children's vital statistics, weights from week to week, diet, innoculations, treatments, and so forth. A possible Watsonian leaning may, however, have been implied by her comment on Bob's "loving" and "affectionate" nature, and by Louie's underlinings in the following paragraph of Jastrow's article:

Watson's conclusion seems to me more baseless still [than Freud's]. His warning that mothers should not fondle their children because some mothers overdo it, fails to recognize the many cases of neglect of children or the records of societies for the prevention of cruelty to children. Apparently he would found a society for the prevention of tenderness to children . . .

Sadly, Watson's parenting techniques may have been part of Dorothy's "wrong handling."

Against these odds, Dorothy and Robert struggled to make their marriage work. With the United States's entry into the war, twenty-nine-year-old Robert volunteered his services on two military boards. He worked as a contract surgeon on the army's Tuberculosis Examining Board and as a member of the Medical Advisory Board for the Selective Service Act, and soon received his commission as a first lieutenant in the Army Medical Reserve Corps. In June of 1918 he was stationed in the Cardio-Vascular Department of the army's Medical Research Laboratory, Hazelhurst Field, Mineola, Long Island.

Over the winter of 1917–18 Dorothy had built a stucco and shingle cottage on a tree-lined ridge west of Laurelton Hall. Louis had given each of his children land near Cold Spring Harbor and, with Black Point an increasingly less attractive option, Dorothy had evidently felt the need for a private hideaway. A lane just wide enough for her Model T Ford wound through the trees to the cottage. Designed by Gurdon Parker, it had banks of windows running its length, a fireplace at each end, and a Canadian snow roof. With Robert nearby but restricted to base, the summer of 1918 might have been a brief respite for Dorothy. Instead, she recalled, "This was the beginning of the end." Bob "minded so" the separation from his father, and Robert suffered another nervous break-down.

Though triggered by stressful conditions, the manic-depressive syndrome is today considered to be the product of a chemical-hormonal imbalance which can be transmitted genetically from generation to generation. Indeed, Robert's disease may have originated with the Lawrences. Louie's older sister, Mellie, had some undefined ailment. More specific is a letter dated 1887 from Richard Hoe Lawrence, Louie's brother, reporting that their father, De Witt (the one who had just five years before abandoned his family for the French widow), was in Paris seeking the attentions of Dr. Jean-Martin Charcot, the greatest neuropathologist of the day. He wrote, "I still think father's condition discouraging, & his mind is certainly unbalanced . . . I gave [Charcot] a sketch of father's life & told him I feared it was drink . . . He, Dr. C., says that stimulants have not caused only hastened this trouble, that he suffers from melancholia & that it is likely that this has been coming on for some time . . . Of course I did not get [home] until very late . . . Father had been acting extravagantly of course."

Thirty years later the disease was still widely misunderstood, and still essentially untreatable. Louie would never even admit that Robert was ill; after a dozen such breakdowns she still insisted that he became "overtired." Indeed, when he emerged from a depression, it was difficult to believe he had ever been sick. The clouds rolled away and his character shone forth once again. But the storms were ferocious, starting with a leap from childlike exuberance to full-blown mania in which it was difficult to predict his behavior. When manic he tended to verbal abuse, rashly charging into situations, confronting people unnecessarily. Then he plunged into an abysmal depression steeped in self-recrimination, blaming himself for his lack of control, and especially for dishonoring his family. Tragically, he seemed to believe that these episodes should have been controllable by the force of his will. Evidence suggests a crisis of faith. In 1925 Robert would write C.C.B., "You wrote a very noble letter to us today, and if I prayed as much as you, who knows, perhaps all this burden and sorrow might not have fallen on your shoulders."

Then the war was over and the armistice signed by the new, socialist-led republic. Fully recovered, Robert received an honorable discharge on February 10, 1919, with the comment, "A capable officer." He joined the staff of the Reconstruction Hospital in New York and resumed the practice of medicine. On March 27, 1919, Katrina Ely (Tinky) Burlingham was born, named for the still childless Katrina Tiffany, whom Dorothy evidently viewed with a mixture of admiration and compassion, naming her and Charles in an early will legal guardians of her children. Things did not improve, however, and on August 20, 1920, Louis remarked in a letter to May-May, "Dorothy . . . is miserable, having a hard time." She was pregnant again, and knew the marriage was impossible. Before the birth of Michael (Mikey) Burlingham on March 16, 1921, Dorothy had left Robert. "Somehow," she wrote, "I could not manage caring for him and doing what I should do for the children."

Dorothy's decision to leave Robert was, however, surely prompted by concern for the children secondarily. People who leave their spouses are motivated by pain, anger, fear, or disillusionment. They have fallen in or out of love, or quit for other visceral reasons. For Dorothy, Robert's lapses of control seem to have invoked the specter of Papa Louis and the tempestuous emotions to which she had been subjected as a child. Robert the doctor had become Robert the patient, husband had merged into father, savior into tyrant—this last the very image that Dorothy had meant to leave behind. Confronted with what must have seemed like another tragic twist of fate, Dorothy was probably beset by old childhood fears. And so one cannot simply rationalize her decision as being in Bob's interest, since, as she later recalled, "the separation made his childhood very difficult for he loved his father as well as myself, so when his father and I lived apart he had all kinds of problems which I could not seem to help him with."

Another woman might have felt her first responsibility to her husband. Instead, confronted once again with the unpredictability, the unreliability of the male sex, Dorothy seems to have done what Mama Lou had not—that is, become for her children the mother denied her, the woman who rated her responsibility to herself above her responsibility to her husband. In the fairy-tale world of the unconscious mind Dorothy may have been packing Mama Lou's bags, saving her from the Kubla Khan and his Xanadu and, in so doing, taking Dorothy away from the suffering which lay in store for her—together entering a real Paradiso.

The reality was not so satisfying. Dorothy was abandoning a man in desperate need of her support, while, for herself and the children, all that loomed ahead was uncertainty. "Somehow" was the operative word: "somehow I could not manage caring for him and doing what I should do for the children." Later she may have viewed her choice with some dispassion, but at the time she was compelled to act as she did. Ultimately her decision to leave Robert was neither callous, heroic, nor Machiavellian. It was a conditioned response; Dorothy was not about to be shocked again.

Ironically, her flight was facilitated by C.C.B.'s having taken over Robert's physical and emotional care, shuttling him from doctor to relatives, city to country; Dorothy knew that he was not uncared for. Her money was essential, also. Hilda had died in 1908 leaving an estate of $61,675; presuming that all of Louis's daughters were similarily endowed, thirteen years later Dorothy may have had somewhat more. In 1918 Louis had settled on an arrangement for the distribution of interest from his securities to his children on a regular basis. Dorothy was receiving $5,000 a year with rights to borrow up to $10,000 more; at the time, these moneys could sustain a comfortable independence. The Burlinghams, however, could never understand how a woman could have left her husband under such conditions, and it was for this that they later condemned her.

Having ripped free of her moorings, Dorothy began a four-year drift, the "search within herself" rising to a keener intensity. If she actually had subscribed to Dr. Watson's theories, her faith in him at this point was shaken, as she swung to a radical, Freudian perspective. In March 1921, acting probably on the recommendation of Katrina Tiffany, Dorothy engaged the services of a pair of Bryn Mawr–based, if not educated, nannies—Florence G. Sheath and Agnes Kenney; and, leaving Bob, Mabbie, and Tinky in their care, Dorothy went off to deliver Mikey. Then, leaving the three eldest children in Kenney's charge, Dorothy took little Mikey to Alfred V. de Forest's Sky Farm in Marlborough, New Hampshire. The son of Lockwood de Forest, Alfred was the twins' age and had been their playmate, not Dorothy's. He was her favorite cousin, nonetheless; an MIT professor and an inventor, she thought him "a genius." Once again the fortunes of the Tiffany and de Forest families intertwined, as Alfred and his wife, Izette, were deeply interested in the "new science" of psychoanalysis, then gaining currency in American avant-garde circles.

Curiously enough, Alfred's interest in psychoanalysis may have been derived from his father's regard for the so-called effortless skill of Indian caste-trained craftsmen—Lockwood's reading, in the twenties, included *From the Unconscious to the Conscious* by Dr. Gustave Galey. Dorothy would not have thought the same of her father, who seemed to her, then as later, "not at all psychologically interested." But the age which had spawned Tiffany glass was, after all, the same age which had given birth to Freud's *Studies on Hysteria,* and Louis's complexities, like his free expression of fantasy in art, had certainly awakened Dorothy psychologically. Robert's helplessness before his own illness may then have confirmed for her the acuteness of Freudian departure from nineteenth-century neurobiology.

Since Robert sought Dorothy out wherever she went, leaving the children with Kenney was probably calculated to minimize his influence on them. By this time she had come to see the separation as essential to the childrens' welfare, which, given the circumstances—Robert's attacks, the marital chemistry, and the interference of his parents in their life—was not altogether a false notion. Dorothy was in a no-win situation, one ironically compounded by her own conscientiousness. Desperately she was searching for a solution. During the winter, from a farm in New Canaan, Connecticut, Kenney had written her employer, "I am not quite sure of Dr. Burlingham's faith and trust in me, perhaps I am a lesser evil than one unknown to him, but I do feel that if Bob who is the pivot of all his joys and misunderstandings, could grow strong and be a living proof that our efforts were just, and . . . thereby regain confidence in himself and us, it would be a blessing from God." On May 30, on the farm with Bob, Mabbie, and Tinky, Kenney reported, "All goes well here, the children are very happy, decidedly browner . . . Bobbie is lively and full of pep, the three crawl around the floor together, they begin to realize they must put their toys out of [the kittens'] reach, just three tomboys they are." This same reassuring, upbeat tone sounded in all of Kenney's reports. "Everything goes nicely here," she again wrote Dorothy, "the children are growing like happy brown mushrooms."

At summer's end Dorothy could only think to flee once more, and farther from Robert. In September 1921, she collected Joy Gilder, eldest of Comfort's four children, who like Bob was asthmatic, and left for Tucson, Arizona, where the dry air would hopefully improve their breathing. After spending the fall and winter there, Dorothy met Comfort, Rodman, and their other children near Sheridan, Wyoming, where Comfort's friends, the Gallatins, had a sprawling ranch. When they saw Dorothy, the Gilders were shocked by the change in her appearance: she had shorn her beautiful waist-length tresses. The flapper bob, britches, high boots, flannel shirt, ten-gallon hat, and horse certainly presented a different side of Dorothy, and the effect must have been liberating, since she always remembered it as "a marvellous summer . . . I had a horse, a big beautiful black horse that ran away with me." The three families rode, camped, and fished, gathering around the bonfire to tell tales of the Sioux and their sacred Black Hills, gold, Custer and Little Big Horn. Comfort, strumming a guitar, led them in song. Yet evidently that idyllic time was the product of some preparation. In August, Louis had reported to May-May that Dorothy had visited Laurelton Hall to settle some of her affairs. But, he added, "she expects to stay west for the winter." Indeed, as winter turned to spring, she kept running and searching.

The summer of 1923 found her abroad with "the Four" (as their grandfather Burlingham affectionately called them). By August they were high in the mountains of Murren, south of Bern, in Switzerland, the children looking healthy in shorts, sweaters, and broad-brimmed hats. By September they were at the foot of Les Granges Mountains. Returning to the States, they repeated the winter in Tucson and summer in Sheridan. Bob was then nine, Mabbie seven, Tinky five, and Mikey three—and none had ever set foot in a school. Their education consisting of a patchwork sewn by successive private tutors, Dorothy realized the time had come: she had to settle somewhere.

As it happened, Izette de Forest was planning to depart for Budapest in January 1925 to begin a training analysis (an analysis undertaken to become an analyst) with Freud's disciple Sándor Ferenczi. Realizing Dorothy's plight, Alfred invited her to spend the winter in Stratford, Connecticut, where the children could attend the local schools. Dorothy jumped at the chance, settling near the de Forest's Salt Marsh House by the Housatonic River. It was there, probably, that Dorothy underwent "some kind of analytic experience."

Dorothy had discovered the nature of unconscious drives the hard way, and by 1924 her life had become a tangled skein. Having had a father but no mother, she had created as if by way of compensation the opposite situation for her children. They had been both protected from and deprived of their father's influence, and they missed him sorely, Bob—the eldest—most demonstrably. With every day he was becoming more and more "difficult," his asthma and allergies overlayed with temper tantrums, petty thefts, infantile habits, and white lies. Unlike Papa Louis, Robert had an exceptional way with children, even as infants, genuinely enjoying their company, doing for them, playing with them, nurturing them. Many years later Dorothy recalled Robert's and Bob's "lovely relationship"—how "[Robert] wheeled [Bob] in his baby carriage & then in the go-chair to the beach & how they played together for hours." Angry at Dorothy for separating him from his father, Bob had become unmanageable.

Robert's illness had meanwhile forced him to give up his private practice, a humiliation that he never truly got over. He had begun a new career of medical research which, unlike the art of surgery, could be structured around his breakdowns. Loyal friends and relations rallied to him, taking him in while he recovered from depression. Grace Lawrence Taylor, his aunt, was particularly devoted. Her husband, Robert Taylor, a professor of romance languages at Williams College in western Massachusetts, arranged for Robert to conduct some research through the Biology Department.

While traveling, Dorothy had succeeded in keeping him at bay, sending him brief, unheaded reports on the children. But once ensconced at Stratford, she was obliged to send them to Black Point. Their first visit, in late summer, passed peaceably, but in the midst of the second, in early fall, Robert collapsed and the children were abruptly returned to her. Meanwhile, in Stratford, Dorothy was growing more interested in the possibilities of psychoanalysis.

Nineteen twenty-four was an active year in America for analysis. Dr. Morton Prince was busy proselytizing, Karl Menninger was inducted into the American Psychoanalytic Association, and Otto Rank, still widely regarded as Freud's right-hand man, arrived in the United States to begin a lecture tour. Dorothy may well have attended his first lecture, delivered after Easter in New York at the Academy of Medicine, or read it in published form, as it presented a compelling case for the psychoanalytic treatment of so-called organic conditions like asthma. This same year also brought word that Freud's daughter had begun the psychoanalytic treatment of children in Vienna, with promising results. Tracing her hopes across the Atlantic seemed worthwhile to Dorothy, even if they proved illusory. She who had defied her father, left her husband, and seemed incapable of helping her son may have felt she had little left to lose.

American friends, Ruth and Arthur Sweetser, had established a small International School in Geneva for English-speaking children, and they invited Dorothy to enroll the Four. Once in Switzerland, Dorothy planned to head for Vienna to interview Anna Freud with the prospect of entering Bob into a brief analysis. Thinking to remain abroad for six months, perhaps a year, she sailed on May 1, 1925—Mabbie's eighth birthday.

Knowing the devastation that her departure would cause Robert, Dorothy left without telling him. He had been a frequent guest over the winter in the Providence household of Dr. William P. Buffum, a graduate of the Harvard Medical School. And when Buffum's wife, Constance, got word of Dorothy's plan she fired off an impassioned note to Robert's physician in New York, a Dr. Amsden, who forwarded it to Louie. "I know it means simply pushing him over the precipice," she began. Apparently, all winter long, Robert had spoken continually of his children; and "to take the children out of his reach this summer when he is in this weakened condition," she wrote, "is like refusing water to a man dying of thirst."

Where did Dorothy get the mettle to follow through with her plan? In a taped conversation fifty-three years later with her nephew Rodman Gilder, Jr., himself an analyst of adults and children, Dorothy spoke of this time. Rodman could remember as an eight-year-old visiting Dorothy in the de Forests' Stratford home shortly before her departure abroad, and hearing her play the record *Titania* over and over again. There was something that he wanted to know of his favorite aunt.

"Aunt Dodo," he asked, addressing her by her family nickname, "what did your father think of your going to Vienna?"

"Well, you know, I know very little about what my father thought about anything, I have discovered," she replied, her voice thick with sadness.

"I mean, he didn't write you . . . telling you what you should and shouldn't do, or anything?"

"Never. I had very few letters from him . . . I'm sure he was sorry that I went. But at that time we weren't very close, I would say . . ."

"It must have been terribly difficult . . ."

"It was, I'm sure," she began. "Well, as a matter of fact it isn't [so difficult], because you know what you want, and damn what the other—"

"Yeah!" Rodman interrupted, excitedly. "That's the way he felt, too! He *knew* what he wanted and *did* what he wanted, so in a way he taught you how to operate!"

This remark met with an awkward silence, and the focus was quickly changed.

VIII

The Choice

Dorothy and the Four arrived in Geneva just as the city was bursting into a glorious spring. Narcissi brightened the sun-splashed air as they rode through the city, the Four like jumping beans on the backseat of the Model T Ford. With a fat British governess—"Zaza" Armstrong—squeezed into the passenger seat, Dorothy cut through traffic as only an American woman could, at thirty-three pilot of her destiny at last.

While arranging to move to the suburbs, Dorothy took temporary lodgings in the city and installed the Four in the International School alongside Ruth and Arthur Sweetser's own children, who were near in age to the Burlinghams and also four in number. The Sweetsers had been brought to Geneva by Arthur's unenviable job as America's unofficial ambassador to the League of Nations, Woodrow Wilson's ambitious peacekeeping fraternity which had been rejected by the Senate. By happenstance Ruth Sweetser knew Constance Buffum, Louie Burlingham's devoted correspondent, and it was not long before letters began arriving in Geneva from the Buffum summer seat in Little Compton, Rhode Island, discreetly sounding out Ruth's attitudes toward Dorothy. To Buffum's disappointment Ruth proved herself Dorothy's staunch ally and, on September 8, Buffum sent Louie the bad news together with a portrait of Dorothy in Geneva, a sympathetic portrait painted by Ruth Sweetser, and overpainted by the adversarial Buffum. Containing as it does two opposed points of view, it may be a reasonable likeness.

Ruth evidently admires & loves Dorothy intensely and can see no wrong in anything she does. The only comforting part of it is that evidently the children are well and happy because she says "The present good condition of the children themselves seems to me proof that Dorothy's judgement *is* to be trusted and *should* be trusted." And in another place "of all the jobs of motherhood well done there is nothing that I have seen that can touch Dorothy's" and again "she has had to make herself a happy, wise mother with calm, well controlled nerves and she has succeeded." The fact that Dorothy's eccentricities have had anything to do with Robert's illnesses evidently has never entered her head. Dorothy must have a magnetic personality to impress anyone so much and I only wish Ruth could talk to Robert or to you and Mr. Burlingham to see that there is another side as well . . . I am afraid that even if we met and talked that we would get nowhere . . . I have no doubt that Dorothy is honestly trying to do her best but she seems to have supreme confidence in her own judgement.

A second letter echoed the first.

I simply cannot understand Ruth Sweetzer's [*sic*] attitude unless she has been greatly misinformed about conditions . . . Ruth evidently has no idea that Dorothy has ever been at all abnormal, and yet the whole trend of her letters seemed to me to show Dorothy as a person with an almost terrifying confidence in her own judgement. With her there can be no other side but her own convictions, regardless of advise from older and wiser people.

Buffum was clearly taking her cues from Louie, and the references to Dorothy's eccentricities and abnormality reflected her view. According to Louie's niece Rosamond Taylor Edmondson, Dorothy then had great difficulty in expressing her affection—to the children as well as to Robert, and this, presumably, together with her abandonment of him, provided the basis for the charge of abnormality. The perception of Dorothy's eccentricities was probably housed in the larger philosophical and stylistic differences between families, an opinion that the flap over Dorothy's choice of a nanny for Bob had done nothing to dispel. With such attitudes, it was a short step to believing that Dorothy had contributed to Robert's illnesses as well.

Dorothy made her first trip to Vienna weeks after landing in Geneva.

Details of her first meeting with Anna Freud are not known, but Dorothy returned with the news that she had agreed to take Bob into analysis after the September International Psychoanalytic Congress. She recalled during her taped reminiscence with nephew Rodman Gilder that "my reason for going to Vienna was entirely because of Bob. Bob was difficult and I was not happy about him, and I heard that analysis was good—so there I was."

"Aunt Dodo," observed Rodman's wife, Mellie, "that sounds to me like a very brave, imaginative thing in those days. Not many people had such courage."

Dorothy demurred, adding that she had decided to go into analysis herself as a means of testing the waters for Bob. If so, Anna Freud would have heartily approved, but for reasons of appreciating the parental role in the etiology of neurosis. Anna Freud (or Annafreud as she signed her name) arranged for Dorothy to begin her analysis with Theodor Reik, her father's gifted colleague and personal friend. And, for the first time in years, Dorothy knew the resuscitation of hope.

That fall she rented the mansion of a Hungarian prince, fully furnished with extensive grounds, on Braungasse, in the Dornbach suburb west of the old inner city. She began an intensive six-hour-per-week analysis with Reik at Lackierergasse 1a, while Bob started his "lessons" with Anna Freud at Bergasse 19. Mabbie followed Bob into analysis almost immediately; then Adelaide Sweetser, second of the Sweetser children, arrived in Vienna for an initial three-week consultation. Soon after, Professor Freud, to whom Dorothy had been proudly introduced by Anna, wryly observed in a letter to his son-in-law, "Anna is treating naughty American children." For her part, before she knew it, Dorothy was immersed in a fascinating new way of viewing human behavior.

Robert, who was informed of his family's departure that June, had immediately written Dorothy, who evidently had suggested that he also undergo analysis—with a "German doctor." But, as Constance Buffum put it, "she is simply discounting Dr. [Amsden's] wisdom in favour of her own." Instead, Robert made a quick visit to Europe, and returned with hopes for his family's imminent return. Whether encouraged by Dorothy, or imagined, his hopes were sufficient for him to begin searching for a family home in Brookline, Massachusetts, while delivering a lecture series in Cambridge. According to a letter to Louie from a Boston-based friend, signed "E.L.B.," "Soon D's letters changed & plans very uncertain from mail to mail until R realized finally that she had no intention of returning with the children to this country."

> He was terribly sad at times but tried . . . to keep hope & not allow himself to give into depression. He took long walks—sometimes at night when he would telephone to my room to say he could not rest. We went sketching, sightseeing, shopping, etc. I would suggest that he would try to rest between lectures. But quickly he began to sag very plainly. He told me he could not concentrate & felt he was making a spectacle of himself before the others; he was nervous & [found it] difficult to control questions. He dreaded the lectures, but felt it was his last chance to show he was equal to the case of his family.

Meanwhile, over the fall and winter, Dorothy and Anna had met frequently to talk about the children, and by the spring were making regular excursions to the Vienna Woods, their discussions of Bob and Mabbie leading the women over carpets of wild strawberries and patches of melting snow to "lonely, beautiful spots." Dorothy's possession of a motorcar, a rarity in postwar Vienna, enabled her occasionally to begin the days of that fateful spring by chauffeuring Professor, as he was known to his intimates, and Anna to the lilac-scented fringes of the city. In return Freud gave Dorothy a beautiful brooch, a blue, red, and green opal set in thick gold, which she promptly lost. This and the "awful moment" when she managed to wedge the Model T (with Freud and Anna) between two trees, may have served as early lessons in the phenomenon of parapraxis, those slips from the unconscious which Freud had formulated in *The Psychopathology of Everyday Life.*

Anna Freud's close friend Eva Rosenfeld later found Dorothy's brooch where it had fallen, weeks earlier, under the leaves of a strawberry plant. Eva's determination to find it may have revealed her jealousy of Dorothy's quick attachment to the Freuds, because Professor declared, "Eva must keep the brooch. I have anyway ordered another one for Dorothy in the meantime, which will be ready in a few days."

Eva had only recently met Anna, in November 1924, when Anna had asked her to take one of her child patients as a boarder, but they had become fast friends. The following year, on Anna's birthday, Eva had given her a long cord to which she had attached thirty gifts, the number signifying the depth of her affection as well as Anna's age. But, as Eva rationalized later:

> In the meantime, Dorothy Burlingham had joined our circle . . . with her four elfin-like children. American children were of course "special" children to me. As for Anna, the Burlinghams came to play a most important part in her life. I had a home of my own, my own children, a circle of friends. Dorothy and her children came as strangers and Anna's mind and heart became their home . . .

Suddenly Dorothy was not as alone in the world as she had thought. Less than nine months after arriving in Vienna, when the Freuds left for the mountainous summer resort at Semmering, Dorothy and the Four were invited along to live next door to the Freuds.

Using the door in the hedge between Villas Schüler and Sophie, Anna introduced the Burlinghams to the Austrian countryside. As her father the mycophile had once led her, she led them to the edible mushrooms which grow among the roots of the Austrian black pine. She led them up steep mountains to *walderberren,* and into valleys where trains began a labored ascent, traversing viaducts, emerging from tunnels, their engines echoing against the mountainsides; and she led them in swimming, and in Halma (a form of checkers). She inspired them with simple healthy habits, and at night invented spellbinding stories, such as how Mabbie had gotten her blue eyes (God had taken a bit of blue sky, she said). At turns charming and frank, merry and austere, spontaneous and disciplined, she was always capable and lucid.

Had Dorothy arrived in Vienna either sooner or later than she did, things might have gone differently for her. But she came at that precisely receptive moment in Anna Freud's life when, as the Austrians say, she had "met her fate," and her destiny was rolled out before her.

Anna Freud had been born four years after Dorothy, in the same year that her father had first successfully interpreted a dream. Like Dorothy Anna was the youngest born, and like Dorothy (after Annie's death), she was one of six siblings; Anna may also have been a lonely child, following her elder brothers and sisters around crying "Me too!" Anna's father had evidently also hoped for a boy, and thus had to discard the name he had chosen to honor Wilhelm Fliess, his sole confidant during the seminal years of "splendid isolation" from the medical establishment. Anna's arrival had apparently not disturbed Freud's three o'clock consultation hour, and he had penned, rather than telegraphed, Fliess the news of his daughter's birth. Though Anna was quick to deny that her father had been disappointed in a daughter, Freud himself once jokingly referred to her as my "only [true] son."

Perhaps in part because Freud had delighted in Anna's cheeky insolence, permitting it as the youngest child's prerogative, she had become the archetypal faithful daughter, loyal in the first and last place to him and his psychoanalytic cause. Her feelings for him as a child had been reflected in enthusiasm for a popular song called "The Grenadiers," which tells of two French soldiers returning from the Russian front who learn that France has fallen and the emperor been taken. The grenadiers weep at the news, but while one speaks fondly of returning to his family, the other thinks only of his emperor, saying, "What matters wife? What matters child?/With far greater cares I'm shaken. Let them go beg with hunger wild. My Emperor, my Emperor is taken!" Anna's identification with this grenadier had horrified one school chum, who herself had sided with the first grenadier's (and—for a girl—more conventional) position. In retrospect, one sees that Anna had been militant from girlhood, committed to the defense of the father, or father-figure, and his higher cause, at the expense, even, of domestic life.

Of Freud's six children, three boys and three girls, Anna was the only one to follow in his footsteps (hence, "my only [true] son"). Her relationship with him had always been harmonious, though her development had "been on deeper and more difficult lines" than Mathilde's, the eldest daughter, or, probably, Sophie's, the beautiful, frail, and feminine daughter, who had been Freud's early favorite. The premier place in his affections had been won for Anna by the force of her will, and by fate.

Their relationship had begun to closen with Sophie's engagement and 1913 marriage to Hamburg portrait photographer Max Halberstadt. Shortly after Sophie's engagement Freud had implied to Ferenczi that "the subjective condition" or impetus for his essay "The Theme of Three Caskets," had been Anna's emergence as his Cordelia, King Lear's youngest and only faithful daughter. And, in 1914, he had declared her "the most gifted and accomplished" of his children. An early interest in children led Anna to a five-year stint as an elementary-school teacher in Vienna's Cottage Lyceum. But already by the second year, shortly after writing her father to ask the meaning of transference, she had begun to study psychoanalysis actively. In 1918 she had attended her first congress and, in the same year, had gone into analysis—with her father. At age twenty-two Anna had been living alone with her parents, the sole unmarried sibling, for five years. Freud had still been hopeful in 1921 that Anna might marry, but in the year of Dorothy's arrival in Vienna wrote Max Halberstadt, "she has just passed her thirtieth birthday, [and] does not seem inclined to get married." The Anna whom her cousin Edward L. Bernays had in 1913 found "feminine . . . gentle and self-effacing" had begun the essential change to the "strong personality" the world would later encounter.

The filial bond which Anna forged in becoming the sole unmarried, psychoanalytically directed sibling had been cemented by Sophie's sudden death from pneumonia in 1920 and, three years later, by the occurrence of Freud's cancer of the jaw. Anna had since attended to him with great devotion, becoming his nurse, secretary, ambassador, and alter ego. Elected to membership in the Vienna Psychoanalytic Society in 1922, she had begun her practice, which included the treatment of children, in the following year.

In *Anna Freud: A Life Dedicated to Children,* Uwe Henrik Peters identifies in her development the ego-defensive mechanism of altruistic surrender. Anna does appear to have illustrated this defense mechanism in her celebrated 1936 book, *The Ego and the Mechanisms of Defense,* with a thinly veiled autobiographical example: Anna, the young schoolteacher, becoming a governess whose analysis revealed obsessional wishes for "beautiful clothes and a number of children." Yet, "when she came to be analyzed, she was unmarried and childless and her dress was rather shabby and inconspicuous." (By her own admission Anna was not then much concerned with clothes, either.) But analysis revealed that the governess was fulfilling her wishes, after all, though vicariously, through the children in her charge and by attending her elder, more attractive sister.

Dorothy's arrival in Vienna coincided, then, with that crucial juncture in Anna's life when the main currents of her life had combined, and her desire for children had reemerged as a transcendent expression of loyalty to her father. Freud believed that neuroses are ego disorders invariably caused in early childhood by the demands of sexual instincts, but with one exception his patients had been adults, and his knowledge of the psyche's developmental stages largely inferred from their analyses. The child analyst was therefore charged with the responsibility of validating or repudiating the psychoanalytic structure which Freud had postulated. Acceptance of this and other responsibilities had molded Anna's character; once, like Dorothy, shy and filled with dread at the prospect of public speaking, she had become a self-possessed, compelling orator. Speaking, like her father, without reference to notes, and with his gift for reducing complex subjects to their simplest terms, she, too, commanded the psychological limelight. To Dorothy, whose father had cramped her educational ambitions, Anna's filial relations must have seemed paradigmatic. Yet, for opposite reasons, Dorothy's and Anna's respective capacities for happiness in marriage had been made impossible by their relationships with their fathers. Anna's filial relationship was all-consuming: there was no place for another man in her life. Dorothy's relationship, on the other hand, had been sufficiently injurious as to have made her marriage unendurable.

Dorothy later characterized her connection to Anna Freud as "a simple and direct" one. Freud's 1925 comment to Max Halberstadt that Anna was "treating naughty American children" struck the note upon which the relationship began, but belied the circumstances. In that same year, according to Anna, child analysis was still "a pioneering venture needing to establish its right of existence even in the psychoanalytic world." The ascription "to the nature of children sexual as well as aggressive impulses . . . [was] . . . an offense against the formerly cherished belief in the innocence of childhood." Thus the bond between Dorothy and Anna was, in fact, an extraordinary one, based on a shared revolutionary concept of children.

Child analysis is generally said to have begun with Freud's 1909 publication of the case of Little Hans, a five-year-old with a fear of horses, who was Freud's first, and last, child patient. After a caesura, child analysis was taken up in earnest by Hermine von Hug-Hellmuth in Vienna, by Melanie Klein in Berlin, and again in Vienna by Anna Freud.

The infantile ego, Freud had discovered, may be no match for the triple threat of instinctual drives, the superego (or watchdog of conscience), and external reality. Caught between the amoral instigations of the id (or one's unconscious libidinal or aggressive urges) on the one hand, and the restrictive demands of conscience and civilization, on the other, the young, weak ego may have no recourse but to repress a drive which, banished to the unconscious, lives on in the form of a neurosis. The aim of psychoanalysis was to free the individual from the pathogenic consequences of repression; and, wrote Anna Freud, ". . . in the analysis of children . . . we can aim at transformations, improvements, and recoveries which we could not even dream of in the analysis of adults." The child, she reasoned, is that much closer to the fork in the path of psychic development where the divergence from normality occurred, crucial life decisions have yet to be made, and the environment is accessible to the analyst's direct influence. In other words if, within the wider psychoanalytic community, there were doubts as to the feasibility of treating children, among the practitioner-pioneers, child analysis was thought to offer the greatest promise—if not of a cure, as one is cured of a physical ailment, then—of a considerably alleviated condition.

Having observed that the young superego is still dependent upon its parental authority, an authority which usually lies at the root of the child's disturbances, Anna Freud had come to believe that the child analyst, unlike her adult counterpart, should play an educative role in addition to the therapeutic one. Of Anna's emerging techniques of child analysis this was, in her own estimation, "perhaps most important." It required that the analyst literally establish herself as an authority "even greater" than the parent, and maintain that authority throughout the analysis—which today remains a surprising concept. Only then, she believed, could the analyst "succeed in putting herself in the place of the child's ego ideal," and hence begin to exert a direct superego influence, in effect installing an improved standard of behavior—or, to put it more forcefully, reprogramming the child's value system. By ministering to the child's internal and external worlds, Anna Freud believed that the analyst of children dramatically improved her efficacy.

Controversy lay in the fact that the analyst then stood before the child, not as the blank slate or opaque mirror of classical adult analysis, but as a flesh and blood role model, and this compromised the formation of a transference neurosis. The idea was essentially that, by remaining neutral in his behavior toward the patient—or analysand, more correctly put—the analyst became the screen upon which the analysand's neurotic emotions, usually toward his parents, were projected. In reliving toward the analyst the conflicted love-hate emotions once harbored for his parents, the analysand paved, if not a "royal road," then, a vice-regal road to his unconscious mind. Anna Freud, at that time, believed that an interpretable transference neurosis did not anyway develop in children while they remained attached to their parental figures; the analyst could at best only "share" transference with the parents. Thus, in this light, her educative approach to child analysis served, in a sense, as its replacement.

The technical development of child analysis by Anna Freud was marked by just this kind of innovation. Dream interpretation—"the royal road to the unconscious"—remained just that for adults and children alike. Once instructed that "no dream can make itself out of nothing; it must have fetched every bit from somewhere," the child, having told his dream, eagerly embarked in search of its origins. But Anna supplemented this classic technique with the analysis of daydreams and drawings. The interpretation of transference phenomena she largely rejected, as she entirely did free association, of which children had proven incapable, turning instead to the home environment for links to the personal symbolic content of dreams. Anna also instigated a period of preparation at the outset of analysis to gain the child's cooperation. And since the child could not reliably furnish his own case history, the parents were asked to do so, and to report continually on the child's doings outside the analytic sessions.

Anna Freud's chief competitor in the field of child analysis was Melanie Klein, whose own approach to child analysis resembled more closely classical adult analysis. She felt that scrutiny of the child's defensive maneuvers at the outset of analysis made the preparatory period unnecessary, that transference did develop and was intepretable, that play therapy could be used to the same effect as free association and, most significantly here, that educative and therapeutic aims were incompatible. Anna Freud's "Continental school of child analysis" was therefore born in controversy, and contradistinction to Melanie Klein's "London school." Klein concentrated primarily upon the child's inner, experiential world, while Anna Freud's educative approach maximized contact between analyst and parent. And in this we see the foundation for Dorothy's and Anna's friendship. Their relationship blossomed in the soil of Anna Freud's theory and technique.

While in Geneva, Dorothy had sent Bob to the French "therapeutist," Emile Coué, known for his work with hypnotism and positive suggestion, whose treatment had consisted of lining ten-year-old Bob against the wall and having him endlessly repeat,

"Every day in every way I am getting a little better." But in Anna Freud Dorothy had found someone willing to march right into her home, and transform it. She had been quick to fire Bob's tutor, an Englishman whom Dorothy had brought from Geneva, and Mabbie's governess eventually met the same fate (each being in some way counteractive to the direction of the therapy). Through Eva Rosenfeld Anna hired a new tutor for Bob, a German biology student in Vienna for a semester's study, and for the *Fasching,* the annual carnival. Subsequently a top New York psychoanalyst and authority on adolescence, Peter Blos proved an exacting teacher. After the fall semester, probably acting on Anna Freud's suggestion, Dorothy had invited him to live in the Braungasse mansion and to join them for that first summer in Semmering, which Blos recalls as "romantic" and "playful."

Dorothy was no doubt relieved to surrender to Anna a share of her parental responsibility and authority. Having shouldered it alone for over four years and, in Bob's case, to such unhappy ends, she virtually hurled herself into the role of cooperative parent, Anna's confidence irradiating her pockets of doubt. Professor Freud was himself cautious about the results obtainable through psychoanalysis, quipping in *Studies on Hysteria* that it could at best transform "neurotic misery into common unhappiness." He felt "a certain indifference to the world," and confessed the view that "my dear fellow creatures—with individual exceptions—are rabble." His discoveries had nevertheless raised hopes in others that understanding the full spectrum of mental processes might ensure mankind a brighter future. And his followers took his pessimism as further proof of his genius. Charged with custody of one of "the greatest secrets of nature," their enthusiasm seemed boundless. Dorothy was young, Anna still younger; they shared that enthusiasm.

When the Burlinghams returned to Vienna at the end of September 1926. Dorothy moved from Dornbach to Hohe Warte, where she rented the Silber Schlossel (Little Silver Castle) at 55 Silbergasse, a wine merchant's mansion, again elaborately furnished with extensive grounds. Having decided to enter Adelaide into analysis with Anna Freud, the Sweetsers arrived to spend a year in Vienna as houseguests of the Burlinghams. With education looming as a problem for both families, Dorothy followed her friends' example in establishing a tiny, makeshift "school" of her own, with Peter Blos the live-in schoolmaster and a miniature Swiss chalet on the grounds serving as the schoolhouse. It was straight out of Grimms' *Fairy Tales,* nestled in snow-blanketed gardens under snow-laden boughs, hung with icicles and warmed by a green tile stove, with lace curtains in the windows and a frieze of fish swimming around the walls. *Das Bauernhaus* they called it, the Farm House: an enthusiastic, sentimental expression of hope for a new start under the psychoanalytic aegis.

The city in which Dorothy's hopes were rekindled was, however, an implausible scene for a renaissance. The great Hapsburg empire, splendid and relatively secure under Franz Josef's pre-War rule, had been humbled to a state the size of Wisconsin, its capital city become a gray, sad phantom. Its manufacturing-oriented economy had been shattered by inflation, reparations, and sudden separation from the raw materials and markets of the successor states. Yet, oddly, the pomp, the grandeur, the glittering court palaces and lush formal gardens, the entire *Thousand and One Nights* panoply, remained.

The cultural and political tides had waned in Vienna as they had waxed in New York, but Dorothy found she vastly preferred the tempo of Austrian socialism to America's frenzied prosperity. The pace was slower in Vienna, and the capacity for enjoyment seemed higher. Vienna's *schlamperei* remained the verso side to its *gemütlichkeit:* an ambling inefficiency went hand in hand with the tourist brochure charm. Hardship existed on easy terms with a wry indifference; music still spilled down the cobbled, winding streets, seeped from homes crumbling within the Ringstrasse; the citizenry kept the same languorous hours, and one could relax. Dorothy appreciated it all. She relished her anonymity, and the newfound latitude to be different without being labeled "eccentric" or "abnormal."

I n the meantime, Anna Freud and Melanie Klein's war of theoretical possession was heating up, and Klein, by dint of having been quicker to boast of the results of her work with children, held the early edge.

At the Eighth International Psychoanalytic Congress in Salzburg in April 1924, Melanie Klein had presented her technique of early analysis; at the First Conference of German Psychoanalysts in Würzburg, October 1924, she had used "Erna's" case to describe her play technique; in December of the same year she had addressed the Vienna Society on the psychological principles of analysis in childhood; and in London over the summer of 1925 she had delivered a series of six lectures to an appreciative British audience. But, due to Professor's illness, Anna Freud had attended neither the Salzburg nor the Würzburg meetings, and at the 1925 Bad Homburg Congress duty had required her to read her father's paper, not her own.

Her answer to Klein came over the winter of 1926–27 in four lectures delivered to the Vienna Society. Supplemented with a fifth lecture presented at the Innsbruck Congress of 1927, they were published in the same year as the now classic *Introduction to the Technique of Child Analysis*.

The Four had of course since stepped into the breach, arriving in Vienna during the crucial three-year span between 1923 and 1926 when Anna Freud was laying the foundation of her child analytic technique on the basis of ten analyses. The private histories of Bob and Mabbie, and also Adelaide, would therefore soon be marshaled as ammunition for Anna Freud's theoretical salvo.

In his 1914 paper, "On Narcissism," Freud wrote that parents who treat their children like princes and princesses are projecting on them their own lost narcissism, the original condition at birth and most primitive stage on the long civilizing journey. Of Dorothy's children Bob and Mabbie, the elder pair, this seemed most demonstrably true. They were her golden boy and girl, as most everyone who knew them agrees. In family parlance they were "Boma," an acronym which their grandfather C.C.B. had devised. (Tinky and Mikey were "Timi"; Dorothy and the Four collectively were "Dobomatimi.") Bob and Mabbie were both sensitive, emotional, and artistic, their charisma such that they virtually eclipsed the younger entente. In Robert's absence, the prince and princess had developed in opposite ways, however, Bob becoming Dorothy's alternately *strahlend* (radiant) and *stürmisch* (stormy) enfant terrible; Mabbie, on the other hand, her adoring soul mate. The rivalry for parental affection is naturally intensified in single parent families, and Bob's rivalry with Mabbie led to the establishment of two lifelong ententes, Bob and Tinky ("Boti"), and Mabbie and Mikey ("Mami"), each *strahlend* child tying the closest sibling knot with the eclipsed child of the opposite sex.

The *strahlend* pair were the children to whom Dorothy was closest, the ones upon whom she most relied as they grew older, the objects of her greatest hopes and fears, the ones she doted upon and set apart the most;

given the marital and emotional strains under which she labored, they were also the most burdened.

Bob of course had brought Dorothy to Vienna. Of the two sons, he was most like his father. He had Robert's gentle sensitivity and effervescent charm. Anna Freud's nephew Ernsti Halberstadt (who later changed his name to W. Ernest Freud) recalled Bob's "open face over which would spread the most engaging smile, lighting up his whole personality so that one could not help taking him into one's heart." Smitten on the Atlantic crossing with the cello of a tea-music orchestra, Bob had taken up the instrument with a prodigious ability, a little boy manifesting the artistry in his blood. It must have seemed a promising development since he had been but ten years old and Vienna the ancestral home of Mozart, Beethoven, Schubert, and Mahler. But, as gadfly, Bob had stung Dorothy to her destiny; and so she would play a determining role in his.

Since to one as perceptive as Peter Blos, Bob was then "a nice fellow whose problems weren't apparent," one may conclude that Bob initially reserved his difficult behavior for Dorothy. Their problems were certainly linked, this the reason Anna Freud had advised her to enter into analysis. Brushing aside Robert's immediate concern that Bob might not be understood by an Austrian analyst, Dorothy had written, "I don't think you need worry that Bob won't be understood. What we should have feared was our lack of understanding of the children—of ourselves & of their reactions to us." More practically, Anna did speak English, Dorothy a passable German, and the Four were meanwhile picking up a mixture of German and Austrian dialects.

If, during their first interview, Dorothy had shown Anna Freud the letters that Bob had sent her from Geneva, Anna would not have missed the revealing postscript, "I wrote to *father*"—the word *father* underlined and terminated with a period twenty times as large as the others on the page. Since Bob's feelings for Robert seemed so charged with emotion, Dorothy might then have recalled for Anna the charming *baromètre artistique* that the boy had sent his father from Geneva. The barometer ingeniously took the shape of a winding road which led to a fairy tale cottage, the glass—somehow—changing color with the weather, from *bleu (beau)* to *rouge (pluie ou brouillard)*, as if (in Bob's mind) to indicate the variably emotional path leading to Geneva. Then, if Dorothy had shown Anna a poem which Bob had composed especially for his father, she might have pieced together the oversized period and the volatile path with the heartfelt love expressed in "The Summer Farm."

> I love to see the summer farm
> upon the planes so green
> With horses, cows and pigs around
> to eat the grasses green.
> I love to see the summer view
> upon the mountains blue.
> But when I look at things so pretty
> It makes me think of you.

Nanny Agnes Kenney's 1921 observation that Bob was "the pivot of all [Robert's] joys and misunderstandings" was also true the other way around. Robert's illness was understandably a source of confusion for Bob, though when healthy he was an exceptional father. If Bob was difficult, it was partially on account of Dorothy's having left Robert, for separating a son from his father.

Anna Freud's clinical diagnosis of Bob exists, at least in fragmentary form, in the examples she drew from her ten analyses to buttress technical points in *Introduction to the Technique of Child Analysis*. In each case mentioned the examples strung together create an approximate psychological profile. Anna Freud protected the identities of her analysands as best she could by changing their names, but vital information such as age and sex could not be altered for obvious reasons. Her biographer, however, Uwe Henrik Peters, incorrectly identified the most frequently cited of these cases, that of the obsessional "Devil Girl," as Dorothy's second-born child. But the Devil Girl began her analysis at six, Mabbie at eight. The Devil Girl, furthermore, had been sent to Anna Freud for an initial "three weeks' observation," and had "lived at the beginning of her analysis with friends of her family." Lastly, the analyst disclosed that this girl, "already knew two children who were being analyzed by me, and she came to her first appointment with her slightly older friend." At the beginning of the next session, when the little girl was alone, Anna Freud had said that "she knew quite well why her two friends came to me: one because he could never tell the truth and wanted to give up this habit, and the other because she cried so often and was angry with herself for doing so." In an instant, then, one knows that the Devil Girl was Adelaide

Sweetser, her "slightly older friend" Mabbie. Bob, of course, was the boy who could "never tell the truth."

Bob appeared again in Table 1, Summary of Ten Early Child Cases, 1923–1926, in *Introduction to the Technique of Child Analysis* as, "Sex: M; Age in Years: 10; Salient Features: Perversions; very diverse anxieties; semi-delinquent." In the text proper, he is described as "a boy of 10 with an obscure mixture of many anxieties, nervous states, insincerities, and infantile perverse habits." She continued:

> Various small and one more serious theft had occurred in recent years. The conflict with his parents was neither open nor conscious, and on the surface any insight into his very uncomfortable condition, or any wish to change it, was not obvious. His attitude to me was thoroughly rejecting and mistrustful; all his strivings were directed toward protecting his sexual secrets from discovery.

According to Anna Freud, Bob had not thought himself to have a problem and, at the outset, had been suspicious of her; for these reasons, the period of preparation during which the analytic alliance was struck had proved unusually troublesome. But she had made herself first interesting, then useful, and finally indispensable to Bob by catering to him and doing him all manner of services and favors—both small, such as typing his letters, and large, like protecting him from punishment and returning money which he had stolen. Eventually, she was pleased to report, he had become dependent upon her, and "I had only waited for this moment to demand of him in return the most extensive cooperation." Bob had then come to understand "the meaning of analysis and its therapeutic aim," as Anna Freud demonstrated with the following example.

> One day in a later period of his analysis he entered into a conversation with one of my father's adult patients in the waiting room. This man told him about his dog, who had killed a fowl for which he, the owner, had had to pay. "The dog ought to be sent to Freud," said my little patient, "he needs analysis." The adult patient did not reply, but afterwards showed great disapproval. What odd sort of idea of analysis did the child have? The dog had nothing the matter with it; it wanted to kill the hen and it killed it. But I knew exactly what the boy had in mind. "The poor dog," he must have thought, "he wants so badly to be a good dog and he can't. Something inside him makes him kill chickens."

To his mind, insight into the inner conflict with forbidden wishes provided a fully sufficient motive for analysis.

A year and a half later, with Bob now approaching twelve, Anna Freud had presumably plumbed Bob's psyche a good bit further, as this long passage from the case study shows. The material reveals the workings of Bob's mind, but also Anna Freud's and, in addition, the analytic process, and therefore seems worth quoting at length.

When he began treatment, he was a passive-feminine character, his original object relationship with his mother being entirely overlaid by identification with her. His original masculine aggressiveness found expression only occasionally in hostile behavior to his brothers [sic] and sisters and in isolated delinquent acts, which were followed by violent fits of repentance and depression. In this period of his analysis he was preoccupied, in numerous ideas, fantasies, and dreams, with the problem of death, or rather the infliction of death.

At that time one of his mother's closest friends was very ill, and one day his mother received a telegram saying that her condition was dangerous. He seized on this event, spinning elaborate fantasies around it. He imagined that a new telegram arrived saying she was dead. His mother was extremely grieved. Then came another telegram [in his fantasy]—she is still alive, it was a mistake. The mother rejoiced. And then he fancied telegrams arriving in quick succession, an announcement of death always followed by another of revival. The fantasy ended with the news [again, in his fantasy] that the whole thing was a joke which someone had played on his mother. It is not difficult to interpret; we see his ambivalence clearly expressed, the wish to kill the person loved by his mother, and the inability to pursue his idea to its real conclusion.

Shortly thereafter he reported the following compulsive action. When sitting in the lavatory he had to touch a knob which he found in the wall at one side three times; but then he had to repeat the process at once with a knob on the other side. This action seemed at first unintelligible, until the explanation was found next day through a fantasy recounted in another connection. He imagined God as an old man, seated in the heavenly abode on a big throne. To right and left of him were knobs or switches protruding from the wall. If he pressed the knobs on one side, someone died; if he pressed one on the other, a child came into the world. I trust that linking the compulsive action with the daydream makes further interpretation superfluous. The number 3 is probably to be explained by the number of his brothers and sisters.

Soon afterward another friend of the family fell ill. He was both close to the boy's mother and the father of one of his playmates. The boy heard the telephone ring just as he was leaving for his session with me, and in the session constructed the following fantasy: His mother had been told that she must go to the invalid's house; she went there, entered the sickroom, went up to the bed, wanting to talk with the patient. But he made no reply, and she saw that he was dead. It was a great shock to her. At that moment the dead man's little son came in. She called him and said, "Come here, look, your father is dead." The boy came up to the bed and spoke to his father. The father was alive and answered him. He turned to my patient's mother and said, "What is the matter? He is alive." Then she spoke again to the father, but again he made no reply and was dead. But when the boy came up again and spoke, the father was alive again.

This fantasy is instructive and transparent, and in addition contains the interpretation of the two previous ones. We see that the father is dead in his relationship with the mother, but alive so far as concerns his relationship with the son. While in the previous fantasies the ambivalence—the wish to kill and to bring to life again—was directed to the same person, though split into two different actions which must cancel each other out, the present fantasy gives us the historical elucidation of the double attitude by specifying the person who is threatened—a man, on the one hand, and a father, on the other.

The two tendencies clearly spring from different phases of the boy's development. The death wish against the father as the rival for the mother's love derives from the normal oedipal phase with its since-repressed positive object love for the mother. Here his masculine aggression turns against the father; he must be eliminated, to leave the way free for the child himself. But the other tendency, the wish to retain the father, stems on the one hand from the early period of purely admiring and loving attitude to the father, undisturbed as yet by the rivalry of the oedipus complex; and on the other from the phase—which here plays the more important part—of identification with the mother, which had replaced the normal oedipal attitude. Owing to fear of castration, threatening from the father, the boy had surrendered his love for his mother and allowed himself to be forced into the feminine attitude. From then on he had to try to sustain the father as an object of his homosexual love.

It would be tempting to go further and describe the transition in the boy from this wish to kill to a fear of death, which manifested itself each evening; and so to find a key to the complicated structure of this neurosis of the latency period. But I have mentioned this fragment only to show that this part of the analysis of a child differs in no way from that of an adult. We have to free a part of this boy's masculine aggressiveness and his object love for his mother from repression and from the overlay by the present passive-feminine character and mother identification. The conflict involved is an inner one. While the fear of his real father in the external world originally drove him into carrying out the repression, the success of this achievement depends for its maintenance upon inner forces. The father has been internalized, the superego has become the representative of his powers, and the fear of him is felt by the boy as castration anxiety. At every step which the analysis takes on the path toward making conscious the repressed oedipal tendencies, it encounters outbreaks of this castration anxiety as an obstacle. Only the laborious historico-analytic dissolution of this superego permits the work of liberation to progress. Thus you see that the therapist's work and attitude are, so far as this part of the problem is concerned, purely analytic. There is no place here for any educational admixture.

Two points stand out particularly in regard to the diagnostic information offered by these analytic fragments. First is the manic-depressive note in the "hostile behavior" and "isolated delinquent acts . . . followed by violent fits of repentance and depression." Bob does seem to have inherited the disease which, as with Robert, manifested itself unmistakably later in life.

Second is the image of a boy whose absent father has led to an identification with his mother, a boy who senses that his father is dead so far as his mother is concerned and is moved himself to fill the emotional space she has vacated; a Freudian textbook case of latent homosexuality, to which "The Summer Farm" had provided the earliest clue. The metrics of Bob's poem were faultlessly iambic with the exception of the additional syllable at the end of the seventh line, the muse abandoning Bob at just that moment when he was bridging, with the conspicuously feminine adjective *pretty*, the bucolic description of the farm to his feelings about his father. "But when I look at things so pretty,/It makes me think of you." *Pretty* had become stuck in Bob's craw, which is to support a Freudian diagnosis with a Freudian method. Anna Freud had immediately seen the tendency to homosexuality, which Freud in his 1905

Three Essays on the Theory of Sexuality had classified under "The Sexual Aberrations." This was the reason, hints Peter Blos, why she had fired Bob's first tutor; the Englishman was too handsome.

As Anna Freud observed, Bob's superego had detached itself from the parental influence it mirrored. Yet by laborious work with his superego, it was her intent to reawaken Bob's original oedipal rivalry with his father for Dorothy, and thereby set Bob back on the heterosexual track. Yet in illustrating an inner conflict calling for purely analytic work, Anna Freud omitted important details from the external world which had greatly impacted on Bob's "passive-feminine character," such as the fact that he had been living with his mother, apart from his father, since age six. And her purely therapeutic work was supplemented elsewhere by just the "educational admixture" the case study rejects, starting, for example, with the handsome tutor's dismissal. In terms of Bob's heterosexual development, Peter Blos was evidently cut from more acceptable stock than his predecessor; this was the cardinal reason for his invitation to live with the Burlinghams, first in Dornbach, then in Hohe Warte. In future Bob would continually be provided with rigorously masculine role models while being assiduously sheltered from the slightest homosexual temptations: Anna Freud later cited Bob's tendencies as a reason not to send him to boarding school.

Anna Freud was unquestionably concerned with treating Bob's neurosis, increasing his self-knowledge, and easing his adjustment to the realities which confronted him. But in so doing she was imposing upon him a Freudian ideology, a particular set of values which, among other things, presumed a heterosexual definition of normality. There are, of course, other possibilities; for example, the view that assigns a greater determining factor to that which is separate from experience, or innate, in human beings; the view in which sexual identity is born, or at least not unmade after the age of ten. In other words, if Bob were homosexual, it is questionable whether anything or anyone, at this point, could have made him heterosexual. Also, since no evidence suggests that Bob's homosexuality ever emerged from latency (as it were), there is the further possibility that the concerns for his heterosexuality were exaggerated, that his homosexual tendencies were a phase in his development. Be this as it may, sexual orientation remained a major focus of Bob's analysis—even after his marriage.

With regard to his manic-depressive symptoms, it is uncertain when exactly Anna Freud diagnosed them as such. That she did so eventually is not the issue; rather, that even after reaching this conclusion, she continued to view and treat him within the exclusive parameters of Freudian ideology and technique. That was Bob's, and Mabbie's, fate.

The didactic ubiquity of Anna Freud's conception of child analysis had been a bone of contention between Anna Freud and her mentor Lou Andreas-Salomé, the literary lion, pioneering analyst, and native of Göttingen, Germany. Anna Freud had met Salomé shortly after making the switch from schoolteacher to analyst, when she was twenty-six and Salomé sixty. Theirs was one of Anna Freud's few genuinely intimate relationships, and it peaked in this period of her analytic gestation. Salomé's positive response to *Introduction to the Technique of Child Analysis* evidently took Anna Freud by surprise, as she wrote, "I was not at all sure that you would be satisfied, especially because they are children, whom I always want to change, while you prefer to leave as they are."

Perhaps in part because Mabbie's character corresponded more closely with Anna Freud's personal standards, she pronounced hers—prematurely as it turned out—the "most successful of [the ten] early cases." Like Bob, Mabbie was *strahlend,* sensitive, emotional, and artistic; she drew beautifully, and with great freedom. But in Robert's absence Mabbie had bonded to Dorothy even more closely than had Bob. At age eight, in Geneva, after having failed to meet her mother for an expected rendezvous, and sensing, evidently, that her feelings had been hurt, Mabbie had left her this brief note: "D'ont [*sic*] feel so unhappy . . . for we won't do it once more . . . I love you so much. I know how you feel." Empathetic and solicitous beyond her years, Mabbie was Dorothy's confidante and helper, possessed already of the selflessness that would earn her the reputation as "the best of the Burlinghams."

Her problem was seemingly quite unlike Bob's. In "Preparation for Child Analysis," the first chapter of *Introduction to the Technique of Child Analysis,* Anna Freud used Mabbie's case to show how loyalty conflicts can prove disruptive to the analysis. She described Mabbie as an enchanting, extremely sensitive child who, for unknown reasons, all too frequently burst into tears. Unlike Bob, Mabbie recognized this as a problem and earnestly tried to be cooperative. But her analysis made no progress and Anna Freud was on the verge of terminating it when she discovered the impediment to be Mabbie's attachment to her old-fashioned nanny, who felt threatened by the analysis. Anna Freud realized that the allegiance to the nanny and resistance to her was a reenactment of the loyalty conflict which had dominated Mabbie's childhood, when she had been forced to choose between her parents after their separation, and had sided with Dorothy. This interpretation did not, however, dissolve the analytic obstacle since the nanny continued to be a very real and influential person in Mabbie's life. And so, in order to save the analysis, Anna Freud set out to shake Mabbie's confidence in her nanny. Only when this had been achieved, through repeated criticisms, did the analysis make progress.

In Chapter Two, "The Methods of Child Analysis," Anna Freud returned to Mabbie's case to illustrate the importance of daydreams, and, in so doing, revealed the root of her character:

> The simplest type is the daydream as a reaction to the day's experiences. The little girl . . . reacted with the following daydream at a time when competition with her brothers and sisters was playing a very important role in her analysis.

> I wish I had never come into the world at all, I wish I could die. Sometimes I pretend I do die, and then come back into the world as an animal or a doll. But if I come back into the world as a doll, I know who I mean to belong to—a little girl with whom my nurse was before, who is specially nice and good. I want to be her doll and I would not mind at all being treated like they treat dolls. I would be a dear little baby and they could wash me and do anything to me. The little girl would like me best of all. Perhaps she would get another doll for Christmas, but I would still be her favorite. She would never prefer any doll to the baby doll.

> Her current situation could not find clearer expression in any account or association than it did in this little fantasy.

Mabbie's and Bob's characters had obviously evolved quite differently, and yet at the root of each lay a parental loyalty conflict, the classic problem for children from broken homes. The angel and the enfant terrible both suffered from their fatherlessness and from resultingly symbiotic ties to Dorothy. Mabbie had been forced (she thought) to choose her mother over her father, the sad rigidity of that choice echoed by her unassailable loyalty to her nanny vis-à-vis Anna Freud. (The nanny was probably Zaza Armstrong, who had been with the Burlingham children since their arrival in Europe.) Thus, in this way,

Mabbie's original choice had made Dorothy's love and approval essential, hence her "favorite doll" persona. Bob's loyalties, on the other hand, straddled a precarious fence. His feminine identification reflected allegiance to both parents.

Contact with the Freuds had nevertheless reinforced Dorothy's decision to live apart from Robert. It seemed that for each of her needs Anna Freud offered a promising solution. Dorothy had arrived in Vienna seeking a therapist for Bob, and that of course she had found. But she had also found an ally and friend and more, someone possessed of and willing to share a solid family life, career, and all-embracing cause. In Anna Freud, of all people, she had found a woman whose values were an extension of "those spiritual things" which Julia de Forest had believed so important to Mama Lou: she had found her true partner in life.

As Dorothy's and Anna's bond had deepened, so too had blossomed the attraction that began in part from opposite stances toward their fathers: Dorothy's antipathy for hers leading to single parenthood and the search for her maternal image; Anna's identification with hers resulting in a symbiosis with him, which had left her with insufficient outlets for her maternal and feminine instincts. As a sort of analytic stepparent to the Four, Anna received the children she otherwise had been denied by fate, while, in Dorothy, she may have found a substitute for Sophie, the elder sister through whom she had vicariously fulfilled her typically feminine desires. The Freuds were keen on these substitutive, wish-fulfilling relationships, encouraging them as conscious, deliberate responses to those things in life which fate inadequately provides, or prematurely denies. Dorothy and Anna certainly fulfilled one another's dearest wishes, and substituted for relationships and roles neglected in their pasts—this was the poetic side to their understanding of the contents of their unconscious minds. They were sharing, Anna wrote her father in 1927, "the most agreeable and unalloyed comradeship."

With the fatherlessness of her children seeming increasingly irremediable, Dorothy grew all the more determined to improve the quality of her mothering. Her time in Vienna had been sufficient to convince her that she and Robert shared responsibility for the children's neuroses, that her unconscious needs had seduced Bob and Mabbie particularly into filling the gap of intimacy in her life which Robert had left. But again, the Freuds had the answer. Analysis, of course, first and foremost. But, also, *"lieben und arbeiten"* (love and work)—Professor's recipe for happiness. When Dorothy had arrived in Vienna she had had neither; a year and a half later she had both.

With her emotional energies mainly focused on the Four, her intellect had gradually, naturally, and inexorably been engaged by analytic thought and the possibility of an analytic career for herself. This, she and Anna concluded, would over time act as a safeguard against the pitfall of single parenthood and a further bond to their friendship. Anna's relationship with Eva Rosenfeld and Lou Andreas-Salomé had been centered respectively on domestic concerns and intellectual affairs, but as a child analyst Dorothy could combine those interests.

She had probably attended over the winter of 1926–27 Anna Freud's "Four Lectures on Child Analysis," the declaration of her professional creed. And Dorothy was an early participant in the Seminar for Child Analysis which Anna Freud began shortly thereafter to clarify the positions of the Viennese group. Now known as the first generation of child analysts, its members had included Anny Rosenberg Angel (Katan), Marie Briehl, Jenny Pollak Waelder, Editha Sterba, Grete Bibring, Marianne Rie Kris, and Anna Maenchen. Though today it is difficult to understand how one could join a clinical seminar on psychoanalysis without either experience, training, or even a college education, these were pioneering days, and the rules were then elastic. Before 1918 analysts had actually not been required to undergo analysis themselves (and many had not), and before 1925, when the Training Institute had opened in Vienna, no standardized course of psychoanalytic instruction even existed. Thereafter, most interested, bright persons, could probably have gained admittance regardless of prior qualifications.

However, given her maternal obligations and personal difficulties, Dorothy did not formally enroll in the Institute at this point, auditing the Monday evening seminars instead. She nevertheless soaked up the earnest discussion in the smoke-filled lecture room of the *Herzstation* in the University District—a center for heart research by day, psychoanalytic headquarters come evening. Sitting silent and inconspicuous, shy and withdrawn, Dorothy admired the radiant brilliance of her new young friend. She and Anna invariably arrived and departed together, so Dorothy was known only as Anna's "American friend," though the suffering and unhappiness etched on her face made plausible the story of a woman who had left America for the sake of her children. Those who did penetrate beyond her facade did not find an altogether pleasing personality. Dorothy Burlingham seemed distant, stiff, and uneasy. Encouraging no intimacies, she barricaded herself behind a wall of reserve and discretion. Analysis had not helped her yet.

Later it was convenient to say that Dorothy's analysis with Sigmund Freud's friend and associate Theodor Reik had ended in 1928 when Reik moved to Berlin, when in fact it had ended in early 1927. Reik by most accounts was a talented lay analyst, that is, one not medically trained. And, according to Dr. Richard Sterba's *Reminiscences of a Viennese Psychoanalyst,* Reik had "developed an open animosity toward physician analysts" and was causing friction within the Viennese Psychoanalytic Society. It might seem fateful, therefore, that in the spring of 1926 a charge of quackery had been leveled against him by a former patient. Although the case had been dismissed, the attendant publicity spoiled Reik's practice, precipitating his move to Berlin two years later.

But Reik's case had also succeeded in bringing to a boil the simmering controversy over lay analysis. Freud's early difficulties with the Viennese medical establishment had shaped a continuing bias against the narrow focus of the medically educated; "as long as I live," he wrote analyst Paul Federn in March 1926, "I shall balk at having psychoanalysts swallowed by medicine." In Freud's opinion psychoanalysis was better served by the broadening influence of other disciplines. In July 1926, he had defended this view in *The Question of Lay Analysis,* but in New York, where the future of psychoanalysis lay, the state legislature had passed a bill declaring lay analysis illegal in autumn of that same year.

Due to this delicate situation Dorothy did not advertise her difficulties with Reik, whatever they may have been. In New York her in-laws had surely grown edgy when legislation had followed the quackery charges (Anna Freud was also a lay analyst), and Dorothy did not want the Burlinghams armed with antianalytic ammunition. But, according to Anny Katan, Dorothy's analysis with Reik had produced "no good results," and, recognizing "the good work of Anna Freud with her children, she broke off her analysis with Reik and asked Professor Freud to take her into analysis."

Freud was then in his seventh decade and, in his own phrase, "beginning to grow inorganic." From the onset of his cancer in 1923 to his death sixteen years later he underwent thirty-three operations, the third of these involving the removal of his right side jaw and palate. The ill-fitting replacement, designed to separate the oral and nasal cavities, which he dubbed "the Monster," made a trial of sustenance and speech. He ate privately and spoke little, no longer able to chair Society meetings or preside over congresses. It was in order to remain within reach of his surgeon that the friends summered at Semmering, two and a half hours from Vienna by car.

Yet, as is also well-known, he took few palliatives for the incessant, often severe pain, the only visible sign of which was, according to Eva Rosenfeld, "an awkward little chewing movement." These privations and the stoic resignation with which he endured them contributed to his almost mythic stature, making those whom he accepted for analysis feel even more privileged. The declining Freud could afford to analyze, and then for a year, or possibly two, only the select few in whom the future of analysis was to be invested. As a result Freud's analysands enjoyed great distinction; their analytic line of descent was considered purest and their training services in turn most coveted.

If personal problems and familial responsibilities had prevented Dorothy's formal enrollment in the Training Institute, the interest she had shown in auditing the Seminar for Child Analysis now worked in her favor. And Anna Freud took care of the rest. As she wrote Eva Rosenfeld, "[Dorothy] would like so much to be entirely a member of our circle and makes such immense efforts with her own self." It is not widely known but Dorothy not only won one of Professor's precious hours but also, as Anna noted much later, "apart from the interruptions caused by his operations on the one hand and the upheavals caused by the Hitler events, emigration, etc., on the other . . . [she] remained in analysis until his death"—twelve years later. With this justification, Dorothy could write, "The years in which I knew him were the most important of my life."

Those twelve years were the years of the visionary prophet captured in Max Pollack's etching; the years of Ferdinand Schmutzer's Old Testament patriarch; of Salvador Dali's extraterrestrial being; of Marcel Steinberger's wizened, hoary image of Pity. They were the late years of the former Jewish medical student who, finding himself expected to feel both inferior and an alien in Catholic Vienna, had refused in the first instance and resigned himself in the second; of a Victorian who had come to view his society of fellows with the benevolent detachment one might reserve for a swarm of protozoa on a microscope slide; of a Victorian who had once described fin de siècle Paris as "a vast overdressed Sphinx"; a Victorian who saw lust in the image of Madonna and Child and counted himself among "fellow unbelievers [who] leave heaven to the angels and sparrows." These were the consummate years of the *gescheiter mensch,* a man of great intelligence, erudition, and insight; the years, also, of an elderly, cigar-smoking Viennese, his hairline retreating behind a lengthening forehead; a small, stooped, lithe, petit bourgeois family man; to Dorothy, a "wonderful, wise and dear" man. For his part, Freud cryptically described Dorothy at the outset of her analysis, in a letter to Lou Andreas-Salomé, as "a quite congenial American woman, an unhappy virgin."

The public and private sides of Freud were dramatized by the two entrances to his Bergasse 19 apartment. Upon reaching the second floor landing, the left-hand door led to the family quarters, the right-hand door to the doctor's consulting room and study. One reason why Dorothy gained access through both doors is the same reason why her only formal account of Freud is so brief: her inbred sense and tact and discretion faithfully served a man who relished his privacy. "During this time," she wrote in 1939, after his death, "I had the opportunity of being in contact with an unusual personality. I felt the greatness of his spirit and the warmth of his feelings, and above all, how he met life. Another quality which I learned to value was his ability to enjoy, whenever there was something to enjoy."

Analysis with Freud and acceptance within the inner circle rooted Dorothy to Vienna with finality. Having been virtually adopted by the Freud family, her future no longer lay in New York with the Burlinghams or Tiffanys. She now knew with certainty: she had left behind her American ancestral identity, two and one half centuries and eight generations in the making. Born to a "lost generation," disaffected from class and country, she had become an expatriate.

As if to stiffen Dorothy's resolve, Katrina Tiffany died suddenly in New York from pneumonia at the age of fifty-one. She had visited the Silber Schlossel in the fall of 1926, in low spirits. She had remained childless, and unhappily so. Charles had publicly maintained that he wanted no children, but considering the pressures on him to produce a male heir, and his childhood bout with mumps, was probably infertile.

He had, at any rate, "taken a gal" on the side, and the marriage was splintering. Katrina had tried unsuccessfully to dispatch the interloper by seeing her socially and publicly scalding her. Katrina died, thought her family, having lost the will to live.

Leaving the Four in Ruth Sweetser's charge, Dorothy had left for New York in April 1927. Katrina had been one of the few people in whom Dorothy had really trusted and confided; in moments of need, she had found herself turning to Katrina more easily than to her own family. A trustee of the Infirmary for Women and Children, a treasurer of the Sunnyside Day Nursery, and a suffragist, she was a precious link to Mama Lou, and Dorothy loved and admired her greatly. The telegram informing Dorothy that Katrina's condition was dangerous had figured in Bob's analysis and been related by Anna Freud in her case study. Wrote ten-year-old Mabbie, "I always hope aunt Katrina would come to life again because then you will be happy again, but you are happy also some time even when she is dead."

The circumstances of Katrina's death, somehow familiar to Dorothy, must have convinced her that the choice she had made was the right choice. On a foreign continent, in an alien milieu, through the most desperate of situations, she had found at last what she had been searching for, "even as a child."

IX

City of My Dreams

T he family in Vienna to whom the Burlinghams were closest, after the Freuds, were the Rosenfelds. The Rosenfelds lived in the suburb of Hietzing at Wattmangasse 11. Valentin ("Valti") Rosenfeld was a lawyer, an unsuccessful one, a socialist who disliked his profession but adored books and was particularly passionate in his pursuit of first edition Goethe, a combination which left his family financially lacking. It was for this reason that Valti's wife, Eva, had taken as a boarder Anna's very first child patient, Minna. Since then, and despite Dorothy's increasingly preemptive friendship with Anna Freud, the Rosenfeld household, which also included a daughter Maëdi and son Victor, had been swelled further by the addition of Vera, another of Anna's little analysands, and Hertha, Eva's young Tyrolean cousin. Others, including Vaslav Nijinski's daughter Kyra, came and went, bringing the Rosenfelds supplemental income or, depending on the arrangement, the cheap labor of an au pair girl or, to use the German, *Haustochter*. Eva proudly described her hostellike home as "our sophisticated replica of the Zellerhaus" (a Berlin institution for homeless children).

At the head of this Zellerhaus stood the *zaftig* figure of Eva herself, sustaining her "vibrating nervous behavior" with constant cups of steaming black coffee. Talkative, energetic, to some overbearing, Eva had a knack for organizing young people into spirited productive groups. "Music was our food of love," she declared, directing from the piano impromptu, larking sing-alongs, winning the affectionate nickname Muschy. Eva was, in her own estimation, the only one of the Freudian inner circle "in no way professionally directed or limited—every subject of knowledge was welcome in our house." Peter Blos saw her as "a resourceful, intelligent, gifted woman who created around her an atmosphere of humanity, culture and music." The Four were immediately drawn to Eva and her *Haustochters,* as Dorothy soon observed. After Mabbie's first overnight visit, when Dorothy and Anna drove to Hietzing to pick her up, she darted onto the balcony shouting, "Hello, hello, I don't want to go home, I want to stay here."

The proximity of the Rosenfeld home proved decisive when Dorothy confronted the dilemma of how to educate the Four properly in Vienna. *Das Bauernhaus* had been a temporary solution at best. The Four needed a comprehensive curriculum, a clear educational philosophy, and rigorous standards applied in a group setting, none of which could be provided by one teacher in *Das Bauernhaus.* Anna Freud later dramatized the situation, writing that Dorothy's "children being American and, worse still, analyzed, experienced a degree of discomfort in the conventional schools of Vienna which threatened to interfere with their intellectual curiosity and pleasure in learning. The—to her obvious—remedy was to found a modern school of her own, a venture not easy to achieve at that period: there was, after all, no place, no house, and there were no teachers." The Four had actually not entered the Viennese school system, as Anna Freud suggested, though a collision of convention and progressive values was inevitable. A teacher was at hand, furthermore, in the person of Peter Blos, and an ideal place existed at Wattmangasse 11. But the kernel of Anna Freud's recollection was incontrovertible: her analytic program for the children was highly progressive for twenties Vienna, and at odds with the rigid, doctrinaire mentality of the educational governors. Should Dorothy subject her children to the analytic bends in shuttling them daily between different cultures, or should she fashion around them an entirely self-sufficient bubble to defy decompression? As Anna Freud observed, to Dorothy the answer was obvious.

Dorothy, Anna Freud, Peter Blos, and Eva Rosenfeld had all met by the winter of 1926–27, and had agreed to found a school supportive of analytic values. A conversation following the meeting had captured their pioneering zeal. Peter had needed a second teacher and had thought of

Erik Homburger, a former schoolmate from their Karlsruhe hometown in Germany. "But," he had warned Anna, "Erik's an artist; he knows nothing of education or teaching . . ."

"So why do you recommend him?" she had asked pointedly.

Blos had not exactly known why but had blurted, "I believe more in gifted people than in trained people." This remark had momentarily frozen Anna because, as it so happened, so did she.

"I would like to meet your friend," she had said.

Dorothy had financed Homburger's trip from Karlsruhe by commissioning portraits of her family. In April 1927, shortly after the death of Katrina Tiffany, the twenty-five-year-old Homburger arrived in Vienna to be interviewed for a teaching post. Author Robert Coles later described him as "a gifted artist; he particularly did etchings, and his subjects were often children; he was widely read, an avid student of history, and a stubborn individualist who was having trouble with his life . . ." Bob, in great excitement, wrote Dorothy in New York, "A friend of Mr. Blos has come and he can draw heads, you know! The Pictures that Mr. Blos showed you one time well! those are the pictures that he made. I wanted to know if he could draw Prof. (Anna Freud's father). Ask A. Freud what she thinks?!" Evidently Anna Freud, Peter Blos, and Dorothy all had a nose for talent because their interviewee turned out to be the young Erik H. Erikson.

After executing his finely rendered pencil portraits, and passing muster, Erikson accepted Dorothy's invitation to spend the summer with the Burlinghams at Semmering, thereby relieving Blos of his masculine role-model duty; indeed, Mabbie would later entertain hopes that Dorothy would marry him. Erikson, at the time, had "hardly any idea who Freud was," and he had never before encountered a self-contained, well-bred American like Dorothy. He observed that she chuckled when amused but never fully laughed, and, more important, was struck by the "strange intimacy," as he put it, which existed between the Burlinghams and Freuds. (Later he realized that it extended to others within the inner circle. Once part of the circle, he recalled, the atmosphere was "unbelievably friendly.")

Anna Freud's thirteen-year-old nephew Ernsti Halberstadt, son of her late sister Sophie, also vacationing at Semmering, recalled a comic image of that intimacy. "The family's Model T Ford was expertly driven by mother," he wrote, referring to Dorothy, "usually loaded beyond capacity with tiers of children (some of them crouching on the floor) . . . This car would negotiate incredibly rough and narrow forest paths and when it came to a standstill it would be put into reverse to ascend even steeper hills."

That magic second summer at Semmering was, however, shattered by the death of Eva's daughter Maëdi in a mountaineering accident, she and a friend having "lost their way and their lives" in western Austria's Salzkammergut. Valti rang Anna Freud, who hastened to Grundlsee, where the Rosenfelds kept a summer cottage. "Anna Freud came," Eva wrote, "and packed up Maëdi's belongings. She knew what had happened to me but [she added, referring to Anna's emotional restraint] she did not suffer with me. She was a friend in need." Tinky recalls the vivid tale that Anna Freud told the children when she returned, about a young girl who went on a hiking expedition and never came back. The children went to sleep thinking the story another of Anna Freud's interesting fictions; the next morning, having subliminally accepted the possibility of such an accident, and thus being better prepared for its actuality, they were told the truth. This was vintage Anna Freud.

When they returned to Vienna at summer's end, Dorothy put up the money for the two-story Norwegian timber schoolhouse constructed in the Rosenfelds' backyard, its diminutive scale suggesting the name the Matchbox School. Years later Eva recalled that "the real spiritual founder of the school is not to be found among the living, for it is in the undying image of my young daughter in whose honor I created the school, and in whose honor I now recall working in it." Fifteen to twenty children were enrolled from families of liberal, cultured backgrounds, and divided into classes that corresponded roughly with the ages of Dorothy's children. Not all were in analysis, nor from analytic backgrounds; the Baers, for example, ran a dance studio in the Laxenburg suburb. However, according to Victor Rosenfeld, the children did promptly split into opposing camps of those in analysis and those not. Joining Bob, Mabbie, and Adelaide on the analytic side, in 1927 and 1932 respectively, were Tinky and Mikey. Also in analysis with Anna Freud were Peter Heller, son of chocolate manufacturer Hans Heller, and Reinhard Simmel, son of Ernst Simmel, founder and director of the first psychoanalytic sanitorium at Schloss Tegel, outside Berlin. Reinhard also boarded at the Zellerhaus, as did Ernsti Halberstadt. Feeling restricted in his stepmother's parochial Hamburg household, Ernsti moved to Vienna in 1928 and went into analysis with Willi Hoffer. Like the Four he was virtually adopted by Anna Freud; later, as W. Ernest Freud, he became an analyst himself.

Though the school functioned under the psychoanalytic aegis, its curriculum was not analytic, and no interpretations were given. The method of study devised by Blos and Erikson was based on the Dalton plan, or Project Method, then gaining popularity. As Eva explained:

> Every child of every age had [a] project to work on, which encompassed a main theme, e.g. England, her history during a certain period, geography, a thorough study of the language, drawing, map-reading, poets and painters, natural and cultural history and so forth. For certain subjects the children would study together and for certain subjects they remained apart. Every month the Headmaster from the local school came to watch and examine their progress so that they should not lose touch with the ordinary requirements of the school authorities. By far the most advanced teaching was accomplished, however, in the arts, owing to the rich gifts and superior interest the Burlingham children showed in drawing, painting and all things visual.

Erikson taught art, German, and history; Blos, geography and nature; Dorothy and child analyst Marie Briehl, English; a Herr Goldscheider instructed the children in Latin, arithmetic, and geometry. The Project Method in turn infused these narrowly prescribed courses of study with an interdisciplinary spirit. One project theme was West Coast, North American Indians; another, for the eleven to fourteen year olds, was the Arctic. During this semester the children dressed like Eskimos, performed Eskimo rituals, made Eskimo art, and sang Eskimo songs; in short, they had a lot of fun. But the theory held that their pleasure acted as a catalyst to learning, that absorption was effortless with their attention thus fully engaged. In the Arctic unit, for example, they covered subjects as diverse as sun clocks, volcanoes, ocean currents, climate, plants and physics, the exploration of Pytheas, ancient world maps, the Vikings, Erik the Red and his sons, Commander Peary, Fridtjof Nansen, the whaling industry, and the biology of whales, dolphins, polar bears, and seals. And, as Erik Erikson recalled in a brief history of the school, "The teacher . . . observed unforgettably what Freud called the *strahlende Intelligenz* (the 'radiant intelligence') displayed by children who for some moments are permitted (by themselves and circumstances) to function freely."

Shortly after the school's October 1927 opening, Mabbie sent her father an enthusiastic letter recounting "an interesting lesson . . . with Herr Erik."

> . . . he read Ighino [a fellow student] and me the storry of how the Ivs [?] thought the world began and then we talked of us people, I said I thought I was ferst a flee then a bee then a cat then a goat then a horse and then a person, and still another way, that when I am dead that my part that makes me move gose to a horse then a goat then a cat then a bee then a flee and that's why the animals can't talk because they should not tell us people that we also one day will be an animal.

It is not known what Robert made of this lesson, which seems to have dealt with creation myths of primitive cultures and transmigration of the soul; but it was pounced upon by the bilingual ten-year-old, who continued to her father:

> Now I am reading a lovly book of a horse it is called "!Smoky!" I go with very often with Erik to the mauseme and he explains the pictures to me and we see all the beautiful colors in one little picture, then I am much more interested in my drawing.

Due to the involvement of Erik Erikson and the prescient emphasis on an unfettered, individualistic, psychologically informed education, there has been a scramble to give and take credit for the Matchbox or Hietzing School. Raymond Dyer, author of *The Work of Anna Freud: Her Father's Daughter,* notes that the school was "associated with Anna Freud's analytical child education group." Undoubtedly the school would not have existed without her influence and guidance; and Anna Freud in turn acknowledged psychoanalytic educators Siegfried Bernfeld and August Aichhorn as her primary pedagogic influences. Aichhorn, for example, was author of *Wayward Youth* (1925), a highly regarded treatise on adolescent delinquency based in part on his experience as head of a Viennese reform school (for a time this book was better known in America than *The Interpretation of Dreams*). There, Aichhorn had replaced blind discipline with psychoanalytically informed applications of freedom; in one instance he exhausted group aggression by allowing it full, violent expression; once vented, the youths turned their energies to productive functions. Another important influence on Anna Freud, one from her preanalytic days, was Dr. Maria Montessori, for her enlightened approach of "freedom within carefully defined limits," and respect for individuality (though Montessori did not, of course, advocate the Project Method, and her Catholicism was at odds with the sexuality inherent in psychoanalysis).

Anna Freud ultimately credited Dorothy for the school's existence, though years later the Rosenfelds bristled at the idea of a "Dorothy Burlingham School." According to Victor Ross,* it was his mother Eva in her role as divinely inspired housemother who "breathed life" into the school, and the "story" that Dorothy had more to do with the school than Eva was "put about" after Eva's death. But Erikson points out that Eva had nothing to do with the curriculum, and Ross concedes that Dorothy's conception and financial backing gave the Hietzing School its start.

Such disputes notwithstanding, the strength of character and resolve required for Dorothy to resist the pressures of conformist society (e.g., the public school system) cannot be overrated; in bypassing the system and entrusting her children to Blos and Erikson, both of whom were untrained and, in Erikson's case, unproven, Dorothy made an essential contribution to the school. Such unconventional instincts placed her in the vanguard of her times, as they had her father before her; and like him, she had the conviction to act on her beliefs. Dorothy would then have been loathe to admit the filial debt, especially one of shared iconoclastic spirit (she undoubtedly saw her life as a departure from the old, but never militantly so). But, as Rod Gilder had guessed, despite Dorothy's antipathy and resistance to her father—or perhaps because of it—he was very much alive and working within her.

In 1918 Louis, then seventy years old, had begun the final phase of his artistic evolution, in bequeathing his beloved Laurelton Hall, its grounds and art collection, along with a million-dollar endowment, to the Louis Comfort Tiffany Foundation, an art school founded "to help young artists of our country to appreciate more the study of nature, and to assist them in establishing themselves in the art world." Nine years before the Matchbox School's founding, therefore, Dorothy's father had conceived

---

*After emigrating to London before World War II, Victor Rosenfeld anglicized his name to Ross. Hence, Rosenfeld will be used only when referring to him before emigration. This also applies to Ernsti Halberstadt, who became W. Ernest Freud.

a school—with no curriculum, no classes, no rules, and no teachers. The young artists (including Bradley Walker Tomlin, Luigi Lucioni, Paul Cadmus, Ilya Bolotowsky, Georgio Cavallon, Chaim Gross, Umberto Romano, and Alan Dunn) arrived at Laurelton Hall to find themselves Mr. Tiffany's "personal guests," served by butlers, and free to work in any way that pleased them. Quite possibly then, the theoretical spirit infusing the Hietzing School may also be traced to Louis and his anti-academicism, even to Louis's conflict with his father, sixty-five years previously, and the Eagleswood Military Academy. It is at least amusing to consider the possibility that if not for the character of Louis Tiffany, Peter Blos might today be a biologist and Erik Erikson a painter of pictures.

Two years after arriving in Vienna Dorothy had neatly wrapped her family in a bubble of self-sufficiency, meeting, insofar as possible, their domestic, familial, therapeutic, and educational needs. Over the winter of 1927–28 the Sweetsers returned to Geneva, leaving Adelaide to continue her analysis with Anna Freud and her studies for an additional year at the Matchbox School. With a diminished household, Dorothy moved for the third time, to Peterjordanstrasse 72, in Vienna's Thirteenth District. Knowing that Vienna and the Freuds were to be their permanent home, Dorothy for the first time let this house unfurnished, and decorated it to her own taste. Unlike the mansions she had previously rented, Peterjordanstrasse 72 was an unpretentious suburban home; it met the family's basic needs but no more. Rather, it reflected a cozy, comfortable, Viennese *gemütlichkeit,* much like that of the Rosenfeld home. (After Mabbie's first overnight visit to Wattmangasse 11, she had gushed about how the Rosenfelds made their own beds and washed their own clothes. "Do you know," she had told her mother, "their house is so small but it is like a castle, it is so big, room for everything. Our house is so big, when you go in one room sometimes there is no one in it, there, whether you go upstairs or down there is always someone there . . .") Peter Blos believes that the new house demonstrated the beginning of the Freudian influence on Dorothy. Initially, he says, she seemed less interested in understanding life than in its "trimmings"—in "organizing it in a big way." Blos, the small-town Weimar product, may speak with some hyperbole when he recalls the "entourage" with which she had arrived, and her "mansion-in-a-park" on Braungasse, and Silbergasse; but his point is fundamentally correct.

Within the Freudian circle, truth evidently lingered in the *Belle Epoque* jingle, *Wien, Wien, nur du allein/Wirst stets die Stadt meiner Traüme sein* ("Vienna, Vienna, you alone will always be the city of my dreams"). Indeed, people tend to recall the circle and the school in fantastic terms, Victor Ross speaking of the "wonderland" in which they all lived and W. Ernest Freud describing the "dream world" of the school. Erik Erikson himself later wrote how Dorothy, Eva, and Anna had together "dreamed up" the school. That the Burlinghams occupied a privileged position even within the school is reflected in the casting of the (first annual) children's Christmas play. The Four were assigned, in descending order of age, the starring roles of Joseph, Mary, Jesus, and an angel, while Victor Rosenfeld and Reinhardt Simmel were cast as shepherds and rabbis. As Dorothy wrote Robert:

> Peter Blos and Erik were responsible for getting it together. Eva did the costumes which consisted of just the things we had in our houses. Herr Winkles played through it on the cello—& Mien Boch at the piano. Peter with Bob's help did the lighting which was beautifully done.
>
> It's going to be done again for Prof. Freud as he could not come, it was so cold then—& everyone told him he should see it. I cannot tell you how lumps came in my throat as I saw Mabbie as Mary rocking the baby—and Tinky as Jesus was so lovely, & preaching in the temple I'll never forget . . . It was beautiful in spirit & in beauty. Mabbie looked like a woman and her beauty was never to be forgotten. Bob was splendid too and Michael adorable.

From their playmates' perspective, the Four seemed to have it all: money, health, talent, good looks and, for them, that rarest of luxuries a motorcar. Hietzing School student Peter Heller recalls, "We children, back in Vienna, all admired the style and grace of the Burlingham family quite uncritically. They were the ruling house in our circle, and to us a model of good taste." To Victor Rosenfeld, the Burlinghams seemed like "pop stars"; their very teeth seemed whiter, their jawline different from the Viennese; they wore the clothing he associated with Hollywood glamour, and seemed filled with a peculiar American confidence in life.

Opinionated and yet well mannered, they were physically stronger and "almost too beautiful." They observed odd occasions like Mother's Day and celebrated an old English Christmas with yule log, carols, acrobats, dancers, boar's head, and mistletoe; they toasted marshmallows and slept under gingham covers; it seemed that they were the only ones in Vienna who had cornflakes for breakfast, bacon with their eggs, and a fireplace in practically every room; "special and strange," they were "objects of interest and veneration." Victor Rosenfeld "learned to love and hate the Burlinghams."

As for Ernsti Halberstadt, they became the subject of his family romance, the idealized family which he fantasized as substituting for his own; and Bob, who seemed to have "a wonderful life without worries and with always something going on," was his ego-ideal. From the shops on the Graben Bob always managed to procure the latest Mickey Mouse and Felix the Cat cartoons, giving shows with his 9.5mm Pathé-Baby projector. He scaled the walls of the Matchbox School, Douglas Fairbanks style, fired blanks at passing vehicles, raced down the Cobenzl—one of Vienna's steepest hills—standing on the seat of his bicycle, used the rim of the Silber Schlossel swimming pool—in winter when drained—to make bank turns, doused a formally attired Peter Blos with bathwater, and once dropped a medicine ball from the top floor of the Diana Baths, the local health club. His high spirits seemed endless, as did his interests, which at a later age turned to cars, photography, and girls. He drew detailed sketches of internal combustion engines, planned a model railway, carried a Leica, developed and printed his own pictures, and flirted madly. Eva's *Haustochter* Hertha Huber was the first of a long succession of girl friends, a love which Victor Ross recalls as being of "long standing" and "fairly passionate."

The bleak interior world of Bob's and Mabbie's analyses, then, as described by Anna Freud, seemed almost unrecognizable beside the enviable world perceived by their contemporaries.

Contributing to this was the natural order of Vienna itself, the sulphur springs, sunbathing, and hiking, and the cultural order of impromptu a capella choirs, politicized youth groups, and street proselytizers. The legacy of the Habsburgs was everywhere and, together with "Herr Erik," the Four plunged into the Belvedere, Hofburg, and Schönbrunn palaces. The young, brilliant Ernest Kris, a newly confirmed memeber of the Vienna Psychoanalytic Society, introduced them to the Kunsthistorisches

Museum, where he was an assistant curator of sculpture and applied arts—appropriately enough, a specialist in cut glass, gems, intaglios, and gold objects. The fairy-land setting and astounding natural beauty of Semmering had also become familiar: during the summer of 1928 the Burlinghams and Freuds for the third consecutive season took the villas Sophie and Schüler.

It was after this summer that Freud wrote his friend Swiss psychiatrist Ludwig Binswanger, "Our symbiosis with an American family (husband-less), whose children my daughter is bringing up analytically with a firm hand, is growing continually stronger so that we share with them our needs for the summer." His use of the word *symbiosis* is interesting, because Freud, as a doctor and vigilant writer, surely intended the biological sense of a close association between different organisms, though not necessarily of benefit to each. At about this time, he nevertheless presented Dorothy with a golden ring set with an ancient Greek intaglio carved in black jasper picturing a chariot and driver. An avid antiquarian, Freud had conceived of this colorful recognition of his closest disciples in 1912, when the "committee" of analysts had been formed (Karl Abraham, Ernest Jones, Sándor Ferenczi, Otto Rank, and Hans Sachs) to deflect from Freud some of the controversy and dissension then wracking the psychoanalytic movement. Freud often seemed to have selected the intaglios with the recipient's personality in mind. Usually they represented one of the Greco-Roman pantheon; and Freud, in full, immodest thrall of his Olympian fantasy, had chosen for himself the graven image of Zeus. The "boyish and perhaps romantic element" which had given rise to the Ring Committee had since broadened to include a few women, among them Anna Freud, Lou Andreas-Salomé, the American analyst Ruth Mack Brunswick, and the great-grandniece of Napoleon I, Princess Marie Bonaparte. Dorothy's chariot and driver would seem to symbolize Dorothy and her Model T Ford; when the stone cracked, Freud replaced it with another, also of black jasper, representing a Viking long ship, testament to the long journey she had taken from her American past.

The morning drives to the Viennese suburbs which had served to introduce Dorothy to Freud continued, and now often included a stop at the kennels at Kragan, dogs having become a sort of common denominator between them. Freud's earliest experience with canines had been Anna's large Alsatian Wolfi, procured shortly before Dorothy's arrival in Vienna to accompany a presumably lonely Anna on her long, solitary strolls at Semmering. As Ernest Jones noted, Jews of Freud's generation usually had "little contact with animals," so for Freud the trips to Kragan and the Semmering pound represented a new interest. Given the fondness of Dorothy's father for dogs, Freud's sudden interest may in part have been calculated as an emotional catalyst for Dorothy's attachment to Freud as a benevolent father-figure, to facilitate a positive transference. It was she who gave him his first dog, a black chow puppy called Lün Yu.

Lün did link Dorothy's future and past, having been acquired through Katrina Tiffany's sister Henrietta Ely, who lived and bred chows in Paris. Since the chow had traditionally been the Chinese emperor's dog, and was marked by its unswerving loyalty to one master, Dorothy must have thought it a fitting companion for the father of a movement which had spawned perhaps more than its share of defectors, the most recent being Otto Rank.

One morning in the winter of 1928/1929, as Professor, Anna Freud, Dorothy, and Wolfi emerged from the street door at Bergasse 19, they unwittingly became the home-movie subject of Phillip Lehrman, one of Freud's analysands-in-training (whose desire to film Freud was interpreted as compulsion). Lehrman caught them again at their destination, a picket-fenced country yard where the pup Lün was quartered that winter, the coldest to hit Vienna in sixty years. Lehrman's footage humanizes Freud. A grandfatherly wisp bundled into a long coat, fur collar, and homburg plays with a passel of dogs while doted upon, it would appear, by his two daughters.

Dogs were the source of much comfort and amusement to the Burlinghams and Freuds. On one occasion after getting lost in the Prater, the large park north of the Danube Canal, Wolfi distinguished himself by jumping into a waiting taxicab. The driver read his tag and returned him to Bergasse 19. "From now on, Wolfi must carry a purse," declared Tinky. As if not to be outdone, a chow later owned by Dorothy once had a false pregnancy, an event duly reported and commented upon by Ernest Jones in his three-volume biography of Freud, with the comment, "Freud . . . must have been amused at this example of the power of wish fulfillment combined with the phenomenon of somatic compliancy." Analyst Felix Deutsch was more direct: "Have you ever heard of a dog with a false pregnancy. I am almost inclined to say: that can only happen to the dog of an analyst!"

Lün was run over during the following summer by a train at the Salzburg railway station, and Freud wrote analyst Max Eitingon in Berlin that the grief which they all felt was similar to that experienced after the loss of a child. The dog had broken free while being escorted home to Vienna by Eva Rosenfeld, whose sorrow was all the greater for having actually lost a child just two years earlier. In addition, this aggravated the injury and feeling of displacement she still suffered over the loss of intimacy with Anna to Dorothy, and a month later Anna wrote her sharply, evidently hoping to jar her from negative emotions, "Why do you play background to Dorothy? And why do you believe that I have only thoughts about Dorothy and want to be reassured only about her condition? Now I don't know at all what goes on in you . . ." This was followed, more kindly, by an offer, made free of charge, to have an analysis with her father, which Eva accepted. Dorothy meanwhile hastily obtained from Henrietta Ely a double replacement: Jo-fi (meaning beautiful in Hebrew) and Lün Yu II, both red chow pups. The second Lün was the dog with the false pregnancy, and the dog to whom Professor found himself humming the aria of Don Giovanni, "A bond of friendship/ Unites us both . . ." To Marie Bonaparte, years later, he explained, "Why one can love an animal like Topsy [her chow] (or Jo-Fi) with such an extraordinary intensity: affection without ambivalence, the simplicity of a life free from the almost unbearable conflicts of civilization, the beauty of an existence complete in itself. And yet, despite all divergence in the organic development, that feeling of an intimate affinity, of an undisputed solidarity."

It was over that summer of 1929 that Freud set down his ideas about these conflicts. They had been brewing, as usual, for some time, had influenced Anna Freud's childrearing philosophy, and were, therefore, put into practice on the Four, influencing and stimulating Dorothy in turn. In *Civilization and Its Discontents* Freud wrote, "The price we pay for our advance in civilization is a loss of happiness through the heightening of the sense of guilt." Freud believed that aggression is innate in man, a by-product of the death instinct he had posited in *Beyond the Pleasure Principle,* and was "the greatest impediment to civilization." He believed that the suppression of aggression is achieved in childhood to the degree that it transfers to the superego, where, as the watchdog of conscience, even uncommitted aggression creates an inescapable sense of guilt: "the price of progress in civilization."

Freud philosophized that civilization, mankind's supreme achievement, itself makes a true, lasting happiness impossible through its demands on our instinctual lives. None of the methods by which mankind strives to win happiness and keep suffering at bay—and among these he includes artistic creation, religion, love, and work—none of these can correct the fundamental condition of civilization which simultaneously permits its forward progress and exacts a toll in human suffering. To Freud, "The fateful question of the human species seems . . . whether and to what extent their cultural development will succeed in mastering the disturbance of their communal life by the human instinct of aggression and self-destruction."

If psychoanalysis could not alter the dynamics of civilization, it did offer certain practical advantages—and for the young especially, advantages with wide cultural implications. Anna Freud's work with children pivoted on softening the demands placed on their instinctual lives, handling them in individually sensitive ways, and replacing authoritarian discipline with a flexible approach based on psychoanalytically informed options.

It happened that Freud wrote *Civilization and Its Discontents* in Berchtesgaden, a beautiful medieval town nestled beneath the jagged, snow-capped peak of Mt. Watzmann in eastern Germany, where some thirty years before he had drafted *The Interpretation of Dreams*. The previous winter, after being fitted for an improved prosthesis, Freud had once again been able to speak without pain, enabling the resumption of scientific discussions with a select group at the Bergasse, and the luxury of a summer beyond the reach of his surgeon. Buoyed by his good health, a coterie of friends and family also planned to visit Berchtesgaden and nearby Salzburg, where the Tenth Annual Mozart Festival would be taking place. Erik Erikson led an advance party of Hietzing scholars to the ancient salt mines, sheer precipices, and dark glacial lakes of the Salzkammergut, where Bob wrote Dorothy, "Now we are on the *Hohen* Salzburg and it is so beautiful here. We can see very far around the country . . . You don't know how I feel. I am all happy and feel just like I feel when I hear music."

Dorothy and Anna had rented Schneewinkel from an eleven-strong family of farmers, the Stockklausers. Once again the Burlinghams and Freuds rented adjoining cottages—chalets actually—on this secluded farm, which Professor described as being "in the middle of the fields in a little corner of forest belonging to it." Among their visitors were Princess Bonaparte and her daughter Eugénie, Max Halberstadt, Gertrude Ely (the middle and politically active of the Bryn Mawr sisters), and Dorothy's old friends the de Forests. Ernsti Halberstadt and Reinhard Simmel were also along, as was Alfred and Izette de Forest's daughter Judy, who had come to live with the Burlinghams and study at the Hietzing School; and the Rosenfelds were at nearby Grundlsee.

Much to the amusement of their Viennese playmates, the Four picked up the Stockklausers' peasant dialect. Wearing dirndls and "antler-stitched" Gams lederhosen, the suspenders hand-embroidered with "Kaiser Blume" flowers, with mid-calf leggings, clogs, loden jackets, and plumed hats, they could easily have been taken for Tyrolean *junge bauern.* "The children have a real paradise here," Anna wrote Eva. It was an unforgettable summer, day-tripping to Salzburg, hiking, harvesting, riding the hay wagon, and singing boisterously from the songbook *Yodlers of the Alps.* At night Mozart's canon echoed between chalets: *"Buona Nox/ Bist a rechter Ochs!/ Buona Notte/ Kleine Motte,"* and later still, the birds and beasts of the forests could have overheard the closing strains of an old Austrian folk song: *"Auf Wieder-Wiedersehen!"*

If the summer of 1929 was the high point of the Burlinghams' Vienna years, it was also the point after which easterly storm clouds threatened to drench their bubble of enchantment. Nineteen twenty-nine was of course the year of the stock market crash, and a boom year for the National Socialists, their seats in the German parliament jumping ninefold between 1928 and 1930. Berchtesgaden, with its exquisite natural beauty, was just the kind of provincial paradise that propagated the most virulent strain of Nazism; indeed, a Nazi was already living openly in town, a major in the German army, and soon the Stockklausers, and millions like them, would join the Nazi Party. Later it was at Berchtesgaden that Hitler would build his Eagle's Nest; and Field Marshal Hermann Göring himself would later buy and renovate the family's beloved Schneewinkel.

The sky began to darken for Dorothy on August 12 when the Burlinghams, Robert and C.C.B., arrived from New York. They had opposed child analysis from the start and had made their views plain. In December of 1925 Robert had sent his father the following note:

What occurs to me is something like this: I believe that as long as [Dorothy] continues to improve under psychotherapy it should be kept up, but I see no reason for keeping the children over there and I would suggest that they come home and remain with me while her treatment is going on . . . I think our attitude should be one of tender solicitude for Dorothy's condition, but at the same time we should make an iron stand on the question of no more psychoanalysis for the children, all four of them, and their return to me while Dorothy is getting the first care she has ever had . . .

Due to Robert's overriding concern for the children's welfare, and his own illness, his position had thus far proved no legal threat to Dorothy, and her aim of minimizing his influence on the Four had been largely successful. The Four remained C.C.B.'s only grandchildren (Charles and Nancy both still being unmarried), and he had not seen them since that fateful spring of 1925. Lately, however, he had stepped up his correspondence, as per the following to seven-year-old Mikey:

I don't know whether you like lions or not. I certainly don't like to see them in small cages, but when they are in a big place where they can move about and have some exercise and enough to eat, I think they are better off than when they are being hunted in Africa with spears and guns. I am sending some pictures of lions on a lion farm out in California, which maybe you will like.

Dorothy had meanwhile been permitting Robert summer visitation privileges. He was again doing well, having taken a research position in the Pathology Department of the Albany City Hospital under Dr. Victor Jacobsen, who "firmly believe[d] that the laboratory side of medicine is where [Robert] is thoroughly at home and hence is where he can do the most constructive work." Erik Erikson had made Robert's portrait in 1927 during his brief stay in Semmering, and a consultation with Professor had resulted in a surprisingly positive diagnosis. Freud had found Robert both likable and well adjusted, which he was, between psychotic episodes. The following year Robert had arrived in Vienna for a longer stay together with C.C.B.'s close friend George Woodward Wickersham, the former U.S. attorney general. This may have been intended as a signal of the Burlinghams' stiffening resolve, as Wickersham was not to be trifled with and would have made an influential witness in court. Robert had suffered more than had Dorothy from the broken marriage as he had been deprived of his children, had neither sought nor found a new mate, and had fallen back on his parents for support. Still in love with Dorothy and devoted to his children, he remained hopeful to the end that they would be reunited, a goal upon which his happiness and self-esteem unfortunately depended. His hopes were reflected by his 1928 Christmas card, a photograph of the family at Semmering, Robert literally at the head of the family as he sat on a fence with Dorothy standing below him, the Four in a descending vertical of grinning heads, ending with little Mikey, kneeling on the grass. William P. Buffum, Jr., middle child of the Providence Buffums, recalls Robert's devotion:

> I remember Dr. Robert very distinctly as a very jovial man delighted to be having a weekend off at Sakkonet. He did the vigorous chores, such as drawing water from my uncle's well, and cranking mother's model T Ford. These events are somewhere in our family movies, or at least very firmly fixed in my memory. I also remember his telephoning . . . Michael on his birthday. This took a lot of planning and impressed me as a very long-long distance telephone call. Yes, missing his children was a great fact of Dr. Robert's life. I remember a lot of talk about and pictures of these children. They were about our ages.

And to Louie Burlingham, William's mother, Constance, had written in 1925:

> I have never known anyone to whom children responded more quickly and with greater affection. My first impression of him was that he was starving (it is the only word that expresses it) for his children and for that reason I gave him ours as much as I could. He had the freedom of the house, [and] when I was not here would frequently come & take my children out to a near-by shop or read to them in the house until I came in. My nurse-maid often spoke of the exceptional way he had with children. On Sunday evenings when she was out he always helped me give the children their supper, and put them to bed, & was a wonderful help to me because he did everything so much more quickly, thoroughly & gently than I did . . .
>
> Often when he first came into the house he would be rather excited and restless but he quickly relaxed in the atmosphere of home life, and

was never irritable with the children, although they often gave him plenty of cause . . .

Between these sympathetically penned lines lurked the reasons for the Burlinghams' resentment of Dorothy. They believed that she had provoked Robert's breakdowns, that (to use an earlier metaphor) she had first driven him "over the precipice" and then starved him of his own children. It was clear to Dorothy that C.C.B. (then president of the New York Bar Association) had in part come to Austria to put muscle into Robert's request for a greater share of his children's time. And, as August 12 approached, Dorothy had grown progressively more upset. Eva Rosenfeld had told her Hungarian friend, musician Marinka Gurewich, that Professor had been pacing his garden. "He's so afraid, so terrified for Dorothy with Robert coming," she had said. According to child analyst Anny Katan, Dorothy "definitely had a great conflict about leaving her husband but felt that she could not have acted otherwise because of the children." Dorothy could not, however, have helped recognizing that Robert's request was not unreasonable.

The Burlinghams' arrival initiated a tense pantomime of colliding values, symbolized, on the one hand, by three-piece Brooks Brothers suits and wool fedoras and, on the other, by the Tyrolean leisurewear of Dorothy, Anna, and the children. According to Judy de Forest Taves, now a Boston-based analyst, Dorothy and Anna were then "down on America and American things," a prejudice partly based on Dorothy's past and present conflicts, and partly acquired from Professor, whose distaste for its materialistic quality was distilled in his quip to Ernest Jones, "America is gigantic, but a gigantic mistake." Nonetheless, judging from C.C.B.'s appointment book for 1929, which now reposes in the Manuscript Division of the Harvard Law School Library, Dorothy did an excellent job of diverting her visitors. She took them to see *Hamlet* in Salzburg's Cathedral Square and Hoffmansthal's *Everyman,* a Festival tradition. She showed them the birthplace of Wolfgang Amadeus Mozart, the Mirabell Palace where the boy prodigy made his debut, the Festival Hall, and the Mozarteum, where they attended performances of *Requiem* and *The Magic Flute.* The Burlinghams visited the summer and winter riding schools, lunched with the wife of the ex-Kaiser, had tea in Berchtesgaden's Grand Hotel with Princess Bonaparte, snacked on chocolate, coffee, pastries, and lemonade at a succession of picturesque cafés, hiked along the Huntersee and Altausee, visited Bishofschofen's Gothic Parish Church, and at night returned not to Schneewinkel, but to Villa Waldrast; there C.C.B. could write *"chez nous."*

The Burlinghams were delighted to see the Four again, C.C.B. especially. "Mabbie lunches with me," he wrote. "Oh, joy, oh rapture!" Bob's fourteenth birthday was celebrated along with his grandfather's seventy-first, at Schneewinkel, on August 25, at a traditional Austrian *geburtstagstisch* or birthday table, set up in the glade between chalets and loaded with gifts. C.C.B.'s appointment book also notes that he hiked along the dark dramatic Königsee with Anna Freud. But nowhere in the book is evidence of the struggle that took place behind the scenes that summer, a struggle that is however made abundantly clear by the notes Robert made after a series of interviews with Professor and Anna Freud. It would appear that Robert made these notes from memory directly after each interview concluded, probably anticipating some sort of legal action. The first interview (between Robert and Anna Freud with Dorothy present) took place on August 26, between eleven thirty and twelve noon.

R.B. to A.F.: I've come to learn from you what progress the children have made with their psychoanalysis during the past year.

A.F. to R.B.: I'd rather know how you think they are.

R.B. to A.F.: Dorothy & I have been talking over their progress this afternoon and Dorothy suggested I confer with you. Let's take up Bob first. Does he show the same tendencies you mentioned last summer?

A.F. to R.B.: I think he is much improved in that respect. Bob is eager to progress, is more open & frank. Finds it easier to get along with other people and with the children at the school.

R.B. to A.F.: Do you agree with Dorothy that puberty is not [*sic*] a period in one's life when children need careful guiding? (To D: I hope I am not misquoting you.)

A.F. to R.B.: Of course I think that period [is] one in which children need especially careful guiding.

R.B. to A.F.: Do you agree with Dorothy that it is unwise for Bob to go to boarding school?

A.F. to R.B.: Yes, I think it would be most unwise to subject Bob to the "temptations" of contact with other boys in boarding school.

R.B. to A.F.: How do you feel about college for Bob?

A.F. to R.B.: That is for him to decide.

R.B. to A.F.: I am not in perfect agreement with you and Dorothy about the education and supervision of the children. I have read some of your books and so am somewhat familiar with your views. Child guidance is your special field. I am a layman as to psychoanalysis. I rather hesitate to express my views, but it strikes me that boys need contact with other boys, and that a father is best fitted to guide his sons throughout their developmental period. Do you think that Bob's work in life should be music?

A.F. to R.B.: That is for him to decide.

R.B. to A.F.: Dorothy has told me that she intends to lay more emphasis on sports for Bob during the coming winter. I think that [is] an excellent idea & though I consider Bob a high strung & sensitive boy, he is muscularly-wirey. Have you anything further to add about Bob?

A.F. to R.B.: I think that covers the situation as regards Bob.

R.B. to A.F.: Let's take up next Mabbie's progress during the past year. Mabbie is an affectionate, sensitive, exquisite little spirit, and I am entirely satisfied with our relationship, in fact with my relationship to all our children. Does Mabbie continue to go to you for psychoanalysis?

A.F. to R.B.: Yes, for a period of a week at a time, followed by an interval of say three weeks, though I keep in touch with her, through Dorothy.

R.B. to A.F.: Dorothy feels sure that Mabbie has begun to menstruate, so I am particularly glad that Dorothy & Mabbie are so close to one another, as I think a young girl needs her mother particularly at this time. I am of the opinion that Mabbie should be seen by a physician who can consult with Dr. Friedjung regarding her posture, eyes & lumps.

A.F. to R.B.: Mabbie is under Dr. Friedjung's care . . .

R.B. to D.B.: If you have no objections, I should like to speak to "Miss Anna" alone for a few minutes. (Exit Dorothy.)

R.B. to A.F.: Dr. Amsden wrote me a long letter before I sailed, saying that after conferring with your father, you & Dorothy, he had gathered that your united opinions were that following my visit of last summer, the children had a shock of excitement which had lasted into the winter & even into early spring. Is this your opinion?

A.F. to R.B.: Yes.

R.B. to A.F.: Did you consider that excitement physiological or pathological? It strikes me that when I see the children for such a brief period & then but once a year at the most, it is only natural that they should anticipate my coming with a certain amount of joy. Of course, I believe there are other factors responsible for any observed excitement.

A.F. to R.B.: The children sense your relations with Dorothy.

R.B. to A.F.: Do you consider, as Dorothy does, that the children have been unduly excited by my presence this summer?

A.F. to R.B.: No. I think their "reaction" has been much more "normal."

R.B. to A.F.: I hope my having asked Dorothy to allow me to speak to you alone has not upset her.

A.F. to R.B.: Oh no, that's quite all right.

R.B. to A.F.: Thank you very much for interrupting your typewriting so that I might have this opportunity to learn your views. You can count on me to cooperate with you. Without that (my cooperation) you cannot accomplish much. I have a deep responsibility to Dorothy & our children which is a bit difficult to fulfill at 4,000 miles. I am pleased at the progress Dorothy has made during the past five years in her relations to our children.

Your father said he would return from motoring about noon, and that he would see me. Would you be good enough to find out if it is convenient?

A.F. to R.B.: Certainly.

The interview with Freud began immediately, and lasted until twelve thirty.

S.F.: Good morning. Have a cigar?

R.B.: Thanks, but it's a bit too near lunch. (S.F. takes out & looks at watch to see if it's too near lunch.) Where would you like to sit? In your office or on your porch?

S.F.: Wherever you prefer.

R.B.: What sort of progress has Dorothy made during the past year?

S.F.: She has improved very much, but she is a very difficult case.

R.B.: Is it your opinion that my presence this summer has unduly excited Dorothy?

S.F.: Your presence is a "temptation." I am trying to teach Dorothy self-mastery. [Her] life is made up of many interests, art, music, children, work, gardening, but when Dorothy wishes sex[ual] satisfaction with you there's no reason why she shouldn't have it. She has a conflict [however] between her physical desires to return to you and her judgment.

R.B.: Do you consider psychoanalysis a barrier between us?

S.F.: No, but your attitude towards psychoanalysis Dorothy may well consider a barrier.

R.B.: I am impressed by Dorothy's poor condition. Do you not believe that it would be advisable for her to see an internist in consultation with you? I suggest Dr. Wilhelm Schlessinger at Vienna. I believe that Dorothy should be built up physically. By the way, how are her gall bladder attacks?

S.F.: Dorothy's physical condition will never improve until her emotional life is stabilized. I do not believe she has any gall bladder disturbances.

R.B.: Possibly spastic?

S.F.: Yes. When you are about, Dorothy has severe diarrhoea.

R.B.: Mucous colitis?

S.F.: I don't know.

R.B.: Do you give her anything for it, such as bismuth?

S.F.: No.

A third interview took place the following day in a hostile atmosphere, C.C.B. joining Robert and Professor.

C.C.B.: What is your diagnosis of Dorothy's condition?

S.F.: Hysterical or obsessive neurosis, with fear.

R.B.: Just what did you mean yesterday, when you told me you were teaching Dorothy to control her sex [ual] feelings. Am I to understand that you are attempting to come between Dorothy and me?

S.F.: I never come between husband and wife.

C.C.B.: What about the children returning home?

S.F.: That is a legal matter.

C.C.B.: Dorothy has at times thought that we might kidnap the children. You consider us gentlemen, do you not?

S.F.: Dr. Burlingham is a gentleman, but you are a lawyer.

The interview ended on this note, and when Robert and C.C.B. left Berchtesgaden two days later the entire Freud circle breathed a collective sigh of relief. Unbeknownst to them, however, a sequel was unfolding to the west, one indicated by C.C.B.'s appointment book. Peter Blos has not forgotten the visitors who arrived unexpectedly on the doorstep of his parents' home in Karlsruhe, Germany, where he was spending the summer. "August 29 to Karlsruhe, Hotel Germanea," noted C.C.B. "August 30 walk w/ Peter Blos." Due perhaps to the elapse of more than half a century, Blos recalls Robert as "a Fifth Avenue lawyer" accompanied by "an attending psychiatrist." Their purpose, however, was and remains clear to him. They had come to enlist his support for the return of at least some of the children to America, probably the boys. But, when Blos flatly refused to help them, they had little choice but to return to their hotel and, after short visits with friends in Paris and London, they sailed via the White Star Line *Olympia* for New York, arriving in Black Point on September 26, less than a month before the stock market crash.

By then Dorothy and the Four had met their American cousins, the Gilders, in Mont-Dore, France, where longstanding arrangements had been made for the asthmatics, Bob, Mabbie, and Joy Gilder, to breathe the fabled health spa gases. (Tinky, the only one of the Four who was allergy-free, remained in Berchtesgaden, drying mushrooms with Freud's wife Martha, called Frau Professor.) Photographs taken that summer by Max Halberstadt confirm Robert's observation of Dorothy's poor physical condition, alluded to also by Anna Freud in her September 30 letter to Eva Rosenfeld, in which she rebuked Eva for believing her to be concerned only with Dorothy's condition. The drawn, gaunt expression in some of the photos indicates a state close to nervous exhaustion, a state perhaps caused by the emotional conflicts surfacing in her analysis, but also no doubt exacerbated by Robert's presence that summer. Professor's and Robert's exchange on Dorothy's health actually drew a neat illustration of Freud's departure from the medical establishment on the subject of (what Freud would have termed) psychosomatic illness. In his view a medicated remedy for an emotionally caused sympton merely complicated the dissection of the underlying cause, a position which, in Dorothy's case, was being practiced without deviation. Spas were acceptable, however, if bismuth was not, and Dorothy was no doubt also benefited at Mont-Dore. The entire family needed to unwind from the Burlinghams' visit. They rode donkeys, and celebrated Bob's birthday a second time at the Château d'Ex. Dorothy's recollection of it as one of the nicest of Bob's birthdays indicates her attitude toward the first, dual celebration at Schneewinkel. After a visit to Henrietta Ely in Paris, they returned with Jo-fi and Lün Yu II to Vienna, where the Burlingham-Freud symbiosis intensified.

T hat fall Dorothy moved once again, this time to an apartment, her first since the Osborne in New York. Five blocks north of the Ringstrasse, Bergasse descended sharply from the twin spires of the Votive Church down a cobbled thoroughfare of shops and apartments to the Tandelmarkt—a flea market sprawled along the banks of the Danube Canal. Sandwiched between Siegmund Kornmehl's butcher shop and a food coöp, No. 19 was an ordinary-looking apartment house in the neo–Renaissance style of the 1870s, five stories high, with triangular lintels surmounting bay windows, a heavy oaken door leading to a typically cool, dark, tiled porte cochere, through which horses had once trudged to a carriage house in back. This apartment house on Bergasse had been home to the Freuds since the year of Dorothy's birth, and it was the home that Dorothy would always love best, the dwelling which "somehow . . . fitted all our needs."

No longer would Dorothy have to shuttle her family daily between the Thirteenth District and the Ninth. Though half the size of the Freuds' second-floor suite, the eastern wing on the fourth floor was wonderfully close to Professor's and Anna's consulting rooms. After a skillful renovation by architect Felix Augenfeld, a friend of Freud's, there was space for all five Burlinghams, Judy de Forest, two live-in maids, and a governess. Being American, they "naturally" required the installation of a fireplace, and replacement of the antiquated plumbing and wiring (the renovation solving the bedbug problem, which continued to plague their neighbors, the Freuds included). Taking the damp northern-exposure bedroom over-looking the courtyard for herself, Dorothy saved the sunny rooms facing Bergasse for her children—a noble gesture, though, considering her physical condition, a risky one. In order to chat privately with Anna after retiring for the night, Dorothy connected a direct telephone line between their bedrooms.

To further relieve her responsibilities Dorothy hired a chauffeur, an English teacher, and a governess for the children: in order, Herr Wimmer, Joan Serson, and Margot Goldschmidt. Joan Serson, a Canadian artist taking dance lessons at the Baers' Laxenburg studio, soon became Doro-thy's good friend, the head of the Hietzing School English Department, and Mrs. Erik Erikson. Margot Goldschmidt, the children's companion, was studying to be a Montessori teacher in a class with Erik Erikson. An inspiring, free-spirited Berliner, she tested Dorothy at every point—premarital sex, socialism, the Bauhaus, all of which she herself endorsed—earning the sobriquet "my revolutionary daughter." Margot soon discov-ered, however, that unlike her former employer, Ruth Sweetser, through whom she had been recommended, she could not "wrap Dorothy around her little finger."

The Bergasse apartment, chauffeur, English teacher, and children's companion collectively served to free blocks of Dorothy's time so that her psychoanalytic training could begin. In addition to the now legendary Wednesday evening meetings of the Society, there were courses three nights a week, technical seminars for both adult and child analysis, and a burgeoning literature to absorb. As Tinky says of this period, "We missed our mother."

Like a medical internship, Dorothy's practice began while still in training, and her Bergasse dining and living rooms were doubled as waiting and consulting rooms—a blind girl and August Aichhorn's son Walter among her first analysands. Her personal analysis with Freud meanwhile shifted to a training analysis, a difference only in its coinci-dence with her studies at the Institute. Dorothy had evidently returned from Mont-Dore in an improved condition, as Anna Freud wrote Eva Rosenfeld, ". . . from Dorothy herself I know that she has again come out of her state and I believe all further matters will go well from now on." This proved to be wishful thinking, however. Judy de Forest Taves recalls the Bergasse as "a pretty gloomy place" throughout the year she remained there. Dorothy apparently fell into black moods while reliving childhood sorrows in analysis, at which time Margot Goldschmidt was obliged to whisk the children away on a *nacht wanderung,* an overnight hike. Dorothy also suffered from the sudden death during the summer of 1928 of Bob's friend Harold Sweetser, stricken by polio while visiting Semmering with the Burlinghams. All the children had come down with colds, but Harold's had worsened while under Dorothy's care and infantile paralysis of the throat had set in. By the time the Sweetsers arrived from Geneva, their son could no longer speak.

Harold's death may have followed on the heels of another tragedy, one recalled by analyst Muriel Morris Gardiner. Gardiner was an American heiress who later became a director of the Freud Archives, but is more widely known for her courageous role in the Austrian anti-Fascist underground, as fictionalized by Lillian Hellman in *Pentimento* and brought to the screen as *Julia.* According to Gardiner:

> I had gone to Vienna in the fall of 1926, and when I moved into my own apartment in the fall of 1927 I needed a cook-housekeeper. My analyst, Ruth Mack (later Ruth Mack Brunswick), told me that she knew of one who was leaving Dorothy Burlingham's employ. This woman was named Mina. Her last name, I think, was Dorn. I know I spoke to [Dorothy] on the telephone about her and may even have talked with [Dorothy] in person, getting a reference. She often spoke of "Mrs. Burlingham," but the only thing I remember of significance was that she told me that Mrs. Burlingham had, through no fault of her own, hit and killed a child while driving her car. Mina said that Mrs. Burlingham never got over this.

Tinky, for one, never learned of this incident. Given the primary source—that is, the cook-housekeeper—it could well have been apocryphal in the sense of explaining Dorothy's evident unhappiness. Few people besides the Freuds knew Dorothy's background, and that was the way she preferred it. But many wondered at her sadness. On the other hand, if the incident was real, it may have coincided with Dorothy's switching analysts from Reik to Freud in early 1927.

After the eventful summer, Freud had evidently deemed it wise to step up Dorothy's program of "self-mastery"; thus, the beginning of her formal studies at the Institute before her neurosis had been resolved. As Freud saw it, Dorothy's independence from Robert could never be assured without the sublimation of her sexual drive. By this he did not, of course, mean the repression of sexuality, but rather "the transformation of object [directed] libido into narcissistic libido." As he explained, "The man who is predominantly erotic will give first preference to his emotional relationships, to other people; the narcissistic man, who is inclined to be self-sufficient, will seek his main satisfactions in his internal mental processes." The cornerstone of Freud's self-mastery program for Dorothy, then, was an intellectual preoccupation so engrossing as to reroute her sexual drive. Desexualization is not an attractive concept, but that was nonetheless Freud's intent. His denials to Robert aside, he was raising an absolute barrier between husband and wife.

As to the nature of Dorothy's neurosis, Freud's response to C.C.B. was not particularly illuminating. The duration of her analysis itself indicates "a very difficult case," and his diagnosis of an "hysterical or obsessional neurosis, with fear," means anything and nothing. Freud held that human sexuality is diphasic: a period of sexual dormancy, or latency, separating childhood sexuality from the drive which begins, or rather resumes, at puberty. Neuroses, in the Freudian scheme of things, are invariably acquired in the "early sexual efflorescence," when the ego is relatively weak in its relations with the id; and the specific neurosis, whether hysteria, obsessional, or paranoia, is determined by the stage at which development is thwarted, causing a fixation at that point in time. Difficulties encountered later in life may cause the individual to regress to that stage, which is identifiable through the symptomatology. Freud likewise traced the development of the normal individual to sexual conflicts in childhood, the ego's mastery of instinct creating character.

After two years of in-depth analysis it is highly unlikely that the father of psychoanalysis was unable to determine whether Dorothy's neurosis was of the hysterical or obsessional type. He clearly intended to reveal nothing that might be used against Dorothy in a custody suit. Knowledge of Dorothy's personality and childhood does make it possible, however, to hazard the proposition that Dorothy's neurosis was of the obsessional type, which Freud called "unquestionably the most interesting and repaying subject of analytic research."

Of the five stages through which Freud saw childhood sexuality passing, the auto-erotic, narcissistic, oral, "anal-sadistic," and phallic, it is to the anal-sadistic stage that the obsessional neurotic regresses, a time when the child's aggressive impulses surge to the fore and sexuality is localized in anal-eroticism. The anal-sadistic stage lies relatively late along the developmental path, which continues through the phallic and oedipal phases to the formation of the superego, at which time, by the sixth year, the sexual slumber of latency sets in, the child's nascent conscience banishing all memory of its early sexuality. Thus, in the Freudian schema, the occurrence of an obsessional neurosis could have coincided with the trauma of Annie's death and Dorothy's subsequent mistreatment by her nanny.

In the obsessional neurotic, wrote Freud, "the ego-ideal displays particular severity and often rages against the ego in a cruel fashion." Dorothy suffered lifelong from feelings of inferiority, and the unhappy American who had arrived in Vienna (with bobbed hair) yet was desirous of the husband she had left behind, recalls (as Freud wrote in his classic monographs) the typical obsessional neurotic with "a strong affinity" with masculinity, at least more so than the hysterical neurotic with an "affinity with femininity," who is "openly afraid of the sexual function." Other obsessional traits are ambivalence (Dorothy was torn as late as 1932 by urges to return to America, and to Robert), and the ego-defensive mechanism of reaction formation. Aghast at the id's regressive anal-sadistic tendencies, the ego of the obsessional neurotic often demands scrupulous cleanliness and order, conscientiousness, sympathy or altruism. Dorothy's pilgrimage to Vienna—for "Bob's sake"—may in this context have been an obsessional act geared to protect him from her unconscious hostility toward him, as a male who had inherited qualities from both her father and husband. Additionally, the twelve-year duration of her analysis may further indicate an obsessional neurosis, as Freud had described it clinically in the year of Dorothy's arrival in Vienna as "a problem . . . not yet . . . mastered," that is, one which he had not yet pursued to a conclusive understanding. Finally, the following, in Freud's 1913 paper, "The Disposition to Obsessional Neurosis," binds this type of neurosis together with the intellectual preoccupation which led Dorothy to the Vienna Psychoanalytic Society.

. . . we often gain an impression that the instinct for knowledge can actually take the place of sadism in the mechanism of obsessional neurosis. Indeed it is at bottom a sublimated offshoot of the instinct of mastery exalted into something intellectual, and its repudiation in the form of doubt plays a large part in the picture of obsessional neurosis.

Dorothy's sublimation also reflected a Freud family practice, and was a link to father and daughter. Because psychoanalysis lays so much emphasis on sex, much has been made of Professor's own sex life. But his belief in the sexual etiology of neurosis did not generate as much enthusiasm for genital love as one might suppose. His prodigious capacity for work alone makes it unlikely that his exploration of sexuality took frequent physical form. He was frank about the midlife death of coital relations with his wife, Martha Bernays, was critical of Wilhelm Reik's advocacy of the curative powers of the "perfect orgasm," and frowned on sexual permissiveness, once writing the American psychiatrist James Jackson Putnam, "I stand for a much freer sexual life. However, I have made little use of such freedom . . ." As for Anna Freud, there was in her truly something of the virgin schoolmarm, an ascetic, moral puritanism that her former analysand Peter Heller calls her "spinsterish holiness." "She was very strong when it came to demanding and furthering sublimation," recalls Professor Heller. "She was not really friendly to sexuality." She disliked kissing or being kissed and, in her eighty-seven-year lifetime, there is no incontrovertible evidence of her having had sexual relations with anyone. This was surely the ulterior point of a remark made by old guard analyst Eduard Hitschmann at a meeting of the Vienna Psychoanalytic Society. Leaning toward Richard Sterba he said caustically, pointing to Anna's chair, "There Freud sat and taught us the *drives,* and now Anna sits there and teaches us the *defenses.*"

Anna's sexuality was, in fact, a cardinal point of worry for Freud in regard to her. In the spring of 1927, when Dorothy had replaced Eva in Anna's affections, he had written Lou Andreas-Salomé about Anna, "Since the poor heart must absolutely have something, it clings to women friends, one taking the place of another." Then, in December, he had added, "Anna is splendid and intellectually independent, but [has] no sexual life. What will she do without her father [i.e., when I am gone]?" And finally during the spring of 1936, in a letter to writer Arnold Zweig,

Freud, referring to Anna, would return to the same worrisome theme of the "passionate woman [who] almost wholly sublimates her sexuality."

S urely it was not to interrupt her analysis at a crucial juncture that Dorothy left Vienna with the Freuds on May 4, 1930, for an expected six-week stay at Ernst Simmel's psychoanalytic sanatorium at Schloss Tegel on the outskirts of Berlin. The purpose of this visit was to have Freud fitted with another prosthesis, but this took much longer than expected. While Dorothy was away Margot and the girls remained at the Bergasse, the boys visited "Tante Evechen" and "Onkel Valti" Rosenfeld in Hietzing, and each child in turn visited Dorothy, Anna, and Professor at Schloss Tegel.

Anna continued to view Dorothy's progress optimistically in correspondence with Eva Rosenfeld. From Tegel she wrote, "Dorothy is now confronted with writing her final rejection to Robert. But even that does not daunt her." This, evidently, was Dorothy's response to the events at Berchtesgaden and Karlsruhe, of which she was surely now aware. Though Robert refused to be rebuffed, the act may have served a therapeutic purpose in clearing Dorothy's mind of any lingering ambivalence toward him. As Anna indicated between the lines and with evident satisfaction, Dorothy was burning her bridges.

Dorothy returned to Vienna on June 24 after Mabbie developed appendicitis. Anna wrote Eva, "Dorothy departed yesterday in a hurry, the final decision about the operation is being made right now in the afternoon. Dorothy is quite calm and reasonable and all must go well." A few days later she wrote again. "Mabbie, apparently, is already feeling very well again; I spoke to Dorothy and she sounds quite calm and reassured. If only there will be no new obstacles . . ."

This last, wistful note would seem expressive of a more tenuous state of affairs for Dorothy and the Four than Anna Freud liked to admit, even to an intimate such as Eva Rosenfeld. While in Tegel she had described Bob to her as "radiant and blossoming," adding, "One could take pictures of him for an advertisement; 'Before analysis . . . and after.' " But just as Anna Freud's early dark diagnosis of Bob had not jibed with the outward impression he had made on his playmates, this updated sunny portrait does not correspond with that evoked by at least one female contemporary, Judy de Forest, who, toward the end of her Bergasse stay became his girl, succeeding Eva's *Haustochters,* Hertha Huber, Ann Neederhoud, and Kyra Nijinski. Judy remembers Bob as "a conceited egoist who thought he was great." While acknowledging his musical talent and good looks, she says he was "difficult and had lots of problems." The observation is interesting in that Bob's problems were now manifesting themselves outside of his relationships with his mother and analyst, and, significantly, in his dealings with a girl friend. It is surely no coincidence that the positive view of Bob emerges from the recollections of his male contemporaries, Ernsti Halberstadt and Victor Rosenfeld, who were united in their awe of his conquests. In other words, fourteen-year-old Bob's promiscuous pursuit of the female gender seemed calculated to impress everyone but the girl in question and, perhaps, himself.

The "obstacles" Anna Freud so fervently hoped to avoid for Dorothy and the children were to a life-style being cultivated on visits to regions like the Salzkammergut-Hohe Tavern, and one reflected in their Tyrolean clothing, hand-painted folk furniture, and their disavowal of anything artificial or unnatural, a life-style that pivoted on an idealized vision of the *bauern,* the peasant farmer. Peter Heller writes that "the [Hietzing] school, like the Burlinghams themselves, cultivated the opposite of what an ordinary person might think of as luxury, namely: simplicity, understatement, restraint, and homespun materials, a stylization in the direction of the expensively unpretentious." This was an extension, really, of the characteristic manner in which Dorothy and her sisters had underplayed the Tiffany life-style, always dressing down, down-scaling, simplifying their lives and personal appearances. When Judy de Forest had arrived from America in January 1929, her lips painted like ripe cherries, her clothes fashionable, her soul evidently bereft of analytic enlightenment, Dorothy was quick to remark how "unnatural" she had become. The censure behind the remark "crippled" Judy, who began a six-month analysis with Anna Freud and changed herself in order to be accepted by her peers.

At the end of Judy's stay in Vienna, Izette de Forest was summoned to Tegel for a conference in which she was "scolded" by Anna Freud for her contribution to Judy's neurosis, an incident emblematic of the philosophic friction building between Freud and Izette's mentor, Sándor Ferenczi. Toward outsiders and those with differing perspectives, clearly,

Dorothy and Anna had little patience. Peter Heller, who later came to know Dorothy as his mother-in-law, recalls her as "always well-intentioned, generous and high-minded," but notes that their relationship was "always one of respect rather than of intimacy, and not without ambivalence. I found her difficult to talk to, and opinionated, even to the point of intolerance."

The Burlingham-Freud quality of life is obviously best measured at its core by the attainment of those who were living it. While Dorothy was at Tegel all four children corresponded with her on a regular basis. These letters are not only fascinating, but in representing the voices of some of the first children to be psychoanalyzed, they are historic. Of these, Mabbie's reflected Dorothy's and Anna's vision most vividly. The angel girl was closest to her mother, and her identification with and belief in their analytic life-style was axiomatic. Mabbie's sensitive empathy also contributed to making her a virtual ambassador of child analysis, a paradigm of the pedagogic analysis envisaged and practiced by Anna Freud. Mabbie in addition had the gift of creative expression; in her own phrase, "the thoughts come like Cornflakes." When English would not serve, she switched to German, sometimes mixing the two languages to create expressions. Her candor and lack of inhibition is startling; nothing seems to have been withheld. Yet the touching honesty of Mabbie's struggle to know herself was overlayed by a burden of responsibility thrust upon her by leading the examined life. She had just celebrated her thirteenth birthday when she wrote, on psychosomatic symptoms:

> Yesterday night and in the morning I had everything of my old pretends. I coughed, blew my nose, had pains in my legs and wheezed [asthma]. I always make believe (but really believe it) that the others don't like me so then I can go to you [in Berlin]. Last night I wheezed. I also dreamed and wanted to ask Margot [Goldschmidt] if I coughed. I thought I did.

In the second week of June Peter Blos took some of his Hietzing pupils on a *nacht wanderung* to the village of Hallstatt in the Salzkammergut, where Mabbie wrote:

> We walked on into another pasture where there was a big herd of oxen and two cows which were always being married. I began to cough but it stopped when I thought it was like me between so many boys.

Back in Vienna she wrote:

> I know most of my trouble must hang together with Daddy because I dreamed about it . . .

On her mother's childhood:

> Sometimes when I look at the pictures of you when you were little I think if I had lived then, I would have been so nice to you so you wouldn't be so unhappy.

On inner conflicts:

> I feel so pullen here and there and don't know on which side I belong.

On analysis:

> It's really nice we have analysis because we could never have written so nicely to each other. I wonder what I would have been without [analysis]. Analysis makes me much nearer to you.

On being her mother's favorite:

> I think you like me best so I like it because before I always wanted to be the only child and get all the love but now . . . I hate it. I think it's a mean and greedy thought.

On Anna Freud:

> How is Anna Freud? Sometimes I could love to have a lesson [analytic hour] with her. But not always. When I think that I usually write to you . . .

> I would like Anna Freud to read my letters but when I think of her reading them I get shy so I thought I won't write it to you [that Dorothy should show Anna Freud her letters], you will do it anyhow.

> When I saw Tinky got a letter from AF I also wanted one but always after that time I have forgotten the very interesting and important thing

I wanted to tell her [Anna Freud]. It's so blöd [silly]. I also am shy of her. But when I write to you some of it is meant for her but really most[ly] for you. It's just like getting a heap of stones off me when I write to you because I think very often in daytime or in the evening, this I must write to Mother, and when I write all the rememberings fall off.

In another letter Mabbie realized she was writing her mother mostly gossip while saving the important (analytic) material for Anna Freud. Struck by this "injustice" to her mother, thinking that it made her jealous, Mabbie began to founder in a sargasso of potential unconscious motives:

Today I have written mostly gossip but the other [things] I have written to Anna Freud. But that doesn't matter because another time I'll write it to you. I hate to write gossip (as Margot calls it) it's most awful. I think you will be jealous of Anna Freud. I am really so queer, I don't write her a letter if not to you . . . Oh it's awfully blöd because everything has its unknown reasons. I with my many troublys and unknown reasons. Everything has an unknown reason. Oh reason after reason, everything with its reasons. It nearly makes me mad. Wide shoes have it, fears have it, things with Daddy and you have it, well . . . nearly everything. But hard to live with these sogenannte [so-called] reasons, it is not only sometimes.

Mabbie's confusion must have been glaringly obvious to her analyst. Indeed it seems that Dorothy and Anna had deliberately cultivated the *bauern* life to counterbalance these analytic complexities. Anna had written Eva Rosenfeld, perhaps as early as July of 1928, "The schoolhouse must only be the beginning; we must have something far more beautiful to share, with all the girls and all the children. Do you think this might come true some day? This would then be your schoolfarm [evidently Eva's original idea for the Hietzing School]."

Dorothy's and Anna's abhorrence of unnaturalness and artificiality in others may have stemmed from a deficiency in their own lives. It was back in 1925, in the Preface to August Aichhorn's *Wayward Youth,* that Professor had referred to healing as one of the "impossible professions," a categorization that obviously extended to psychoanalysis, perhaps particularly so. The intense microscopic scrutiny of others and oneself, day in and day out, was simply not healthful and, to Dorothy and Anna, the pursuit of naturalness and simplicity appeared to be the necessary antidote.

As Marie Antoinette and her ladies-in-waiting had once escaped the mannered court life at Versailles by dressing as shepherdesses and milk-maids in the Petit Trianon, so did Dorothy and Anna (and the children) need to escape the labyrinthine introspection at the Bergasse. This aspect of the *bauern* quest was not lost on Margot Goldschmidt, whose comment to Mabbie was relayed to Dorothy at Tegel. "Margot is all against you," snitched Mabbie, "She . . . says that even if we wear dirndls and have *bauernfurnitur* we won't be *bauern*."

The summers at Semmreing, Berchtesgaden, and Grundlsee had, never-theless, inspired Dorothy and Anna sufficiently to begin searching for a real farm. The first move in this direction was a rented weekend cottage in the countryside beyond Vienna called Neuhaus; Margot and the Four moved there in the spring of 1930 while Dorothy was still at Tegel, and they seemed to love it. Mabbie sent Dorothy a cartographic rendering of its flowering gardens; Tinky drew the house. But as Anna would later cryptically write Eva, "Neuhaus was not beneficial to Dorothy." Thus the Burlinghams spent their second consecutive summer in the Salzkam-mergut, again in a chalet adjacent to the Freuds, but along the mirror-smooth Grundlsee. In September Margot Goldscmidt hiked with the children through the Gesäuse en route to Vienna, reporting to Dorothy, "I wished you could have seen us walking along with our big 'ruck̈sacke' through this wonderful part of the world. The children were *fabelhaft* [marvelous], never tired and so free and happy . . . The only thing was, it was too short. When they really began to feel how one must feel when one is living a natural life, we had to go back."

Dorothy was meanwhile driving Anna in her new Daimler through Switzerland and Italy; then, in late 1930 they bought Hochroterd, a six-acre farm in the Wienerwalk above Mauer, forty-five minutes from Bergasse by car.

Professor's deteriorating health would cancel any further forays to remote regions, making Grundlsee the last enchanted Salzkammregut summer. Managed by Fritsl and Josefa Fadenberger, the tenant farmer and his wife, Hochroterd (High Red Earth) had a glorious view over a valley of woods and fields that ascended to distant rolling tiers of blue-misted mountains. Come that next summer, 1931, the two families rented adja-cent villas in the Viennese suburb of Pötzleindorf, in the Eighteenth District, while Dorothy and Anna commuted to Hochroterd, spending every spare moment there. They stabled a cow and housed a flock of chickens, renovated and furnished the *bauernhaus,* adding an L-shaped wing for the children.

Having burned her bridges, Dorothy literally began to put down roots. The planting began: oats, cucumbers, beans, peas, tomatoes, clover, carnations, and roses; below the two-story stucco farmhouse, pear trees and a rock garden. To Dorothy Anna declared, "I like it about farm life that it brings down to a simple formula, even psychic things." Seven years commenced, years of planting, harvesting, weaving, preserving, canning, milking: fruitful years in more ways than one.

X

A Trustworthy Witness

Even as Dorothy shot roots into Austrian soil, winds were eddying nervously overhead, gathering a force to loosen even the oak's tenacious grip on the land. As if to illustrate the eternal struggle between the life and death instincts posited by Freud, Dorothy's professional work bore its first fruit while the sky seethed. She became a member of the Vienna Psychoanalytic Society, wrote up her early clinical observations, collaborated with Anna Freud. But even before Anschluss, the joining of Nazi Germany and Nazi Austria, her dream city had turned nightmarish, and the lovingly wrought bubble of enchantment had burst around her head.

In May 1931, the same dark hand that had humbled the New York Stock Exchange, inaugurating the Hooverville era in America, reached across the Atlantic and collapsed Austria's greatest banking institution, the Rothschilds' Kreditanstalt. Overnight the painstaking gains made by the Austrian Republic in the years following the war were erased, and the country once again plunged into an abysmal economic crisis. A maturing Bob chronicled the family effort to help provide the poor with food and clothing that Christmas. On December 4, he wrote, "I just had a sweet talk with Mother about everything under the sun. She talked a lot about the Winter *hilfe* [relief] and what we are going to do for the different families." By December 12 the children had piled a table with clothes and collected money at school. Professor and C.C.B. respectively donated $15 and $100, and Hans Heller contributed forty boxes of chocolate; a "circus" put on by the children raised $20 more. On December 23 Bob wrote, "The boxes have all been delivered and [the chauffeur] Herr Wimmer told me that the families are so poor and the houses so smelly that he won't want anything to eat for supper."

Like wildfire the Depression spread from country to country. Thinking the downfall of capitalism at hand, Marxists erupted in jubilation. But in Austria, as in Germany, the crash effectively doomed the incumbent socialist regime. In "Red Vienna" the beggar's cry "He, too, has to live," sounded incessantly as the political pendulum swung to the Right. With the balance of power tilting from the Social Democrats to the Christian Socialists, the paramilitary arms of the parties clashed with increasing fury. When German President Paul von Hindenburg appointed Adolf Hitler chancellor of the Weimar Republic in January 1933, many refused to take the situation seriously. On February 27, Dorothy heard on the radio that Berlin's Reichstag was on fire and immediately called Eva Rosenfeld, who had moved in 1931 with her family to Berlin to work at Simmel's psychoanalytic sanitarium. Bob was then a visitor in the Rosenfeld household. "The Reichstag burning?" was Eva's reaction. "Surely I would have known about this!" she later wrote.

> How could it be true? I had not read any paper for weeks. I knew there was some book called *Mein Kampf* by some ridiculous fool who threatened to destroy the Jews—but who was going to listen to such nonsense?

Yet after the German parliament passed the Enabling Act permitting Hitler to rule—legally—by dictatorial decree, and a staged incident in May where in public squares, to the accompaniment of torchlight parades and impassioned speeches, the Nazis consigned psychoanalytic and other blacklisted literature to flames, Theodor Reik, René Spitz, Berta Bornstein, Hans Lampl, and Jeanne Lampl-de Groot were among the analysts soon arriving in Vienna. But Austrian Chancellor Engelbert Dollfuss had also begun a de facto Fascist rule in an effort to steer a perceived "middle course" between the shoals of German Nazism and Austrian socialism. Tensions ran high within the psychoanalytic community itself, especially given the large numbers of Jews and socialists within it. And so began the exodus which made America the world center of psychoanalysis, the unlikely happenstance which Freud particularly had not foreseen.

There were other, nonpolitical pressures, as well. With each passing

year the demands on Dorothy to be more generous to Robert with regard
to the children were increasing. Some of that stress was reflected in a letter
to Louie Burlingham from her English friend Helena Hirst, wife of
Francis W. Hirst, editor of *The Economist*. In June 1930 Helena had
written after hearing that Robert was not planning to visit Vienna that
summer, and would not therefore be stopping in London.

> Of course in my selfish soul, I hope [Robert] may have come over here,
> though in my inner and better soul I do realize that happiness would mean
> to him and to you if Dorothy would go back and *with* his children. I think
> it is wonderful how he bears it all, for it must be a constant gnawing at
> his heart. I can't think how she can act as she does, and such a complete
> separation from him, and from her side no sign of meetings, even if she
> only arranged them for a short time! Of course I can't judge, but it strikes
> me that if there is no real separation there should be some [meetings]
> mutually arranged and very definitely acknowledged by her and that mere
> humanity and the sense of *his* right (and not only for his sake, but for
> the justice of it and for the children themselves) . . .

The following June Dorothy relented. With trepidation and a wrenching sense of loss she sent Bob back for a visit, hoping that the identity
of her sixteen-year-old was sufficient to withstand the inevitable cultural
and familial buffeting. Bob's father and grandfather naturally pounced on
their opportunity, as she had known they would, registering Bob for the
preliminary set of college entrance examinations and selling him on the
glories of American education. Bob, however, "flunked" every subject
but German, and he did not go over on a personal level, either. "He has
been so much together with girls and women," offered Mabbie.

From that summer onward the children took turns visiting their father
in America, Dorothy never sending them all at once, fearing they would
be abducted. These trips reopened the old wounds of loyalty and identity
which grew angrier as the atmosphere in Vienna grew more poisonous.
It did not help Dorothy's position that the political climate in America
had turned more enlightened; with Austria heeling to fascism and America to Franklin Delano Roosevelt's brand of progressivism, Robert's sense
of righteous conviction hardened as did Dorothy's anxieties.

But perhaps the most constant source of concern for Dorothy stemmed
from Professor's now terminal illness. Freud's ritualistic lighting of the

cigar was a familiar part of Dorothy's analysis, and a welcome one, as the sharp aroma frequently celebrated a analytic milestone. But the Olympian's sword and buckler in life, as he once put it, was also his Achilles heel. The cigar had caused his cancer, and he had shown himself unable to give up the habit. Although Freud's mortality may have deepened her—to know that Thanatos was working in her idol was genuinely to admit the universality of his laws—it is more likely that the certain imminence of his death was profoundly unsettling. In fact, it was probably in the summer of 1932 that Anna wrote Eva from Hochroterd, "We are lying peacefully in our garden . . . Dorothy is not a giant of strength as yet, but thinks that she has been achieving enormous things in the way of resting," a comment which reveals the continuing precariousness, since Berchtesgaden, of Dorothy's own health. With Professor warning her of the interrelatedness of physical and emotional health, the severity of his illness threatened not only her psychic growth in analysis, but also her physical health; a terrifying prospect. In retrospect it seems that her very life was at stake in these years.

Dorothy was bound to Professor to a far greater extent, of course, through Anna Freud. At the first sign of his cancer eight years before, he and Anna had made a pact to spare him the ordeal of professional nursing. He would allow her to help with the daily insertion and removal of his prosthesis, which he was unable to manage alone, and to assist with the often agonizing medical procedures, if she agreed to conduct herself with strict professional detachment, an arrangement which she honored to the end, and which irreversibly bound them to each other. Eva later related an incident from her analysis, in which Freud, through his vehement protests, inadvertently revealed Anna's preëminent place in his affections among his six children:

> One day, I—reclining on the couch—looked up at the candelabra in the middle of Freud's consulting room. There were six glass shades, one of them different from the other five. I said to Freud: "One of those glass shades is different from the five others."
> He said: "No."
> I said: "Yes, it is."
> He insisted: "No, it isn't."
> So he got up from his chair, switched on the electric light and had a look for himself. He switched it off and went back and sat down.

"You are right," he said, "the sixth one is different from the others," and he added with emphasis: "This fact will, however, not prevent me from saying that you meant to tell me that Anna's position among my six children is different from all the others."

On another occasion he quoted Goethe's *Mephistopheles:* "In the end we all depend/ On creatures we ourselves have made," adding to Lou Andreas-Salomé, "In any case it was very wise to have made [Anna]." Her unblinking fidelity and emotional restraint in nursing Freud are well known; not so the anxieties, for Dorothy as well as Anna, which must have attended his ups and downs.

For Dorothy, the positive side to this symbiosis was naturally the stimulation which the Freuds generated in her. In Professor's late years Anna was closest to him emotionally as well, and by virtue of this intimacy, Dorothy's intellectual development was nurtured in the blazing sun of a true genius. Dorothy herself credited him with her productivity, discovering to her great relief after his death that her fears of intellectual sterility had been unfounded.

Anna Freud of course also exercised a nurturing influence on Dorothy's intellectual development, perhaps the major influence. Victor Ross makes the intriguing comment that Dorothy was not, in his family's opinion, a born intellectual, rather "she metamorphosized herself out of love for Anna Freud." The Rosenfelds were certainly in a position to form such a judgment; and it does appear that Dorothy's feelings for Anna were grounded in an identification with her. W. Ernest Freud observed that his aunt "may have 're-created' a sibling, if not a twin relationship, with Dorothy Burlingham, her close friend and co-worker throughout a long period of her life." Perhaps he was thinking of Anna's relationship with Sophie, his mother. And had he known better the circumstances of Dorothy's childhood, he could have been more certain. Long frustrated by the exclusivity of her sisters' twinship, "Me-Too" had of course yearned for a twin of her own.

Finding one word which evokes both the rigorous sense of duty and schoolgirl romance so peculiarly mixed in their relationship is difficult. Instinctively one turns to German. *Freundinnen* (girl friends) conjures an Anna Freudian image of fierce loyalty, sorority, Platonic love, and patriarchal devotion, while *doppelgänger* (double) best describes the character of Dorothy's needs. In this context Dorothy's analytic career was an extension of her bonding with Anna Freud. And to have planted her life's work in this promised land was, despite the gathering clouds, another wish fulfilled.

D orothy's career as an analyst was as informed by her role as a mother as it was by her connection to the Freuds. As Anna Freud would later observe, "So far as child analysis was concerned, Dorothy Burlingham came to it the hard way."

> Any mother with children in analysis—and in her case there were four— has to meet the inconvenience of ferrying them to and from their treat- ment hour; to sit around in waiting rooms; to meet the difficulty of sharing responsibility; to tolerate their allegiance to a stranger; to have her own attitude and actions scrutinized, etc. She tolerated all these hardships admirably and, in later days, after changing roles and becoming a child analyst herself, she extracted from this period the ability never to criticize the mothers of her patients for complaining about or even breaking down under the inevitable strain. Several sensitive papers . . . stem from this period.

Indeed the impact of personal experience on Dorothy (and the Four) was evident as her primary influence in the field beginning with her first long paper, "Child Analysis and the Mother," which in 1932 won her associate membership in the Vienna Psychoanalytic Society.

Dorothy followed Anna's lead in focusing her energies along two sometimes overlapping avenues: substantiating with hard clinical data suppositions about childhood which Professor's analyses of adults had led him to formulate, and investigating areas which he had neglected. The subjects which Dorothy knew best from personal experience fell into the latter category, however, so the nature of her work was more exploratory than buttressing. It is widely recognized that Freud emphasized the fa- ther's role at the mother's expense; but this granted Dorothy license to venture freely into the waters of her maternal experience without fear of treading on the master's toes. The mother-child relationship, in this way, became the unifying theme of a variety of subjects which interested Dorothy in the half-century span of her professional life.

"Child Analysis and the Mother" was published in 1932 in the *Journal for Psychoanalytic Education,* edited, among others, by August Aichhorn and Anna Freud. The paper was at once an endorsement of Anna Freud's "educational admixture" and an attack on the exclusivity of Melanie Klein's focus on the child's inner, experiential world. "Let us see . . ." wrote Dorothy, "how the child is after he has been treated in this [Melanie Klein] manner."

> When one talks to him he can recite to you at length all the conscious and unconscious reasons for all his actions and where they come from; but if one watches him in his surroundings, he seems like a ship at sea. He has no connection with reality. He cannot use his newly acquired understanding of himself to adjust to reality, even if he has lost his symptoms. His world is changed for him only so far as his symptoms interfered with his ability to meet it; but his environment, the atmosphere which was conducive to the formation of his neurosis, has not changed.

Although emphatic about the necessity of dealing with the child's home life, Dorothy recognized that of the two approaches, Anna Freud's was by far the more demanding. Dorothy was especially convincing in the portrayal of the reaction of the mother to analysis.

> She feels herself being dragged into the analysis. Her relationship toward her child, her actions and behavior toward him, what she says to him, and how she says it, her moods and her tempers, everything is studied from the analytic angle. That is bad enough, but when she realizes that her whole private life is also being brought in, she naturally feels abused. She can understand why all that concerns the child is necessary material for the analyst, but when it comes to her private life—that seems to her to be going one step too far. She will not stand for it and struggles against it. Naturally, she feels injured, criticized, misunderstood. Furthermore, she feels jealous even of the attention which is now being given to her child. It was she who suffered from her child's behavior, and now it is her child who gets all the sympathy and help. She, who was most affected by his difficulties, now not only is not being considered, but an even more difficult situation is being made for her. Moreover, she feels her child loving someone else more than herself, turning to someone else with all his troubles as he previously did to her. It does not make it easier for her

to realize that this person really does understand her child better than she does. She feels humiliated. And then, added to all of this, the child begins to look at her, the mother, with newly opened eyes, even criticizing her, her actions, her very thoughts; and she knows that her child finds sympathy in all of this with his newfound friend, the analyst. Is it astonishing that the mother resents the analyst's efforts? Is it strange that analysts often lose cases just because parents cannot stand the analysis and suddenly break off the treatment?

At the heart of Dorothy's conviction that these tribulations were essential to the child's analysis lay a familiarity with the power of unconscious forces which tack between mother and child, a power "so subtle and uncanny that it seems at times to approach the supernatural." Where it is found, she wrote, "it must be taken into account as an unknown quantity that will bring many uncertainties into the analysis." While recognizing that this depth was not invariably present, she called it "a phenomenon which demands investigation."

Given Professor's bitter controversies with C. J. Jung over the occult, and Freud's continuing scorn for the "mystic *Weltanschauung,*" Dorothy's dalliance with the supernatural may have seemed confrontational. Surprising, then, is Freud's comment in *New Introductory Lectures:* "A short time ago, Dorothy Burlingham, a trustworthy witness [*eine vertrauenswürdige frau*] in a paper on child analysis and the mother published some observations which, if they can be confirmed, would be bound to put an end to the remaining doubts on the reality of thought transference."

This riddle was created and is solved by a paradox in Freud himself. Otto Weis, founder of the Italian Psychoanalytic Society, observed that Freud's interests extended far beyond his published works—to parapsychology, telepathy, extrasensory perception, and clairvoyance. Dorothy may have been influenced by these interests to which she was privy, unaware perhaps of the striking conflict with his public stand behind the "scientific *Weltanschauung.*" Analyst Helene Deutsch believed that Freud insisted on the rational because irrational elements were so strong in him. Deutsch in 1932 had assumed the helm of the Technical Seminar for Adult Analysis, of which Dorothy was a regular participant, and her ideas may have been influential. Deutsch stressed the value of creative intuition as a therapeutic tool, an unorthodox view, as it allowed for a meeting of the unconscious minds of analyst and analysand. According to one who underwent a training analysis with Dorothy in later years, she was indeed highly intuitive, which does not surprise, given her paternity, and also supports Victor Ross's theory of an intellectual metamorphosis.

Freud may have acted to reaffirm Dorothy's credibility. But, in observing that Professor couched his tribute on the condition that Dorothy's observation be confirmed, one realizes that he also intended a subtle warning. Dorothy might as well have been asked to prove scientifically the existence of God.

Three years later, when she returned to the subject in "Empathy Between Infant and Mother," Dorothy backed away from the telepathic view. Rather, she attributed the startling ability of some children to plumb their mother's private emotions to an ultrasensitivity of the prelatency period which had not been fully appreciated. "We do not maintain," she wrote, "as we did before, that the child's unconscious has made contact with the unconscious of the mother. We say instead that the child is an acute observer of all those overt reactions of the mother which betray what happens in the depth of her mind." This did not alter the fundamental fact which concerned Dorothy, however: "The mother's unconscious is no less vital for the child than what happens in her consciousness . . . The mother's character, her neurosis, her obsessions, anxieties, symptoms, in short, her affects as well as her repressions have passed from mother to child with lightning speed and power." Focusing, then, upon the simultaneous analysis of mother and child as a tool for the scientific dissection of this empathy, Dorothy wrote, "His apparently intuitive understanding for the mother's unconscious can be traced back to earliest observations and conclusions drawn from them, i.e., to repressed impressions which are lifted once more into consciousness as a result of analytic work." She concluded with the observation that she herself had undergone such a simultaneous analysis with her children. "More than once I was struck by the fact that sometimes the subject which played a major role in my analysis at the same time dominated the analysis of one of the children."

With these remarks Dorothy concluded her first cycle of experience and began the cycle of justification which lent the latter part of her life its meaning. Atonement for the mistakes she had made as a mother would motivate Dorothy as an analyst, weaving into her life's work with children a pattern of penance. Equally vivid was the desire to light the path for others, to help others see where she had been blind. Dorothy's failure and triumph were both evident in "the periodically depressed mother," who

> reported that her child excelled in naughtiness, irritability, and provoking behavior whenever she felt worst, a change in the child noticed not only by her but confirmed by all other members of the household. According to this mother, it felt as if the child had every intention of increasing her depression. This happened so regularly that the mother had learned to use the child's reaction as the first indication of the recurrence of her depression, even if at the time she had not yet become aware of it herself.

Two additional papers rounded out this early literary phase. "A Child at Play" (1932) reported the case of Gerda, a verbally uncommunicative child whose unconscious processes Dorothy was able to reach through the game of tiddlywinks. There seemed here a conciliatory note toward Klein, as it was she who had championed play therapy. Already by 1927 Anna Freud had realized that the effect of her aggressiveness toward Klein in "Four Lectures on Child Analysis" had been divisive to the wider cause of child analysis; at the Innsbruck Congress her tone had been distinctly mellower. Anna Freud agreed that play therapy had a value, but did not consider it the equivalent of free association, as Klein seemed to. In the case of Gerda, Dorothy outlined parameters in which play therapy was clearly effective, while demonstrating that this seven-year-old's superego control was still dependent upon authority figures. She concluded, "To win or lose a game means . . . a very real success or defeat. It is this very confusion between fantasy and reality, play and life situations, which turns every observation of this kind into a useful piece of material for analytic investigation."

"The Urge to Tell and the Compulsion to Confess," presented on the evening of December 30, 1933, won Dorothy full membership in the Vienna Psychoanalytic Society. The paper, both a respectful nod to her first analyst and a furtherance of his ideas, delineated Theodore Reik's theory on the compulsion to confess from the child's urge to share infantile discoveries. Unlike the compulsion to confess, a pathological process geared to the expiation of guilt, the urge to tell represented a positive effort in the pursuit of a partner, rooted in the exhibitionistic instinct. Even in the face of parental prohibition—for example, against scatology—the urge proved irrepressible, diving underground only to reappear in the form of a nonsensical "involuntary confession." As Anna Freud wrote Bob, "It has given [Dorothy] a lot of work, but it was very good and everybody in the meeting recognized it as such. I think she . . . won a lot of respect for herself that evening."

Dorothy's final contribution in Vienna was made possible by the economic conditions. In 1937, finding twenty or so mothers poor enough to fit Dorothy's description of being "beyond the dole," and, in consequence, delighted to have their toddlers fed, bathed, clothed, and medically examined daily without charge, and to be freed themselves to work a full day, was not difficult. These circumstances made possible the so-called Edith Jackson Project, a psychoanalytic, pre-kindergarten day-care center named for the wealthy American analyst who financed it, "out of gratitude to Freud." The opportunity to observe one- and two-year-olds over an extended period in a clinical environment was a rare one, and a chance for Anna Freud to test her theories on instinctual restriction further. In a 1929 lecture to teachers at after-school day-care centers, or *Horts,* she had dealt with the latency period:

> Evidently, to raise children to be "good" is not without its dangers. The repressions which are required to achieve this result, the reaction formations and the sublimations which have been built up, are paid for at the price of originality and spontaneity. Thus, if the older [latency period] children, compared with the younger ones, strike us as duller and more inactive, the impression is absolutely correct. The limitations which are placed upon their thinking, and the obstacles put in the way of their primitive activities, result in restrictions of thinking and inhibitions of acting.
>
> While, thus, parents need not be too proud of their successes, in another respect as well it is somewhat doubtful how much credit they deserve. We seem to have no guarantee at all whether the good behavior of the older child is the product of education or simply the consequence of having reached a certain stage of development. So far we have no evidence to help us decide what would happen if young children were allowed to develop without interference. We do not know whether they could grow up like little savages or whether, without any external help, they would spontaneously pass through a series of successive modifications.

Seven years after posing this question Anna set out to answer it in space rented from a Montessori kindergarten. Edith Jackson was in Vienna during the summer months, and then descended from the Grinzing vineyards in a chauffeur-driven limousine to "the Children's Home" on Rudolfplatz. The actual day-to-day operation of the "creche," or *krippe,* represented Dorothy's second collaborative venture with Anna Freud (the first had been a psychoanalytic seminar for the nursery-school teachers who had attended the *Hort* lecture); they were assisted by the analytically trained pediatrician Josephine (Fifi) Stross, the American analyst Julia Deming, and some volunteers. Deming, in charge of feeding schedules, was the children's "Pappitante" (Auntie Porridge), and so on. Freud commented dryly to his son Martin, "Anna is enjoying her so-called vacation—i.e., she is playing with the little babies instead of the big ones."

"[The children] got pretty quickly used to us," Dorothy recalled,

> and some of them of course did cry a lot, but I think they enjoyed the activities they were allowed, which they didn't have in their closed quarters [at home], but at that age most of them were only interested in moving, I mean [at the toddler] age, what else do they want? They were either sleeping at certain times or creeping around the floor or running around or sitting on people's laps.

Dr. Stross recalls that the children responded better when attended by the same person rather than being shuttled from one person to the next. And she cites an example which would seem to have confirmed Anna's suspicion that children may indeed "spontaneously pass through a series of successive modifications." In one experiment each child was allowed to crawl to his or her own individual buffet and select food without interference. Each space was divided so that the child was not influenced by the choices of his neighbors. And, after a brief, bacchanalian chocolate fest, the children were observed to begin feeding themselves a balanced diet. Unfortunately, Dorothy's and Anna's meticulous records were not published, as the Anschluss halted the project after just one year. Soon afterwards, however, they would found its more ambitious progeny, the Hampstead War Nurseries.

Another experiment in the application of greater freedom came to a natural end in the spring of 1932. With Peter Blos and Erik Erikson looking to their futures and their eldest class nearing college age, the Hietzing School closed its doors. Five years hence, after the Four had made the transition to other schools and to colleges, Dorothy would conclude a paper delivered at the Psychoanalytic Pedagogy Review Symposium with a poignant plea to the future educators of such analytically "protected" children.

> Owing to the understanding upbringing they have had . . . it is precisely these children who are especially oversensitive, who are not readily inclined to accept restrictions, who in particular can scarcely tolerate any criticism or admonition, and who frequently experience inconsiderate and unkind behavior on the part of their agemates as a profound rejection. Thus they must negotiate a particularly long and difficult path before they can adapt to the ordinary demands of school and attain a good level of performance.
>
> The teacher's task in relation to these children is again a very special one. What these protected children have so far not been able to gain— their lack of resilience—must now be made up within the community and with the help of the teacher. Here, then, in addition to the usual goals of education—for work and appropriate behavior—there is a new air: the gradual accommodation to the demands of external reality, and these demands are no longer attuned to the special needs of the individual.

These words of course reflected the Four's entry into regular educational systems, and in a 1940 letter to Bob Dorothy actually called the Hietzing School "a mistake." But in 1932 the realization lay ahead that the bubble of enchantment which she had fashioned around her children would inevitably postpone and possibly prevent their acclimation to the world beyond. As "Bomatimi" rose from their nether world of labored introspection, they discovered another which prized tangible accomplishment and outward impressions above all. Given that their innate sensitivities had been fine-tuned to exquisite receptivity by analysis, it is not surprising that they got an especially bad case of the bends. The external world not only devalued their precious inward accomplishments, but it found them conspicuously lacking in the broad spectrum of knowledge imparted by ordinary schools. Five years in wonderland had come to an end and the piper had to be paid; and it was the Four who did the paying.

Michael's decompression seemed the smoothest, as he was the youngest and most adaptable child. By common consensus Mikey was a sweet, sturdy, confident boy, and the least problematic of the Four. Dorothy had left Robert before his birth, and presumably Mikey had been the least affected by his father's illness. He had, relatively speaking, certainly been analyzed the least, having spent but two years in Anna Freud's consulting room. The influence of Herr Wimmer had nurtured Mikey's mechanical bent, manifested first in his infatuation with Matchbox toys, then in a fantastic series of car drawings, each lower-slung, lengthier, and more aerodynamic than the past. Many years later, Michael would explain that the *Realschule der Schottenbastei* in which he enrolled at age eleven was "a school which prepares you for a scientific upper education . . . I went there because I already knew I wanted to be an engineer."

Tinky had more difficulty. In part because Mabbie was Dorothy's favorite child and the family's second mother, Tinky had become the contrary daughter, her favorite expression having given her chow, Ono, his name. Although Tinky appeared less colorful than her *strahlend* brother and sister, Anna Freud had told Robert in Berchtesgaden that "she has the most affectionate and 'passionate' nature of any of the children." Asked about her progress, she had responded, "I am not of the opinion that Tinky is remote, inaccessible or 'negative.' She has shown improvement during the last year. Whereas, formerly, her 'negativism' was marked, now when asked if she would like to do something, she answers 'if you wish.' "

Tinky's opposition to psychoanalysis, the crux and crucible of their lives, was nevertheless apparent as late as the summer of 1937, eight years later. (Her analysis had ended after three years, a year in adolescence following the pair ending at age ten.) Dorothy wrote Bob, "I took [Tinky] out to the nursery school—but I guess it's too analytical for her. I felt her hair standing on end . . . Analysis has done a great deal for Mabbie this year, and she is very happy about it—so perhaps that makes it harder for Tinky." As for school, Tinky found the Albertgasse Realgymnasium as "unpleasant" as the Doblinger Realgymnasium to which she progressed, and increasingly so, as the schools became polarized between children from Fascist and socialist homes. She remembers being failed by her Latin teacher, who was a Nazi.

Mabbie's decision to attend the *Kunstgewerbeschule* (College of Applied Arts) was as characteristic as would be Bob's decision to attend college in the States. While Dorothy's gadfly in 1933 buzzed over to that "gigantic mistake" of a land where his father happened to reside, the angel girl resisted Judy de Forest's entreaties to join her at Bennington, presumably in order to remain loyal to her mother in Vienna. The *Kunstgewerbeschule* however made good sense for the artistically inclined Mabbie in that it was allied through designers Josef Hoffman and Koloman Moser to the Wiener Werkstätte, a spiritual successor to the Tiffany Studios.

Blessed with talent discovered at an early age, and nurtured by regular lessons in a city which virtually perspired music, Bob's transition to the world beyond Wattmangasse 11 could have been the swiftest, but was the stickiest by far. The same teenager who went to concerts and sat "shivering all over with excitement and joy" was in a jam over his future, writing Dorothy in the spring of 1930, "I just can't make a decision on Techniker or Musiker. . . ." When Bob's ambivalence became unendurable Dorothy wrote Pablo Casals to request an audition. But the master declined, reflecting "that unless [Bob] was someone who could give all his energy to the enormous amount of practice needed, etc. & etc., he should not follow it as a career," Dorothy recalled. "I think," she continued, "we as well as himself did not have that type of character . . . and this was what led him to architecture & now I believe [it was] a mistake. I think if he had been under the influence of a man like Casals he would have given his all to music."

It was at this time that Bob, though afflicted with severe asthma, took up smoking. The cigarette gradually became as indispensable to him as his cello had been, and soon no dawn broke without a torturous hacking of lungs. One therefore reads with some skepticism Bob's journal entry for December 3, 1931—Anna Freud's birthday:

Hoch [Cheers] Anna Freud!
    It is really not understandable for anyone, except the person who has been through it all, to understand what analysis has done for me. If I think about the way I used to steal and lie, and that now just because I am able to understand why I did it, I am able to stop! well! it seems . . . a miracle.

This was followed on December 7 with an account from his analysis.

> In my lesson with Anna Freud I found out that all my dreams were about Mother, when she was out or went away from me (when I was 6 months old) and that she refused me, as I felt then. I wanted her milk that she had given me up to then and she refused. Mother tells me now that I refused any eatable [*sic*] when in that state & they had the time of their life trying to feed me.

Bob's best friend, Ernsti Halberstadt, presently got a very different message from him. Having left for boarding school the previous winter, Ernsti was "very surprised" to hear from Bob an uncharacteristic note in *"Hier in Wien ist immer das ewig selbe los"* ("Here in Vienna it is the same old thing"). Ernest places Bob's outburst "in the context of increasing school work," but Ernsti was seeing new vistas while Bob, in his seventh consecutive year of analysis, and prevented from going to boarding school—ostensibly by his homosexual tendencies—was flogging the same dead horse.

Between the closing of the Hietzing School and Bob's and Mabbie's college starts, a year elapsed in which they were tutored each morning at the Bergasse by Joan Erikson. Come summer the Freuds moved to Pötzleindorf and the Burlinghams to Casimir Villa in nearby Grinzing. Tinky recalls "the beautiful house of an artist," set in an impressionist purple and green canvas of vineyards.

Dorothy and Anna had presented their *"gemeinsamen vater"* ("common father") with a booklet of pictures and commentary extolling the virtues of the Hochroterd "oasis." And on May 8, 1932, Freud reclined in a lawn chair to write Arnold Zweig, "Where am I writing from? From a small farmhouse on a hillside, forty-five minutes by car from the Bergasse, which my daughter and her American friend (who owns the car) have bought and furnished as a weekend cottage." This was the first of six glorious summers at this *Bauernhaus,* a locus for family and friends.

Among the first visitors were Dorothy's niece Comfort Parker and her Brearley classmate Rosilla Hornblower. Of the Boston, Miller & Hornblower legal dynasty, Rosilla recalls feeling constricted in a company which, she thought, analyzed her every breath, and with her hostess, who finally declared, "There is a wall between us, Rosilla." Then, too, that wall of culture was no less real for Mabbie and Tinky in Black Point.

Soon after they had arrived for their first stateside visit, Mabbie exploded, "It is dumb that we live with the Burlinghams and can't do as we like!"

The summer residents at Black Point regarded Mabbie's and Tinky's freewheeling ways with equal measures of curiosity and incomprehension. The Lords, Windlows, Montgomerys, Hopkinses, Iselins, Garrisons and Lincolns, a thoroughbred stable of old-guard families, did not subscribe to the importance of the instinctual life. The manner of behavior regarded at the Bergasse as enlightened was considered barbaric on the Point. Mabbie promptly reported, "Bompa [C.C.B.] . . . trys to teach us good manners like not speaking with full mouth and he also teaches us English." And, "I am trying not to blow my nose so often and so loud because Aunt Nancy said she had never seen (or heard) such a family who blew their noses so much and so often." A general but in fact pointed topic of dinnertime conversation was the shortcomings of unorthodox upbringing and education.

The Old Black Point community also tended to denigrate psychoanalysis, and Jews. "They all make a lot of remarks about analysis," wrote Mabbie. As did those at Cold Spring Harbor. "Uncle Rodman [Gilder] made jokes about dreams and Professor. I always laugh and say nothing." When reminded of *Jokes and Their Relation to the Unconscious,* C.C.B. would roar, "Humor? What does Freud know of humor? He *has* no sense of humor!" Thinking it best to avoid Robert herself, Dorothy had delegated the responsibility of chaperoning the children to the States to Margot Goldschmidt; a (non observant) Jewess, socialist, and Berliner, she was disturbed to see a RESTRICTED sign posted at the entrance to Old Black Point. Freud of course was a Jew in the cultural sense only, having characterized religion in *The Future of an Illusion* as "the universal obsessional neurosis of humanity." This point of view, now ingrained in the Four, added another tender spot to relations with the devout Burlinghams, which *New York Times* headlines such as RELIGION DOOMED/FREUD ASSERTS had done nothing to alleviate. The degree to which Tinky, for one, had been braced to withstand their values was evident in her first letter home. "It is really not so bad as I thought it would be," she wrote. "We don't have to pray at table and don't have to go to church. But perhaps that will come soon." Mabbie echoed her sister's guarded suspicion. "They are really awfully nice if I did not have to say they are my family."

Raised in the spirit of Anna Freud's "spinsterish holiness," the girls recoiled at the Burlinghams' physical demonstrations of affection, Robert, having been separated so long from his children, being particularly anxious to express his affection for them, and to have them return it. Cried Tinky, "We have to give so many kisses it is terrible." "Daddy still tells me how much he likes me and asks me if I know it," Mabbie wrote. "I hate that he kisses me so much and nearly on my mouth. He does not always do it but sometimes, really only once last night, but I hate it. I don't think a father has to do that."

After Bob's return to Vienna the previous summer, Robert had suffered another nervous breakdown, forcing him to give up his Albany post and return to New York. He had since recovered and had taken the position of assistant in pathology at the New York Hospital–Cornell Medical Center, but the repeated separations from his family and the strain of living under his parents' roof continued to take its toll. Mabbie wrote, "Yesterday we went shopping and Daddy had a kind of *tick*. I think he also had it in Semmering when he was restless."

Mabbie was in violent flux. She confessed to her mother, "Daddy is so nice. He really is lovely when he is not sick . . . He loves us very much but is not too sweet. In reality he loves you because all the things he likes in us is because they are like you . . . Bompa is so queer. He encouraged us to be wild at meals and then all at once yesterday he told Daddy that we *had* to be more formal at meals. Queer! Now we are so proper! . . . Bompa is as nice as he was [before]." She added, "I think that I have changed already. Perhaps not outside but inside. I don't look at people and criticize as narrow-minded[ly] as I did."

The effects of C.C.B.'s dominance over his children were increasingly evident. Charles, the eldest sibling, had been "saved" only by his recent marriage to Cora Weir Carlin. The daughter of American impressionist painter J. Alden Weir, Cora had had the gumption to stand up to C.C.B. and insist that Charles and she were entitled to a life of their own. But neither his plain spinster sister nor his excitable, spouseless brother had been as fortunate. Nancy, who was afraid of her father, had developed a wan identity, and Robert was now clearly unwell. Although "absolutely the nicest man," thought Margot Goldschmidt, he appeared a remote figure, taking little part in the goings-on. His anger, Margot suspected, was inwardly directed.

Dorothy, following the proceedings from Grinzing and Hochroterd, was relieved when the time came for Mabbie and Tinky to visit briefly with her family at Cold Spring Harbor. "I like all the people terrible much in Oyster Bay," wrote Tinky, "and I like them all much better than [those at Black Point]." Mabbie agreed. She wrote:

> One thing I and Tinky are always doing and that is seeing you in [Aunt Comfort and Aunt Julia]. You have the same bony thinness, the same elbows, the same *gesichts schnitt* [facial expressions], the same nose and chin and the same movements. They sit and look at things exactly as you do. It is awfully funny.

Cold Spring Harbor was especially rewarding for Tinky, who looked most like Dorothy. "When I played tennis at Aunt Julia's, Aunt Com-Com [Comfort] told me that I played tennis just like you did," she wrote. "And when I went into my bed Mabbie said I have a Tiffany nose."

These comments surely awoke Dorothy to the ineluctability of heritage, despite the distance of four thousand miles and seven years. This realization was strengthened by Mabbie's and Tinky's news that her eighty-four-year-old father was now stooped and weak, his eyesight and hearing failing. "That visit to Pa made me very unhappy," wrote Mabbie. "I think he would love to see you but I really don't know. I can't see clearly if he loved to see us because he is so old and not clear himself." After the girls' return in August, Dorothy realized that she could delay no longer if she was to see her father alive. And, shortly thereafter, together with Tinky she set off on the *Berengaria* for New York. Little is known about this reunion except that it was a good one, that Louis was happy to see his daughter, and Dorothy was glad to see him.

More important, perhaps, was the newly confrontational spirit which motivated Dorothy to face the painful feelings inevitably aroused by the trip. Comfort Parker recalls that her aunt had begun to preach the general importance of feeling life's pains as well as its pleasures, and specifically, that she came to loggerheads with the twins over her opposition to the use of anesthetics in childbirth, decades before the revival of natural childbirth. Dorothy, who above all valued the way in which Freud "met life," was under the influence of his reality principle—the postponement and abandonment of short-term gratifications for a more farsighted balance or constancy of stimuli. "My father lived very much under the Pleasure Principle," Dorothy acknowledged near the end of her own life. But in 1932 she struggled to master his influence, her devotion to Freud, her substitute father-figure, helping to heal the emotional gap and start her down the path to rapprochement.

From Laurelton Hall Dorothy journeyed to the upper reaches of Park Avenue and the new home of her distinguished in-laws. In 1929, after a rising hotel had darkened their Murray Hill town house, the Burlinghams had moved to 860 Park, taking the rambling, parqueted apartment on the fourteenth floor. Tinky is not likely to forget the scene that night when Dorothy, evidently hoping to bring about a complete severance of relations, asked Robert for a divorce.

Dorothy's life had by then been so radically restructured that she, at least, realized that a reconciliation with Robert was not merely undesirable, it was impossible. With the opportunity to make the request, and new confidence in herself, she may have felt finally capable of winning Robert's agreement, and perhaps even of making him see that it would be in the best interest of them all; that he too could start a new life. Also, Dorothy must have been incensed when even Mabbie had joined the hue-and-cry for Bob to spend a year in New England before college. "Aunt Com Com also believes that Bob should learn over here because they know how to bring children through [the college entrance] exams," Mabbie had written, citing the example of Comfort's eldest son. "Richard came through his examinations with 2 highest honors and 2 plain honors. It hasn't been done since 10 years." Perhaps she hoped that an end to relations would change Bob's mind about attending an American college, that he would join Mabbie at the *Kunstgewerbeschule,* and with an end to summer visitations, their insulated existence could continue as before.

But she had grossly miscalculated Robert's reaction. To ask Robert for a divorce was to ask him to relinquish the hope that gave meaning to his life. Her demand bored into him like a drill and, locking the door to his bedroom, he trapped her inside with him. "He could do that," Tinky recalls, "corner a person." The commotion was muffled, though furious, and halted only by C.C.B.'s intervention. When they emerged Dorothy realized that there could be no divorce; they would never even become legally separated.

On September 3, 1932, Dorothy was reunited with Anna Freud in Wiesbaden, Germany, for the Twelfth International Psychoanalytic Congress. They caught up on events in their room at the Hotel Rose. Herr Wimmer had been teaching Anna Freud how to drive, and she reported her first unaccompanied trip to Hochroterd, where the harvest had been bountiful. Professor had just finished writing his *New Introductory Lectures,* and Anna had read Melanie Klein's new book, *The Psychoanalysis of Children;* meanwhile Sándor Ferenczi, feeling that he had moved too far from the common psychoanalytic ground, had refused the presidency of the International Psychoanalytic Association. This was sad news; but Dorothy was soon back in familiar terrain, listening to Anna's lecture, "The Neurotic Mechanisms under the Influence of Education"; on September 6, they joined their colleagues on a boat trip along the Rhine. The following day, at the conclusion of the congress, Dorothy's transition to everyday life in Vienna was seamlessly effected.

Then, just four months later, Dorothy's emotions were again riveted stateside, when her father died on January 17, 1933, after a ten-day bout of pneumonia. Having visited him so recently, Dorothy did not return for the funeral at Brooklyn's Greenwood Cemetery, where Dr. Henry Sloane Coffin laid Louis to rest between May and Lou under a blanket of pink carnations.

Taste had changed with the times. The Tiffany Studios, established in 1902 as the umbrella for all of Louis's productive and marketing operations, including the "vast central workshop" to which Siegfried Bing had made reference, had dwindled through a series of cutbacks and relocations to the size and site of a single department, the Ecclesiastical, on 23rd Street. World War I had hastened what the landmark 1913 Armory Show had begun; and, for the first time in his life, Louis had found himself unable to embrace, much less lead, the new art. It had done no good to rail against the Modernists. To Louis's conviction that "the Cubists and Futurists do not belong to art; they are not artists; they are untrained inventors of processes of the arts," *The New Republic* had satirically responded, "Woman, had Mr. Tiffany created her, instead of having two only, would have had many breasts, and each breast, instead of having one only, would, if Mr. Tiffany had created woman, have been all encrusted in nipples."

The reversal of Louis's fortunes had not flushed out of hiding any of his father's penurious qualities. He had ensured the future of Laurelton Hall with a costly concern for young artists, yet had also continued to live his extravagant life. On paper Dorothy and her siblings made out decently; fifty shares of Tiffany & Company stock each, plus equal shares of the residual estate. But after payment of his debts, even the $10,000 cash bequests to his thirteen grandchildren could not at first be fully honored; and Dorothy received not a penny until after the 1938 sale of the Lenox Hill mansion, a transaction which resulted in its demolition. But this came as no surprise to one who had witnessed the death of the King of Diamonds and birth of the Kubla Khan. In his last-born child especially, Louis's death provoked no feeling of spurned avarice. Dorothy's nonmaterialism and disregard for Laurelton Hall were both reflected in Bob, who, when offered any of its treasures, whether it be a Tiffany lamp, vase, or window, chose instead a potted camellia from the greenhouse.

Dorothy would appreciate her father only after she herself had struggled lifelong in behalf of a cause and had experienced both the waxing and waning of its popularity; and after weighing her private and public lives on the scales of conscience. In the eleventh hour the memory of her father in his came flooding back to Dorothy. Buried in her files, in the margin of a documentary film script on her father's artistry, is a startling insight into the two men most influential in her life. "There is a drive to catch his ideas," she wrote, indicating her father. "It is what genius is made of, facts & creativity. What opposites [are] my father & Freud, both are drawn by an idea; nothing else matters, what people think, money is unimportant." But if the analyst in Dorothy had perceived that her father's extravagance had belied a contempt for money, the comparison with Freud required a daughter's transcendence.

In the far future Dorothy could verbalize, "He did what he meant to do, and that's not crazy," but at the time she grieved silently. When her sister Julia visited Vienna that winter she brought Dorothy their father's (and, before that, her grandfather's) chiming Tiffany & Company pocket watch; also, at Dorothy's request, one of the snarling polar bear rugs from the inner court at Laurelton Hall. It found a new home at Bergasse 19 before the hearth of Dorothy's consulting room, where it served her analysands as a catalyst for the primeval contents of their unconscious minds.

Adolf Hitler came to power in Germany twelve days after the death of Louis Tiffany, and within a matter of months Dorothy found herself living in a Fascist state, with repercussions swift in the coming. In the midst of a July heat wave, Dorothy boarded a train in Cherbourg, France, where she put "Matimi" and Margot Goldschmidt on the *Pennland,* as had been arranged, for another Black Point summer. On August 21, Anna Freud wrote Eva Rosenfeld, "Bob will leave tomorrow with Erik [Erikson] for Normandy to the seashore . . . That is a very good thing. I have been doing my best to promote this." Dorothy later met Bob in Copenhagen, and together witnessed a beginning to the analytic migration as the Eriksons boarded a Moore-McCormack freighter for New York. After a special time together in London, Dorothy and Bob parted tearfully, Bob boarding the SS *Olympic* for New York, and from there traveling to Yellow Springs, Ohio, and Antioch—the college of his choice. The school's experimental charter was no doubt a factor in Bob's acceptance, considering his poor showing on the college entrance exams, as was the influence of the Burlinghams, who considered it a triumph to have Bob in *any* American school.

Dorothy had meanwhile returned to Vienna, where, childless for the first time in eighteen years and wrenched by desolate feelings, she devoured her children's letters. Despite the girls' initial reservations, the previous summer at Black Point had ended on a warm note, Mabbie writing of "romantic picnics, lovely swims, driving lessons and rides on bridle paths." But the summer of 1933 started out badly. Mabbie's test scores came back and were no better than Bob's had been. And Robert was still depressed. "I don't know what to do to cheer Daddy up," Mabbie wrote. "He is sad all over and worries all the time." By mid-August she was homesick. "I can hardly stand the sweet voices around me. I pity Daddy so much. The older I get, the more I see what a horrible life he is leading. I would have shot myself long ago—or ran away to some far-off country. I miss the farm too terribly. I feel just like a fish on land here."

Meanwhile in Austria, Chancellor Dollfuss struck a deal with his *Fascisti* neighbor Mussolini. In return for protection from Nazi Germany Dollfuss agreed to unleash the *Heimwehr* (the Christian Socialist private army) on Vienna's Social Democrats. At Black Point breakfast began with descriptions of an Austria "where Nazi bombs wreck the peace of quiet evenings, where Nazi banners wave at unexpected points to flout the law and swastikas are strewn on the pavements and painted swastikas deface public buildings."

On August 25 Mabbie wrote frantically:

Mother! It is just impossible to get at Bompa and make him tell us which boat to take home. I can't speak to Daddy because he always gets so sad, disturbed and excited! All Bompa says is that he will ask Bob what you want and all you want is that we be home on the 10th [of September]. I've told him this 100 times. Well! He is coming from N.Y. today and promised he would speak to Bob today.

The following day she reported:

At last today we all talked with Bompa and Daddy. It was horrible. Daddy was white with anger, Bompa laughed! Oh horror. All we got out of them was this: they want us to stay longer because of politics. We all knew it would come. Mother I am sick of it all. I can't look at any of them without feeling [sick]. . . . Well anyhow [Bompa?] sent you a telegram asking for us to stay longer with Bobs and my syllables [signed 'Boma'].
I hope that didn't make you think we really want to stay here longer!

On the twenty-eighth she added:

You don't know how unsure it makes me over here about going back to Europe. I understand perfectly their point of view and gosh it is hard to have two points of view. But believe me! I would rather live with you in a Nazi camp than here in this sweetness! Of course it is crazy to go to a country where there are dangers when I could stay in this safeness. But we have family reasons. *Nicht wahr?*

Feeling inwardly stronger than ever before, Dorothy settled the matter by demanding, and effecting, "Matimi's" return in early fall. Vienna was not as volatile as the press reported, she told them, and for Americans especially there was little danger. Behind this claim of course lay the "family reasons" to which Mabbie had referred. Freud had resolved to live out his days in Vienna and, as he had observed, their families were not casually but symbiotically linked. Dorothy would quit Vienna with the Freuds, or not at all. C.C.B., for his part, had not only his son's feelings to consider, but also his position that fascism was a negative influence on the children. Though these custody battles were waged on the higher ground of the children's welfare, it was the children who increasingly seemed like hostages to the ideological impass of a broken marriage.

Despite Dorothy's strong feelings the Four were now three. Agreeing to write at least once a week and to return to Vienna for summer analysis, Bob had left for college in high spirits. But in Ohio he discovered that he was unlike his fellow Antiochians. They shrank from his analytic vision and introspective confidences. All "lightness, gayness, laughter, fun, dancing, clothes and artificiality," he pronounced them "masters of acting." Feeling very much the outsider Bob began to reexamine the Bergasse life-style. To his mother, he reported the comment of one professor, "It is good that you have to come over here; you are now going to get away from the influence of Psychoanalysis and see other kinds of psychology that are much more advanced in their methods." Why was it, demanded Bob, that the Freuds avoided the subjects of Adler, Jung, Stekel, and the rest? Were they afraid of dissent? Few Americans could understand Dorothy's viewpoint, Bob continued. Surely she must realize that the experiences of her youth had prejudiced her against the United States. He advised her to read *Brave New World,* despite, he wrote, its being among other things "a mockery of analysis." Evidently, Bob wanted to test Dorothy's resolve on this most crucial aspect of their lives.

Continuing to play the devil's advocate, Bob prophesied a Nazi Austria, and passing along to Dorothy the following words from her father-in-law, which he knew she was certain to find nettlesome:

> The Versailles Treaty was a cruel as well as foolish affair and it is no wonder that the Germans have revolted from it and are determined to get rid of it as soon as possible; but their methods are most unwise.
>
> I don't know much about the German people, but I believe they like to be ruled and always have liked it, which makes it easier for their rulers to determine policy.

C.C.B. continued:

> What I have said about the Germans is, I fancy, not true of the Austrians; but Dollfuss seems to be having his troubles. Professor Redlech [of law, at the University of Vienna, afterwards Harvard] was here the other day and, although he is very reserved in his statements, he appreciates the seriousness of conditions and will not be surprised to see the Nazis push

their way into the cabinet and unseat Dollfuss. The fact is that Dollfuss is a Fascist and there isn't much difference between a Fascist and a Nazi, is there?

Bob did not hesitate to note that while writing he was listening to Richard Wagner's martial *Walküre* work toward its howling, blood-curdling "Ride."

Dorothy might have taken Bob's obvious attempt to bait her with a grain of salt, as his crowing was if anything overdue. Instead, to help him "clarify" his ideas about analysis, she sent him a boxload of analytic texts. And when a week passed without a letter from Yellow Springs she wrote Bob that he must be in a state of depression. Anna Freud's response was typically more measured, a dispassionate litmus test of his feelings. "Do you think we put too much on you to send you out in a world with an analytic background when the world outside has so little use for it?" And yet the asking makes the question seem rhetorical, as if she had begun to fear that it was so.

In February 1934, Vienna's socialists staged a workers' revolution. Brutal bite was added to Dollfuss's reprisal by Nazis within the police force. Among those arrested was Valti Rosenfeld; Herr Wimmer turned out to be the informant and was fired. Otherwise, at the Bergasse, the worst of the revolution seems to have been the inconvenience. Freud wrote Arnold Zweig, "Our little bit of civil war was not at all nice. You could not go out without your passport, electricity was cut off for a day, and the thought that the water supply might run out was very unpleasant. Now everything is calm, the calm of tension, you might say: just like waiting in a hotel room for the second shoe to be flung against the wall."

C.C.B. had cabled Dorothy at the first report of street fighting, ordering her to return the children to America forthwith. Instead, to satisfy his concern for their safety, she sent them to Italy with Margot Goldschmidt, a trip which led them through Florence and Venice before landing them, penniless, on the steps of Tiffany & Company's Paris branch. Dressed in their *bauern* garb, laden with bundles of Venetian bullrushes, looking, quite possibly, like Nazi youth, they entered the glittering palace, identified themselves as Tiffany grandchildren, and requested emergency funds. The distance which lay between the children and their heritage was crystallized in the startled clerk's incredulous stare. Eventually, however, they were recognized and advanced the trainfare home to their mother.

Back in Vienna, Dollfuss had outlawed all political parties except his own "Fatherland Front," in hopes of staving off the Nazis, setting the stage for the summer of 1934. In early July, with the 1932 Lindbergh kidnapping and the impending 1934 Gloria Vanderbilt custody battle probably also on her mind, Dorothy sent Mami to Black Point, keeping Tinky back in case the Burlinghams tried to snare the Four at a stroke. "[Bompa] cannot quite understand that Tinky is not coming with the others," wrote Bob. "He also does not seem to believe that she is held [behind] because of exams." As soon as they had all arrived, Robert—"all sunburnt and looking his best"—called a conference, telling the children that he begrudged Dorothy for taking advantage of his unselfishness. Had he been firmer in the past he could not be separated from them now, he said. He felt like a summer parent; that his relationship with them lacked the depth and intimacy a father deserved. His career had been made a shambles by his shuttling about, and he missed having a home of his own. Now, he said, he aimed to see each of them at least once a year and he was already looking for a house where they all could settle when they finished their schooling.

"How can he think we would do that?!" Mabbie wrote Dorothy. "He said he has so often been treated meanly and that's why he is so sensitive now, and his nervous breakdowns were not because he is a maniac but because his heart was broken—it was very sad and I cried."

On July 25, 1934, a group of Nazis burst into Dollfuss's chancellery and shot him point-blank in the throat. As the Germans prepared to intervene only Mussolini's quick march to the Brenner Pass prevented a coup d'état. With the Mariahilferstrasse draped in black, Kurt von Schuschnigg assumed both the chancellorship and Dollfuss's "middle course" of Austrian fascism. And the assassination was followed by Hitler's consolidation of the offices of chancellor and president under the title Der Führer. One result of these developments was Margot Goldschmidt's decision not to return to Vienna at summer's end. If Dorothy wanted her children back, she realized, she would have to come and get them herself. She did, and shortly after she joined Romami in Lake Placid, C.C.B. penned her the following letter, by turns charming, blunt, disingenuous and blistering.

I have had no opportunity to talk with you alone, and I did not wish to introduce any disharmonious note in our welcome to you here, which, as you must know, always is and always will be most sincere and hearty. It was sweet of you to come down and see Mother. She was touched by it and so was I. I hope it was not hard for you to come, and it is always a delight to have you in our house.

I have knocked at your door often, and to make a bad pun, I don't want to be a continual knocker. But I am getting very old, and while I never stand on rights, which I consider vastly inferior to duties, I have a right to talk plainly to you and we have always talked to each other plainly and frankly, have we not?

1. You have done wonders with the children; the Freudian influence has been all to their benefit; they are four remarkable personages.

2. I have not now and have not had, except momentarily when the news looked particularly bleak, any fear for your personal safety in Vienna, but I do not think the atmosphere of Vienna is salubrious or proper for the bringing up of children in their teens. I appreciate that a riot or bombing or shooting in one district does not reach to another one; it is like a race riot in Negro Harlem, which we should not hear of at 77th Street except from the papers. What I think is serious is the psychological effect of the sad condition of Vienna—poverty, oppression, suppression of liberty of speech, writing and action, cruelties worthy of the Nazis themselves— these are the things that subconsciously affect us, even joyous children in their teens.

3. I am far more interested in the children than I am in either you or Robert. I think the younger ones are now being deprived of opportunities which they are entitled to. They have got all the German or Austrian Kultur they need. I think they should be in American schools in the winter and visit Europe in summer. There are schools in this country which are wise and enlightened. There are teachers like the headmaster of Deerfield, who are marvellous men, and the same is true of some of the girls' schools. And then there is the companionship of young and happy children doing things together. We have tried to bring the girls and Michael into contact with the fine children there are at the Point, but without much success. When Margot was here last year they were with her very much and Tinky was shy. Then, naturally, Robert, having been deprived of their society so long, loves to do things with them instead of leaving them free to find themselves with their contemporaries. That is inevitable. In school it would be different. They would get on famously with other children.

4. If you are adamant against their entering American schools, then they should be in Switzerland or France and acquire the *Latin* culture.

Well, I have written you perhaps too much and in too great haste. I recognize that you are acting according to your best judgment and your conscience, but some of the bitterest suffering in this world, from the Middle Ages down, has been caused by people who were following their conscience. It would not be fair for me to close this letter without my telling you plainly that while Mother and I have always and inevitably told Robert that he must do nothing which would break up the unity of the family, even at the greatest cost to himself, we have never spoken of you to him or to anyone else except in kindness and love. But notwithstanding this, I feel it my duty to put down in black and white my opinion, which is that you have failed to treat him fairly and justly in the matter of the children. You observe that I leave the rest of us out. We adore the Four and you know how little we have seen of them.

Dorothy's confidence was pierced by none of this, however, and she did not veer from her course. Professor's influence was now plainly evident in Dorothy's confrontations, in rising to face painful situations head-on. From Yellow Springs came confirmation of this progress report from Bob, who wrote, "Mother, you really have changed a good deal during the year '34. You seem to get so much more out of life than you used to. I am so pleased. You seem to be so much happier and contented within yourself, and with your friends. I was surprised that you are able to enjoy America, although it must have been fearfully unpleasant at times."

Dorothy's tenacity was, however, fetched at the price of her husband's stability. After Mami's departure Robert had collapsed once again, and Bob, arriving in New York in early October en route to Yellow Springs, had found his father "so thin and run down that I didn't know what to do. . . ." A year later Robert was still "not well altogether." Under the circumstances, remembered Anny Katan, "Dorothy did not want to go back . . . to face her husband or his family that summer." So Katan agreed to see Timi over herself. Mabbie, with Bob—after summer analysis—followed in August. It was then, with the Four in Black Point, that Dorothy decided to visit the U.S. Legation and speak with George S. Messersmith, the tough, combative foreign minister.

Dorothy knew that Messersmith and C.C.B. were acquainted, but may not have known that C.C.B. had secured Messersmith's promise, upon his transfer from Berlin, that "Mrs. Burlingham's personal welfare will be a matter of solicitude for me." Messersmith told Dorothy that he did not consider her family to be in imminent danger, and that he would do everything in his power to assist them in the case of an emergency. But he had discouraged his own teenage nieces from visiting him as they had the previous winter, not wishing to subject them to any unnecessary danger. And as her children were already in America, he advised her to let them remain.

But, Messersmith informed C.C.B., "Mrs. Burlingham seems to have some rather strange ideas about our own country and I feel that she does not know it quite as well as some of the rest of us . . . I could readily see . . . that she did not like what I said and that what she really wished me to say was that it was perfectly all right in every way for the children to come back. I told her that she must not expect me to say merely what she wished me to say, but that as she asked my opinion I must give it to her frankly. She made it clear to me that she would insist on the children's returning." They did, with the exception of Bob.

Bob was increasingly Dorothy's concern as he began to fall under the spell of his grandfather, who was never more influential in New York than in his seventies, when he was known as its first citizen. Oswald Garrison Villard was first to use the epithet, writing in *The Nation*, "If any man deserves the title of the first citizen of this municipality, it is Mr. Burlingham. If there is a good, liberal cause which has not had his aid and support, I should like to know what it is." The many crusades to which C.C.B. had lent his support had included a federal child labor amendment, the establishment of a minimum wage, and public welfare programs. Harvard law professor Andrew L. Kaufman writes that "whether it was on a small scale, like orchestrating the admission of [Benjamin] Cardozo to the Century Club in the face of at least some latent anti-semitism or getting Harvard to award honorary degrees to women, or on the somewhat larger scale of opening the Columbia and Harvard Law Schools to women, or the American Bar Association to blacks, C.C.B. was ever ready to lead or join the effort." C.C.B. had fought with greatest vigilance, however, for the cause of an independent and qualified judiciary, and was largely responsible for advancing to the federal bench such jurists as Learned Hand, Charles M. Hough, and Henry Galbraith Ward. He had refused a unanimous third-term nomination as president of the New York Bar Association, instead replacing Robert de

Forest as president of the Welfare Council. This and a brief tenure as president of the Board of Education were his only public offices, his influence otherwise wielded wholly as a private citizen. After starting Thomas Dewey on his racket-busting career, C.C.B. went on to orchestrate the mayoral nomination of Fiorello La Guardia, to whom, according to a bemused Felix Frankfurter, C.C.B. became "the Madame Pompadour, the Eminence Grise, the Colonel House and the Jim Farley, all rolled into one. . . ." C.C.B. was reportedly the only one of La Guardia's advisers who "never fell from grace." He listened to C.C.B., said Whitney North Seymour, a former bar association president because "he had no personal ax to grind. He never asked for anything for himself. If he recommended someone for the bench, it was not because he was a friend, but because he thought he would make a good judge." His friendships ranged from F.D.R. to Hermann, the doorman at 860 Park. Even Mabbie had to admit, "Bompa is too wise and sharp for me."

In October 1935, C.C.B. landed Bob a work-study job with F.D.R.'s brain truster Thomas Corcoran. Before long, Bob was dining in the White House, having tea with Supreme Court Justices Charles Evans Hughes, Louis Brandeis, and Benjamin Cardozo, and rapturously writing Dorothy that "Washington is like a fairy city where luck is always with you, and you are always having your every wish fulfilled . . ."

C.C.B. could not let well enough alone, however. Despite the fact that Antioch seemed increasingly right for Bob, C.C.B. could see it only as the place for Bob's "re-Americanization," and as a stepping-stone to Harvard. Already by Christmas of Bob's first term at Yellow Springs, C.C.B. had sent him up to Cambridge to chat with Professor Frank Taussig, author of the classic text *Principles of Economics.* Taussig had transferred with C.C.B. from St. Louis's Washington University into the Class of 1879, and had obligingly compared Antioch's work-study program to "what the Nazis are doing in Germany." C.C.B. had been chipping away at Bob ever since, despite a protest from Antioch's dean of men. The Gilder boys, Richard and Rodman, were enthusiastic about Harvard, and Erik Erikson had met there with a warm reception; that bridged two worlds. But Bob, with a track record of false starts and distracting interests, was rightly concerned about leaving Antioch another unfinished symphony. He could not choose.

B
ob was in fact still gripped by the conflict which had brought him to analysis ten years earlier. His decision to return to America for college, his repeated insistence to Dorothy on the inevitability of a Nazi Austria, and especially his application to Washington of glowing terms once reserved exclusively for Vienna, all indicated his burning wish for a reconciliation between his parents, or, as he may have thought, for the two halves of himself to be fused once again. At Christmas 1935, Bob compared photographs of Dorothy in the year of her marriage with the young Katharine Hepburn, and reported Robert "alive and natural . . . I can well understand that people find it hard to believe that he can get sick." As Anna Freud must have known, Bob's wish was the source of his agonizing ambivalence—*techniker* or *musiker?* Harvard or Antioch? heterosexual or homosexual?—as well as the wrong choices he made, in the instances of architecture and Harvard, and possibly in his heterosexual life as well. With unerring accuracy Bob often seemed to choose a path suited to someone else. He denied himself; that was the final word and language of his dissatisfaction. He could not blast his life-support system, after all; the anger he had directed toward Dorothy for leaving his father, like his anger toward Anna Freud for "replacing" him, had to find another outlet. Under such circumstances even the two-thousand-hour dose of psychoanalysis which, conservatively estimated, he had thus far received, had not prevented, and may have actually catalyzed, the transformation of a Milquetoast delinquency into a drive of self-destructive capability.

One problem was that Anna Freud was a prime player in the drama she was obliged to critique. Analytic neutrality had gone by the boards long ago; stepmother, friend, ego-ideal—Anna Freud was all of these things to Bob; but disinterested party she was not. The same person urging Dorothy to reject Robert was trying to help Bob adjust to his fatherlessness. Hindsight makes it obvious that Bob's sense of loss could not be eased by one who had a personal stake in perpetuating it.

But analysis was new then, and the early analysts as *schlampig* as Vienna itself, the pioneers relatively easygoing, humane, and freewheeling in their clinical approaches. If a patient walked into a consulting room with a broken arm, the Viennese did not fear for the transference, they voiced their sympathy and concern. Professor and Anna Freud in particular cheerfully ignored this measure of analytic orthodoxy, fraternizing with their patients, weaving in and out of the transference and "non-transference" relationships quite naturally. Anna Freud often attended to her knitting during her analytic sessions and, at the conclusion of one hour with Erik Erikson, presented him with a sweater for his newborn son; and the Four were treated to so many tasty treats during their hours that Frau Professor dryly exclaimed, "A costly affair, child analysis." The Freuds, in other words, did not allow the analytic process to exclude extra-analytic contact, and vice versa. Professor's analysis of his own daughter was surely the most conspicuous flouting of the laws he had laid down for others, though, perhaps, *Quod licet Jovi non licet bovi* ("What is permitted Jove is not permitted the ox").

In 1925 Anna Freud had been the brilliant analyst in the making, optimistic, young, and undaunted, her heady confidence reflected in a technique which blended therapeutic and educational aims. But to the Four she assumed the role of surrogate parent as well, which she saw as an opportunity to carry her technique of analytic pedagogy to its logical extreme, to stretch her control—and efficacy. This may explain why, once her friendship with Dorothy had cemented, she did not refer the children to other of Vienna's qualified analysts. She believed then, and always, that she was best qualified for the job of analyzing Dorothy's children.

At first her methods were richly rewarded. Bob's delinquency vanished as its underlying reasons were revealed to him, and by the summer of 1929 Anna Freud touted him as a living advertisement for psychoanalysis. It is not clear exactly when she began to appreciate the bind she was in; but even before Bob's first stateside visit, he had already been in analysis three times as long as the norm for the twenties. But the therapeutic process only grew more complicated. As early as the summer of 1932 Mabbie wrote Dorothy that Bob was almost finished with his analysis, an idea again voiced three years later by Bob himself; year after year he felt himself at the brink of a conclusion, yet unable to "turn the last stone."

The same was true of Mabbie. Ten years after Anna Freud had proclaimed hers the most successful of the first ten child cases, she was still in analysis and, like Bob, still suffering from the conflict which had brought her to analysis in the first place. Traumatized, too, by the severance of relations between her parents, Mabbie had continued to deal with her conflict of loyalties by in effect banishing it, choosing mother over father and clinging hard to Dorothy. While her agreeableness had made her dearly loved, she desperately needed to be more selfish, to stop lavishing herself upon others.

But Anna Freud was also in a compromised situation with Mabbie. Anna was, in fact, dead opposed to the influence of Mabbie's father. She was also considered Dorothy's "better half"; that is, her partner, friend, and double, an idealized version of everything that mother represented to Mabbie. Therefore, in reality and in Mabbie's fantasy, Anna Freud was identified with the very side of the conflict on which she was trapped, Mabbie's absolute loyalty to Dorothy extending through association to Anna Freud and psychoanalysis. It is not surprising that this same blurred twin image of motherhood impeded Mabbie's treatment. Anna Freud may have correctly fathomed her own ability to juggle her analytic, educational, and parental roles, but she had probably overestimated Boma. The convoluted circumstances definitely made analysis more difficult for them. Thus Mabbie's cri de coeur to Dorothy takes on new, tragic meaning. "Oh it's awfully blöd because everything has its unknown reasons. I with my many troublys and unknown reasons. Everything has an unknown reason. Oh reason after reason, everything with its reasons. It nearly makes me mad." This was hardly the desired result of her analysis.

But by the time that Anna Freud realized the effect of her clinical sloppiness, neither Bob nor Mabbie could do without her clinical support. They had become vulnerable for the protection they had received, and dependent on it. Snatching away the crutch she had fashioned for them would have been cruel, and it would have been an embarrassment and an indiscretion to turn them over to a colleague, and concede defeat. The Four were living proof of the effectiveness of her methods, and if she would boast the results, she could also take the heat. Anna Freud had little choice but to stick to her guns and hope for a kindly turn of fate.

Unfortunately even that hope was nurtured in the soil of cross-purposes. Far better that Bob and Mabbie had struck an analytic alliance with a neutral third party than with one so charismatically possessed of a cause, so brilliantly proselytizing a creed, and so totally invested in a blueprint for the future. The irony is that Dorothy, who had yearned to find just such a person, was by virtue of her age free to accept or reject the values that Anna Freud represented, while Boma had been indoctrinated into her program as children, without much choice or consent. Had Boma been of an analytic bent, like Ernsti Halberstadt, or Judy de Forest, or even capable of the kind of metamorphosis that Dorothy had achieved, Anna Freud might have harvested some lucky quirks of fate, since their grooming had been in psychoanalytic thought. But when it came to the artistic spirit little nourishment was to be found at the bosom of the Freud family.

It might seem that Freud, at least, was passionate about art; he was an avid collector of Egyptian sarcophagi, Chinese Buddhas, Attic vases, Roman busts, mythic figurines, and other fragments of mankind's archaic heritage. But Freud was actually condescending, if not outright scornful, of the artistic *Weltanschauung*. His intellect seemed almost befuddled when confronted with it. "The enjoyment of beauty," he wrote, "has a peculiar, mildly intoxicating quality of feeling. Beauty has no obvious use, nor is there any clear cultural necessity for it. Yet civilization could not do without it." He considered art an illusion, like religion, one offering quick, evanescent, aim-inhibited satisfactions, the real object of which is sexual in nature. In Freud's view, the artist is essentially a neurotic whose symptoms assume the form of art, a view which surely cast an unending, if indirect, drizzle on Boma's creative impulses. Although Anna Freud, and likely through association with Dorothy, did cultivate an appreciation of nature and music, she was cut from the same cloth as her father. And it is one thing for a parent to instill a behavorial code; it is another for an analyst to do the same; concocting an educational admixture that rubs against the grain of character is something else again. Herein lay quicksand for one "who always want[s] to change children."

The nature of the Freuds' gravitational pull on Dorothy only complicated the problem. Part of their attraction to her, one realizes, came from their endorsement of those spiritual things so dear to her mother and their rejection of the solipsistic artistry embodied by her father. Therefore by association Anna Freud was to Boma a reflection of Dorothy's childhood wish for the ascendancy of Lou (Mother-Healing) over Louis (Papa-Art). So far as Boma were concerned, Anna Freud, both as a person and an analyst, was positioned at the crux of Dorothy's fundamental conflict.

Dorothy knew well the "lightning speed and power" with which a mother's "affects" and "repressions" pass to her children. It was for this reason that she had worked on herself so diligently. But now, even as the bubble was beginning to burst around them, came a sobering realization. Uwe Henrik Peters describes it:

> Early psychoanalytic educational theory . . . raised the hope that it was possible to raise conflict-free people, if only disturbing influences—in particular those of family and environment—were eliminated or rectified early enough through child analysis. This inadmissibly simplified idea held the family, especially the mother, responsible for every disturbance and change in the child. The mother was thus expected to raise her child to be an emotionally well-balanced person. Anna Freud later explained that those were unrealistic and unrealisable expectations and that it was fundamentally impossible to reach this goal.

With this admission, the original object of Dorothy's pilgrimage effectively vanished. After ten long years, she as well as her children were stuck with many of the same old problems; problems that had once shuttled between them under cover of darkness now did so in the light of consciousness. They saw them; they knew them; they called them by name; but they could not necessarily make them disappear.

In place of a dramatic accession to freedom people began to look to analysis for more moderate gains over a longer term. Aaron Green, Janet Malcolm's pseudonymous, modern-day Freudian, says that "analysis leaves the patient with more freedom of choice than he had before—but how much more? This much: instead of going straight down the meridian, he will go five degrees, ten degrees—maybe fifteen degrees if you push very hard—to the left or right, but no more than that." Gradually, the two-year analysis of the 1920s gave way to the five, ten, fifteen, twenty years of the heyday fifties. And the increase altered the nature of the analytic alliance. The analyst became more of an ongoing support system, an outlet for and clarifier of day-to-day emotive confidences. In this sense, at least, the analysand became less self-reliant, less independent or *selbstandig*—to use a word which reverberates continuously throughout Mabbie's correspondence, a word that clearly echoed a prime concern of Anna Freud's.

Dorothy was struggling to become *selbstandig* every bit as hard as Mabbie and Bob, and in 1935 she terminated her analysis. But no sooner had she quit than it resumed again. In September she consulted with Freud's former physician Felix Deutsch, who reported to his wife Helene, Dorothy's seminar professor, "I find she is not in the best psychic condition—the analysis is finished, and the transference is unsolved. She is now having me treat her organically—a feeble substitute. A poor shadow creature; can't live without the light that Professor infuses in her. It will be no different with the children."

Dependency had become an issue for the entire family. The extent to which Dorothy was dependent upon her children became apparent only after she was separated from them, when she observed that she had in part taken up a career to guard against this pitfall of single parenthood. Then it was clear that her longing for them was uncontrollable. She must therefore have been haunted by the specter of the Nazis finishing what her in-laws had begun. Already by September 1936 Bob was at Harvard, Tinky was eyeing Bennington, and Michael, the most enthusiastic of the Four about America, was destined for MIT. Nonetheless Dorothy knew it was highly improbable that the Freuds would also end up in a country that Freud disliked, and this was her problem. And so Dorothy's anxieties escalated as Hitler began systematically stripping German Jews of their rights of citizenship, renounced the military provisions of the Versailles Treaty, reinstated conscription, and began rebuilding the German war machine. And when Austria, still shaking in the jaws of the Great Depression, began to benefit from the flush of economic prosperity engendered by the remilitarization, she must have truly been concerned.

Of her children it was Boma, the elder pair, upon whom Dorothy relied the most, and whose attachment was to her in turn the most reinforcing. That is why Dorothy had responded as she had to Bob's challenges to analysis and the Bergasse life-style, and the reason also why he tested her so provocatively. They shared an uncommonly close bond plied by impulses neither of them could easily do without. Between them of course stood the figure of Anna Freud, doing her judicious best to deliver the conscious from the unconscious and separate the normal from the neurotic, while also trying to honor their individual needs, which, at times, naturally conflicted. Amidst the increasing political turbulence, it was inevitable that Anna would eventually have to weigh in the balance the urgency of their respective emotional needs, and decide in favor of one or the other.

The prelude to this sounded in early summer 1937, when Bob discovered that he had flunked out of Harvard. Evidently carried away by an atmosphere where his charm and background had made him very popular, he had neglected to open a book. His social calendar, on the other hand, had been so full that on one occasion Richard Gilder's roommate, David Rockefeller, had resorted to telegram in order to reach him.

Dorothy, by this time missing Bob "dreadfully," impulsively called for his immediate return to Vienna—naturally for more analysis. But when she learned that he had instead determined to win readmission through summer school, she wrote:

> I guess everyone has such jolts in one thing or the other, they are never pleasant, but they are something that makes one fight with all one's might against those destructive qualities in oneself—& analysis is what one turns to as a help towards unravelling those tendencies, but you are right in first seeing what you can do for yourself. . . .

Likewise anticipating Bob's early return that summer, Anna Freud had reserved for him an analytic hour, the first of which she now used to establish, via correspondence, a starting point for those to follow.

> I feel it should be very possible to solve the puzzle and . . . I still feel confident that you can do it. Not because I believe in that outside [facade] that impresses the others, but because of some hidden energy in you that has to be set free some day. Also because I know that it is so very worthwhile to become all right.

When Bob finally returned to Vienna in late summer, he did so triumphantly, reinstated in the Class of 1939. Like a general returning from a successful campaign, he had piloted his Gilder and Parker cousins through the vineyards of Champagne in his spanking new yellow Oldsmobile convertible, rising every so often from behind the wheel to shout *aber ja!* [but yes] at flabbergasted flocks of sheep. One might suppose that Bob's elbow grease and high spirits were token enough of his intentions and state of mind, and a brief respite was probably in

order before the start of a second year at Cambridge. Instead, while his
peers basked at the Salzburg *Festspiel,* Bob was obliged to introspect at
Grinzing; and, in September, it was decided—by Bob, with Anna
Freud's council—that he would not return to Cambridge after all, but
would remain in Vienna for analysis full-time until he had decided
how better to manage his life.

The news provoked a flood of telegrams from an irate C.C.B., and one
even from the Viennese-born Felix Frankfurter. In light of Bob's rein-
statement, it was a puzzling decision. Surely, adding Harvard to his
growing list of "unfinished symphonies" was not in Bob's best interest.
But, as it happened, one of those quirks of fate for which Anna Freud
had been on the lookout had seemingly materialized in the form of
Rigmor "Mossik" Sørensen, a young Norwegian whom Dorothy would
recall as having about her "something so alive, brilliantly charming &
glowing." Anna Freud had witnessed the beneficial effect on Mabbie of
her romantic involvement with Simon Schmiderer, a fellow architectural
student at the *Kunstgewerbeschule.* The son of a locomotive engineer,
steeped in the craftsman ethos of his Hohe Tauern village, Simon seemed
so right for Mabbie that her analysis ended even as she prepared to
announce their engagement. And Mossik, the daughter of an industrious,
small-town merchant, likewise embodied many of those wholesome
qualities which Anna Freud had so faithfully labored to instill in the Four.

If Anna Freud had indeed foreseen Mossik as the potential match for
Bob, Dorothy had not, since she knew Mossik only as Mabbie's and
Tinky's friend. After learning that Mossik's application to the University
of Wisconsin had arrived too late for consideration that fall, and knowing
that she did not want to return to Norway, Dorothy had sympathetically
invited her to stay with them while taking courses at the University of
Vienna. But then, when she learned that she and Bob had become intimate, her attitude had changed dramatically. Citing her responsibility in
loco parentis, she had told Mossik that she would have to make other
arrangements. This had been followed by another abrupt about-turn.
When Mossik returned from a long, contemplative walk, Dorothy apolo-
gized profusely, and said she could stay, after all. Mossik later suspected
Dorothy of having learned of their liaison through a breach of analytic
confidence, Anna reporting to Dorothy what she had learned from Bob
in analysis. Then, believes Mossik, after hearing of Dorothy's jealous
reaction to their romance Anna Freud must have given her a good

scolding. This was Mossik's first glimpse of the submerged cable which bound her future husband and mother-in-law.

It was later, with the decks cleared for serious courtship, that the decision was made for Bob to remain in Vienna. From this it would appear that Anna Freud believed Bob at that point to have been more in need of a relationship than an education. In reality, however, the matchmaking provided a handy rationale for Bob's return to the Viennese fold. Anna Freud had at last been forced to weigh in the balance and urgency of needs, and Bob's needs at that time were pale beside Dorothy's.

Oddly enough, it was Robert who divined the underlying reason for "Bob's decision." From Lake Placid he wrote his father that ". . . from the humanitarian view-point, and especially during these disturbed times . . . Dorothy probably needs Bob's guidance and love." The extent of Dorothy's neediness was vividly demonstrated within weeks when she was diagnosed as having tuberculosis.

Her illness had any number of possible somatic causes, starting with the damp northern exposure of her Bergasse bedroom. Then, too, the Freuds' devoted housekeeper, Paula Fichtl, previously in Dorothy's employ, had had a tubercular history. And of course the disease ran in Dorothy's family. Though she was then unaware of it, pulmonary X-rays subsequently revealed tubercular scars in Dorothy's lungs from childhood.

The Freudian view would assign these factors a secondary place, however. Freud himself had predicated Dorothy's physical health upon her emotional well-being, and he surely related the incursion on her lungs to the fragmentation of her stabilizing world. One can anyway imagine the pitched psychological battle which must have preceded the illness, and the resigned soul-searching which must inevitably have followed it, together with a welter of conflicting emotions—anxiety, rage, futility, despair, depression, words which only cloak the reality they are meant to convey. Dorothy's friends doubted that she would survive the year.

Thus it was from the removed perspective of a hospital bed in the Cottage Sanitarium near the Turkenschanzpark that an incapacitated, helpless Dorothy observed the dénouement to her life in Vienna.

Chancellor Schuschnigg had struck a deal with Hitler in July of 1936 conceding Austria to be a German state in return for self-determination, a maneuver that allowed each side to carry on exactly as before. Nazi cells within Austria had continued to pave the path to Anschluss, but Hitler had grown impatient, having expected Austria to fall bloodlessly into his hands long before.

This was the state of affairs on Christmas Day 1937 when, without a breath of prior warning, Robert arrived at Dorothy's bedside, considerably agitated by the death of his mother on December 7 from a protracted illness. That fall he had evidently suffered another attack and had taken a leave of absence from his new position as curator of the Pathological Museum at the Cornell Medical Center. He had gone, as he so often did, to the Adirondacks, where he had sufficiently recovered to put in a half day at the Saranac Laboratory under Director Leroy U. Garder—the subject of Robert's research all these years having been the particular illness which Dorothy had just contracted. He had been researching "the relation of antibody formation to silicosis" when he received word of Mabbie's engagement, which had destabilized him further. He had actually written C.C.B. to instruct Messersmith to instruct his boss, Grenville Emmet, to stop the marriage, which was possible as Mabbie was not yet twenty-one. He had cited three reasons: "I. Mabbie's youthful age. 2. Mab. an American (I am opposed to international marriages). 3. S.S. an Austrian, probably a Catholic. His social background." But the following day, after receiving a special delivery letter from his father, Robert had reversed himself. "I have written Mabbie by the Queen Mary, and though I wish that the engagement and marriage turn out happily, I do not retreat from my position regarding international marriages, and express my wish to see & talk with the young man, before giving my paternal blessing." This was presumably another reason for his visit which, with the extinction of the maternal check on his impulses, C.C.B. had been unable to prevent.

Dorothy had just observed (for she could hardly celebrate) Christmas Eve. With the exception of Tinky, who had started at Bennington, a family swollen by marital prospects had gathered around her bed before heading off to Simon's hometown of Saalfelden for a fortnight's skiing. The next day Dorothy had received a cable from C.C.B. alerting her to Robert's impending arrival, and she had in turn wired Boma to head him off at Paris. He had arrived in Vienna, nonetheless, with his son and daughter the very next day.

Robert may have come with visions of healing her and taking charge of his family in their hour of need, though Dorothy probably figured his was a last-ditch effort to achieve by force what he had been unable to finesse otherwise. Refusing all entreaties to return to New York, he further unbalanced the family equation. His children tried to avoid him, and Mabbie, who had taken an apartment with Simon, kept up the pretense that she was still sleeping at home. Mossik each morning rumpled Mabbie's bedclothes before Robert arrived from his Ninth District hotel. Then, after breakfast, leaving the Bergasse, he invariably took a tram to the Turkenschanzpark, and there would have spent the entire day had Dorothy not quickly arranged a research project for him at the university. After a month Robert still showed no inclination to return to New York.

Then the wheel of an independent Austria began its final revolution. On February 12, Hitler summoned Schuschnigg to Berchtesgaden and there served him with an ultimatum. He had either to fill five key cabinet posts with Nazis and pardon Nazi political prisoners, or face invasion. Schuschnigg struggled to escape the Führer's trap, appointing men who favored a Nazi Austria separate from Nazi Germany and granting socialist prisoners amnesty as well. And he called for a plebiscite for the Austrian people to decide their own fate. But Hitler learned that Austrian Nazis could deliver no more than 35 percent of the vote, and ordered the invasion. Dorothy heard it on the radio that day, March 11. "Austrians!" shouted Schuschnigg. "Chancellor Hitler has asked me to cancel the plebiscite and to resign. If I do not yield within the hour, German troops will invade Austria. To avoid bloodshed and destruction I have tendered my resignation. God save Austria!" Even as Nazi thugs hustled Schuschnigg off to prison a rain of paper leaflets fell from bombers in the sky: "Nazi Germany welcomes Nazi Austria!" Austria was now part of "Greater Germany."

The following day Adolf Hitler made a clamorous reentry into the capital city. He appeared in triumph on the balcony of the Hotel Imperial, where the year before Thomas Mann had read a tribute on the occasion of Freud's eightieth birthday. Today, however, the air trembled with the thunder of black leather boots goosestepping on the cobbles of the

Ringstrasse. As Schuschnigg would write in his memoirs, though born in Austria, Hitler had hated his mother country from boyhood, and was determined to destroy her: "as an empire, as a tradition, as an idea, and as a culture." But most awful to Dorothy, huddled by her wireless, must have been the din of approval issuing from all those Austrian throats.

Back at the Bergasse Paula Fichtl knocked softly on the door of Professor's study, and when he bade her enter handed him a bouquet of flowers. *"Für* meinen *führer,"* she said ("For *my* leader").

It galled Dorothy to be bedridden at exactly that time when, as an American, she could have been especially helpful. Still she could speak— in labored gasps—on the telephone, and she informed Marie Bonaparte in Paris and Ernest Jones in London of Professor's intransigence. He refused to emigrate, wishing to die peacefully on Austrian soil. On March 12 the American chargé d'affaires in Vienna, John Cooper Wiley, called on Freud to work out a plan for his protection. It was agreed that at the first Nazi provocation, Anna Freud would use the private telephone line between her bedroom and Dorothy's to alert one of the Burlinghams to call the American embassy, which in turn would dispatch an official to "drop in" casually on the Freuds.

The following day a meeting of the Executive Committee of the Vienna Psychoanalytic Society, chaired by Anna Freud, voted to dissolve the Society and urged its members to flee. Told of the committee's decision to relocate wherever he decided to settle, Freud did not reveal his intentions. They must do as the Jews had done after the destruction of the Temple in Jerusalem, he said, "open a school at Jabneh for the study of the Torah."

Of Dorothy's family, Mabbie and Simon were first to leave; Simon's socialist activities were well known to Viennese Nazis—he had been arrested on at least one occasion. Posing as an architect hired by Dorothy to investigate Dutch properties, he slipped across the Swiss border with Mabbie, joining Anny Katan.

On March 15 the Nazis burst into the psychoanalytic publishing house, arresting Anna Freud's brother Martin, its director. Another posse invaded the Bergasse and made off with six thousand shillings from Freud's safe; a week later the Gestapo returned and this time made off with Anna Freud herself. That day—March 22—may have been the worst of Dorothy's life. Flat on her back in a horrible apprehension, she learned of events in snatches over the phone. Child analyst Anna Maenchen had just left the Bergasse after trying to reassure Anna that the Nazis would not dare arrest Freud on account of his years. Anna had responded that they had already arrested Felix Frankfurter's elderly brother. As she departed Maenchen had seen the Gestapo loitering on the street nearby, but had also noticed a limousine from the U.S. Legation, the stars and stripes fluttering conspicuously from the antenna.

Anna Freud had brought the sedative Veronal with her to Gestapo headquarters, but was not tortured. Upon her return at day's end, however, Freud bowed to the wishes of Bonaparte and Jones and agreed to emigrate; he chose London, where his youngest son, Ernst, lived. Aided by the American ambassador to France, William C. Bullitt, Jones and Bonaparte set about the long, tricky business of securing exit permissions, immigration visas, and work permits for Freud and his entourage.

"Both Freud himself and Anna were never realistic about politics," recalled Anny Katan:

> I had tried to warn them before I left Vienna for Holland and also before the Nazis occupied Austria. I was not naive in politics and I told them exactly what would happen. Freud's humorous fantasy was that the Austrians were so disorderly in every respect that they would also be disorderly in applying Hitler's ideas, views, and laws. I told him that the disorderliness of the Austrians would play no role because the Germans would follow. I could not persuade him. Freud and Anna really tried to prove that nothing bad would happen. It is interesting what a great role denial can play even in personalities like Professor Freud and Anna.

Dorothy meanwhile made provisions for her own family. After Mossik had left for Norway, Dorothy convinced Robert to escort Michael to America, knowing it was his cherished goal to see Michael properly prepared for the college entrance examinations. Michael, the youngest of the Four, was seventeen. They arrived in New York on March 29, Robert writing Dorothy that "Michael has gone on to Cambridge to see Alfred de Forest regarding admission requirements to the Massachusetts Institute of Technology." He added that he would also take Dorothy's X-rays around to various diagnostic experts. Dorothy had intended to remain in Vienna with Bob until the Freuds were safely out, but the new regime extended to non-Austrians a law forbidding the possession of foreign-held assets. Dorothy could either forfeit her New York trust fund, go to jail, or flee. So on April 1, one month shy of thirteen years after leaving New York for Geneva, she rose from her hospital bed, motored to the Westbannhof station, and boarded a Zurich-bound train. In Switzerland she could still help the Freuds.

XI

The Blitz

Dorothy and Bob had left Zurich for southern Switzerland's Ital-
ian-speaking Ticino by April 9. For the rich blueness of the lake,
the majesty of Mount Savatore, and the purity of air at nine
hundred feet especially, Dorothy chose Lugano. The canton of Ticino has
been described as resembling "an udder drooping from the vaccine body
of Switzerland," and Lugano as "the teat of the udder . . . dripping *milch*
or *lait* or *latte* into the mouth of northern Italy."

At the Carleton Hotel, joined by Mabbie and Simon, Dorothy posted
a Vienna watch. Reports of the anti-Semitic pogrom, deportations, and
suicides wound her to high tension, toughened her defenses, and probably,
aided her own survival. The Nazis had been busy, seizing the psychoanalytic library and property of the publishing house, confiscating Freud's
private assets and holding his library and antique collection against their
demands for further ransom. Marie Bonaparte eventually paid the moneys
in Freud's behalf, but Dorothy continued to fear for the discovery of his
foreign holdings. Within months, galvanized by the perilous situations,
Dorothy was back on her feet, and by year's end, fully recovered,
astonishing those who had anticipated her demise.

She occupied herself with the plethora of affidavits required for her
emigrating colleagues, a delicate business since the Nazis were opening
all mail, even that delivered in care of the U.S. Legation. And by phone
she kept in daily contact with Anna Freud, on whom the strain had
evidently begun to tell also. To American analyst Edith Jackson, whom

Dorothy would contact repeatedly in the difficult days ahead, she wrote on April 13, "Please don't repeat this—but I wanted to warn you. We all know how much Anna Freud has done & can do to help people in need—but there are times when she is not herself."

The month of April passed with malevolent intent, the Nazis continuing to "exact their pound of flesh" (Ernest Jones's phrase). Finally Freud wrote his son Ernst in London, "It is time for Ahasuerus [the Wandering Jew] to come to rest somewhere." The picture was brightening. On May 5 Dorothy returned to Vienna briefly in order to fetch Professor's sister-in-law, Minna Bernays, herself an invalid suffering from glaucoma and heart disease. And that same day Bob left for London, where Mabbie and Simon were arranging the details of their wedding with the help of Gertrude Ely. In Paris Bob stopped to visit Princess Bonaparte, who said that the Freuds ought to be out within two or three weeks. From the Hotel Louvois he informed Dorothy of this, but added, "The anti-Jewish propaganda has become much worse. There are many suicides still, and the Princess feels very strongly that they should somehow be prevented because it's just what the G's [Nazis] want." Bob wrote again late in the day from London's Stafford Hotel.

> Tomorrow is Professor's birthday. I do so wish that he could know the good news. I have just heard from Ernst [Freud] and [Ernest] Jones. [U.S. Ambassador to France William C.] Bullitt was here for a day, and Ernst took the opportunity to see him, and tell him as much as he knew, and in turn was told that Bullitt would do everything he possibly could, even if necessary go to Berlin and there see Neurath and Göbbels. He will immediately get in touch with Wily when he gets to Paris to report on the conditions [in Vienna] . . . Ernst and Jones both think that the Fs will come sooner than 3 weeks, perhaps in 10–14 days.

Dorothy remained in Lugano despite these reassurances. Even Mabbie's wedding on May 8 did not budge her from her post. Not until May 28 did she feel assured enough of the Freuds' safe passage to depart with Tante Minna for London. But that day proved to be a disaster.

Suddenly, the trail of footprints was clear for her to see. She had been certainly forewarned by numerous, inescapable signs; and she had probably always half-expected and feared it. But at that moment, with her concern so totally concentrated on the Freuds, it hit her from the blind side.

Mabbie had told Dorothy back in the summer of 1932 that had she been in her father's place she would have "shot myself long ago—or run away to some far off country." Both options had evidently been on Robert's mind. One Christmas he had sent to Vienna a recording of Mendelssohn's "Oh for the Wings of a Dove," saying it had made a great impression on him when he had first heard it in London, the summer before starting medical school. The title, as Robert well knew, was from Psalm 55. "Fearfulness and trembling are come upon me,/ And horror hath overwhelmed me./ And I said, Oh that I had wings like a dove!/ For then would I fly away, and be at rest." And as C.C.B. had written Dorothy upon her arrival in New York in 1934 to fetch the children, "Mother and I have always and invariably told Robert not to do anything which would break up the unity of the family, *even at the greatest cost to himself. . . .*" To these sketchy strokes had soon been added broader lines: the death of Robert's mother on December 7, 1937, the failure of Robert's final bid to be reunited with them in Vienna, and then, with Mabbie's engagement, the knowledge that his children would soon have families of their own and would no longer need him; that it was too late. Still he had clung to the thread of hope that events might somehow propel Dorothy back to the States. On April 1, he had met Comfort Gilder's daughter Helena for lunch and poured out his troubles to her, as if she knew "the whole story." She did not. Four days later he had read in the *New York Times* of the Freuds' intention to emigrate to London.

At the end of the month when Robert had visited Tinky at Bennington he had told her that he had given up all hopes for his family; shortly afterwards a friend found him "a jigsaw puzzle of disconnected pieces." His final letter to Dorothy, however, had shown no trace of distress. He had thanked her, profusely, for the letter she had sent him on Mabbie's wedding day, by which he had learned the details third-hand. He had especially liked her description of Mabbie's "serious radiance." Then, for nine days, he could not sleep. On the evening of May 27 he had gone for a brisk walk and later had played cards with his father. At midnight, as he was turning in, C.C.B. had tried to persuade him to take the sleeping pill his doctor had prescribed. "He would not tell you to take it if it would do you any harm," he had said. But Robert had refused and tossed through his tenth night. Rising at dawn he had padded into the library, presumably to look for a book. But he must have glanced at the spring dawn breaking over the apartment tops to the east, and opened the window for some fresh air. He was found hours later, crumpled in blue pajamas on the sidewalk fourteen floors below. A wingless dove, he had flown at last.

"You will go over so many things & it will be agony for you," Comfort wrote, anticipating Dorothy's stabbing guilt, "for you will imagine things you could have done differently. But you have always done the very best you knew how—the best you could for him and for the children. You must be thankful that you let him know that you loved him. He knew it—he told me."

The arrival the following week of a weary but unharmed Freud family helped Dorothy through the shock. And after a fortnight she could write Edith Jackson, "Life is very curious, and at times very sad."

> Perhaps you who met Robert will understand a little the tragedy that his whole life has been. My one sorrow is, & has been, that I could not help him or do anything to give him happiness. I would have given a very great deal to have been able to do so, especially this winter when he was over with us. We had hoped, the children and I, that the future would contain more happiness for him—and we had often talked over & planned what we could do for him. But surely he never could have been satisfied & would have continued to suffer. You who know all the children will surely understand that they have many of his qualities—of sensitiveness & fineness of spirit. They have always been a blessed reminder of his loveliness and have proved to me the tragedy of his illness.

Forty-six now, and with a potentially long and productive life ahead of her, it would have served no purpose for Dorothy, publicly or privately, to have assumed a responsibility for Robert's death. She met the pain and carried on, as she had been taught to do by the Freuds. Without them, Dorothy doubted the chances for her own survival.

A letter written by Mabbie a year later indicated the direction taken by their mourning. "I am so happy that we are all able to absorb and soften our feelings," she wrote. "It is so hard and of no use really to always only think of Daddy with sorrow."

Eventually, however, little remained of "Dr. Robert's" life but the circumstances of his death. The Lethe of time washed so inexorably at his memory that his grandchildren were later hard-pressed to find a shard of his existence, such as a photograph to tell his appearance. Like a radioactive pellet trapped inside the body of the collective family, only his suicide remained, doing its silent damage.

I nstalled at 39 Elsworthy Road on Primrose Hill, near Regent's Park, the newly liberated Freud exclaimed, "I am almost tempted to cry out 'Heil Hitler.' " The heroic welcome which London accorded Freud lifted Dorothy's spirits, too.

From her own apartment on nearby Norfolk Road she wrote Edith Jackson, "The house is lovely & Professor has not looked so well for years. He is so pleased with everything & his eyes sparkle and it is a joy to see him."

> Anna is naturally tired but she too is happy with the possibilities here with Jones's & the group's wonderful cooperation. We really are all very fortunate. The friendliness is so delightful & we are indeed lucky to have come to a land where we are wanted & welcomed. I feel sorry for the others who have it less easy. Of course it is because of Anna & the Professor, but it has also to do with the English. When they decided to take us in, they made the real decision & they all back their decision with enthusiasm and do not seem to regret it.

Cheered by the prospect of a new start, Dorothy's optimism knew no bounds. "Melanie Klein as a person is really very nice," she wrote. "I am sure Anna will be able to manage that situation."

Despite her prematurity as to Klein, it was fortunate that Dorothy had learned to savor life's bright moments, as by early fall the skies were again darkening, and would not truly lift until Germany and Japan had been defeated. For Dorothy these were the first years of professional duty taking precedence over family life, and though the logical outcome of her colleagueship with Anna Freud, this was somehow difficult for her to swallow. Dorothy by mid-September was already touching on the inner conflict that would dominate her war years. Again to Edith Jackson she wrote:

Sometimes lately I have had the feeling that I am making a mistake in not returning to my own [country]. I long for it sometimes—but I might be very unhappy & would certainly miss the home I have made here around the Freuds—& then I am quite convinced that I could only work here, & that if work is the center of one's life, then here is the place for me.

The Four meanwhile swirled in uncertain eddies around her. Mabbie and Simon spent the spring semester at the Architectural Association School of Architecture before heading off to the States in search of work. Bob, who had joined them at the *Kunstgewerbeschule* the previous winter, joined them again at Bedford Square, leaving for the States that summer, but returning—married to Mossik Sørensen—in time for the fall semester. For Tinky the events of 1938 had been "too much." Taking a leave of absence from Bennington she steamed to England, in late summer visiting the Isle of Wight with Dorothy. Only Michael was entirely absent from London that year, cramming summer long in Cambridge. After starting at MIT, he wrote C.C.B. that "the sun is shining and the Charles is as blue as the Danube." Later, when he too had begun to founder academically, he admitted that his father and grandfather had been right, that a year in a New England prep school would have been helpful.

Bob had also found new merit in C.C.B.'s advice, writing Dorothy, "I think Bompa is right about one thing. I have always taken analysis as if it were a dose of pills that makes you well, and when I have gone back to it I have done it as I would to a protecting Mother. This is all wrong, and I realize it and have realized it, and if I realize it enough perhaps I shall be able to finish it in a very short time." Analysis was the sole reason Bob had given C.C.B. for starting at the Architectural Association rather than Columbia, his decision to practice architecture now being final. He had told C.C.B. that "the sooner I get into a school here the better," that he would remain in London only so long as it took to finish analysis. Thus did Bob guarantee for himself another false start, as Dorothy managed to skirt around her the remnants of the old family in the nervous interim preceding the outbreak of hostilities. The fall of 1938 found Dorothy, Tinky, Bob, and Mossik ensconced at 2 Maresfield Gardens, Bob and Mossik occupying an upstairs flat, Dorothy and Tinky setting up house below.

Dorothy in Vienna, 1925

With "The Four"

Anna Freud

The Burlinghams at
Semmering, 1928

With the Freuds. *(From left to right)*
Professor Freud, Tinky, Ernsti Halberstadt,
Mikey, Anna Freud, Dorothy, and Bob

Dorothy and Anna with Alfred de Forest

Berchtesgaden, 1929

Bob

Mikey and Mabbie

Tinky

Robert Burlingham in 1927

C.C.B., 1931

At Black Point, 1933. *(From left to right)* Tinky, Mikey, Mabbie,
Robert, Nancy, and Charles Culp Burlingham

Dorothy and her Bergasse
consulting room

Dorothy with Professor Freud and chow, mid 1930s

Anna Freud, 1951

Dorothy weaving in her Maresfield Gardens bedroom

Dorothy and Anna in the Maresfield Gardens library, 1979

A week after Dorothy moved into 2 Maresfield Gardens, the Freuds took possession of No. 20, a vine-wreathed Edwardian residence made brilliant by a battery of bay and dormer windows, poised above and beyond the worldly roar of traffic on Finchley Road—an altogether appropriate resting place for the father of psychoanalysis. The street, midway between Swiss Cottage and Hampstead Heath, was tree-lined and the house "so ideal, the Professor was depressed because it was too perfect," Dorothy reported to Edith Jackson.

But by then Freud also had real reason to be depressed. On September 8 he had undergone his most severe surgery since the radical excision of 1923, some thirty operations and fifteen years previously, and from this one he never fully recovered. Anna Freud was "so terribly tired."

September 1938 is of course remembered for the Munich crisis, and, in that tense period, as the British mobilized and war seemed imminent, the Viennese got a taste of what it was like to be, in the British vernacular, "bloody refugees." "You should have seen the parks," Dorothy wrote when it was over, "suddenly they were dotted with guns pointed to the skies and then in certain places the ditches were dug, looking ugly and sad. You can imagine our friends the immigrants, all so unhappy that they had chosen England, all so frightened at what would happen to them." As winter replaced fall Dorothy and Anna became increasingly aware that London was not Jabneh. By December most of their colleagues had "one foot already in America," and Dorothy was wondering "if they are not all really right." The prospect of being isolated in an analytic community dominated by Melanie Klein could not have been heartening.

D orothy noted in a terse sentence to Edith Jackson on October 20 their first contact with the British Psychoanalytic Society. "The Society meetings have started, and we miss Vienna more than ever." The differences with Klein were both technical and theoretical, Klein dating the Oedipus and superego formation a full two years ahead of Freud, and also methodological, Anna Freud moving with the greater caution of an empiricist. At times the dispute had grown bitterly personal. The Kleinians had suggested that Anna Freud had avoided the treatment of prelatency children and neglected the Oedipus complex because her own "inverse Oedipal" strata had remained unpenetrated by analysis.

Ernest Jones must have known that Anna had been analyzed by her own father when he had written Freud after publication of *Introduction to the Techniques of Child Analysis,* "It is a pain to me that I cannot agree with some of the tendencies in Anna's book, and I cannot help thinking that they must be due in part to some imperfectly analyzed resistances. . . ." Freud had responded acidly, "Who is really sufficiently analyzed? I can assure you that Anna has been analyzed longer and more thoroughly than, for instance, yourself." But Jones was president of the British Society; and his children had been analyzed by Klein.

Having no wish to reward with a bitter struggle those who had orchestrated their immigration and been so warmly welcoming, Anna Freud was forced to curb her dominant instincts and lie low at British Society meetings. Echoing her father, she declared, "We are guests in this country and were not brought here to cause trouble." She adopted instead a separatist stance, holding the traditional Wednesday evening seminar at 20 Maresfield Gardens rather than at Society headquarters. With analytic candidates Elisabeth Geleerd and Mary Hawkins, Anna and Dorothy also began a *kinderseminar.* Dorothy's first case was "a wonderful one, a charming child with tics."

At the December 7 meeting of the British Society, in an atmosphere of "electrifying tension," it by happenstance fell to Dorothy to voice the continental viewpoint for the first time. Invited to open discussion of "Temper Tantrums in Early Childhood in Their Relation to Internal Objects," by stalwart Kleinian Susan Isaacs, Dorothy hesitated, "but decided sometime we must break our silence and this was a good opportunity."

> I did not criticize her paper but showed how far we could go with her and where and how our views separated, giving examples of my own and trying to show that the temper tantrums were like an orgasmus. Jones was very polite to me but when Hawkins brought . . . a confirmation of my view he lost his temper, saying after all we were there to discuss Isaacs' case and not to bring new cases. Anna spoke too and I think it was a very good beginning. We were told afterwards that for the last ten years there had not been such a meeting where sexuality was mentioned in that way, so freely. Since then [Sylvia] Payne and [Ella] Sharpe have asked Anna whether she would not have a small seminar, perhaps the Stracheys [Alix

and James] will come beside our group. That may be a beginning. The English group will now become definitely divided and that is the only way.

These comments to Edith Jackson reflected a new degree of professional assurance in Dorothy, but transcendence on the emotional level was more difficult. In her analysis, which continued amidst the familiar, seminal clutter of Professor's antiquities and books, Dorothy was now specifically dealing with the difficulty of sharing her *strahlend* son with his wife. Or so it would appear. One morning, after inviting Mossik into her bedroom, she began to apologize before the mirror where she stood brushing her hair, which had again grown long. Her apology, interrupted by wracking sobs, was for her unconscious hostility to Mossik, since to all appearances she had been perfectly pleasant. Then at Easter, Bob and Mossik drove to Cornwall for a belated honeymoon. Three days later, Dorothy arrived at their hotel together with Tinky and a friend. Stung by the understandably frosty reception, Dorothy declared that she would never again spend a holiday with them.

By then she was probably in a bad way. A swelling on Professor's jaw in early February had indicated a possible new malignancy, and soon afterwards the atmosphere at No. 20 and No. 2 Maresfield Gardens had grown thick, as a diagnosis of "inoperable, incurable cancer" was reached. Under these circumstances, at the end of July, Dorothy's analysis of twelve years came to an end, her anxieties then evidently transposing themselves from the specter of death to the promise of birth. Dissatisfied with Mabbie's obstetrician, she pushed so hard for another recommended by Ruth Mack Brunswick that Mabbie snapped, "Why do you always want only to believe someone whose voice you can hear and not voices I can hear?" The following day, Mabbie continued more gently, "Do give Prof. my love & I do hope he will enjoy his great-grandchild through you and me and our relationship pact." On August 14 Dorothy reported, "The Professor has continual ups & downs, a lot of pain—and sleeps a lot from medicines. Anna Freud is continually with him. He is no worse."

Anna no doubt wished to spare Dorothy the end, for Dorothy arrived in New York in late August for the birth of her first grandchild, Timothy Schmiderer. Better that she focus on a positive human drama than again be overwhelmed by negative emotions, she and Anna must have agreed.

A month later, on September 23, Freud died in his sleep. Suddenly desperate to return to Anna, who now surely needed her, Dorothy found herself unable to do so despite C.C.B.'s admiralty connections. "The most important years" of Dorothy's life had ended as World War II had begun.

In London Dorothy had briefly known a life in which work was the primary focus, but in New York her children and grandchild again took center stage. For the first time since Vienna she was reunited with all four children, Bob having transferred to Columbia at the outbreak of war, and Tinky returning with Dorothy to begin teacher's training in Greenwich Village. Michael was in his second year at MIT, and Mabbie was happily mothering in Riverdale. At the Hotel Volney on East 74th Street, Dorothy had ample time to reflect upon her future, and her past. In early January she moved closer to her roots, taking an apartment with Tinky at 242 East 72nd Street. But the spatial proximity only dramatized the psychic distance between Dorothy and her background, a distance which found an objective correlative in the thirties modern apartment building which rose on the site of her Lenox Hill birthplace. Simon's first architectural job, designing the rear-exit stairwell of the vaultlike Tiffany & Company building at Fifth Avenue and 57th Street, had come through the influence of Charles Tiffany. But again it was that distance which Mabbie had expressed to Dorothy in June. "In New York we saw Uncle Charles Tiffany and didn't agree on a single subject."

One clear perception for Dorothy, perhaps, was the increasingly schismatic aspect to her life with Anna Freud, and the family life in which current she was now floating, somehow oddly disconnected and coreless. And so, despite the pleasures of her family and outings to Cambridge and New Hampshire, when the opportunity of returning to London finally presented itself, Dorothy did not hesitate.

She traveled via Italy in April of 1940 to a city where, once again, the parks were dotted with guns pointing to the sky. The sky was itself dotted with "barrage balloons," and the streets dark, sandbagged, and clanking with weaponry. But despite this and Hitler's blitzkrieg through Denmark and Norway, Dorothy's spirits were soaring once again. She wrote Bob:

Life for us all is so different because [Freud] is gone—but at the same time
I am surprised how unchanged everything goes on. Even now I don't take
it in. I think it is partly because my relationship with Anna is not changed
in the slightest . . .

I can only admire Anna, how very wonderful she is. She goes on with
life more intensely than she ever has, has many ideas & plans. She is
building up her life without her father & yet somehow it is still his
personality & his life which you feel in everything she does. Everything
is simple, natural, and real that she does . . .

I am glad to be here. It is surely right for me to be where perhaps I
can really be of help to Anna. I know it means a lot to her that I am here
& that is enough for me.

Anna Freud had retrieved the psychoanalytic standard which had
slipped from Freud's grasp, and Dorothy joyfully heeded the call. The
relief—palpable in Dorothy's comments to Bob—over the continuity of
her relations with Anna Freud offset her regret at being "without chick
or child." By May 1 Dorothy had "three very worthwhile" analysands,
and had been made a training analyst for the first time. The power to
influence future analysts was a signal achievement, and Dorothy was
"very pleased." "I've never seen anything the way the time goes here,"
she wrote, "and never enough time to get everything done I want to."
Soon, "as a way of cutting down expenses as well as living together,"
Dorothy moved into 20 Maresfield Gardens, the home where she was to
live out her days.

The fleeting pleasures of an "unbelievably beautiful" spring, shared by
the two friends, helped to bridge their new, mid-life beginning in England. After a Sunday drive to Suffolk with Anna's brother Ernst and his
wife, Lux, Dorothy wrote Mossik, "I don't really like the too perfect
English countryside. I like the imperfections of our [American] rougher
countryside. But perhaps I don't know England well enough." She
compensated, gleefully, by reverting the garden at No. 20 to its "normal
wildness." Though she attributed this urge to her father's influence, her
description of the English countryside as "too perfect" echoed Freud; the
garden may therefore have been something of an analogy to her psychoanalytic thinking on the subject of instinctual restrictions.

Dorothy's respect for the British people was rapidly won by their
Churchillian spirit. "You know," she wrote Bob, "I have more & more

admiration for the way the British behave. Their background & conventions & good manners does mean something. At such a time you realize that. I've never seen such calmness & courage & determination as they show. It's good to know there are such finalities in this mad world."

One positive development following Freud's death was a quickening of Dorothy's feelings for the seventy-nine-year-old Frau Professor. Anna's preëmptive relationship with her father had indubitably created some friction with her mother over the years, which had extended by association to Dorothy. Martha had frequently criticized their "messy" and "incorrect" appearance, which, from the cotton chemises which they wore in place of brassieres, to a total absence of makeup, to their "undone" or natural hair, to the rounded toes of their "sensible" shoes, was certainly idiosyncratic, at least through Martha's petit bourgeois eyes. And Dorothy, in the throes of transference, had surely found plenty of fault in Frau Professor. During the Munich crisis, Martha had refused to accept the masks which were being offered door-to-door as protection against poison gas attack, declaring herself unafraid. Mentioning the incident to Edith Jackson, Dorothy had snorted, *"Echt* ['Genuine'] Frau Prof.! I then ordered them for the whole household." But later, after Freud's death, Dorothy saw Martha in a different light. "I love Frau Prof.," she wrote. "She is a wonderful person & so very dear & not fussy at all anymore . . . She certainly has qualities that I never knew she had. Such quiet determination & meeting things as they come & no fear & right values, one can only admire her."

With the invasion of the Channel Islands in June came the beginning of real hardship, as sentiment turned hard on émigrés. By July even the "A-Class" aliens were being arrested and shipped to internment camps. Though Anna, Martha, and Minna were spared, Anna's brother Martin; Martin's son, W. Ernest Freud; and Paula Fichtl were imprisoned. "Anna has not been feeling very well & she's depressed too," Dorothy wrote Bob on July 7. "Altogether these weeks have been the hardest since I arrived." A plea to Ambassador Bullitt brought Dorothy a gentle rebuke: "You must not forget that the British are fighting for their very existence." For the first time in Anna's life, observed Dorothy, she was confronted with an obstacle which she could not surmount.

A ground swell of popular sentiment quickly led to the release of all but a small percentage of the internees. Nevertheless, to judge by the regularity with which Dorothy declared either herself or Anna to be "depressed," the next five years proved extremely taxing on both women. Anna, in particular, seems to have aged sufficiently to fit Jones's description of "a tough and perhaps indigestible morsel." Jones aside, Anna Freud's postwar appearance did suggest the opposite of leavening, as if the ingredients of her life had been altered in various measures to produce a settling and thickening compression of self.

The question arises, Why did Anna Freud not emigrate to America, where life might have been easier? Dorothy's correspondence is unclear on this point. In one instance, without stating reasons, she wrote, "Neither Anna nor I would enjoy the analytical work in the U.S." This may have indicated an emotional knot in Anna's reasoning and, on Dorothy's part, a deference to her will, since most of their colleagues, lay analysts included, were making the transition, and Dorothy would have jumped at the chance to be with her family. But psychoanalysis had priority in the life that Dorothy had chosen, and Anna, it seems, felt bound to uphold the standard in the country that her father had selected, the country whose diplomatic stance prior to World War I had provided Freud with the phrase "splendid isolation."

On the evening of August 15, 1940, feeling depressed, Dorothy and Anna decided to treat themselves to supper out. Deep in the tube, heading for Piccadilly Circus to meet Anna, Dorothy did not hear the siren. The Luftwaffe had been edging ever closer to London since the July runs on the airfields, factories, and repair shops of southeastern England, and now they struck the suburb of Biggin Hill, and nearby Croyden. "Isn't it curious," wrote Dorothy the following day, "when you are expecting something, when it comes you don't take it in?"

With metropolitan London yet to be specifically targeted, Dorothy could adopt the same mollifying tone which she had perfected during the political upheavals in Vienna, except that now it was her children she was pacifying. On August 18 she wrote Bob, "Certainly many districts knew nothing of the air raid warnings. No one seemed the slightest bit excited . . . everyone went about their normal lives as far as possible. Patients appeared like clockwork & were annoyed when we sent them to the shelters down the street. The main emotion one feels during an air raid when you don't hear anything is boredom and annoyance. It's quite queer." One clear day Dorothy and Anna went rowing in Regent's Park, and the evenings passed peaceably enough, the women occasionally interrupting their studies to watch what Dorothy referred to as the "show."

Oddly, Dorothy's possession of an imaginative eye is confirmed for the first time in her descriptions of aerial bombardment.

> You could hear the planes—follow them by the lights from the search lights which caught little clouds. We saw a flare dropped & then soon after the sky glow red in the distance from a fire. Several times we went downstairs when the planes seemed nearer . . .
>
> We always can tell where the planes are by the search lights which are turned on them & follow them about. Sometimes rockets are thrown from the planes & it's just like watching fireworks . . .
>
> Search lights flashed over parts of the sky like summer lightning & sudden sparks around the spot where the searchlights were all focused. It's a beautiful sight even if its object is dreadful. Then the searchlights went off one by one. The drone of the plane receded into nothingness & all was still & we went to bed. A quiet night.

Then, on the afternoon of September 7, in reprisal for four consecutive strikes on Berlin, an armada of Dornier and Heinkel bombers sweeping westward above the Thames at sixteen thousand feet unleashed a rain of fire that left London's East End glowing like a setting sun. Before long the Germans were regularly blasting all parts of the city, forcing the occupants of 20 Maresfield Gardens to bed down in the first floor hall between kitchen and dining room. "I understand better [why] soldiers exhausted, will sleep through anything," Dorothy remarked after spending a few nights continuously checking the roof for incendiaries.

Dorothy's acknowledged "weak point" was noise, and yet she withstood the worst of the blitz and remained stoutly calm, at least in correspondence. Viewing an exhibit of war pictures a year hence, Dorothy found not one image which captured the essence of war for her. But shortly thereafter, "down in the city walking," she and Anna chanced upon a scene which did, of "yellow light streaming through a beautiful archway, in the background a spire of a church. It was unbelievably beautiful. When we came near we realized the light effect was due to the fact that [in] back of the doorway was emptiness . . . the effect was beautiful due to the destruction." Dorothy's single-minded focus upon the aesthetics of destruction reached beyond the desire to relieve her children's concerns for her safety. It was her genuine perspective. In times of war, she discovered, the mind seemed to chart an almost opposite course from its surroundings. "It's interesting," she wrote, "that when one dreams, one dreams not of the war but of the most peaceful and harmless events."

With the Battle of Britain raging overhead, Dorothy and Anna were aroused by the plight of the "poor little mites of humanity" below. At the outbreak of war two million of the city's children had been evacuated to foster home billets in the country. Many infants and younger children had, however, remained in the city with their mothers, and by the fall of 1940 some two thousand evacuees were returning daily, adding to their number. The blitz hit the working-class families clustered around the city's docks, arsenals, and munitions factories especially hard, and it was the progeny of these bombed-out, homeless East End working mothers and soldier fathers who gave Dorothy and Anna the idea for the Hampstead War Nurseries.

Dorothy had first mentioned it on September 3, writing Bob, "I went off to see a friend of Marinka's [Gurewich] about an idea we've had, to start a night shelter for mothers and little children with the furniture from the Krippe"—the Edith Jackson Project. Gurewich's friend, Lilian Bowes-Lyon, a cousin of the Queen, was "delighted with the idea & is taking it up with someone who could give us advice about the possibilities," Dorothy wrote. A week later she added, "We still have not found a proper shelter for our night shelter; we have something in view, but everything always takes so long although the demand is so great & everyone anxious that we should go on with our plans." Money was quickly proffered by "some English friends," and "a Swedish Committee" followed with the loan of a suitable house near Maresfield Gardens, and equipment, which included a complete Montessori nursery school. As Dorothy had indicated, pint-sized furniture from the Edith Jackson Project was also at hand, and that was enough to start. Led by Anna's "electric energy" and "fascinating magnetism," the *Freundinnen* set to work. They had "such fun getting everything in order."

The "Rest Centre" at 13 Wedderbourne Road opened before Christmas, and by March 1941 the Foster Parents for War Children, Inc. had assumed complete financial responsibility for its operation. An international, professionally staffed organization headquartered in New York, the Foster Parents had been founded in 1937 to provide for children victimized by the Spanish Civil War, and was currently sponsoring some twenty-five British hostels and shelters. Being dependent upon support from the private sector, the Foster Parents were presumably under pressure to produce the kind of propagandizing publicity which elicits generous donations, though, according to Anna Freud, the only condition imposed on them by the charity in return for its support was the submission of detailed monthly reports. The Foster Parents was therefore probably not responsible for the crucial change made in the second month of the Centre's existence, when the house was hastily converted from a family night shelter into a twenty-four-hour children's sanctuary. From its inception, Anna Freud had viewed the Centre as an opportunity for scientific investigation, this concern again mixing with the desire to do public service in much the way the Edith Jackson Project had. As a family night shelter, its clinical scope would have been limited to the study of trauma caused in children by reasons of war; but in the context of a residential nursery, in war as in peace the focus was directed toward the more universal problem of separation anxiety. And, after fifty-six months of continuous observation, the first and foremost conclusion the women reached was that, for a child, the horror of war pales beside the horror of separation from the mother. In fact they discovered that "the war itself was no more than . . . a precipitating and aggravating agent." Whether the change in direction was made for scientific or practical reasons, or a combination of the two, is not clear. But the death of Dorothy's mother and illness of her infant son had made separation trauma a subject close to her heart, and she may therefore have had a shaping influence on this pioneering child development study.

On March 2, 1941, she wrote Bob:

Today we are already planning a second venture for babies under 1 & younger around the corner in [No. 5] Netherhall Gardens. We will then have the toddlers and kindergarten children in the present one and the younger ones is the new one. We feel a little dizzy at the speed of the way things develop but since Mr. Muggeridge is encouraging us and wants to further these schemes we are naturally delighted.

The Baby Home, as it was affectionately called, opened in July. In August, again at the urging of Eric G. Muggeridge, the Foster Parents' British representative, they opened a third center for older children called New Barn, with Alice Goldberger in charge, sixty miles from London, at Lindsell, near Dunmow in Essex. And suddenly Dorothy and Anna found themselves custodian to some eighty children ranging in age from ten days to ten years. The press printed such quintessentially British headlines as FREUD'S GIRL CARRIES ON, Dorothy reporting that "life was a bit too full, even for [Anna]."

The Hampstead War Nurseries did, however, become an emotional bridge for both Anna and Dorothy, easing the transfer of their loyalty and affection from Austria to England. Dorothy voiced this revisionism to Mabbie. "There were very few qualities of the people, except the Freuds, around us [in Austria] that you could respect or admire," she wrote. "Here you can admire fundamental qualities practically in everyone—courage, audacity, initiative, not letting you down . . ."

The nursery staff were virtually all refugees, relieved to be working at all, if, in some cases, for room, board, and pocket money, an arrangement which made it possible to circumvent the obstacle of work permits. Personnel increased as the number of children swelled to 120 and, after the Baby Home's opening, 13 Wedderbourne Road was revamped as a staff facility. Among the staff was but one former colleague, pediatrician Josephine Stross. No continental analyst had remained in London to assist them with the nurseries. Heddy Schwartz, superintendent of the nurseries for the first six months, had run a Montessori school in Vienna; her replacement, Ilse Hellman, had been a student of child psychology at the University of Vienna, a field separate from and then antagonistic to child analysis; the German Dann sisters, Sophie and Gertrude, charged with the babies and "junior toddlers," had been trained as a nurse and cook respectively. Virtually the entire staff had therefore to be retrained in the basic tenets of psychoanalysis, and, by October 1941, "a purely private and unofficial training scheme" was instituted for this purpose. However, in the instances of Ilse Hellman, the Danns, and the young Viennese Hansi Engel (Kennedy), the instruction was rewarded with lifelong colleagueship.

By day 5 Netherhall Gardens functioned much like any good nursery school, but at night the children were bedded down in a basement fortified to withstand all but a direct hit. The Marie Curie Hospital on the corner of Maresfield Gardens and Fitzjohns Avenue was obliterated one evening by just such a strike. The blast opened the front door to the Baby Home and brought shouting down the street the area warden, poet Stephen Spender, whose job it was to enforce the blackout. Another thousand-pound bomb landed thirty yards from the doorstep of 13 Wedderbourne Road, but did not explode, and a fighter narrowly missed crashing into New Barn. At 20 Maresfield Gardens the worst was broken windows, a spilled ink bottle, and "the dust of ages" roused from nooks where it had long been settling. They were lucky: from 5 Netherhall Gardens, high in Hampstead, one could see the whole of London stretched out below, the entire smashed panorama. According to Gertrude Dann, "One could see more than one wanted to."

The intensity of the blitz gradually diminished; by early November 1940, Dorothy and Anna had returned to their beds three nights a week, and by summer the skies had entirely cleared. The staff continued to write their observations on file cards, which Anna and Dorothy used when writing up the Foster Parents reports. "Quite a task," recalled Dorothy. The reports became the basis for *Young Children in Wartime* (1942) and *Infants Without Families* (1944), which they coauthored, volumes containing the observations of five years. When in 1973 the material reappeared as Volume III of *The Writings of Anna Freud,* the Foreword observed:

> Since World War II, when these reports were written and the conclusions drawn from them, they have been followed by a long line of studies of young children who have to pass through their infancy deprived of family care. Some of these publications contain material which is more impressive in its tragic impact than the observations recorded by us; or which has had a much wider impact on the public mind; or which surpasses us by far in scientific accuracy. Nevertheless, we can claim the merit to have been first on the scene, and thereby to have initiated the series.

One can imagine Dorothy's and Anna's astonishment, therefore, when even the cacophonous raids of April 16 and May 10, 1941, failed to disturb their charges, and their surprise when children snatched from the rubble of their former homes showed absolutely no sign of war trauma, or "shell shock." Anxiety which was in fact caused by conditions of war was usually traceable to the attitude of the parents: the frightened mother often had a frightened child. Children were just not susceptible to war in the way people had imagined. Rather, they believed:

> Children have to be safeguarded against the primitive horrors of the war, not because horrors and atrocities are so strange to them, but because we want them at this decisive stage of their development to overcome and

estrange themselves from the primitive and atrocious wishes of their own infantile nature.

The most tragic effect in these war children turned out to be separation from their parents. In the case of "Billie," "We were shocked to see an apparently healthy child develop a compulsive tic under our very eyes." And "Dell" reacted by behaving "exactly like a stray dog who has lost its master." Probing further, they found that these reactions were determined by the manner of separation, the worst cases being abrupt departures for which the child had been unprepared. From the psychoanalytic viewpoint, the sudden and inexplicable absences seemed an intolerable confirmation of the child's murderous impulses. A gradual separation, on the other hand, sensitively handled, made it possible for the child to accept and adapt to new surroundings and surrogate parents. In the case of under-threes, it was repeatedly possible, and in a relatively short time span, to forget their real parents entirely.

With Anna "the most fascinating part of the whole work," the nursery's first year passed quickly for Dorothy. And, on October 11, 1941, she celebrated her fiftieth birthday, writing Mossik, "I don't feel old & I don't feel young. I feel somehow very content & not a bit anxious to have life end but at the same time not too anxious to hang on to it." She continued to Bob, "It really is true that analysis never stops working in oneself. I find that even this year I have learned more about myself & have at times a greater peace than I have ever had. Age does not seem to do away with problems or with personal difficulties but it also does not seem to make progress impossible, which is very wonderful."

Dorothy's equilibrium was soon to be undermined by a procession of difficulties, however. The first sign of a shifting wind came, as it so often did for Dorothy, from New York. On December 21, in a letter to Bob, she complained:

Now . . . we only get criticism from the Foster Parents for not being what they want us to be: a propaganda asset. They do not appreciate in the slightest our value as something really scientific, & doing interesting work. Since from the start we always said we never could be of any use as propaganda & wished to have nothing to do with it, they should not be so astonished. It is only too bad to be backed by a society who considers you only a liability. Too bad we never could get backed by the Rockefeller Foundation. I suppose we should only consider these things like pin pricks, but they are annoying & take away from the pleasure of the work. We of course will go on just as we have been going on, but we are quite aware that some day we will be told there is no money for us & then we will have to close, which would certainly be a great shame.

That day arrived in early March 1942, when they were ordered to close the Baby Home. But, due to the pioneering nature of their scientific study of under-threes, the Baby Home was the one they least wanted to close. On March 11 an emotionally tried Dorothy wrote, "In another two weeks we may have to throw [the babies] out to real destitution and horrible conditions. We are really very disturbed and unhappy. It's been a ghastly time. Somehow [it is] our fault that we started such a venture without better security." Their dander up, they cast about for alternative financial means, throwing themselves into the "unpleasant work" of getting in touch with "the right people." Long after midnight Anna's typewriter continued to rattle in the attic of 20 Maresfield Gardens, and Dorothy, on the slender thread of a nearly forgotten Tiffany-Roosevelt acquaintanceship, telegraphed Eleanor Roosevelt—to no avail. March passed with the salaried staff agreeing to work without wages and, on April 4, Dorothy wrote Bob, "Both Anna Freud and I feel [the "very hard time"] . . . [we] are tired, discouraged & depressed. It's wonderful working so long as you have no money worries, but as soon as you have, the pleasure is all gone, it's simply a day to day strain & most of the time we wish we had never started." The crisis was averted when the Foster Parents, for reasons unknown to that organization today, abruptly resumed their support; but, in the meantime, had begun—to quote child analyst Grete Bibring—"the blitz with Melanie Klein."

At the outbreak of war, Klein and Jones had led an analytic exodus to the hinterlands, lulling the British Society into hibernation. But they had returned after the blitz to transform the British Society, in one member's words, "into an absolute hotbed of crazy fury," which it remained throughout the war. Dorothy had written Mossik on January 11, 1942, "The psychoanalytic society here [is] dreadful—and so few who really stand for real analysis." She added on October 25, "We have had such disagreeable times in the Society lately. It makes you really quite sick the way the name of Freud is thrown mud at. I think Anna always knew England would be difficult but I guess she did not realize how difficult it would be." She continued on November 16, "We are rather depressed at present. I think mostly because the Psycho-analytic society situation is so very unpleasant at present. There is no constructive work possible in such an atmosphere and so much energy [is] spent on what seems futile work." And adding insult to injury was the decision of Eva Rosenfeld—who had migrated to London with her family before the war—to have a second, Kleinian, analysis. While Victor Ross acknowledges his mother's disappointment over the loss to Dorothy of intimacy with Anna Freud, he defends Eva's actions by pointing out her eclectic predilection. Indeed, Eva herself went on to become a good analyst, he says, because she "put humanity into analysis rather than letting analysis drive it out." Nevertheless, Eva's "defection" chilled her relationship with Anna Freud for years.

By mid-1944 the situation with the Society had gotten so bad that Anna and Dorothy stopped attending its meetings; Anna resigned in the same year from the Training Committee, the Society's locus of influence and controversy. Not until after the war was an agreement reached for the purposes of training analytic candidates, and the Society split—much as Dorothy had predicted in December of 1938—into a Kleinian "A-Group," an Anna Freudian "B-Group," with a third "C-Group" of "Independents" treading the no-man's land between.

For Dorothy the attacks served only to inflame her partisan spirit. On the third anniversary of Freud's death, she wrote:

It seems like ages & ages ago in so many ways. It's hard losing someone in one's life who in no way can be replaced, but the memory of such a personality does enrich one's life forever. It's a kind of assurance to know such a person has lived & has looked at life & met life as he did. One knows, although it is so rare, that such a personality is possible & it gives me faith in human nature to have had the privilege of having known such a person. We are lucky in Anna Freud. It's amazing that there should be two such personalities in one family. It had to be a woman, only a woman could have been able to enjoy & grow from such a father & yet to be able to keep independent of thought & to continue as she does now growing & giving out. I have often seen a person who has lived for another person, sort of shrink & lose whatever they had gotten when that person is gone—but there is none of that with Anna Freud. Her meetings are brilliant . . . I often look around at those young faces and enjoy their enthusiasm, their earnestness and appreciation of what has come their way.

The fervor of this praise, however, itself suggested the opposition confronting them. By the time of the Japanese attack on Pearl Harbor the war had already seemed endless to Dorothy and, as 1942 had unfolded the Baby Home crisis and Kleinian controversies, her spirit had begun to drag. Life at the Freud home was not without disadvantages, she discovered. Upon the death of Minna Bernays in June of 1941, Dorothy had become third lady of a household in which the functions of a political headquarters took precedence over domestic concerns. Dorothy discussed with Anna the possibility of a separate place, "something small & simple & [requiring] less care," perhaps the duplex or "twin house" that Dorothy had "always dreamed of," but in any case a place where she and Anna "could at times have private lives."

"There are times when we do want to ask someone for instance to a meal and the other one does not necessarily want to be there. I know there are times when I long for my personal things around me and my way of doing things. Here in this house it would be difficult. . . ." As if to illustrate the problem, Mossik's brother Einar Sørensen arrived in London in March of 1943 after escaping from a train bound for a Nazi concentration camp and stowing aboard a Swedish freighter. Dorothy had wanted to show him a warm welcome, but in frustration wrote Mossik, "It's impossible to invite [Einar] here for a meal and he can't meet me at lunch time . . . That is the difference of having a home of your own. It's so easy a way to invite someone & see them & be hospitable, everything else for me has a flavor of artificiality." This confession may have been the closest that Dorothy ever came to criticizing Anna Freud. They did make plans for renovating one of the garages flanking the house, but nothing came of them. Dorothy adjusted her sights instead, concluding gamely, "Well, one cannot have everything and it is very wonderful that I don't have to live alone but here with Anna Freud."

But fatherless, embattled, and faced with the "dropping away of all her father's and analytical first friends," the war years were especially hard on Anna Freud and, consequently, on Dorothy as well. Anna Freud of course knew how to carry on, retreating into the nepenthe of incessant labor. But, with the war entering its fourth year, Dorothy could not help feeling the emptiness of a life which made work its sole object. She tried to place her feelings within the context of the extraordinary, transitory times in which she lived, but was overwhelmed. She knew the direction of her thoughts when she caught herself repeatedly humming "Home Sweet Home." She tried to absorb her feelings, planting spring bulbs, junketing to antique stores, even reading mysteries, a genre she had despised. To Bob she confided, "I get into a sort of dreamlike contentment as I write you as if you were playing on the piano and I was listening and feeling all is well with you." Her correspondence, by the fall of 1942, had become the palliative for her homesickness. "Sometimes," she wrote Bob, "I feel very lonely for you all and get very upset when I realize how much I miss seeing my Grandchildren [who now numbered three] in these most important years of their lives. But when I look back & try to see whether or where I made a mistake in judgment I realize I would under the same circumstances make the same choices. Then I feel quieter again."

But four months later she was again voicing her regret. "I seem to repeat this song in each of my letters, but the wish gets louder & louder & at times I feel very depressed over the length of this separation & what I miss in these years of you children & my grandchildren." By summer, what had begun as scattered chirps of remorse had become a full-blown threnody. Her grandchildren, Mabbie's Timothy and Dorothy Anna, and Bob's Christine and the newborn Randi, were then rich in garments which she and Anna Freud had knitted especially for them. But the knitting, like her sudden, vicarious enthusiasm for Gertrude Dann's "junior toddlers," and the steady flow of correspondence, could not substitute for the little ones themselves.

Tinky's marriage to her Hietzing School sweetheart, Peter Heller, in January 1943 had made hers the third wedding which Dorothy had missed. Michael had meanwhile enlisted in the Army Air Corps, had quickly made first lieutenant, and was soon to move with the 419th Fighter Squadron "up the slot" to the Philippines. Dorothy was worried that he so rarely wrote. A suggestion from Mabbie that her architect husband might join the postwar reconstruction of London was enough to turn Dorothy "quite crazy with happiness & longing. I [imagine having] not only Mabbie here, but [Bob] . . . & the others, & then I have my heart's desire. . . ." In August she felt she could no longer stand the separation. "Such a terribly long time, 4 years almost."

And then, as if to crush her anticipation and hope, the Nazis renewed their aerial bombardment on London. Once again at night, "to avoid flying glass & to be near the door in case of incendiaries," they resorted to the downstairs hall. "We have had two years of quiet & it seems difficult to get used to the raids again," Dorothy reported with characteristic understatement.

By the spring of 1944 Dorothy was "quite sick with craving," and physically enervated. And, on May 28, the sixth anniversary of Robert's death, in a remarkable letter to Bob, her crisis reached a fever pitch.

> I think a lot of the future these days. How on earth I am going to arrange my life so that it is sensible & not cutting me off from those I want to be with. I realize more & more that I will have to adjust to a not too strenuous a life. I cannot make out whether my so often feeling tired is due to physical reasons or simply due to a conflict—the wish to be with you which expresses itself that way. There is nothing the matter with me from the doctor's point of view which is reassuring, so probably it is psychical. The future will probably make it easy to make decisions one way or the other. Who knows perhaps Anna will eventually land in the U.S., though I doubt it, there is always that possibility. She certainly does not love it here, but she has patients & [a] house & she has made a place for herself & to pick up stakes again would certainly be very hard for her. So I cannot want it for her. I don't think I even want it for myself. To make new beginnings in the U.S., it looks too terribly strenuous when I try to imagine it. But then I want to be near you all so very much. After all there is no real need for me to work. I could settle down someplace with a wee place. But of course I can't imagine that either & I would be miserable without work I know very well, & I also cannot imagine not sharing Annafreud's life. I think we need each other probably more than ever. She will surely use her energy for analysis wherever she feels it is most needed, that is her main purpose in life & I will have to adjust to her life more or less. So in the end I can only imagine working where Anna is, and spending long holidays with you & having a place waiting with open arms here if ever you can, in your turn, have long holidays & want to divide them between your in-laws & here.

The genesis of a psychosomatic illness could hardly have found clearer expression. Dorothy coughed her way through the first week of June, the advent of the V-1 rockets offsetting the euphoria of D-Day. "I know you have heard that I am flat on my back again as I was that last year in Vienna," she wrote after learning that she was again ill with tuberculosis. "It really is very stupid to repeat such an experience and I am awfully sorry about it."

Dorothy had long recognized the limits of analysis, once writing, "I have many inhibitions that I can never be rid of." The illness was sobering, rather, because from the Freudian standpoint the neurotic repeats rather than remembers, and to repeat this particular conflict was to flirt with death.

Dorothy was not to recover completely until the mid-fifties, after the introduction of drugs such as Ionazid INH. But her survival in those ten years was largely creditable to the power of her will. From the middle of June to the middle of July 1944 there was but one day on which the buzz bombs did not fall, a pounding which Dorothy endured from the master bedroom on the second floor of 20 Maresfield Gardens. Psychologically, the missiles were harder to bear than gravity bombs, because once the air-raid siren had warned of their approach there was no respite, no blessed all-clear signal to end one's anxiety. Like swarms of deranged doodlebugs they flew to all parts of London, and at all hours of the night, the ghastly buzzing ceasing exactly twenty seconds before impact. For months on end Dorothy lay absolutely still on the side of her unafflicted lung, violently reacting to the antibiotic prescribed for her, pondering her mortality in those harrowing intervals.

Being heir to Professor Freud's bedroom boosted her spirits, however. The bright and spacious room overlooking the garden adjoined Anna's own tiny "birdcage" bedroom, formerly the maid's quarters. Anna did "everything a mortal can do to see that I have all that I need, & besides that all the pleasant things that are not necessary but that make life lovely. I have flowers in my room continually; she has planted flowers in boxes on the balcony & the nasturtiums are growing [in] just the kind of tangle I enjoy."

To occupy herself Dorothy made scientific studies of everything within sight—flowers, birds, clouds. And in September she underwent a pneumothorax at the University Hospital, a procedure in which air is pumped into the chest cavity—"just like a tire," wrote Dorothy—laying down the lung to heal. Two months later she could spend half an hour of each day out of bed, and take two baths a week. But in February 1945 she was still "ridiculously tired," and shortly after V-E Day discovered that her other lung was infected. "It's lucky I have only two," she groaned.

In desperation she got out her paint box and, in painting the flowers in her room, was reminded of her childhood. "It's very curious & fascinating," she wrote, "the unconscious seems to hold the brush." After a second pneumothorax she was able to walk on the street a hundred yards. "That means that I can go & buy something, but still not without a taxi." After V-J Day Anna began closing the nurseries, the prospect of seeing her children and grandchildren cheering Dorothy immeasurably. Her revisionism now came full circle. She wrote, "In this generation to be an American is one of the greatest assets there can be. It's wonderful to belong to a country that is not bogged down by centuries of conventions. I realize that more than ever since I have lived here." Dorothy even allowed herself to speculate once again on the possibility of their moving to the States. "I immediately think of settling down on some little farm near New York, enjoying my family & having enough work so that I am not quite out of it . . . it would be a happy fate for me."

XII

"I Have Been Very Lucky"

From the war emerged a Dorothy Burlingham whose course was fixed and whose future was indissolubly bound to Anna Freud. Dorothy might have thought to undertake a new beginning in America for family reasons, but Anna Freud would not or could not have joined her. And Dorothy found herself in times of sickness "frighteningly" dependent on Anna Freud. Left with a fraction of her former lung capacity, Dorothy resigned herself to an invalid and semi-invalid existence by turns. Frail and pinched-looking, confined to bed for extended periods, one could not have guessed at her athletic girlhood. Few suspected her determination, either, which beat her affliction, restored her to productivity, and became part of the Hampstead legend. Because she came to life again, her friend pediatrician Josephine Stross called her Sleeping Beauty.

In London, Dorothy's connection to Anna Freud also had, if anything, intensified the almost Spartan life-style they had previously shared. Freud had predicted this in 1935 to Lou Andreas-Salomé, writing, "What will [Anna] do after she has lost me? Will she lead a life of ascetic austerity?" Dorothy had, for example, in 1943 lived on a total earnings of $3,764, a figure which included taxes of $1,244. Before falling ill, her trust fund income had been strictly reserved for expenses which she considered investments, a category which included analysis. Her financial arrangements with the Freuds for analytic services rendered are not known, but, as one colleague slyly put it, "Surely she got a group rate." Dorothy continued to live simply even after the death of the last of her father's generation, Uncle Burnie, in Beverly Hills, on September 22, 1945. Burnie had never reformed his ways, and the entire trust fund of $1.5 million which had been established for him in 1902, plus the interest which had accrued in the intervening years, was split among the seven surviving children of Annie Mitchell and Louis Tiffany.

During the war Dorothy and Anna had begun to miss Hochroterd with great intensity and, in the last and darkest year, they had begun to comb the classifieds for "a bungalow by the seashore or [an] old mill." It became their favorite pastime. But in January 1946, after the war nursery had closed its doors and the last of its staff had been placed, lapsing into relief, Anna Freud succumbed to a severe viral pneumonia, from the effects of which she never fully recovered. Their search was temporarily postponed. In late May they went to Brighton for their first holiday in nine years, and in July they returned to Ernst Freud's Hidden House in the village of Walberswick; this time Dorothy did not find the countryside "too perfect." Whether six years of confinement or six years of acclimatization was responsible for the change, they fell in love with Suffolk's "wild & glorious" landscape. Dorothy wrote of the train shooting "through fields of grain, fields of flowers . . . fields of sweet peas . . . unbelievably beautiful in their riot of colors," of "sitting in a field with our backs against a gun emplacement looking out over the dikes, then the beach & then the ocean. It's unbelievably beautiful—two windmills are in the middle of the dikes & just at our feet in the water swim ducks & herons."

Walberswick was the kind of village that Dorothy's father might have stopped to paint. A hamlet of neighboring Blythburg at the time of the Norman invasion, by medieval times a prosperous fishing port, its gorse-scented bridle paths led past windblown marshes, prickly thickets, and heather hollows to beaches strewn with carnelian and amber. The "old & original houses" would have arrested Louis also, for their flintstone and thatch composition, and their crumbling Cromwellian faces. On July 7 Dorothy wrote:

This is the happiest time Anna Freud and I have ever had together. She feels free from responsibility & duties and can thoroughly enjoy each minute and I, well I can only say it seems almost like a dream—it's one of those precious moments of life that one can grasp wholeheartedly & then look back on as a wonderful present of fate. As one grows older I think you realize how precious these moments are—that life is often so full of self-made difficulties & problems caused by fate that in reality these perfect moments are really few & therefore to be treasured as they come.

Dorothy bought the first of what would be three Walberswick cottages before returning to London. Of the three, Far End, purchased jointly with Anna Freud, was Hochroterd's heir. The trip from Maresfield Gardens to Far End was two hours longer than that between Bergasse and Hochroterd. But scaled to British proportions and with the ocean's advantages, Far End offered many of the same attractions as Hochroterd— the gardening, the weaving, the contemplation, the retreat from artificial and unnatural perplexities. At the farthest reach of arm extending from the main street ("The Street," aptly called), encircled by a thick, high hedge, its back to the North Sea: this was the essence of Far End. Within their removed and fortified dominion Dorothy's and Anna's poetic side appeared; their spirits lightened, at times turned almost frivolous. Dorothy poked fun at Anna's perfectionism, referring to mistakes in her knitting as "calamities."

With the death of Martha Freud in November of 1951, Dorothy's relationship with Anna Freud reached its final dynamic. For twenty-eight years they lived together much like a married couple, an arrangement which logically caused some speculation. The true nature of their relationship is, according to Victor Ross, "the question that everyone wants to know," and opinion on the subject is divided. Some, like Tinky and W. Ernest Freud, find the idea of a lesbian relationship between her mother and his aunt ridiculous. Others, particularly the generation of Dorothy's grandchildren, think it a possibility, or even likely. The question had, however, originated within the Vienna Psychoanalytic Society itself. In response to a request for information, Dr. Richard Sterba wrote, "The relationship between [Dorothy] and Anna was obviously a very close one. Max Schur took my wife and me once in his car to Hochroterd in the Wiener Wald, where Anna and Mrs. Burlingham owned a little house together. He showed us the inside and we were astonished to find only one double bed in the only bedroom of the house." There was, in reality, a separate wing for the children, and for Dorothy and Anna two single beds in one room which they had evidently, the previous evening, pushed together; but to what purpose? The body of evidence makes it seem profoundly unlikely that they were lesbians in the sexual sense of the word: Anna's asceticism and Dorothy's program of sublimation certainly argue against it, as does Anna's concern for Bob's heterosexuality. It would have taken a hypocrite to discourage homosexuality in him while reveling in it herself; and Anna Freud was not hypocritical. One accurate description of Dorothy's and Anna's relationship, perhaps, is that offered by Peter Heller's father, John. He calls them "intellectual lesbians," an oxymoron which may nevertheless describe a relationship between two women whose attraction for one another is primary, and limited only in its sexual expression.

Curiously enough, after the war, Dorothy and Anna each seemed to adopt something of the other's former identity. The protector and protected exchanged roles, the pressures of duty and fame driving Anna Freud crablike into a shell, and Dorothy emerging from hers. Child analyst Alice Colonna recalls Dorothy's "amazing job" of buffering and insulating Anna from those constantly trying to get at her. Dorothy took care of Anna, running their domestic lives as smoothly as possible. In later years when the housekeeper became "difficult," Dorothy "bore the brunt of Paula." Anna Kris Wolff, daughter of Marianne and Ernest Kris, speaks of the gradual unfolding and warming of her personality.

To Simon Schmiderer, his mother-in-law remained the same person he had met in Vienna in the mid-thirties, "a very stern, serious person with penetrating eyes, a little frightening I thought and at the same time a little shy or embarrassed." Of her relationship with Anna he writes, "There was great mutual concern for each other, each knew exactly what each wanted & needed and that was the law as far as anybody else was concerned. Somehow I felt that D.B. was more in a 'servant' relationship to A.F. and A.F. was god to D.B." Mossik would agree with that assessment. Referring to 20 Maresfield Gardens, she says, "In that house Anna Freud came first, second and last." Helena Gilder Miller also thought it "sad" the way her aunt was "subservient" to Anna, constantly catering to and making things right for her.

Anna Freud's directorial style was no doubt part of her attraction to Dorothy. And whether by reason of sheer force of personality, coincidence with Dorothy's maternal image, or both, that attraction was fierce. It had always been stronger than any other for Dorothy, and had finally triumphed over her imaginary "happy fate" in America. Their connection was subterranean and psychical, and for that reason had weathered even violent changes in external circumstances, like Anschluss, emigration, and Professor's death, and such gradual shifts as the Four coming of age. Most telling perhaps was Dorothy's resignation to a childless life at Maresfield Gardens, a house into which she had detected artificiality creeping, and which, with the preservation of Freud's consulting room and study, had taken on a shrinelike atmosphere. To Erik Erikson, one who had both known the Bergasse and gained perspective on it, the Hampstead house felt "cold" and "tense." Princess Bonaparte had perhaps felt this when, directly after V-E Day, she had "arrived with one of those new creations of hats. But now that she is here," Dorothy wrote, "she does not dare wear it, it looks so incongruous here." Dorothy was also sensitive to her surroundings, but for her Anna's magnetism conquered all.

L ife with Anna did offer productivity and self-respect, and this was vitally important to Dorothy. During her convalescence Dorothy began work on her first independently authored book, a psychoanalytic study of twins, no doubt inspired by, as well as dedicated to, her siblings Comfort and Julia. At the war nurseries had been four pairs of identical twins, two pairs of nonidentical twins, and one set of nonidentical triplets. Of these Dorothy concentrated on three pairs of identical twins, making a highly detailed examination of their behavior. She had written Mossik in May 1942, "What interests me especially is their character development. Whether it has to do with the way the children are to each other or the mother's preference of one." Three years later she published "The Fantasy of Having a Twin," which became the first chapter of her book. The fantasy, she wrote, is compensatory for oedipal disillusionment, an idealized mirror image with whom to dally, narcissistically, in daydreams of absolutely loving and understanding partnership. This sanguine fantasy and the popular perception of twinship overlap, though the reality, she discovered, is frequently opposite. The competition, mimicry, and domination patterns between twins are far more intense than those between regular siblings, as is the tendency in stressful situations to "team" or "gang" together. Focusing, as usual, on the mother–child relationship, Dorothy concluded with the importance of the

294 THE LAST TIFFANY

mother individualizing her relations with each twin. Three years in the writing, *Twins* was published in 1952, the year that Dorothy and Anna founded their renowned clinic.

In 1947, fed up with the wranglings at the British Psychoanalytic Institute, Anna Freud had started an independent college for child analysts based on the Viennese model, the Hampstead Child Therapy Course, at 12 Maresfield Gardens. At the British Institute one began the child analysis program after becoming an analyst of adults. This added eight years of training to the years already spent in college and, frequently, medical school as well. Although lay analysis was legal in England, the number of medical and lay analysts was split roughly fifty-fifty. As Anna and Dorothy saw it, the British Institute candidate, when first learning to analyze children (and then, as if they were miniature adults, à la Klein), was typically approaching middle age with a mind crammed with pre-conceptions. Much better, they thought, to put fresh college graduates through an intensive five-year course devoted solely to the particulars of child analysis. And this is what they did. Dorothy was able to conduct some of the first training analyses while recuperating from her illness. (Inventing a twist on classical technique, she sat former war nursery staffers Ilse Hellman and Hansi Kennedy, facing the wall, at the foot of her bed.)

Financial support for the not-for-profit enterprise came (ironically perhaps) from America, notably through the efforts of analyst Helen Ross and the Field Foundation, which then administered grants in the areas of race relations and child welfare, and also stalwart Freudians Kurt Eissler and Muriel Gardiner. Neither the course nor clinic ever achieved recognition by the International Psychoanalytic Association, however, and was unrecognized by the British Institute for thirty years. This was the price of independence, according to Hansi Kennedy, now codirector of the recently renamed Anna Freud Centre.

Called "the Mecca for the psychoanalytic treatment of children," the Hampstead Child Therapy Course and Clinic was the legacy of Anna's and Dorothy's lifework. To this enterprise they channeled a great share of their energies (without ever drawing a salary), expanding the facilities on Maresfield Gardens to Nos. 14 and 21; eventually, some fifty to seventy children were in treatment at the clinic, four to eight analysts annually completed the course, and a staff of forty-five analysts were put to the tripartite task of research, therapy, and training.

The extent of Dorothy's contribution to the course and clinic is not easily determined since, as Anna Freud wrote, "during her lifetime she was much too modest to either demand or expect adequate recognition for her work." She was underrated, said Ilse Hellman, because she was shy and "didn't make loud noises at the congresses." Dorothy had been battling this condition since St. Timothy's and, during the war, had observed:

> It's so curious how much I enjoy control hours and seminars where I just have to listen and make conclusions out of the material that the students bring, and what a torment it is for me to teach theory. . . . Of course I know enough to teach, but I feel as if I know nothing & get into a terrible state, and the day of the course I am in a panic all day.

"She was underestimated," according to Marinka Gurewich, "because she underestimated herself."

Dorothy was, however, just as happy to leave the limelight to Anna Freud and to exert on affairs an indirect influence, an influence that Ilse Hellman believed was "enormous." This complementary style was already evident at the war nurseries; when matters called for criticism of the staff Anna Freud would mount the podium and do so publicly, while Dorothy tended to draw the individual discreetly aside. From this emerged Dorothy's reputation as "the human being" behind the "duty-bound," "formidable teacher." Dorothy always had a sympathetic understanding of the obligations and concerns imposed by one's personal life. Hansi Kennedy, for example, recalled that Dorothy reacted positively to the news of her marriage, while Anna could see it only as a loss to the clinic, and thereafter could rarely recall her married name.

Dorothy's comments on the child with twins for elder siblings provide a clue to this dynamic. This child

> will be impressed above all by the fact that the twins always have each other as companions, that they are never alone, and that they make an intimate pair just as the parents do. The child may believe that the world is made of couples, feel left out, and decide that he is lacking something and at a great disadvantage in consequence. He may feel his oneness as a state of incompleteness, and have yet another situation in which to play out his fantasies that he has been deprived of some essential part of his own

body, e.g. castration complex. Consequently he will look for other objects and try to make up for his deficiency either in real substitutes or in fantasy relationships.

Behind these words of course lay the genesis of Dorothy's professional interest in twins. Indeed, one sees that Dorothy's search, even as a child, had initially been for a twin substitute; only later had her maternal image settled over her twin image, fusing their faces and Dorothy's search into one. The extraordinary part is that Anna matched both faces; she was both a partner to identify with and an authority to respect and admire. Wrote Dorothy:

> Many of the differences that appeared in the first two years seemed to follow the division between the pairs of twins into one active and one passive partner. To adopt these different roles meant that the twins developed opposite characteristics which they brought into play in their relationship with one another. The active twin would develop dominant, aggressive, selfish characteristics, whereas the passive one would increase the gentle, submissive, altruistic traits which fitted his role.

There can be little doubt that both women were keenly aware of the depth of this aspect to their relationship. From the time that analysis had unearthed Dorothy's wishes from her unconscious, Anna had consciously tried to fulfill them. She was ideal for the part; that is, the part of Julia, the one who had always gotten her own way. Comfort, on the other hand, had made herself agreeable, resembled Mama Lou more closely, and had been Dorothy's favorite. The point here is that both Dorothy and Anna were fulfilled in their relationship and functioned as an effective team.

Dorothy was also an efficient and skillful organizer, and in the early fifties turned her talent to the creation of the Hampstead Psychoanalytic Index. Culling material from the clinic and cross-indexing it under case and subject headings, she fashioned a research archive once referred to by Anna Freud as a "collective analytic memory." Another project which Dorothy is specifically known to have initiated was the simultaneous analysis of mothers and children. Here again personal experience bore professional fruit.

Struck from the start by the importance of dealing with the mothers of children in analysis, Dorothy reaffirmed her conviction in "Present Trends in Handling the Mother-Child Relationship During the Therapeutic Process" (1951). While acknowledging the inherent difficulties, such as the mother who reacts with a venging hostility to the probing of her private life, she concluded that the parent's gain in insight outweighed the risks. Citing the first project case, begun in 1950, that of "Bobbie N," Dorothy focused on his mother, describing her previous treatment as representing the present trend of child guidance clinics. These clinics were then assigning a separate psychiatric social worker to the mother so that she too received help, but without directly contacting her child's therapist. The social worker and therapist instead exchanged notes, which did of course eliminate the problems bred of interaction between the mother and her child's therapist, but also, Dorothy believed, the benefits to the child due to the mother's increased understanding, which direct contact provided. When it became apparent that Bobbie's mother had forgotten much of the social worker's advice, the superficiality of the treatment was also revealed to Dorothy.

Her project called for an in-depth psychoanalysis of both mother and child, with each analyst reporting her findings to an independent coordinator, the content of the analysis melding for the purposes of research rather than therapy. In some cases vital information was exchanged between analysts, but the scientific control had priority. In 1955 Dorothy published Bobbie's case under the title "Simultaneous Analysis of Mother and Child," for which she served as coordinator for Alice Goldberger and Andrew Lussier. Ilse Hellman, coordinator on four of nine subsequent cases, confirmed Dorothy's own conclusion, later writing that "these cases have shown in detail how the mother's fantasies which are acted out physically with the child constitute a major pathogenic factor."

A day nursery for blind children, begun in 1958, was the most ambitious of Dorothy's projects. Though her study of the blind was the principal occupation of the final two decades of her life, it had begun with her studies at the Vienna Psychoanalytic Institute. "Entirely on her own," recalled Anna Freud, "she opened contact with the Headmaster of a large Jewish Residential Home for Blind Children" (Siegfried Altmann of the Israelitisches Blindeninstitut), "observed their educational methods and accepted her first blind child into analysis." The child, a three-year-old named "Sylvia," had been Dorothy's first analysand—blind, sighted, adult or child. This must have been in late 1929 or early 1930, because

Sylvia had visited Dorothy when "in the summer I moved to a house in the suburbs" (Neuhaus), and by winter Dorothy also had been analyzing another patient, Walter Aichhorn. These analyses were followed by that of an eight-year-old blind boy named "Jacob," and her prolonged observations at the Blindeninstitut by those at the Perkins Institute of Watertown, Connecticut (1939–1940), which she conducted while waiting to be reunited with Anna after Professor's death.

The years 1929–1930 had been a period of great upheaval in Dorothy's life, her analysis of Sylvia coinciding with perhaps the most crucial juncture of her own analysis, the struggle for self-mastery and health, and rejection of Robert. Unlike her subsequent psychoanalytic interests, there were no links to the blind from her past experience, but in blindness she may have discovered a metaphor for neurosis, which is to the capacity for enjoyment and fulfillment what blindness is to vision.

But to understand her empathy for the blind one must recall that according to prevalent cultural attitudes during the thirties, forties, and fifties, they were considered to be passive, bored, unspontaneous, withdrawn, depressed, dishonest, and masturbatory. This was of course realized profoundly by Dorothy herself and reported in her papers on the blind; to which Doris Wills adds, "The blind child was [then simplistically] regarded as merely a sighted child without one sense. Dorothy Burlingham['s] . . . work has given great impetus to the study of such children *in their own right.*"

Her earliest observations revealed an entirely separate developmental profile, and a sighted world which preferred to mold rather than to understand the blind. Convinced from birth of the omnipotence of the sighted, the blind child strove to accommodate an educational apparatus which sought to conform him to sighted standards. Taking a group of blind children for a drive one day, Dorothy had been struck by the fact that their questions were uniformly directed to the acquisition of visual knowledge. "Where are we going? What are we passing on the road? Are there any trees? What color is the sky? Are there any animals in the field?" Her observation, that what they heard was evidently more important to them than what they had themselves experienced, had led her to conclude that these children were living "double psychic lives." The laborious construction of a "false self," a cosmetic front for the sighted world, drained their energy from their experiential selves, plunging them into fantasy and make-believe, thwarting their normal development.

On this foundation, over almost fifty years, Dorothy built her understanding of the blind. A baby group, study group, and individual cases were included in Dorothy's blind program, and together they formed the matrix for eight of nine articles she penned on the subject between 1940 and 1979. In 1972 when International Universities Press published in book form a retrospective selection of her papers, Dorothy titled them *Psychoanalytic Studies of the Sighted and the Blind.* Part II, "Development of the Blind," represented the best of Dorothy's work: crisply written, clearly reasoned, intellectually sound, the case material was well integrated with its theoretical underpinnings.

Above all, Dorothy felt the enormity of visual deprivation. Sound is by contrast intermittent and relatively abstract, hence a less reliable tool for reality testing—obviously one of the most important functions of the ego. Furthermore, contrary to popular opinion, the lack of sight can detrimentally affect the other senses. And the mother often compounds the problem. Confused and upset by her infant's blindness, she tends to depression and withdrawal at just that moment when her child needs her active stimulation most urgently. At a later stage she may interrupt his intent listening with feverish sound-making, or take for nonsense his creative and skillful experimentation with sound. Other achievements and abilities of the blind child may also go unrecognized, such as their ingenuity, determination, restraint, and excellent memory, which Dorothy called "phonographic":

> . . . they *remember* the position of stable fittings in their environment to avoid running into them; they *listen* acutely for sounds or echoes to tell them what has been moved from its accustomed place; they *take note* of sidewalks and fix them in their minds; later on they *count* steps; above all, they constantly control their desire for quick movement. While normal children learn about the dangers of fire, water, [and] heights, guided by adults who have passed through the same experiences in their own lives, the blind learn to protect themselves from harm in ways that are unfamiliar to their custodians and which are therefore not taken over by identification with them, but acquired painfully, and independently, by methods of individual trial and error.

Withdrawal, she realized, can be a state of heightened receptivity to sound, passivity self-restraint, and submissiveness a matter of survival. The familiar swaying, rocking "blindisms" are not, as commonly supposed, a normal characteristic of the blind, but rather the result of understimulation in infancy and restricted mobility in childhood.

These insights were brought to bear in the establishment of yet another schoolhouse, this one in back of 21 Maresfield Gardens, where "the mother's wish to make the children conform [was] replaced by the teacher's and observer's desire to see them develop at their own pace and on the basis of their own perceptions." Writes child analyst Anna Maenchen, "When I saw these children running to their school in back of the Hampstead Clinic I could hardly believe that they were blind—so sure and happy they moved."

These postwar years, especially the fifties and sixties, when psychoanalysis was at its height, were the years of Dorothy's personal and analytic fulfillment. As Anna Freud's closest friend and colleague, as well as for her personal qualities, she was respected, admired, and liked on both sides of the Atlantic. She was a power within the psychoanalytic world, the coleader of a matriarchal society of child analysts. Dorothy had, in a twentieth-century idiom, realized the dream for which her mother had sacrificed herself. Her personal attainment was reflected in the remarks of her old friend Marinka Gurewich, now a voice coach living on Central Park West. To Marinka it was "the truthfulness and clarity" which Dorothy put into her relationships which distinguished her. There was nothing of "social artifice" in her. She stayed away from those she did not like and was "lovely" to her friends. Said Marinka, "She was immaculate in her being." How curious, she added, that she managed this without speaking of her inner self, of her personal life or her deepest emotions. Her private life—particularly her Tiffany blood—was, in fact, a cipher to all of her colleagues and analytic friends. Anna Freud was the only one on terms of equal intimacy with Dorothy's public and private sides.

To her family on the west side of the Atlantic, and especially to what would finally number thirteen grandchildren, she was also enigmatic. But the enigma of this great lady called Grandmother lay not in her personal observations and emotions which arrived, with great regularity, *par avion*. The blue aerograms, flowing ink, and rhythmic looping script were terribly familiar, as was the feeling, cultured, creative way in which she expressed herself. She was perhaps at her best at a distance, deeply interested in each family member, positive in her responses to new developments, and eternally hopeful for the future, as loving, thoughtful, philosophic and reliable as a correspondent could be. Her enigma was housed, rather, in the professional sphere. Her Freudian orthodoxy had decisively stamped the family, and yet she was physically removed from it. Her grandchildren felt that distance, and not the sacrifice she had made of a family life. Her letters arrived, inexplicably almost, like persistent ancestral spirits, and they replied as such, hardly guessing that the *kinderbrief* file in which she deposited them was her greatest joy. When Grandmother did materialize on American shores, as she did every other year starting in 1950, her first priority was business. More often than not, the attraction worked the other way. Dorothy was "a powerful magnet."

After more than six years of separation, Tinky was the first of the children to return to London for a postwar visit, arriving in July 1946 with her two-year-old daughter Annie, followed in August by Mabbie, seven-year-old Timmy, and little Dorothy Anna, now six. Dorothy discovered that "it is easier to be a grandmother than a mother & very wonderful just to watch & not have to be on the go every minute of the day." Her pull was meanwhile plainly at work in both its conscious and unconscious aspects. To Bob she wrote, "To see two of my children makes me long. To see two of my children again makes me long for those I haven't seen, even more." She inadvertently repeated herself, probably after pausing to consider her cathexis in longing "for you," or even, "for you and Michael," settling instead on the more measured "others I haven't seen."

The years of separation do leave a gap that writing does not make up for. Letters are wonderful—it is hard to imagine the years without them, but I realize now after having seen Tinky & now Mabbie that letters do not make you understand these years of separation . . . Perhaps you can give me faint glimpses into these years but I don't believe I will ever understand as fully, as if I had step by step followed your lives. This may have had advantages. Probably I could have made life at times easier for each one of you if I had been aware of your needs. But that is all of the past, what is important is the present & future. Now that I have seen Tinky & Mabbie I hope I know enough of their present lives to be able to picture them more realistically, & I hope there won't be such long separations again.

However, Dorothy's dilemma still remained "the structuring of a life around Anna Freud that is sensible & not cutting me off from those I want to be with." Bob was probably first on that list, and on his thirtieth birthday she wrote of planting an acorn at 20 Maresfield Gardens in his honor. But Bob was to be strong, solid, and firmly rooted in British soil in fantasy only. Neither he nor Simon joined the postwar reconstruction of London; instead they began working for I.B.E.C., a New York–based Rockefeller development company. Peter Heller was likewise held in New York by his teaching commitments, and Michael had returned to MIT after marrying Sara Ruth Reid of Orlando, Florida. Dorothy missed their wedding also.

It was then, in the spring of 1946, that the Four broached with Dorothy their plan for a family camp in the Adirondacks, a place, like the Lusks' Camp Comfort, for all to convene together for rest and relaxation. There had been an exchange on the subject of an American farm throughout the war years, with Dorothy (whose trust fund, augmented by her inheritance from Burnie, the scheme relied upon) often raising objections of a practical nature. Her reply on July 18 ran over three single-spaced typewritten pages. She had taken a hard look and gauged the future as follows:

> How often will I really come over to the U.S. and at what time of year? I believe that my visits will often be determined by meetings, congresses, [and] lectures that Anna Freud will come over for. I will certainly want to be over then, not to attend meetings but to be with you during those periods; not that I won't come separately too. Anna Freud will never be over the long periods of time because of patients, and when she does come it will be only partly for pleasure. I cannot imagine that she would be able to be free for more than 2 weeks at any one time. And probably she would not come during July and August because those months would not be possible for lecturing nor for any kind of analytical work nor for meeting the people she will want to see.

In other words, the camp was not a good idea from her perspective. Evidently, Dorothy felt unable to visit her children in America for a few weeks each summer, if it meant leaving Anna to her own devices.

Knowing the Four would not wish to act against her interests, she added:

> Will you not enjoy spending some of your summer holidays in England
> just as much as in the U.S.? Especially when we have found such an ideal
> place for children as well as grownups. A marvellous stretch of sand beach,
> beautiful wild country, a charming village where everybody is friendly.
> I simply cannot imagine anything lovelier.

Thus, with a wave of her wand, Dorothy scuttled the camp, and with
it an independent unity for the family in America. Taking a direct tack,
she then bought Amber Cottage and Thorpeview in Walberswick, effec-
tually making Suffolk—and England—the familial *axis mundi*.

I n 1947 Mabbie became the first to return to analysis with Anna Freud.
Ostensibly she returned that summer to resolve issues of child rearing
which had arisen in her marriage, Mabbie leaning toward permissiveness and Simon to disciplinarianism. But more fundamental still was the
character trait which would remain with Mabbie for life. At the time
Dorothy put it simply in a letter to C.C.B. "She really lives too much
for others, don't you think?"

It is not certain that C.C.B. agreed with her; he seldom did, it seems,
and perhaps especially when it came to selflessness, which, with his record
of public service and his Christian frame of reference, was a virtue. It is
amazing that he and Dorothy were corresponding at all. He had been
deeply wounded by Robert's suicide, suffering a heart attack by summer's
end. On at least one occasion, he flatly stated that he held Dorothy
responsible for Robert's death. But his indomitable faith made it possible
for him to survive without rancor, and accept even the mental illness and
institutionalization in 1940 of his "darling daughter" Nancy. Shattered
by Robert's suicide, she had said to C.C.B.'s face that she hated him, that
he had ruined her life. "It hurt," says C.C.B.'s fifth grandchild, Charles
Burlingham, Jr., "because there was truth in her accusations." After
Nancy's release from Brooklea Farm, a private psychiatric home in
Portchester, New York, C.C.B. bought Nancy a home of her own in
Greenwich, Connecticut, where she became "the monarch of all she
surveyed."

Under these circumstances it would have been entirely human for C.C.B. to have stuck Dorothy's image with pins and set it aflame. But he did not make a scapegoat of her, instead remaining warmly solicitous, and for that she was forever grateful. "One of my greatest sources of pleasure," she wrote, "is that you never turned from me. I do appreciate how wonderful you have been to me. It would be another world if everybody was as loving as you."

He continued to speak his mind, however. "Your grandchildren seem to regard knives and forks as interesting but rather curious implements which have little relation to food. They prefer the primitive methods of the uncivilized." His edge remained keenly stropped and his concern for the family furious, as gradually he grew deaf and blind.

In 1946 he had appraised the situation at a glance. The wartime separation had indeed been hard on Dorothy, but the Four had meanwhile established independent lives and families on their own to which her maternal attractions, at a distance of three thousand miles, seemed disruptive. To C.C.B. the solution was obvious. But, on June 14, he wrote, "[Mabbie] explained to me why Anna prefers England—the confusions and wranglings here among analysts might involve her and give her trouble, so I withdraw my suggestion that she come over here. It was none of my business anyway." Two days later Dorothy wrote:

> You ask why Anna does not come to the U.S. My problems would be gone then I'm sure. But to change lands more often than forced to, is too difficult. She is settled here and professionally has made a new start, in many ways it is not perfect, but to start once more at her age is for her unthinkable. Of course I myself would come to the U.S. and I would far prefer it, but the children do not need me any more, though I know they would love to have me near, and so I do not want to build my life around them. I hate living alone and I am terribly fortunate to have found someone who needs me and wants me to share her life.

C.C.B.'s ire was again aroused, however, when he learned that Mabbie was returning for more analysis. "I appreciate that you want Mab to finish or continue her analysis," he wrote, "but are there not analysts here who could carry it on? . . . I don't like her plan of being separated from Simon for so many weeks and M. says he doesn't like it either." Work naturally made it impossible for Simon to spend three months abroad while Mabbie was being analyzed. But Dorothy saw things differently. She had always wanted her children to have the best, and to her mind Anna was "the best"; and having Mabbie to herself for the entire summer was a dream come true. Shortly after Simon's arrival for his brief visit, Dorothy demonstrated the intolerance to which Peter Heller referred. She reported to Bob, "It is terribly difficult for [Simon] to understand [the reasons for Mabbie's analysis] especially as he would not like to understand what it means." Simon next encountered Anna Freud's law of cohabitation: the Four were themselves always welcome to spend the night at 20 Maresfield Gardens, provided they were alone; but, for the sanctity of Anna Freud's "spinsterish holiness," with spouses the Four had to find other lodgings. Once again, it seems, a Freud was coming between husband and wife. Unfortunately, none of this was an anomaly, and 1947 became the first of Mabbie's annual summer analyses.

Thus a way of life which had been natural in Vienna resumed in London by force of habit. But, as C.C.B. noted, the easy congruence no longer existed. Being separated by the breadth of the Atlantic, resumption of the old ways was like pushing a square peg through a round hole. The priorities were reversed, and now the Four came last. At 20 Maresfield Gardens nothing and no one was more important than psychoanalysis. And, with Anna Freud serving psychoanalysis and Dorothy serving Anna Freud, the Four could in turn only serve Dorothy. She was deprived of their company and they of hers, and analysis was an inviolate rationale for their visitations. This is not to say that Dorothy should have gone along with the Adirondack plan, although it is conceivable that Mabbie might then not have been torn between her husband and mother, as she absolutely was, convinced that she could satisfy neither. For her infinite compassion, Mabbie was adored, but helped only insofar as she fit Anna Freud's temporal, spatial, and ideological schedule. That had of course always been the case. Anna Freud was a busy woman with an enormous burden of responsibility. In retrospect, what should have been handled differently was Mabbie's analysis. Anna Freud should not have been the one analyzing Mabbie, or Bob, or possibly any of Dorothy's children.

Tinky was next. In 1950, feeling depressed, her marriage to Peter

Heller on the rocks, she returned, not to the protective mother of analysis, but to her mother first, and then to analysis with Anna Freud. In Hampstead she developed her talent for photography in a documentary study of the day-nursery blind, and eventually became a first-rate portraitist. In Hampstead, also, vanished the last trace of her ambivalence toward psychoanalysis. She met and married Arthur Valenstein, an American analyst-in-training with Anna Freud. Settling in Cambridge, Massachusetts, she bore him a son, Tinky's physical resemblance to Dorothy deepening into identification with her ethos.

Captain Michael Burlingham returned from the Pacific theater "in fine form," wrote C.C.B., "broadened out, very handsome and self-possessed and self-reliant. He looks very much like Robert and startles me sometimes as he comes up and looks over my shoulder, and I look up and think it is Robert himself." Dorothy evidently demurred, because C.C.B. responded, "Yes, Michael's resemblance to Robert is more in looks than otherwise. And Bob has R's charm." C.C.B. was a judge of character, however, and he saw an essential difference in her sons. "I don't think Bob has as strong and determined a will as Michael, do you?"

After graduating from MIT with honors, Michael worked in microwaves and mechanical timers before relocating in California, a move that seemingly signaled his independence from the family. But, he noted, "my independence was from Mother not the family & it came when I moved to America in March of 1938." In California, through various industrial ventures, he made himself the family's first successful businessman in three generations, owning a ranch house nestled into the foothills of the Sierra Madre, as well as a working ranch named Far End situated across the Mojave Desert. Though a dutiful and loving son, a clue to his perspective on Freud used to hang in his former one-story Northridge home, a sign that read: PSYCHOANALYST: ONE FLIGHT UP.

Bob did not go to war on account of his asthma, and was not happy about it. He started out in the Philadelphia office of architects Kahn & Stonorov (Oscar Stonorov was a friend of Erik Erikson's), but the wartime construction slump soon forced him into city planning for the Tennessee Valley Authority in Johnson City, Tennessee. Neither he nor Mossik liked the South, and in 1947 moved to Hopewell, New Jersey, for a job with the State Planning Commission. In Trenton Bob chafed over not seeing his designs actualized, planning being to architecture what the tortoise is to the hare, but felt he could not begin anew at the drafting table. Creatively blocked and depressed, he quit the job without prospects of another. A period of planning housing projects in the Bergen-Passaic area led him in 1950 to I.B.E.C., and Riverdale, New York. But his frustration with planning followed him there, and within three years he was in effect fired. Father to five, he took to writing the definitive planning book—and to drink—and had a nervous breakdown shortly after Christmas 1953. Paranoid and shaken with delirium tremens, he spent a year at home, Dr. Max Schur pumping him with vitamins. Analysis with Kurt Eissler followed a second breakdown.

By this time his marriage was teetering under the strain, and Mossik came to realize that they had little in common; these then were probable reasons for her own analyses, with Drs. Kronold and Kris (Marianne). Bob spent the next two years vacillating between two jobs (New York Urban Renewal and the London County Council), two analysts (Eissler and Anna Freud), and two women (Mossik and a Hampstead Clinic staffer). He was in London on May 6, 1956, for the celebrations attending the centennial of Freud's birth, and the following spring settled on the L.C.C., Anna Freud, and Mossik. If not for the urgings of loyal Anna Freudians Eissler and Kronold, Mossik might have remained in Riverdale with the children, as the marriage was effectively over. Instead she joined Bob, settling with the children on Queen's Grove in St. John's Wood, a short walk down Finchley Road from Maresfield Gardens. Six years later Bob started another affair and Mossik returned with the children to America.

The reasons for Bob's emotional difficulties are not elusive. He did not, of course, want to be healthy. One recalls Anna Freud laboring in 1925 to win his confidence and establish herself as his ego-ideal, and one is again reminded of her comment about preferring to change children. But in Bob's case Anna Freud's superego modification created a façade of values; Bob the husband, father, and city planner were inventions of her educational admixture, superimposed over the musician, who was perhaps also bisexual, but was in any case most definitely still at odds with himself. To believe this, one has only to read a letter which Anna Freud sent Bob a year after his wedding.

I am sure you are right that your relations in marriage are the center of your other difficulties. Of course it is also true the other way around: all your other difficulties are reflected there. From your description it seems

to me as if you still expected to find Mossik a man and as if most of the
disappointment arose from that. It was just this men's side that we were
trying to work out when you left. Still, you must not forget how different
you are now from the boy you once were. I do not know whether you
remember him (yourself) still but I do. That should make you more
confident about the bits that are still to come.

Though Anna Freud's belief in her approach never wavered, Bob's
example may serve as a reminder of the dangers of such direct efficacy.
If one is to annex to analysis the moral and ethical roles traditionally
assumed by the family, church, and school, does one impose one's personal
values or the values of a broader society? Does one repair the parent's code
only where deleterious to the child, or remake him or her entirely? Or
does one settle on some combination of approaches? With the Four, Anna
Freud seemingly chose to instill her own familial code, grafting it, as it
were, ready-made.

Bob could not be chalked up to science like an unfortunate lab experiment. "With Annafreud," wrote Dorothy, "he was one of her patients,
but besides or [as] part of that relationship [she was] a second mother,
a helper & at times the one person who could give him the support he
needed." Bob had been ten when Anna Freud had established herself in
his eyes as "a very powerful person," when "I had made myself indispensable to him and he had become dependent upon me." But now, three
decades later, instead of seeing his hidden energy released, she was obli-
gated to putting Humpty Dumpty back together again. If this hurt her
pride, she certainly sacrificed a great deal to his restoration, including
Mossik's right to privacy in marriage (imagine, if possible, one's mother-
in-law and one's spouse's analyst being the same person).

Bob eventually found himself in his father's shoes, frequently manic
or depressed, the Atlantic Ocean separating him from his family, and
viewed by them with similar uneasiness. Since there was the appearance
of repetition compulsion and sympathetic illness in this, Anna Freud
continued to treat him from the psychoanalytic angle, despite the increasing suggestion of a biochemical, genetic etiology. In that sense, her
treatment was limited by her ideology and training. Psychoanalysis directly treats the mind, not the body or brain.

Bob was remarried in May 1964 to Annette Müller, a German nurse
with whom he shared a cramped, dark apartment in Regent's Park. They

had no children. Annette recalled, "We . . . had three wonderful weeks together until I encountered for the first time, for me, a depression and following that a manic phase."

> This became more and more frequent during the following seven years of our lives together and worsening heart condition, which he suffered from. Nevertheless, whenever it was possible we shared our lives and interests to the full. Apart from working in the hospital, I learned technical drawing to continue Bob's work when he was unable to work in his office.
>
> He was such an extraordinary person, so highly gifted in so many ways, foremost being music and painting. It was a delight to roam galleries and museums with him and attend concerts, hearing his sharp critique afterwards. And then his wonderful way with other people, so considerate, always able to listen to their needs and detecting their slightest wishes.

Nevertheless, she adds, "It was not always easy for both of us to see life in a positive way . . . My request, at the time, for him to change his analyst must have really meant my death warrant as [far as his] feelings [for me] were concerned." Bob continued to smoke heavily despite his asthma and emphysema, gradually becoming a gaunt, sickly shadow of his former self. Reduced to working a half day, then hospitalized with increasing frequency, he died of an asthma-induced heart attack in January 1970, at age fifty-four.

This was hardly the result that Mabbie had expected when she had managed her divided affections by throwing in her lot, unequivocally, with her mother, Anna Freud, and psychoanalysis. Bob's death was particularly depressing in light of her own problems, the loyalty conflicts which had resurfaced in her marriage. She now also felt an obligation to fill the void in Dorothy's life which Bob had left, tipping the scales further against her marriage.

I.B.E.C. had brought Mabbie and Simon to San Juan, Puerto Rico, in the mid-fifties, where she felt comfortable and he was stimulated by his work. But later Mabbie felt increasingly drained and plagued by the realization that since her college years she had done virtually nothing with her artistic talent. When Simon's most ambitious housing project was then abruptly canceled, they returned to Riverdale, and hit bottom. In late winter 1974, after trying to resolve her problems in analysis with Marianne Kris, Mabbie returned alone to Hampstead. According to Tinky, "Yes Mabbie . . . returned to Mother and A.F. Mabbie had been depressed before leaving Puerto Rico—but even more so by being uprooted from there and by the desolate move back to the old house in Riverdale. You know Simon had himself been depressed before Mabbie—as his excellent last major project folded (we saw its first building) and he quit his job before retirement age. It was sad and depressing for both of them."

Mabbie's last letters were alternately hopeful for the future, and suicidal. Perhaps she remembered the case of the woman whose body had been found washed up on the banks of the Seine in the twenties. Her rapturous expression in suicide had prompted an artist to lift a death mask which had been copied and widely admired as *l'Inconnue de la Seine*. In 1930 Mabbie had written Dorothy in Tegel, "When I get the feeling of loving somebody *unermesslich viel* ['immeasurably much'] I think of that face, you know, of the girl who made *selbstmord* in the Seine by Paris. She had such a lovely smile on her face. Really heavenly." In July, in her bedroom at 20 Maresfield Gardens, Mabbie took an overdose of sleeping pills, and two weeks later died in the hospital.

The following morning Gertrude Dann and a few others were sitting in the staff room at 21 Maresfield Gardens and, knowing that Mabbie had died in the night, were amazed to see Dorothy—drawn and shaken—nevertheless walk purposefully along the path to the nursery school in back to keep an appointment with a little blind girl.

Dorothy wrote a nephew of Mabbie's in late August:

I am surprised that Mabbie was a vague picture to you, because she was such an outgoing, generous loving person and was interested in you and your activities & you were a precious son of your father's & mother's whom she loved dearly & were an important part of her life. I think her end & suicide is what spoilt your picture of her for you because it was exactly the opposite of what you thought of her. She was a happy person, loved by everybody who came in contact with her and she loved being needed & helping where she could.

As you know life always has complications and problems & I think what upset Mabbie so much was that she felt she could no longer help the people she loved. And life no longer had a sense to her—that was the tragedy. How wrong she was. We all needed her so much & miss her continually.

The deaths of Bob and Mabbie severely strained Dorothy's relationships with some of her grandchildren in the last decade of her life. Amidst the shambles, Bob's and Mabbie's children particularly found it hard to see Dorothy and Anna Freud in a positive light. When the turbulence subsided, what remained was a nagging image: that instead of, or perhaps in addition to, having received a golden key, Bob and Mabbie had been loaded with an enormously heavy cross, and bear it they did, to the very altar of psychoanalysis. There remains the ironic conclusion that psychoanalysis had been foisted upon them unnecessarily, and when dependent upon it, had not helped them. Then, when they had really needed help, Freudian ideology had discouraged them from seeking it, for example, in the realm of pharmacology.

Despite Dorothy's every effort to reverse the priorities of the Tiffany imperative, she had remained in its thrall; ultimately she was more successful at work than life; and she wounded her family with the radical change she had wrought upon it. She was herself a pivotal figure, a bridge, the violence surrounding her life a reflection of the profound change which the ideas she had embraced represented. Intellectually she was a Freudian, but emotionally she had remained Victorian as she and her family were swept irrevocably into the twentieth century.

I n the late sixties Dorothy and Anna had bought another country cottage in southwest County Cork, Ireland, a spot "even wilder and more beautiful than Walberswick." "It is the southern part where we go," wrote Dorothy.

It is very near Baltimore, a very lively small port and beyond there are many lovely islands. The country is very beautiful, very rocky and between the steep rocks [there are] many beautiful beaches. There is something very fascinating about the atmosphere & clouds and colours . . . it is so paintable and the people are unspoiled, very friendly and expecting everybody to be as kindly as they are themselves. It gives one such a feeling, that's the way people should be.

From Ireland, in the spring of 1975, Dorothy wrote her grandson; she was celebrating that year the fiftieth anniversary of her first meeting with Anna Freud:

> I am glad you had that avocado present from Annafreud. She loves to give pleasure & this was an opportunity for her. She is like that. She is an amazing person . . . She has a talent like her father's to see things clearly, to see further than others, and to follow what she believes in without reservations. She loves to fulfill needs. She can enjoy so much too, beauty of the intellect as well as the soul. I have been very lucky.

The honorary degrees bestowed on Anna Freud by Yale, Harvard, Columbia, and the University of Vienna, and the Queen's Commander of the British Empire, attest to an extraordinary contribution to society. The awards came, however, as they often do, in the eleventh hour, when psychoanalysis was on its way to becoming what Harold Bloom called "an isolated and disputable theory . . . a small sub-branch, almost a sect, within . . . psychiatric medicine." And in her lifetime, certainly, Anna Freud was viewed as the guardian of an increasingly vulnerable position. Fated for ingestion into popular psychology, psychoanalysis had spewed forth again in a thousand (to the Freudian mind) bastard forms. But Anna Freud never wavered in defense of "real" analysis, once comparing herself with the Spartans who had fallen in their valiant but unsuccessful defense of Thermopylae, asking her nephew W. Ernest Freud to quote Simonides' epitaph to her friends in America. "Go tell the Spartans, all ye who pass by,/ That here, obedient to their laws, we lie." Entrenched, embattled, and outnumbered, yet undaunted and prepared to die before surrendering the pass; these were Anna Freud's vestal robes.

For Dorothy, who shared in the contribution, honor, and defense, one pleasure was seeing her father's star rise after decades of neglect and derision. His foundation had auctioned off the contents of Laurelton Hall and sold it—in the rarest of white elephant transactions—for $10,000, to an absentee owner. The three-day fire which consumed the place in 1957 was perhaps enough to make one believe in karma (Sanskrit, literally, for "Comeback"), as with the next decade, Laurelton Hall would probably have been designated a national landmark. Indeed, in 1977, Dorothy—the last Tiffany since the death of her half siblings and, more recently, in 1973 and 1974, of twins Julia and Comfort—found herself asking almost helplessly, "Why is my father so in the air at present. I get so many clippings, & I do not understand why the present interest in him." And yet, she who had also been a pioneer, would now draw hope from his renaissance.

Ultimately the life that Dorothy and Anna shared together made everything else acceptable. The human scale of their relationship was captured in a moving vignette by analyst Susan Vas Dias. "On the road to Skibberdeen," she wrote,

along a particular stretch, the fuchsia climbs so high on either side that it almost meets overhead. The world seemed to consist of green leaves through which are glimpsed blue sky, fast racing clouds and horses grazing in the heat of the far-off fields. Mrs. Burlingham and Miss Freud stood next to their white Mini, which was stopped almost in the centre of the road. I was concerned that they might have run into difficulty, pulled over and asked if they needed any help. Miss Freud smiled and said, No, thank you. We're just two old ladies who both want to see. We take turns, one drives, one sees. This is our changeover point. Beautiful, isn't it? I agreed, and feeling almost an intruder, said good-bye and left them standing together in the stillness.

At 20 Maresfield Gardens, forty years after Professor's death, his aura hung in the house like smoke; an immaculately quiet, still, thick pregnancy tasting of immortality and death. It hung in the eaves and vines, on the blue historic marker by the front door, in the water-spotted wallpaper, in the frayed, discolored lampshades and worn *bauern* furniture, and grew overwhelming among the leather-bound volumes and antiquities of his study and consulting room. In such an atmosphere, one's very thoughts took on special resonance.

Then it was October 11, 1979, Dorothy's eighty-eighth birthday; a tiny woman with a wrinkled, pinched face, breathless at the top of a flight of stairs, but with the same twinkling eyes, pageboy hair, and will of the girl born on Lenox Hill. A table in Freud's study served as her *geburtstagstisch,* and Dorothy opened her gifts sitting on the rug-draped couch.

Deciding to retire the old Polaroid given her by "a friend of Mr. Land," Anna Freud presented Dorothy with a One-Step. Afterward Dorothy returned to bed, where she spent much time. She was in bed when Anna Freud interrupted her supper one evening to stare at the leaves drifting bright yellow and red through the wet twilight in the garden beyond. A visiting grandson had brightened Dorothy's birthday, but now the end seemed near. Even so, Anna Freud's words startled her interlocutor, perhaps because they were unsolicited and welled from deep silence, punctuated by the scraping of silver on china. "The leaves are falling," she said, "just like the last act of *Cyrano de Bergerac*."

Anna Freud had used Edmond Rostand's play to illustrate altruistic surrender in *The Ego and the Mechanisms of Defense,* but in telling the plot had curiously neglected to tell the ending. Only as Cyrano lies dying in Roxane's arms, does approaching death break his resistance, and he finally declares his love for her. Grandson, he understood Anna to say, you have come at last and declared your love, but only now as your grandmother lies upstairs dying. But, in retrospect, with her history of altruistic surrender, Anna Freud probably meant it the other way around. She had always loved the family, but from a clinical distance, through Dorothy, and this was her declaration of love.

Her words were oracular. Dorothy collapsed a few days after the first Annual Hampstead Clinic Symposium, through which she had remained active. She died on November 20, 1979; her ashes were laid in the Freud crypt of the Golders Green Crematorium. The music played at her funeral was played again three years later at Anna's: the eerie "Farewell" to Mahler's *Das Lied von der Erde* ("The Song of the Earth"):

> I stand here waiting for my friend
> I wait for him to take a last farewell
> I long, my friend, to enjoy the beauty
> Of the evening at your side
> Where are you? You have left me alone for so long!

Notes and Sources

Direct quotations and some other passages in the text are identified here by page number and a quoted phrase. For certain references the following abbreviations have been used:

M-TP	The Mitchell-Tiffany Papers Sterling Library Manuscripts and Archives Department Yale University
T&Co. Archives	Tiffany and Company Archives Parsippany, New Jersey
TFA	The Tiffany Family Archives Anonymous private collection
CCBP	Charles Culp Burlingham Papers Harvard Law School Library Manuscripts Division Harvard University
EBJP	The Edith Banfield Jackson Papers The Schlesinger Library Radcliffe College
S.E.	*The Standard Edition of the Complete Psychological Works of Sigmund Freud*

I THE TIFFANY IMPERATIVE

Page 3   *7 East 72nd Street* —The address was later changed to 27 E. 72nd Street.

    3   *"I find invitations . . . Hurrah!"* —Josephine Balestier to Mary W. Tiffany, April 9, 1891. TFA.

    3   *"closest and most valued friend"* —Edmund Gosse, *Portraits and Sketches.*

    3   *the Kiplings* —The Lockwood Kiplings, Rudyard's parents.

    3   *"the greatest . . . sculptor."* —Josephine Balestier to Mary W. Tiffany, n.d. TFA.

4   *"My life is broken . . . crippled."* —Josephine Balestier to Mary W. Tiffany, December 30, 1891. TFA.

4   *"I am so pleased . . . 'Dorothy.' "* —Josephine Balestier to Mary W. Tiffany, December 30, 1891. TFA.

5   Mail and Express.—"Mayoralty Gallery: No. 10. C.L. Tiffany, a Representative Citizen and a Good Man for Mayor," July 5, 1890. Tiffany & Company Archives.

5   *"standing . . . these times."* —The *Globe* (n.d.). T&Co. Archives.

7   *"very imposing and elegant,"* —Charles L. Tiffany to Annie T. Mitchell, March 12, 1885. M-TP.

8   *"decorative jungle."* —Quoted in Robert Koch, *Louis C. Tiffany: Rebel in Glass,* p.68.

8   *"Arabian Nights in New York,"* —Quoted in *Rebel in Glass,* p.69.

8   *"cinnabar red,"* —[Charles DeKay,] *The Art Work of Louis C. Tiffany,* p.59.

9   *"not bad . . . worst kind."* —Charles L. Tiffany to Annie T. Mitchell, March 9, 1887. M-TP.

10   *"Into eternity . . . go."* —Records of the Massachusetts Bay Colony. Quoted in Joseph Purtell, *The Tiffany Touch,* p.12.

12   *"the future . . . ambition."* —George Frederic Heydt, "Charles L. Tiffany and the House of Tiffany," pp.8–9. M-TP.

13   *"All . . . as death."* —The Diary of Philip Hone, p.258. The New-York Historical Society.

16   *"something like a picture,"* —See Gertrude Speenburgh, *The Arts of the Tiffanys,* p.18.

16   *"the very show . . . art."* —Ibid., p.18.

17   *"the finest . . . secured"* —Annabel A. Groan, "An Appreciation [of Charles L. Tiffany]," 1902. T&Co. Archives.

17   *"absolute . . . the business."* —Ibid.

18   *"cheap . . . badly made,"* —Paraphrased in *The Tiffany Touch,* p.18.

18   *made to order . . . abroad* —See *The Tiffany Touch,* pp.19–20.

19   *One Tiffany . . . porcelain.* —In the 1842/1843 *Longworth Directory of New York.* The New-York Historical Society.

19   *"of taste and utility,"* —New Mirror, May 11, 1844. T&Co. Archives.

19   *"for sale . . . only"* —Tiffany, Young & Ellis Catalog of Useful & Fancy Articles, 1845. T&Co. Archives.

19   *"Tiffany, Young & Ellis . . . imitation."* —Ibid.

19–20   *"since . . . in this country."* —New Mirror, May 11, 1844. T&Co. Archives.

20   *"have always . . . Atlantic."* —Tiffany, Young & Ellis Catalog of Useful & Fancy Articles, 1845. T&Co. Archives.

21   DIAMONDS —New-York Commercial Advertiser, December 18, 1848. The New-York Historical Society.

21   *Overnight . . . diamond merchants.* —The defensive tone of the following advertisement, which appeared in the December 18, 1848, *New-York Commercial Advertiser,* would appear to signal some uneasiness over their good fortune in only their second or third year in the gemstone business. "Feeling that our extraordinary opportunities of buying in quantities, for cash, during the late revolution and subsequent depressions in various European markets; enables us, with entire propriety, to assert the great superiority of our stock of Diamonds and other rich jewelry, over any collection ever seen in this country, and our ability to sell at lower prices—and that we are fairly entitled to any benefit that may arise from the matter of fact . . ." the ad began.

II DIAMOND OF THE FIRST WATER

Page 23 *as Charles . . . 1848 Revolution.* —Although Diamond Ledger #1 in the Tiffany & Company Archives shows diamonds purchased as early as January 21, 1848, a big jump occurs on October 3, this presumably the day that John Young returned from France.

23 *"learned to cope . . . craftsmen."* —Gertrude Speenburgh, *The Arts of the Tiffanys*, p.18.

24 *had moved back . . . Norwich.* —The 1850/1851 *Longworth Directory of New-York* lists a Connecticut address.

24 *American shores.* —Barnum auctioned the tickets to Lind's Castle Garden concert, claiming a moral duty to deprive scalpers of their livelihood.

26 *"the fetish idols . . . trade"* —*Mail and Express.* "Mayoralty Gallery: No.10. C.L. Tiffany, a Representative Citizen and a Good Man for Mayor," July 5, 1890. T&Co. Archives.

27 *"chaste."* —Contemporaneous press clipping, unheaded (n.d.). T&Co. Archives.

27 *"plowed . . . the sea."* —From a plaque at 550 Broadway. See *The Arts of the Tiffanys*, p.20.

28 *"Of course . . . laid."* —*New York Times*, September 3, 1858.

29 *"for ornamenting . . . offices,"* —Quoted in Joseph Purtell, *The Tiffany Touch*, p.34.

29 *"policemen . . . order."* —Quoted in *The Arts of the Tiffanys*, p.30.

29 *"a social . . . art."* —Annabel A. Groan, "An Appreciation [of Charles L. Tiffany]," 1902. T&Co. Archives.

29 *"a very quiet . . . gentleman"* —Quoted in *The Tiffany Touch*, p.55.

29 *"It is not . . . stiff . . ."* —From Annie O. Tiffany's diary, 1865–1867. Quoted by Alfred M. Bingham on page 8 of "Alf and Annie," a chapter from his work-in-progress on his family. Published, in revised form, as *Portrait of an Explorer: Hiram Bingham, Discoverer of Macchu Picchu*.

30 *"the synonym of fashion"* —James D. McCabe, Jr., *New York by Gaslight*, p.78.

30 *"articles . . . and luxury"* —*Frank Leslie's Illustrated Weekly*, January 5, 1861.

31 *"Celtic,"* —The Diary of George Templeton Strong. The New-York Historical Society.

32 *"Louis . . . its existence."* —Charles de Kay, *The Art Work of Louis C. Tiffany*, p.5.

34 *"stiff . . . cramped."* —Charles L. Tiffany to Louis C. Tiffany, November 23, 1862. TFA.

34 *"good and bold"* —Quoted in *The Tiffany Touch*, p.54.

34 *"I went . . . time."* —Louis C. Tiffany to Annie O. Tiffany, December 24, 1857. M-TP.

35 *his solicitor . . . Kingsland.* —Daniel Kingsland, lawyer, apparently acted in Charles's behalf on at least one occasion. Louis wrote, "Mr. Kingsland put up 'Post no bills' on the fence." Louis C. Tiffany to Annie O. Tiffany, December 24, 1857. M-TP.

35 The Eagleswood Military Academy has a curious history. For an excellent account, see "Louis C. Tiffany and His Early Training at Eagleswood, 1862–1865," by Doreen Bolger Burke, *The American Art Journal*, Volume XIX, Number 3 (1987), 29–39. I am indebted to Ms. Burke, Associate Curator of American Paintings and Sculpture at the Metropolitan Museum of Art in New York, for kindly providing me with an early draft of her article, together with much of the primary source material from which it was drawn.

35 *"organized . . . Battalion drill."* —*Catalogue of the Officers and Students of the Eagleswood Military Academy* (1863), p.5.

35 *"not for bad . . . forgetfulness."* —Louis C. Tiffany to Annie O. Tiffany, November 24, 1862. M-TP.

35 *"I don't sleep . . . tired."* —Louis C. Tiffany to Annie O. Tiffany, November 11, 1862. M-TP.

35 *"On Friday . . . myself."* —Louis C. Tiffany to Annie O. Tiffany, November 14, 1862. M-TP.

36 "*I was much . . . haste.*" —Charles L. Tiffany to Louis C. Tiffany, November 23, 1862.
TFA.

36 "*I feel confident . . . lustre.*" —Ibid.

36–37 "*The weather . . . here.*" —Ibid.

37 "*I have written . . . here.*" —Louis C. Tiffany to Charles L. Tiffany, January 14, 1863.
M-TP.

38 "*good mark . . . speaking.*" —Louis C. Tiffany to Annie O. Tiffany, n.d. M-TP.

38 "*for drawing well.*" —Louis C. Tiffany to Annie O. Tiffany, December 24, 1857. M-TP.

38 *natural philosophy . . . favorite subject.* —"I like philosophy ever so much better than
any other for our teacher is so kind and explains so nicely that you understand all about
what you are learning and that is not the case in all studies." Louis C. Tiffany to Annie
O. Tiffany, November 14, 1862. M-TP. The course to which he refers must have been
natural philosophy, as this was the only "philosophy" course offered at Eagleswood
until the senior year.

38 "*Figure . . . and Painting.*" —*Triennial Catalog of the Eagleswood Military Academy, and
Prospectus for 1864–1865* (1864), p.3.

38 "*inspiring quality.*" —[Charles DeKay,] *The Art Work of Louis C. Tiffany*, p.7.

38 "*I agree . . . most.*" —Louis C. Tiffany to Annie O. Tiffany, October 13, 1863. M-TP.

38 "*I think . . . foliage.*" —Ibid.

38–39 "*When do . . . sketching.*" —Louis C. Tiffany to Harriet Y. Tiffany, June 11, n.y. M-TP.

39 "*How does . . . him.*" —Louis C. Tiffany to Annie O. Tiffany, n.d. M-TP.

III ALONG THE HUDSON RIVER

Page 40 *earliest extant work.* —This painting was brought to my attention by Amanda Austin,
Curator of Decorative Arts, Indianapolis Museum of Art.

40 *five feet six* —This is an approximation made specific for interest. The Tiffanys were
all short. Louis's brother Burnie was exactly five feet six, and Louis was not much
taller, if taller at all.

41 "*whenever there was time.*" —From Annie O. Tiffany's diary, 1865–1867. Quoted in
Alfred M. Bingham, "Alf and Annie," p.10.

41 "*one . . . I ever knew.*" —"Alf and Annie," p.10.

41 "*You're a . . . head?*" —Emile Kingsland to Louis C. Tiffany, October 2, 1865. M-TP.

41 "*I have seen . . . you.*" —Ibid.

41 *The result of their meeting* —As told in "Alf and Annie," Louis saw Harry Gray at
Columbia College the following year and "proposed to Papa to ask him to be his
teacher for the summer." This led to Harry's flirtation with Annie, and the offer by
Henry Peters Gray to paint her portrait, "for many favors to my dear son." Gray also
painted a view of the Tappan Zee from Tiffany Hall.

41 "*darling Papa*" —From Annie O. Tiffany's diary. Quoted in "Alf and Annie," p.11.

41 "*The Great River in the Mountains.*" —See John K. Howat, *The Hudson River and Its
Painters*, p.22.

42 "*Divine Architecture . . . Hudson River Painters.*" —Ibid, p.23.

42 "*Ça commence là-bas.*" —Quoted in David C. Huntington, *The Landscapes of Frederic
Edwin Church*, p.4.

42 "*a complete condensation . . . mountains.*" —Quoted ibid., p.5.

42 *the 1867 International Exposition in Paris* —Church won a gold medal, Tiffany &
Company a bronze.

42 "*Nature . . . always beautiful.*" —Louis C. Tiffany, "Color and Its Kinship to Sound,"
The Art World, No.2 (1917), 142–43.

42 "*to overspread . . . experiment of liberty?*" —Quoted in Daniel Aaron, Richard Hofstadter, and William Miller, *The Structure of American History*, p.140.

43 *wangled his way back ... Inness* —The date of Louis's studies with Inness (and, for that matter, Colman) have yet to be conclusively documented. [Charles DeKay,] *The Art Work of Louis C. Tiffany* states only that Louis was then "at the age when a youth in his circumstances is pretty sure to be at the university," p.5.

43 *whom Louis ... colorist.* —See *The Art Work of Louis C. Tiffany*, pp.7 and 75.

44 *"the true use ... civilization."* —Quoted in *The Art Work of Louis C. Tiffany*, p.6.

44 *"The true ... divine."* —Ibid.

44 *a watercolor called* Afternoon. —Identified as a watercolor (evidently on the basis of a contemporaneous press clipping) in Hugh F. McKean, *The "Lost" Treasures of Louis Comfort Tiffany*, p.3.

44 *a favorable one.* —Ibid.

44 *"the Paris way,"* —Quoted in "Louis Comfort Tiffany: the Paintings," essay by Gary A. Reynolds, p.10.

44 *"the old students ... plebes."* —Quoted in Dorothy Weir Young, *The Life and Letters of J. Alden Weir*, p.22.

44 *"study hard ... young American."* —*The Art Work of Louis C. Tiffany*, p.8.

45 *"the finest château in France."* —Louis C. Tiffany, Brittany Journal (unpublished), p.114. Katrina B. Valenstein.

45 *"school of art taste"* and *"teacher of art progress."* —Quoted in Joseph Purtell, *The Tiffany Touch*, p.82.

46 *"The pictures ... story."* —Mark Twain, *The Innocents Abroad.*

47 *"When first I ... my attention."* —Louis C. Tiffany, "The Quest of Beauty," *Harper's Bazaar*, December 1917.

47 *"I returned ... neighbor."* —Ibid.

47 *"sovereign importance."* —Ibid.

47 *"the 'legitimate' ... freely."* —*The Art Work of Louis C. Tiffany*, p.8.

47 *"It is curious ... sky."* —"The Quest of Beauty."

48 *"received more praise ... collection."* —From an undated press clipping in Louis's scrapbook. Quoted in *The "Lost" Treasures of Louis Comfort Tiffany*, p.29.

48 *"beyond question ... flattery."* —Ibid.

48 *"I believe ... splendidly."* —*The Life and Letters of J. Alden Weir*, p.127.

48 *"This exhibition means revolution."* —Quoted ibid., p.139.

49 *"I have ... Ella Morton ..."* —Louis C. Tiffany to Annie O. Tiffany (n.d.). M-TP.

49 *"the loveliest ... knew."* —Quoted in "Alf and Annie," p.10.

49 *"the love of a ... sister."* —Mary W. Goddard to Henry P. Goddard, October 11, 1871. TFA.

50 *"spotless purity,"* —Quoted in "Alf and Annie," p.21.

50 *"I ... Annie have been ..."* —Mary W. Goddard to Henry P. Goddard, October 11, 1871. TFA.

50 *One of Louis's landscapes* —Fuller's Country Store, Norwich (1872).

50 *"inland city."* —"The Inland City" was the title of a poem about Norwich which May transcribed in her notebook (author and date unknown). TFA.

51 *"nearly twelve years ... earth,"* —Julia Goddard Piatt to her cousin Kate M. Trott, January 28, 1884. Quoted in *The "Lost" Treasures of Louis Comfort Tiffany*, p.15.

51 *"the only drawback ... health,"* —Ibid.

51 *"she would not ... earth."* —Ibid.

51 *"I ... scrambled egg,"* —Mary G. Tiffany to Annie T. Mitchell, May 12, 1874. M-TP.

51 *"sun ... nice table."* —Ibid.

51 *"and they ... particularly."* —Ibid.

51 *"remarkably poor"* —Ibid.

52 *"but ... being rebuilt,"* —Ibid.

52 *"warm & lovely"* —Ibid.

52 *"lovely little ... embroidered."* —Ibid.

52 *"lost her child ... time ..."* —Ibid.

52   *"very large fine"* —Mary G. Tiffany to Annie T. Mitchell, December 27, 1874. M-TP.

52   *"remarkably strong"* —Mary G. Tiffany to Annie T. Mitchell, January 1, 1875. M-TP.

52   *"I . . . as I am."* —Mary G. Tiffany to Annie T. Mitchell, December 27, 1874. M-TP.

52–53   *"Tomorrow . . . in these countries."* —Mary G. Tiffany to Annie T. Mitchell, December 27, 1874. M-TP.

53   *"finishing May . . . too fast,"* —Louis C. Tiffany to Charles and Harriet Tiffany, January 3, 1875. M-TP.

53   *"one of the . . . ladies."* —Ibid.

53   *"as Annie has none."* —Ibid.

53   *"God has taken . . . weeks."* —Mary G. Tiffany to Annie T. Mitchell, January 1, 1875. M-TP.

53   *"all . . . worse than before."* —Louis C. Tiffany to Charles and Harriet Tiffany, January 3, 1875. M-TP.

53   *"We shall go . . . well."* —Ibid.

53   *"I do not . . . original."* —Louis C. Tiffany to Annie T. Mitchell, January 10, 1875. M-TP.

54   *If they did . . . season.* —An envelope addressed in May's hand to Mr. and Mrs. Robert W. de Forest is postmarked Algeria. Paris and New York postmarks on the back clearly indicate the date as March 21, '76. TFA.

54   *and Louis . . . season.* —See *Louis Comfort Tiffany: The Paintings,* p.53.

IV   THE CULTURED DESPOT

Page 55   *"missionaries . . . the philistine."* —See Roger B. Stein, "Artifact as Ideology: The Aesthetic Movement in Its American Cultural Context," in John P. O'Neil (ed.), *In Pursuit of Beauty: Americans and the Aesthetic Movement.*

56   *"fine arts workman"* —Quoted in "Celebrating William Morris's Work," *New York Times,* March 15, 1984.

56   *"Have nothing . . . beautiful."* —Ibid.

56   *"all items . . . manufacture,"* —See Robert Koch, *Louis C. Tiffany: Rebel in Glass,* p.10.

56   *"indigent gentlewomen."* —Ibid.

56   *"reaction . . . commercial element"* —[Charles DeKay,] *The Art Work of Louis C. Tiffany,* p.xvi.

57   *"Saracenic"* —This was Moore's term. See Siegfried Bing, *Artistic America, Tiffany Glass, and Art Nouveau,* p.3.

57   *"I am trying . . . existence."* —Louis C. Tiffany to Annie T. Mitchell, January 10, 1875. M-TP.

57   *"to those living . . . delight."* —Quoted in *In Pursuit of Beauty,* p.184.

57   *"the finest . . . continent."* —Boston *Evening Transcript,* February 9, 1877.

57   *"the flye-eye of New York."* —Quoted in Lou Gody (ed.), *The WPA Guide to New York,* p.206.

58   *"would see the world"* —Ibid.

58   Artistic Houses . . . States." —New York: Appleton and Company, 1883–84.

58   *"welded . . . harmonious whole."* —Quoted in *Rebel in Glass,* p.17.

58   *never studied interior design* —According to *Artistic Houses,* Louis's decoration of the Bella led him to "the systematic study of the principles of the profession which he is now practicing." Quoted in *In Pursuit of Beauty,* p.124.

58   *"attracted . . . Corliss engine"* —Quoted in Milton Glaser and Lally Weymouth, *America in 1876: The Way We Were,* p.33.

59   *"the proud position . . . world."* —Quoted in *In Pursuit of Beauty,* p.260.

59   *"As to those . . . around."* —*The Art Work of Louis C. Tiffany,* p.xxiv.

59   *"There is . . . after all."* —Candace Wheeler, *Yesterdays in a Busy Life.*

59 *"any work . . . exceptionally well done"* —"Domestic Indian Architecture," by Lockwood de Forest (draft manuscript of *Indian Domestic Architecture,* published Boston: Heliotype Printing Co., 1885), p.2. Courtesy of Kellam de Forest.

60 *"I . . . light black."* —*Yesterdays in a Busy Life.*

60 *"Mr. Tiffany . . . ways and means."* —Ibid.

60 *"The beauty . . . look."* —Quoted in Hugh F. McKean, *The "Lost" Treasures of Louis Comfort Tiffany,* p.107.

60 *"we . . . need of money."* —Quoted in facsimile in *Rebel in Glass,* p.44.

61 *"I . . . haven't time."* —Charles L. Tiffany to his children, February 22, 1882. M-TP.

61 *"The wave . . . receded."* —*Yesterdays in a Busy Life.* Quoted in *Rebel in Glass,* p.49.

62 *"A name . . . Louis XVI."* —*Artistic America, Tiffany Glass, and Art Nouveau,* p.148.

62 *"I think . . . all,"* —*Yesterdays in a Busy Life.* Quoted in *Rebel in Glass,* p.50.

62 *"Soon after . . . hand."* —"Domestic Indian Architecture," p.165.

62 *"does not . . . Mr. de F.,"* —Mary W. Tiffany to Annie T. Mitchell, August 4, 1883. M-TP.

62 *"Mr. Armstrong . . . Mrs. W."* —Ibid.

63 *"The facts of art . . . despot."* —From "The Truth of Masks: A Note on Illusion." Quoted in *Rebel in Glass,* p.61.

63 *"master hand"* —Oscar Wilde, "An Unequal Match," *The World,* November 7, 1882. Quoted in *Rebel in Glass,* p.60.

63 *"There may be . . . mind."* —Quoted in *Rebel in Glass,* p.61.

63 *"I congratulate you . . . again."* —Samuel Colman to Louis C. Tiffany, August 27, 1879. M-TP.

63 *"laid up and coughing badly."* —Mary G. Tiffany to Annie T. Mitchell, August 4, 1883. M-TP.

64 *"I have not . . . depressed."* —Charles L. Tiffany to Annie T. Mitchell, September 5, 1883. M-TP.

64 *"It took our . . . improving."* —Mary G. Tiffany to Annie T. Mitchell, September 23, 1883. M-TP.

64 *"Louis . . . God knows."* —Julia Goddard Piatt to Kate M. Trott, September 24, 1883. Quoted in *The "Lost" Treasures of Louis Comfort Tiffany,* p.15.

64 *"angel now,"* —Julia Goddard Piatt to Mrs. Levi Hart Goddard, January 22, 1884. TFA.

65 *and in Florida* —The letter written by Charles L. Tiffany to his children, September 22, 1882, indicates that they were then all vacationing in Florida with their families.

65 *by the winter . . . 1882,* —See Mosette Glaser Broderick and William C. Shopsin, *The Villard Houses: Life Story of a Landmark,* p.45.

65 *"The great aesthetic . . . crest."* —Quoted in *In Pursuit of Beauty,* p.177.

65 *He claimed . . . 1872,* —See Robert Koch, *Louis C. Tiffany's Glass-Bronzes-Lamps,* p.25.

66 *"there was . . . stop to it."* —Quoted in *The "Lost" Treasures of Louis Comfort Tiffany,* p.32.

66 *"the commercial element"* —*The Art Work of Louis C. Tiffany,* p.xvi.

68 *minimize . . . flesh tones.* —See *The Art Work of Louis C. Tiffany,* p.19.

69 *"The most inspiring . . . other."* —*Artistic America,* p.135.

69 *"one of the greatest . . . Ages."* —Alice Cooney Frelinghuysen, "A New Renaissance: Stained Glass in the Aesthetic Period," in *In Pursuit of Beauty,* p.185.

69 *"Mr. Lewis . . . me."* —Quoted in H. Barbara Weinberg, *The Decorative Work of John La Farge,* p.365.

69–70 *"not to . . . extent."* —"American Art Supreme in Colored Glass," *The Forum,* Vol. XV (July 1893), p.623.

70 *"the prejudice . . . of glassmakers"* —"The Quest of Beauty," *Harper's Bazaar,* December 1917.

70 *"represented himself"* —*The Art Work of Louis C. Tiffany,* p.19.

70 *but a . . . photograph* —This photograph proudly opens Chapter II, "The Maker of Stained Glass," in *The Art Work of Louis C. Tiffany.*

70 *"an indefinite period."* —La Farge quoted in *The Decorative Work of John La Farge,* p.363.

71 *"the negotiations . . . pieces,"* —Ibid., p.364.

71 *Since Louis . . . glass,* —*Eggplants* and *Squash,* made in 1879, contain variously colored opalescent glasses made at the Tiffany Glasshouse. See *The "Lost" Treasures of Louis Comfort Tiffany,* pp.51–57. Also *In Pursuit of Beauty,* pp.186–89.

71 *juggernaut,* —Alistair Duncan, *Tiffany Windows,* p.13.

71 *"I wish . . . Jebusite."* —John La Farge quoted in *The Decorative Work of John La Farge,* p.369.

71 *"considered as settled."* —Ibid., p.366.

72 *"The use of glass . . . vision."* —Quoted in *Rebel in Glass,* p.55.

73 *"How many years . . . glass?"* —Quoted in *Rebel in Glass,* p.52–53.

73 *As to flesh tones . . . 1912.* —This was *The Bathers.*

74 *"It would break . . . him."* —Julia Goddard Piatt to Kate M. Trott, January 28, 1884. Quoted in *The "Lost" Treasures of Louis Comfort Tiffany,* p.15.

74 *"fast . . . living."* —*Rebel in Glass,* p.59.

74 *"enjoyed the enthusiastic . . . chorus"* —Ibid.

75 *"like fire . . . emeralds,"* —Ibid., p.61.

75 *"master hand . . . ultra-aesthetic."* —Ibid.

75 that *"dreadfully . . . yours."* —Charles L. Tiffany to Mary W. Tiffany, July 23, 1889. TFA.

75 *"an endless . . . complete,"* —Charles L. Tiffany to Annie T. Mitchell, March 12, 1885. M-TP.

75 *"were* much applauded." —Charles L. Tiffany to Annie T. Mitchell, February 16, 1886. M-TP.

75 *"the Tiffany house . . . America."* —Quoted in *Rebel in Glass,* p.63.

75 *"the most beautiful . . . seen."* —Ibid.

77 *A scrapbook* —Gilder family memorabilia.

78 *"I knew . . . loves."* —Julia B. de Forest to Annie T. Mitchell, September 28, 1886. M-TP.

78 The Pennsylvania Canal is now the Delaware and Raritan Canal. Mauch Chunk is now Jim Thorpe.

79 *Their jaunt was chronicled* —The result was an album of photographs accompanied by Holt's LOG OF THE MOLLY POLLY CHUNKER: *Showing forth the Perilous and Thrilling Adventures of her Company in a Voyage through Strange Countries never before Visited by any Similar Expedition.* Privately printed (New York, 1887). Gilder family memorabilia.

79 *"moon and clouds . . . too."* —Log of the Molly Polly Chunker, p.3.

79 *"began . . . so long."* —Ibid., p.7.

79 *"The power . . . after.'"* —Ibid., p.40.

80 *"Lou smiled . . . solemn."* —Julia B. de Forest to Annie T. Mitchell, November 14, 1886. M-TP.

80 *"Louis looked . . . radiant."* —Ibid.

80 *"Here we are . . . everything."* —Louis C. Tiffany to Annie T. Mitchell, November 10, 1886. M-TP.

80 *"supremely happy."* —Julia B. de Forest to Annie T. Mitchell, November 12, 1886. M-TP.

80 *"all together . . . happy"* —Ibid.

81 *"the manufacture of glass . . . kinds."* —Certificate of Incorporation, December 15, 1886.

81 *"nine out . . . houses."* —Quoted in *Rebel in Glass,* p.78.

81 *"Hoffman Bible pictures . . . abominable."* —Ibid., p.80.

82 *"was based . . . Christian art."* —Ibid.

82 *Congregationalists . . . Tiffany windows.* —See *Tiffany Windows,* p.135.

83 *"We are neither . . . lilies."* —Louis C. Tiffany to his children, August 22, n.y. TFA.

83 *"the great innovator . . . one. . . ."* —*Reports of the International Jury of the Exhibition of 1889,* Group III, p.179.

84 *"This is . . . work of each."* —Louis Comfort Tiffany, "American Art Supreme in Colored Glass." *The Forum,* Vol. 15 (1893).

84 *"Do you realize . . . century!"* —Quoted in Burke Wilkinson, *Uncommon Clay: The Life and Work of Augustus Saint-Gaudens*, p.242.

84 *"something not of this world."* —Richard Watson Gilder to Edmund Gosse, May 1893. Quoted in Rosamond Gilder (ed.), *The Letters of Richard Watson Gilder*, p.241.

84 *"Looking down . . . means."* —"Domestic Indian Architecture."

85 *"The damage . . . if not longer."* —Quoted in *Uncommon Clay*, p.242.

85 *"A very false idea . . . color."* —*The Art Work of Louis C. Tiffany*, p.48.

85 *"the parent of stained glass."*—"American Art Supreme in Colored Glass."

85 *"more realistic . . . exhibit."* —Ibid.

86 *Stained glass had not . . . piece,* —Colors had begun to shift, subtly, as early as 1879 in the *Eggplants* and *Squash* windows, but not as distinctly and dramatically as did this amber fish and turquoise water. By 1898, as many as seven different molten colors were being ladled onto an iron sheet to make a single sheet of glass.

86 *"the introduction . . . done,"* —Quoted in *Rebel in Glass*, p.76.

86 *"the best American . . . windows."* —Ibid., p.79.

86 *"bizarre manifeste,"* —Ibid., p.75.

86 *"of a perfection . . . Ages."* —Quoted in *Tiffany Windows*, p.106.

86 *"It would be . . . factors."* —Cecilia Waern, "Industrial Arts of America: The Tiffany Glass and Decorative Co." *International Studio*, Vol. 2 (1897), p.156.

86 *"We are . . . extravagant lives."* —"The Quest of Beauty."

87 *"Too much Stourbridge"* —Quoted in *Louis C. Tiffany's Glass-Bronzes-Lamps*, p.41.

88 *"the first name . . . mind"* —Quoted in *Artistic America*, p.152.

88 *"While glass . . . ideas."* —Ibid., p.146.

88 *"Alas . . . jack-hammer."* —Quoted in *The Decorative Work of John La Farge*, p.369.

88 *"mere form"* —Quoted in *Rebel in Glass*, p.79.

V THE KUBLA KHAN, MAMA LOU, AND ME-TOO

page 91 *"I am so sorry . . . ill."* —Josephine Balestier to Mary W. Tiffany, January 2, 1892. Tiffany Family Archives.

91 *"marvellous Annie."* —Dorothy T. Burlingham in a taped interview with her nephew Rodman Gilder and his wife Mary Ellen, June 4, 1978.

92 *She . . . never would,* —She made this statement in a letter to her son, Robert Burlingham, Jr., November 16, 1942. Author's collection.

92 *"the Ugly Duckling."* —Gilder interview, June 4, 1978.

92 *"Dorothy is six . . . glad."* —Julia de F. Tiffany to Annie T. Mitchell, October 1897. M-TP.

92 *"divided"* —Dorothy T. Burlingham, "Memories of My Father," p.1. Author's collection. Also quoted in Robert Koch, *Louis C. Tiffany: Rebel in Glass*, 3rd edition.

92 *white enamel tabletop . . . cabinetwork.* —For this information I am indebted to the Institute's Field-McCormick Curator of American Arts, Milo N. Naeve.

93 *"run riot . . . woodland"* —"Memories of My Father," p.2.

93 *"Immediately . . . greatest pleasure."* —Ibid., p.1.

94 *"passionately . . . with flowers."* —Gilder interview, June 4, 1978.

94 *"and they greeted . . . side."* —"Memories of My Father," p.1.

94 *"a complex . . . points of view."* —Ibid.

94 *"autocratic"* —Author's interview, July 1978.

94 *"about fifteen . . . top."* —Louis Tiffany, Brittany Journal, pp.25–26. Katrina B. Valenstein.

94–95 *"kept coming . . . again."* —Ibid., pp.75–76.

95 *"an enchanted world . . . beautiful,"* —Ibid., pp.64–65. This refers to Cap Frehel, outside Dinard.

95 *"the world of everyday."* —Ibid., p.93. This refers to Nantes.

95 *"I can see . . . yeah."* —Quoted in Robert Koch, *Louis C. Tiffany's Glass-Bronzes-Lamps,* p.64.

95 *considered a crime.* —Author's interview, July 1978.

95 *But the greatest crime . . . unpunctuality.* —"Memories of My Father," p.2.

95 *"his ideas . . . crazy."* —Gilder interview, June 4, 1978.

95 *"Crazy is not . . . slightest."* —Ibid.

95 *"Originality . . . and creativity."* —Dorothy T. Burlingham writing (in 1977) on the margin of the filmscript "Tracking the Life of An Artist: Louis Comfort Tiffany," by Michael John Burlingham.

96 *"rather stern . . . lovely too."* —Gilder interview, June 4, 1978.

96 *The first . . . their wedding,* —As pointed out by Gary A. Reynolds in the catalog essay to the exhibition *Louis Comfort Tiffany: The Paintings* (p.58), "Although usually dated circa 1896, the Seventy-Second Street mansion was completed almost ten years earlier. The woman depicted is thought to be Tiffany's second wife, Louise, whom he married in 1886. Tiffany exhibited *A Study in My Studio* at the SAA, 1890." The spirit of this painting is certainly more consistent with the ardor of a husband for his newlywed bride.

97 *a fact recalled by Dorothy,* —Author's interview, July 1978.

97 *It was reported . . . tenement.* —James D. McCabe, Jr., *New York by Gaslight,* is the source here throughout.

98 *"a communist . . . property."* —Quoted in Rodger Butterfield, *The American Past,* p.268.

98 *"the public . . . damned!"* —Ibid., p.234.

98 *"the makers . . . underclad."* —Ibid., p.259.

98 *"the first . . . service."* —Kristina Argiros, (ed.), "A Look at the Past with an Eye to the Future," *Vital Signs: Newsletter of the New York Infirmary* (1964 supplement).

98 *Chrysanthemum Festival . . .* —This was the April 1888 event, often referred to as the *Paasch-Feest,* or Dutch Easter Festival.

99 *"a liberated woman,"* —Author's interview, July 1978.

99 *"disgusted"* —Alice S. Rossi, (ed.) *The Feminist Papers from Adams to de Beauvoir,* p.328.

99 *"at the arrogance . . . sect"* —Ibid., p.330.

99 *"The Committee . . . sex."* —*New York Infirmary for Women and Children (36th) Annual Report.* New York (1889). The New York Public Library, Rare Book Division.

100 *A Short History of Art.* —See "Lockwood de Forest: Painter, Importer, Decorator," catalog essay by Anne Suydam Lewis, Heckscher Museum, Huntington, New York (1976).

100 *"Oh no . . . person."* —Author's interview, July 1978.

101 *"Every piece . . . beautiful."* —Jimmy Stewart quoted in *Louis C. Tiffany's Glass-Bronzes-Lamps,* p.65.

101 *Years later . . . road.* —Dorothy T. Burlingham to Michael J. Burlingham, May 6, 1972.

101 *"My grandfather . . . money."* —Interview with Hugh F. McKean, May 1983, (who received the information in an interview with D.T.B.).

102 *"a terrible . . . Burnie,"* —Louis C. Tiffany to Annie T. Mitchell, n.d. M-TP.

102 *"whoop it up . . . power."* —Quoted in Joseph Purtell, *The Tiffany Touch,* p.109.

102 *"My business . . . so."* —Ibid.

102 *"It . . . and health,"* —Quoted ibid., p.111.

102 *"In return . . . week."* —Ibid., p.112.

103 *"the lying . . . libidinous."* —John A. Kouwenhoven, *The Columbia Historical Portrait of New York: An Essay in Graphic History,* p.441.

103 *"Then . . . rush of wealth!"* —"Daffodils," by Comfort T. Gilder. Author's collection.

103 *Burnie's $1.5 million . . . executors.* —Louise's $1.5 million was also put in trust.

104 *"not touched . . . years,"* —*New York Times,* January 30, 1904.

105 *"Grandpa . . . left him!"* Charles L. Tiffany II to Annie T. Mitchell, August 5, 1932. M-TP.

106 *considerably "advanced" price.* —*New York Times,* May 22, 1904.

106 *"In Xanadu . . . decree."* —Samuel Taylor Coleridge, "Kubla Khan."

106   *"Why train . . . privately."* —Alice Freeman Palmer, "A Review of the Higher Education of Women." *The Forum,* Vol. XII (September 1891–February 1892), p.33.

106   *"When I see . . . me!"* —Ruth McAneny Loud (ed.) *The Brearley School: Seventy-Five Years,* (1959), p.40.

107   *"the public mind . . . goose."* —"A Review of the Higher Education of Women," p.40.

107   *"Girls need . . . someday?"* —Comfort T. Gilder, "The Sewing Room," p.11. Author's collection.

107   *"Well . . . a doctor!"* —Ibid.

107   *In 1904 . . . the United States.* —See *Rebel in Glass,* p.130.

107   *"Papa . . . than school."* —"The Sewing Room," p.11.

108   *"very sickly . . . groaning."* —Gilder interview, June 4, 1978.

108   *"Tomorrow."* —"The Sewing Room," p.13.

108   *"Though . . . to be fine."* —Ibid.

108   *"about the same."* —Ibid., p.13.

108   *"self-sufficient . . . understanding."* —Ibid., p.5.

108   *"while Papa's . . . control."* —Ibid., p.7.

108–109   *"One day . . . could be."* —Ibid., pp.13–14.

109   *"Your mother . . . too."* —Ibid., p.16.

109   *"I'm glad . . . anymore."* —Gilder interview, June 4, 1978.

110   *"I think . . . missed."* —"The Sewing Room," pp.9–10.

VI DOROTHY

page 111   *"the fundamental idea"* —"The Quest of Beauty," *Harper's Bazaar,* December 1917.

111   *"a cross . . . barn"* —"Tiffany's Houses Odd—But Then So Was He," by Nixon Smiley, Miami *Herald,* April 14, 1968, p.6-B.

111   *"the perfume . . . America."* —Quoted in Gertrude Speenburgh, *The Arts of the Tiffanys,* p.98.

111   *Pullman railroad coach,* —Hugh F. McKean makes this comparison in *The "Lost" Treasures of Louis Comfort Tiffany,* p.113.

112   *"Mr. Tiffany . . . estate."* —Quoted in *The Arts of the Tiffanys,* p.95.

113   *"Can you do . . . know."* —Quoted in Joseph Purtell, *The Tiffany Touch,* p.150.

113   *"While . . . in succession."* —[Charles DeKay,] *The Art Work of Louis C. Tiffany,* p.77.

114   *"Garden . . . to be loved."* —"Daffodils." Author's collection. Another version of this poem, privately printed in the volume *Points of Light,* ends, "was one single flower loved?"

114   *or so said . . . children* —Dorothy Stewart Pierson, granddaughter of Robert and Emily de Forest, recalled this, and other details presented here, in a privately printed reminiscence, *Uncle Louis and Laurelton Hall* (Christmas 1981).

115   *"dreadful creatures . . . colored."* —"Memories of My Father," by Dorothy T. Burlingham, pp.2–3. Author's collection.

115   *"dimming the horrors."* —Ibid., p.3.

115   *"torpedoed"* —New York Times, June 9, 1916, p.21.

116   *"Every night . . . others."* —Comfort T. Gilder, "Worse Than the Others," p.2. Author's collection.

116   *"terrified . . . our understanding."* —Ibid., p.1.

116   *lifelong fear . . . alcohol.* —Interview with Katrina Burlingham Valenstein, April 29, 1983.

116–17   *"dared the most"* —Gilder interview, June 4, 1978.

118   *"searching for something . . . child."* —Gilder interview, June 4, 1978.

118   *"Ideas penetrate slowly . . . completed."* —Julia B. de Forest to Dr. Graham Lusk, June 24, 1908. TFA.

118 *"The beautiful way . . . do."* —Emily J. de Forest to Mary T. Lusk, n.d. TFA.

118 *"You must not . . . children."* —Julia B. de Forest to Mary T. Lusk, September 2, 1904. TFA.

118 *I sleep . . . Beds.* —Interview with Comfort Parker Lord, April 24, 1983.

119 *"I have looked . . . way."* —Julia B. de Forest to Mary T. Lusk, July 13, 1908. TFA.

119 *"done a good deal . . . families."* —Ibid.

120 *"It was horrible . . . there"* —Gilder interview, June 4, 1978.

120 *"I would . . . mistake."* —Ibid.

120 *"something preposterous . . . all."* —Dorothy T. Burlingham to her children, November 30, 1941. Author's collection.

121 *"five miserable years"* —Gilder interview, June 4, 1978.

121 *"a four page . . . way."* —See *The "Lost" Treasures of Louis Comfort Tiffany*, p.15.

121 *"a good scholar and athlete."* —According to Miss Louise M. Pennington, Class of 1910.

121 *Living . . . to her son.* —Dorothy T. Burlingham to Robert Burlingham, Jr., May 28, 1944. Author's collection.

122 *"the weather . . . Cold Spring Harbor."* —Louis C. Tiffany, Brittany Journal, pp.125–26. Katrina B. Valenstein.

122 *"he was afraid of illness."* —Comfort T. Gilder, "The Sewing Room," p.7. Author's collection.

122 *"very beautiful . . . tragedy."* —Gilder interview, June 4, 1978.

122–23 *"go again . . . grumpy."* —Ibid.

123 *"we . . . our way back."* —Louis C. Tiffany to Mary T. Lusk, February 12, 1908. TFA.

123 *"I am so troubled . . . more."* —Ibid.

123 for *"sacrificing . . . pleasure."* —Comfort T. Gilder, "The Pleasure Trip," p.2. Author's collection.

123 *"He brought on . . . T.B."* —Ibid., p.1.

123 *had events . . . 1910.* —St. Timothy's records from that era, and of the Class of 1910 in particular, are sketchy. Since she is not listed as an "ex-graduate," it is possible that she was awarded a diploma, regardless.

123 *"My father . . . finish . . ."* —Gilder interview, June 4, 1978.

124 *"I didn't dare."* —Ibid.

124 *"It was . . . out."* —Author's interview, October 1979.

125 *"stayed with him . . . ways."* —"Memories of My Father," p.3.

125 *"To Patsy . . . years."* —Quoted in *The Sarah Hanley Collection of Tiffany and Related Items,* catalog of Phillips, New York (1985), p.17.

125 *"he wished . . . resent it."* —"Memories of My Father," p.3.

125 *The family . . . accepted it."* —For the sake of appearances, Patsy later became "engaged" to Stanley Lothrop, resident director of the Louis C. Tiffany Foundation, who was homosexual.

125 *"Patsy got him . . . on her."* —Interview with Comfort Parker Lord, April 24, 1983.

125 *"Padre."* —The *"Lost" Treasures of Louis Comfort Tiffany*, p.16.

125 *"He was a god on earth."* —Ibid.

125 *He once . . . Enthroned.* —See *The Sarah Hanley Collection of Tiffany and Related Items,* p.28.

125 *"What do you think . . . daughters?"* —Charles Burlingham, Sr., in conversation with Michael J. Burlingham, c. 1979.

126 *"the first young . . . education."* —Autobiographical sketch, by Aaron Hale Burlingham. CCBP.

127 *"Baptist pup,"* —Interview with Rosamond Taylor Edmondson, July 25, 1983.

127 *"most admired . . . loved."* —Gabish Holmes to Charles C. Burlingham, February 28, 1944. Timothy Schmiderer Collection.

127 *"Annie . . . fellow men."* —Charles C. Burlingham to Annie Corbin Hoe, March 2, 1879. Schmiderer Collection.

127 *"messing about . . . business."* —Quoted in *Charles C. Burlingham: Twentieth Century Crusader,* Harvard Law School Library exhibit catalog (1980), p.3.

127 *"that awful . . . d'hote."* —Brittany Journal, p.70. Katrina B. Valenstein.

127 *noting . . . waxing late . . ."* —Charles C. Burlingham to Mark A. DeWolfe Howe. Quoted in Helen Huntington Howe, *The Gentle Americans, 1864–1960. Biography of a Breed,* p.405.

127 *"there was . . . horrible."* —Author's interview, October 1979.

128 *"the malefactors . . . wealth,"* —Quoted in Rodger Butterfield, *The American Past,* p.313.

128 *"smash into little pieces"* —Quoted in Robert Koch, *Louis C. Tiffany: Rebel in Glass,* p.21.

128 *"no jews"* —Louis C. Tiffany to Mary T. Lusk, n.d. TFA.

128 *a "setter up . . . kings."* —William Shakespeare, Henry VI, Part III.

128 *"slummish"* —"Where and How We Lived," autobiographical sketch by Charles Culp Burlingham. CCBP.

129 *"equal the case"* —Undated letter to Louisa L. Burlingham, c. 1926, signed "E.L.B." Schmiderer Collection.

129 *"I hope . . . nice letters."* —Robert Burlingham, Sr., to Charles C. Burlingham, n.d. Schmiderer Collection.

129 *"every nerve . . . aggressiveness."* —"On a Dutch Steamer, S.S. *Veendam,* outward bound, August, 1892." Unidentified newspaper clipping, signed "Lookerabout." Schmiderer Collection.

130 *On Shrove Tuesday . . . Cleopatra.* —On June 26, 1911, couturier Paul Poiret and his wife Denise had hosted an ethereal costume party, the "1002nd Night," which may well have served Tiffany with some inspiration.

130 *"acknowledged authorities . . . art."* —Union and Advertizer, Rochester, N.Y., February 5, 1913.

130 *"ransacked for ideas","* —New York *Tribune,* February 5, 1913.

130 *"authoritative books . . . town."* —Ibid.

131 *"four colossal Ethiopians"* —New York *Sun,* February 5, 1913.

131 *"an Egyptian . . . pharaohs"* —Ibid.

131 *"so free . . . the place."* —Uncle Louis and Laurelton Hall.

131 *once suggesting . . . burned.* —Author's interview, July 1978.

131 *"men of genius"* —Quoted in *The Tiffany Touch,* p.145.

131 *"to inspect the spring flowers."* —New York *Herald,* May 9, 1914.

132 *"lovely smile,"* —Author's interview, October 1979.

132 *"a delight,"* —Interview with Louise Lusk Platt, January 19, 1985.

132 *"a heroine . . . romantic!"* —Interview with Clarinda Garrison Binger, August 7, 1983.

VII MOTHER LOVE

Page 134 *"who crawls over whom,"* —Binger interview, August 7, 1983.

135 *"uptight . . . casual eye."* —Ibid.

136 *Bob . . . those he loved.* —Dorothy T. Burlingham to Michael J. Burlingham, April 3, 1975.

137 *"under care . . . work."* —"Where and How We Lived," autobiographical sketch by Charles Culp Burlingham p.8. CCBP.

137 *"never to eat . . . dinner."* —Ibid.

137 *"the close preserve"* —"Notes on the History of Burlingham, Veeder, Clark and Hupper." CCBP.

137 *in spite . . . myself out.* —Records of the Class of 1879, Harvard University, Report IX (1929), p.79.

138   *"like a cricket,"* —Binger interview, August 7, 1983.

138   *"a pea in the griddle."* —Interview with Cora Weir Burlingham, March 1983.

139   *"I was just . . . Louie Lawrence."* —Edmondson interview, July 25, 1983.

139   *"a great . . . lady."* —Interview with Charles Burlingham, Jr., July 27, 1983.

139   *"a pyramid . . . to her toes."* —Edmondson interview, July 25, 1983.

139   *"wasn't greatly interested"* —"Where and How We Lived," p.7. CCBP.

139   *"distinguished . . . generosity,"* —"First Decade of Married Life," autobiographical sketch by Charles C. Burlingham, p.6. CCBP.

139   *"walking off . . . down the block,"* —Edmondson interview, July 25, 1983.

139   *Louie's father . . . the block,"* —C. C. B.'s marriage to Louisa Weed Lawrence on September 29, 1883, occurred shortly after the Lawrences had been abandoned by De Witt.

141   *"were rich . . . way."* —Holly Day to Michael J. Burlingham, November 12, 1983.

142   *"A hundred years . . . difference."* —Charles Burlingham, Jr., interview, July 27, 1983.

143   *"wrong handling"* —Dorothy T. Burlingham to Robert Burlingham, Jr., October 28, 1941. Author's collection.

144   *"everything so much worse"* —Ibid.

144–45 *"Freud . . . and objectively."* —Professor J. Jastrow, "Mother Love." *The Saturday Evening Post,* n.d.

145   *"Watson's . . . to children . . ."* —Ibid.

145   *"This was . . . the end."* —Dorothy T. Burlingham to Michael J. Burlingham, April 3, 1975.

145   *"minded so"* —Ibid.

146   *"I still think . . . of course."* —Richard H. Lawrence to Charles C. Burlingham, September 6, 1887. Schmiderer Collection.

146   *"overtired."* —Edmondson interview, July 25, 1983.

146   *"You wrote . . . shoulders."* —Robert Burlingham, Sr., to Charles C. Burlingham, December 28, 1925. Schmiderer Collection.

146   *"A capable officer."* —Discharge Certificate of the United States Army. Schmiderer Collection.

147   *"Dorothy . . . a hard time."* —Louis C. Tiffany to Mary T. Lusk, August 12, 1920. TFA.

147   *"Somehow . . . the children."* —Dorothy T. Burlingham to Michael J. Burlingham, April 3, 1975.

147   *"the separation . . . with."* —Ibid.

148   *"a genius."* —Gilder interview, June 4, 1978. De Forest was known for his development of the magnaflux test, a magnetic method for discovering the defects in ferrous metals.

149   *Curiously enough . . . Galey.* —See "Lockwood de Forest: Painter, Importer, Decorator," catalog essay by Anne Suydam Lewis, Heckscher Museum, Huntington, New York (1976). p.35.

149   *"not at all . . . interested."* —Gilder interview, June 4, 1978.

149   *"I am not . . . God."* —Agnes Kenney to Dorothy T. Burlingham, c. February 1921, n.d. Dorothy T. Burlingham memorabilia.

149   *"All goes well . . . are."* —Agnes Kenney to Dorothy T. Burlingham, May 30, 1921. Dorothy T. Burlingham memorabilia.

149   *"Everything goes . . . mushrooms."* —Agnes Kenney to Dorothy T. Burlingham, n.d. Dorothy T. Burlingham memorabilia.

150   *"a marvellous summer . . . me."* —Gilder interview, June 4, 1978.

150   *"she expects . . . winter."* —Louis C. Tiffany to Mary T. Lusk, August 20, 1922. TFA.

150   *"some kind . . . experience."* —Valenstein telephone interview, May 1988.

151   *"difficult,"* —Gilder interview, June 4, 1978.

151   *"lovely relationship . . . hours."* —Dorothy T. Burlingham to Michael J. Burlingham, April 3, 1975.

152   *"I know . . . precipice,"* —Constance A. Buffum to Dr. Amsden, April 17, 1925. Schmiderer Collection.

152   *"to take . . . thirst."* —Ibid.

152–53   *"Aunt Dodo . . . operate!"* —Gilder interview, June 4, 1978.

VIII   THE CHOICE

page 155   *"Ruth evidently . . . judgement."* —Constance A. Buffum to Louisa L. Burlingham, September 8, 1925. Schmiderer Collection.

155   *"I . . . wiser people."* —Constance A. Buffum to Louisa L. Burlingham, September 10, 1925. Schmiderer Collection.

156   *"my reason . . . courage."* —Gilder interview, June 4, 1978.

156   *"Anna . . . American children."* —Quoted in Lucy Freeman and Herbert S. Strean, *Freud & Women,* p.81.

156   *"German doctor."* —Constance A. Buffum to Louisa L. Burlingham, September 10, 1925. Schmiderer Collection.

156   *"she . . . of her own."* —Ibid.

156–57   *"Soon D's letters . . . family."* —"E.L.B." to Louisa Burlingham, n.d. Schmiderer Collection.

157   *"lonely, beautiful spots."* —Untitled, undated typescript by Eva Rosenfeld, p.24. Victor Ross collection.

157   *"awful moment"* —Author's interview, October 1979.

157   *"Eva must keep . . . days."* —Rosenfeld typescript, p.25. Ross Collection.

158   *"In the meantime . . . home . . ."* —Ibid., p.29.

158   *"splendid isolation"* —Sigmund Freud, "On the History of the Psycho-Analytical Movement." S.E., Vol. 14, p.22.

159   *"only . . . son."* —Erik Erikson, "Tribute to Anna Freud." *Bulletin of the Hampstead Clinic* (1983), Volume 6, Part 1, p.52.

159   *"and the Emperor . . . taken."* —Quoted in Uwe Henrik Peters, *Anna Freud: A Life Dedicated to Children,* p.17.

159   *"been on deeper . . . lines"* —Lou Andreas-Salomé quoted in *Anna Freud: A Life Dedicated to Children,* p.45.

159   *"the subjective condition"* —Quoted in *Anna Freud: A Life Dedicated to Children,* p.15.

160   *"she has just passed . . . married."* —Quoted in *Freud & Women,* p.81.

160   *"feminine . . . strong personality"* —Ibid., p.78.

160   *"beautiful clothes . . . children."* —*Anna Freud: A Life Dedicated to Children,* p.19.

160   *"when she came . . . inconspicuous."* —Ibid., p.19.

161   *"a simple and direct"* one. —Quoted in Raymond Dyer, *Her Father's Daughter: The Work of Anna Freud,* p.67.

161   *"treating naughty . . . children"* —Quoted in *Freud & Women,* p.81.

161   *"a pioneering venture . . . childhood."* —*The Writings of Anna Freud,* Volume 1, p.vii.

162   *"in the analysis . . . adults."* —Ibid., p.68.

162   *"perhaps most important."* —Ibid., p.50.

162   *"even greater"* —Ibid., p.60.

162   *"succeed . . . ego ideal,"* —Ibid.

163   *"no dream . . . somewhere,"* —Ibid., p. 25.

164   *"Every day . . . better."* —In conversation with Rigmor S. Sheldrick.

164   *"romantic . . . playful."* —Interview with Dr. Peter Blos, April 20, 1983.

164   *"neurotic misery . . . unhappiness."* —Sigmund Freud, *Studies on Hysteria.* S.E. Vol. 2.

164   *"a certain . . . world,"* —Quoted in *Freud & Women,* p.104.

164   *"my dear fellow . . . rabble."* —Quoted in Peter Gay, *Freud: A Life for Our Time,* p.529.

164 *"the greatest . . . nature,"* —Freud quoted in *Freud & Women*, p.14.

164 *"Having decided . . . Anna Freud,"* —According to Elizabeth Young-Bruehl's *Anna Freud: A Biography*, Harold Sweetser also entered into analysis with Anna Freud at this time.

167 *"open face . . . heart."* —Eulogy to Robert Burlingham, Jr., by W. Ernest Freud, January 30, 1970.

167 *"a nice fellow . . . apparent,"* —Blos interview, April 20, 1983.

167 *"I don't think . . . us."* —Quoted by Robert Burlingham, Sr., to Charles C. Burlingham, November 5, 1925. Schmiderer Collection.

167 *"I wrote to father"* —Robert Burlingham, Jr., to Dorothy T. Burlingham, n.d. Dorothy T. Burlingham memorabilia.

168 *"I love . . . you."* —Robert Burlingham, Jr., to Robert Burlingham, Sr., June 25, 1925. Dorothy T. Burlingham memorabilia.

168 *"three weeks' observation,"* —*The Writings of Anna Freud*, Volume I, p.8.

168 *"lived . . . of her family."* —Ibid., p.28.

168 *"already knew . . . friend."* —Ibid., p.8.

168 *"she knew . . . doing so."* —Ibid.

169 *"Sex: M . . . semi-delinquent."* —Quoted in *Her Father's Daughter*, p.58.

169 *"a boy of 10 . . . discovery."* —*The Writings of Anna Freud*, Volume I, p.11.

169 *"I had only . . . cooperation."* —Ibid., p.13.

169 *"the meaning . . . aim,"* —Ibid., p.17.

169–70 *"One day . . . analysis."* —Ibid., pp.17–18.

170–72 *"When he began . . . admixture."* —Ibid., pp.163–67.

174 *"I was not . . . as they are."* —Quoted in *Anna Freud: A Life Dedicated to Children*, p.xi.

174 *"most successful . . . cases."* —*Her Father's Daughter*, p.58.

174 *"D'ont . . . how you feel."* —Mary T. Burlingham to Dorothy T. Burlingham, dated 1925. Dorothy T. Burlingham memorabilia.

174 *"the best . . . Burlinghams."* —Interview with Victor Ross (formerly Rosenfeld), June 26, 1983.

175 *"The simplest type . . . fantasy."* —*The Writings of Anna Freud*, Volume I, pp.27–28.

176 *"lieben und arbeiten"* —Quoted in Alice S. Rossi (ed.), *The Feminist Papers from Adams to de Beauvoir*, p.337.

178 *"developed . . . physician analysts"* —Richard Sterba, *Reminiscences of a Viennese Psychoanalyst*, p.82.

178 *"no good results . . . analysis."* —Dr. Anny Katan to Michael J. Burlingham, May 17, 1983.

178 *"beginning . . . inorganic."* —Sigmund Freud to Lou Andreas-Salomé, May 10, 1925. Quoted in *Sigmund Freud: His Life in Pictures and Words*, biographical sketch by K. R. Eissler, p.237.

179 *"an awkward . . . movement."* —Rosenfeld typescript, p.28. Ross Collection.

179 *"[Dorothy] . . . her own self."* —Anna Freud to Eva Rosenfeld. September 1927?. Victor Ross Collection (translated by Peter Heller).

179 *"apart . . . until his death"* —Eulogy to Dorothy Tiffany-Burlingham by Anna Freud, n.d. Author's collection.

179 *"The years . . . my life."* —Quoted in *Sigmund Freud: His Life in Pictures and Words*, p.261.

180 *"a vast . . . Sphinx"* —Sigmund Freud to Martha Bernays, December 3, 1885. Ibid., p.120.

180 *"fellow unbelievers . . . sparrows."* —Sigmund Freud, quoting Heinrich Heine, in *The Future of an Illusion*, S.E. Vol. 21, p.50.

180 *"wonderful . . . and dear"* —Dorothy T. Burlingham to Edith B. Jackson, February 16, 1939. MC 304. EBJP.

180 *"a quite congenial . . . virgin."* —Quoted in *Freud: A Life for Our Time*, p.540.

180 *"During this time . . . enjoy."* —Spoken on the occasion of Freud's death. Quoted in *Sigmund Freud: His Life in Pictures and Words,* p.261.

180 *Born . . . an expatriate.* —Early references to Dorothy's grandfather as an Iron Chancellor reflected his great admiration for the discipline, efficiency, and organization of the German people. Prior to World War I, sharing that enthusiasm, Louis had named one of his ponies Bismarck. Dorothy's move to Austria, then, grounded her in the familiar territory of German culture, though in Vienna she was significantly subject to the well-known Viennese disposition to *schlamperie.*

181 *"taken a gal"* —Phone interview with Elizabeth Ely Shedd, 1986.

181 *"I always . . . dead."* —Mary T. Burlingham to Dorothy T. Burlingham, n.d. Dorothy T. Burlingham memorabilia.

IX CITY OF MY DREAMS

Page 182 *"our sophisticated . . . Zellerhaus"* —Untitled, undated typescript by Eva Rosenfeld, p.15. Ross Collection.

182 *"vibrating . . . behavior"* —Ibid., p.5.

182 *"Music was . . . love,"* —Ibid., p.79.

183 *"in no way . . . house."* —Ibid., p.37.

183 *"a resourceful . . . music."* —Blos interview, June 6, 1983.

183 *"Hello, hello . . . here."* —Transcribed by Dorothy T. Burlingham, March 6, 1927. Dorothy T. Burlingham memorabilia.

183 *"children being . . . teachers."* —Anna Freud, "Tribute to Dorothy Burlingham." *Bulletin of the Hampstead Clinic* (1980), Volume 3, Part 2, p.76.

184 *"But . . . your friend,"* —Blos interview, April 20, 1983.

184 *"a gifted artist . . . life . . ."* —Robert Coles, *Erik H. Erikson: The Growth of His Work.* Quoted in Rosenfeld typescript, p.44. Ross collection.

184 *"A friend . . . thinks?!"* —Robert Burlingham, Jr., to Dorothy T. Burlingham, April 25, 1927. Dorothy T. Burlingham memorabilia.

184 *"hardly . . . Freud was,"* —Interview with Erik H. Erikson, July 31, 1983.

184 *"strange intimacy,"* —Ibid.

184 *"unbelievably friendly."* —Ibid.

184–85 *"The family's . . . hills."* —Eulogy to Robert Burlingham, Jr., by W. Ernest Freud, p.1. Author's collection.

185 *"lost . . . their lives"* —Rosenfeld typescript, p.10. Ross Collection.

185 *"Anna Freud came . . . need."* —Ibid., p.15.

185 *"the real spiritual . . . it."* —Ibid., p.37.

186 *"Every child . . . visual."* —Ibid., p.39.

186 *"The teacher . . . freely."* —Erik and Joan Erikson, "Dorothy Burlingham's School in Vienna." *Bulletin of the Hampstead Clinic* (1980), Volume 3, Part 2, p.94.

187 *"an interesting . . . animal."* —Mary T. Burlingham to Robert Burlingham, Sr., 1927. Dorothy T. Burlingham memorabilia.

187 *"Now I am . . . drawing."* —Ibid.

187 *"associated . . . group."* —Raymond Dyer, *Her Father's Daughter: The Work of Anna Freud,* p.67.

188 *"freedom within . . . limits,"* —Quoted in Uwe Henrik Peters, *Anna Freud: A Life Dedicated to Children,* p.65.

188 *"breathed life . . . put about"* —Ross interview, June 26, 1983.

188 *"to help . . . art world."* —Quoted in *The "Lost" Treasures of Louis Comfort Tiffany,* p.265.

189 *"personal guests,"* —Hugh F. McKean, *The "Lost" Treasures of Louis Comfort Tiffany,* p.xii.

189 *"Do you know . . . there . . ."* —Transcription by Dorothy T. Burlingham, March 6, 1927. Dorothy T. Burlingham memorabilia.

189 *"trimmings . . . big way."* —Blos interview, April 20, 1983.

190 *"entourage . . . in-a-park."* —Ibid.

190 "Wien, Wien . . . *dreams").* —Quoted in the Museum of Modern Art, *La Belle Epoque,* exhibition essay by Philippe Jullian, p.12.

190 *"wonderland"* —Ross interview, June 26, 1983.

190 *"dream world"* —Interview with W. Ernest Freud (formerly Halberstadt), June 21, 1983.

190 *"dreamed up"* —"Dorothy Burlingham's School in Vienna," p.91.

190 *"Peter Blos . . . adorable."* —Dorothy T. Burlingham to Robert Burlingham, Sr., December 25, 1927. Schmiderer Collection.

190 *"We children . . . taste."* —Peter Heller to Michael J. Burlingham, September 21, 1986.

190 *"pop stars"* —Ross interview, June 26, 1983.

191 *"almost too beautiful."* —Ibid.

191 *"objects of . . . Burlinghams."* —Ibid.

191 *"a wonderful . . . going on,"* —Eulogy to Robert Burlingham, Jr., January 30, 1970.

191 *"long . . . passionate."* —Ross interview, June 26, 1983.

192 *"Our symbiosis . . . summer."* —Quoted in *Anna Freud: A Life Dedicated to Children,* pp.119–20.

192 *"boyish . . . romantic element"* —Freud quoted in *Sigmund Freud: His Life in Pictures and Words,* p.24.

193 *"little contact . . . animals,"* —Ernest Jones, *The Life and Work of Sigmund Freud,* Volume 3, p.141.

193 *"From now on . . . purse,"* —Rosenfeld typescript, p.36. Ross Collection.

193 *"Freud . . . of an analyst!"* —See *The Life and Work of Sigmund Freud,* Volume 3, p.212.

194 *"Why do you . . . in you . . ."* —Anna Freud to Eva Rosenfeld, September 30, 1929. Ross Collection (Heller translation).

194 *"A bond . . . us both . . ."* —Sigmund Freud to Marie Bonaparte, December 6, 1936. Quoted in *Sigmund Freud: His Life in Pictures and Words,* p.271.

194 *"Why one can . . . solidarity."* —Ibid.

194 *"The price . . . guilt."* —Sigmund Freud, *Civilization and Its Discontents,* S.E. Vol. 21, p.134. p.123.

194 *"the greatest . . . civilization."* —Ibid., p.122.

195 *"The fateful . . . self-destruction."* —Ibid., p.145.

195 *"Now we are . . . music."* —Robert Burlingham, Jr., to Dorothy T. Burlingham, May 13, 1929. Dorothy T. Burlingham memorabilia.

195–96 *"in the middle . . . to it."* —Sigmund Freud to Marie Bonaparte, May 2, 1929. Quoted in Celia Bertin, *Marie Bonaparte: A Life,* p.179.

196 *"The children . . . here,"* —Anna Freud to Eva Rosenfeld, c. June–July, 1929. Ross Collection (Heller translation).

197 *"What occurs . . . ever had . . ."* —Robert Burlingham, Sr., to Charles C. Burlingham, December 28, 1925. Schmiderer Collection.

197 *"I don't know . . . like."* —Charles C. Burlingham to Michael Burlingham, December 25, 1928. Schmiderer Collection.

197 *"firmly . . . constructive work."* —Dr. Victor Jacobsen to Charles C. Burlingham, December 19, 1929. Schmiderer Collection.

198 *"I remember . . . our ages."* —William P. Buffum, Jr., to Michael J. Burlingham, June 10, 1986.

198–99 *"I have never . . . cause . . ."* —Constance A. Buffum to Dr. Amsden, April 17, 1925. Schmiderer Collection.

199 "He's so afraid . . . coming," —Interview with Marinka Gurewich, January 28, 1984.
199 Dorothy . . . of the children." —Dr. Anny Katan to Michael J. Burlingham, June 6, 1983.
199 "down on America . . . things," —Interview with Judy de Forest Taves, July 26, 1983.
199 "America . . . gigantic mistake." —Quoted in Peter Gay, *Freud: A Life for Our Time*, p.563.
200 "Mabbie . . . oh rapture!" —Appointment book of Charles C. Burlingham, August 15, 1929. CCBP.
200–202 "R.B. to A.F. . . . certainly." —Interview with Anna Freud, August 26, 1929. Author's collection.
202–203 "S.F. . . . No." —Interview with Sigmund Freud, August 26, 1929. Author's collection.
203–204 "C.C.B. . . . are a lawyer." —Interview with Sigmund Freud, August 26, 1929. Author's collection.
204 "August 29 . . . Germanea," —Appointment book of Charles C. Burlingham, 1929. CCBP.
204 "August 30 . . . Blos." —Ibid.
204 "a Fifth Avenue lawyer" —Blos interview, April 20, 1983.
204 "an attending psychiatrist." —Ibid.
205 "somehow . . . our needs." —Dorothy T. Burlingham to Robert Burlingham, Jr., December 28, 1942. Author's collection.
206 "my . . . daughter." —Telephone interview with Margot Goldschmidt, June 1983.
206 "wrap . . . little finger." —Goldschmidt interview, June 2, 1983.
206 "We missed . . . mother." —Interview with Katrina B. Valenstein, January 30, 1985.
207 "from Dorothy . . . now on." —Anna Freud to Eva Rosenfeld, September 27, 1926. Ross Collection (Heller translation).
207 "a pretty gloomy place" —Taves interview.
207 "I had gone . . . this." —Muriel M. Gardiner to Michael Burlingham, August 17, 1984. Author's collection.
208 "the transformation . . . libido." —Sigmund Freud, *The Ego and the Id*, S.E., Vol. 19, p.30.
208 "The man . . . processes." —*Civilization and Its Discontents*, S.E., Vol. 21, p.83–84.
208 "early . . . efflorescence," —Sigmund Freud, *An Outline of Psychoanalysis*, S.E., Vol. 23, p.86.
209 "unquestionably . . . research." —Sigmund Freud, *Inhibitions, Symptoms and Anxiety*, S.E., Vol. 20, p.113.
209 "the ego-ideal displays . . . fashion." —*The Ego and the Id*, S.E., Vol. 19, p.51.
209 "a strong affinity" —*Inhibitions, Symptoms and Anxiety*, S.E., Vol. 20, p. 143.
209 "affinity with feminity," —Ibid.
209 "openly afraid . . . function." —Ibid., p.88.
209 "a problem . . . mastered," —*Inhibitions, Symptoms and Anxiety*, S.E., Vol. 20, p.113.
210 "we often gain . . . neurosis." —Sigmund Freud, "The Disposition to Obsessional Neurosis: A Contribution to the Problem of Choice of Neurosis," S.E., Vol. 12, p.324.
210 "perfect orgasm," —See Richard Sterba, *Reminiscences of a Viennese Psychoanalyst*, p.87.
210 "I stand for . . . freedom . . ." —Quoted in Lucy Freeman and Herbert S. Strean, *Freud & Women*, p.51.
210 "spinsterish holiness." —Quoted from *Eine Kinderanalyse bei Anna Freud* (1929–1932), in Wilhelm Salber, *Anna Freud*, p.136. Translation by Rigmor S. Sheldrick.
210 "She was very . . . sublimation," —Ibid.
210 "She was not . . . sexuality." —Ibid.
210 "There Freud sat . . . defenses." —*Reminiscences of a Viennese Psychoanalyst*, p.130.
210 "Since the poor . . . another." —Quoted in *Freud: A Life for Our Time*, p.541.
210 "Anna is splendid . . . life." —Ibid.

211 *"passionate woman . . . sexuality."* —Ibid., p.613.

211 *"Dorothy is now . . . her."* —Anna Freud to Eva Rosenfeld, June 1930 (n.d.). Ross Collection (Heller translation).

211 *"Dorothy departed . . . well."* —Anna Freud to Eva Rosenfeld, June 25, 1930. Ross Collection (Heller translation).

211 *"Mabbie, apparently . . . obstacles . . ."* —Anna Freud to Eva Rosenfeld, late June 1930 (n.d.). Ross Collection (Heller translation).

211 *"radiant and blossoming . . . after.'"* —Anna Freud to Eva Rosenfeld, June 25, 1930. Ross Collection (Heller translation).

212 *"a conceited egoist . . . great."* —Taves interview, July 26, 1983.

212 *"difficult and . . . problems."* —Ibid.

212 *"the [Hietzing] school . . . unpretentious."* —Recollections of the Burlingham-Rosenfeld School, by Peter Heller, p.6.

212 *"unnatural"* —Taves interview, July 26, 1983.

212 *"crippled"* —Ibid.

212 *"scolded"* —Ibid.

213 *"always well-intentioned . . . intolerance."* —Peter Heller to Michael J. Burlingham, September 21, 1986.

213 *"the thoughts . . . Cornflakes."* —Mary T. Burlingham to Dorothy T. Burlingham, letter to Tegel, "D," 1930 (n.d.). Dorothy T. Burlingham memorabilia.

213 *"Yesterday night . . . asthma."* —Mary T. Burlingham to Dorothy T. Burlingham, letter to Tegel, "D," 1930 (n.d.). Dorothy T. Burlingham memorabilia.

213 *"I always make . . . did."* —Mary T. Burlingham to Dorothy T. Burlingham, letter to Tegel, "E," 1930 (n.d.). Dorothy T. Burlingham memorabilia.

213 *"We walked on . . . boys."* —Mary T. Burlingham to Dorothy T. Burlingham, June 10–13, 1930. Dorothy T. Burlingham memorabilia.

214 *"I know most . . . it . . ."* —Mary T. Burlingham to Dorothy T. Burlingham, letter to Tegel, 1930 (n.d.). Dorothy T. Burlingham memorabilia.

214 *"Sometimes when I . . . unhappy."* —Mary T. Burlingham to Dorothy T. Burlingham, letter to Tegel, "A," 1930 (n.d.). Dorothy T. Burlingham memorabilia.

214 *"I feel so . . . belong."* —Ibid.

214 *"It's really nice . . . you."* —Mary T. Burlingham to Dorothy T. Burlingham, June 10–13, 1930. Dorothy T. Burlingham memorabilia.

214 *"I think you . . . thought."* —Mary T. Burlingham to Dorothy T. Burlingham, letter to Tegel, "A," 1930 (n.d.). Dorothy T. Burlingham memorabilia.

214 *"How is Anna . . . you . . ."* —Mary T. Burlingham to Dorothy T. Burlingham, letter to Tegel, "E," 1930 (n.d.). Dorothy T. Burlingham memorabilia.

214 *"I would like . . . anyhow."* —Mary T. Burlingham to Dorothy T. Burlingham, letter to Tegel, "A," 1930 (n.d.). Dorothy T. Burlingham memorabilia.

214–15 *"When I saw . . . off."* —Mary T. Burlingham to Dorothy T. Burlingham, letter to Tegel, "D," 1930 (n.d.). Dorothy T. Burlingham memorabilia.

215 *"Today I have . . . sometimes."* —Mary T. Burlingham to Dorothy T. Burlingham, letter to Tegel, "C," 1930 (n.d.). Dorothy T. Burlingham memorabilia.

215 *"The schoolhouse . . . schoolfarm"* —Anna Freud to Eva Rosenfeld, July 8, 1928. Ross Collection (Heller translation).

216 *"Margot . . . won't be bauern."* —Mary T. Burlingham to Dorothy T. Burlingham, letter to Tegel, "B," 1930 (n.d.). Dorothy T. Burlingham memorabilia.

216 *"Neuhaus . . . to Dorothy."* —Anna Freud to Eva Rosenfeld, 1930 (n.d.). Ross Collection (Heller translation).

216 *"I wished . . . go back."* —Margot Goldschmidt to Dorothy T. Burlingham, September 20, 1930. Dorothy T. Burlingham memorabilia.

217 *"I like it . . . things."* —Anna Freud to Dorothy T. Burlingham, summer 1933 (n.d.). Dorothy T. Burlingham memorabilia.

X A TRUSTWORTHY WITNESS

Page 218 *"I just had ... families."* —Journal of Robert Burlingham, Jr., December 1931–January 1932. Author's collection.

219 *"The boxes . . . supper."* —Ibid.

219 *"The Reichstag burning . . . nonsense?"* —Untitled, undated typescript by Eva Rosenfeld, p.78. Ross collection.

220 *"Of course . . . themselves) . . ."* —Helena Hirst to Louisa L. Burlingham, June 1, 1930. Schmiderer Collection.

220 *"He has been . . . women,"* —Mary T. Burlingham to Dorothy T. Burlingham, Black Point Letter "B," 1932 (n.d.). Dorothy T. Burlingham memorabilia.

221 *"We are lying . . . resting,"* —Anna Freud to Eva Rosenfeld, summer 1932 (n.d.). Ross Collection (Heller translation).

221–22 *"One day, I . . . others."* —Rosenfeld typescript, p.61. Ross Collection.

222 *"In any case . . . [Anna]."* —Sigmund Freud to Lou Andreas-Salomé, May 16, 1935. Quoted in *Sigmund Freud: His Life in Pictures and Words,* p.267.

222 *"she metamorphosized . . . Freud."* —Ross interview, June 26, 1983.

222 *"may have 're-created' . . . life."* —W. Ernest Freud, "Funeral Tribute to Anna Freud." *Bulletin of the Hampstead Clinic* (1983), Volume 6, Part 1, p.5.

223 *"So far as . . . period."* —Anna Freud, "Contribution Read During the Dorothy Burlingham Memorial Meeting at the Hampstead Clinic." *Bulletin of the Hampstead Clinic* (1980), Volume 3, Part 2, pp.75–76.

224 *"Let us see . . . changed."* —Dorothy T. Burlingham, "Child Analysis and the Mother," in *Psychoanalytic Studies of the Sighted and the Blind,* p.8.

224–25 *"She feels herself . . . treatment?"* —Ibid., pp.6–7.

225 *"so subtle . . . analysis."* —Ibid., p.5.

225 *"a phenomenon . . . investigation."* —Ibid., p.26.

225 *"mystic Weltanschauung,"* —See Richard Sterba, *Reminiscences of a Viennese Analyst,* pp.108–10.

225 *"A short time . . . transference."* —Quoted in Ilse Hellman, "Contribution Read During the Dorothy Burlingham Memorial Meeting at the Hampstead Clinic." *Bulletin of the Hampstead Clinic* (1980), Volume 3, Part 2, p.81.

225 *"scientific Weltanschauung."* —See *Reminiscences of a Viennese Psychoanalyst,* pp.108–10.

226 *"We do not . . . mind."* —Dorothy T. Burlingham, "Empathy Between Infant and Mother," in *Psychoanalytic Studies of the Sighted and the Blind,* p.63.

226 *"The mother's unconscious . . . power."* —Ibid.

226 *"His apparently . . . work."* —Ibid., p.64.

226 *"More than once . . . children."* —Ibid., pp.68–69.

227 *"the periodically depressed . . . herself."* —Ibid., p.62.

227 *"To win or lose . . . investigation."* —"A Child at Play," ibid., p.32.

228 *"involuntary confession."* —"The Urge to Tell and the Compulsion to Confess," ibid., p.34.

228 *"It has given . . . evening."* —Anna Freud to Robert Burlingham, Jr., December 30, 1933. Author's collection.

228 *"beyond the dole,"* —Gilder interview, June 4, 1978.

228 *"out of . . . Freud."* —Interview with Dr. Josephine Stross, June 23, 1983.

228 *"Evidently, to raise . . . modifications."* —Anna Freud, "The Latency Period," in *The Writings of Anna Freud,* Volume 1, pp.112–13.

229 *"Anna is enjoying . . . ones."* —Quoted in Uwe Henrik Peters, *Anna Freud: A Life Dedicated to Children,* p.145.

229 *"[The children]* ... *laps."* —Gilder interview, June 4, 1978.

230 *"Owing* ... *of the individual."* —Dorothy T. Burlingham, "Problems Confronting the Psychoanalytic Educator," in *Psychoanalytic Studies of the Sighted and the Blind,* p.78.

230 *"a mistake."* —Dorothy T. Burlingham to Robert Burlingham, Jr., June 1940. Author's collection.

231 *"a school which* ... *engineer."* —Michael Burlingham to Michael J. Burlingham, April 1985.

231 *"she has* ... *children."* —Interview with Anna Freud, August 26, 1929. Author's collection.

231 *"I am not* ... *wish.'"* —Ibid.

231 *"I took* ... *Tinky."* —Dorothy T. Burlingham to Robert Burlingham, Jr., July 4, 1937. Author's collection.

231 *"unpleasant"* —Valenstein interview, April 30, 1983.

232 *"shivering all over* ... *joy"* —Robert Burlingham, Jr., to Dorothy T. Burlingham, April 6, 1936. Dorothy T. Burlingham memorabilia.

232 *"I just can't* ... *Musiker....* " —Robert Burlingham, Jr., to Dorothy T. Burlingham, May 23, 1930.

232 *"that unless* ... *music."* —Dorothy T. Burlingham to Michael J. Burlingham, April 3, 1975.

232 *"Hoch* ... *a miracle."* —Journal of Robert Burlingham, Jr., December 1931–January 1932. Author's collection.

233 *"In my lesson* ... *me."* —Ibid.

233 *"very surprised* ... *school work,"* —Eulogy to Robert Burlingham, Jr., January 30, 1970. Author's collection.

233 *"the beautiful house* ... *artist,"* —Valenstein interview, April 30, 1983.

233 *"gemeinsamen vater"* —See Wilhelm Salber, *Anna Freud.*

233 *"oasis."* —Ibid.

233 *"Where am I* ... *cottage."* —Quoted in *Sigmund Freud: His Life in Pictures and Words,* p.261.

233 *"There is* ... *Rosilla."* —Interview with Rosilla H. Hawes, May 7, 1983.

234 *"It is dumb* ... *like!"* —Mary T. Burlingham to Dorothy T. Burlingham, U.S. letter "A," 1932 (n.d.). Dorothy T. Burlingham memorabilia.

234 *"Bompa* ... *teaches us English."* —Mary T. Burlingham to Dorothy T. Burlingham, U.S. letter "B," 1932 (n.d.). Dorothy T. Burlingham memorabilia.

234 *"I am trying* ... *so often."* —Mary T. Burlingham to Dorothy T. Burlingham, U.S. letter "D," 1932 (n.d.). Dorothy T. Burlingham memorabilia.

234 *"They all make* ... *nothing."* —Mary T. Burlingham to Dorothy T. Burlingham, U.S. letter "A," 1932 (n.d.). Dorothy T. Burlingham memorabilia.

234 *"Humor?* ... *humor!"* —Sheldrick interview, May 4, 1983.

234 *"the universal obsessional* ... *humanity."* —Sigmund Freud, *The Future of an Illusion,* S.E., Vol 21, p.43.

234 *"Religion* ... *Freud Asserts"* —Quoted in Peter Gay, *Freud: A Life for Our Time,* p.535.

234 *"It is really* ... *soon."* —Katrina E. Burlingham to Dorothy T. Burlingham, U.S. letter "C," 1932 (n.d.). Dorothy T. Burlingham memorabilia.

234 *"They are really* ... *family."* —Mary T. Burlingham to Dorothy T. Burlingham, U.S. letter "A," 1932 (n.d.). Dorothy T. Burlingham memorabilia.

235 *"We have to* ... *terrible."* —Katrina E. Burlingham to Dorothy T. Burlingham, U.S. letter, 1932 (n.d.). Dorothy T. Burlingham memorabilia.

235 *"Daddy still tells* ... *that."* —Mary T. Burlingham to Dorothy T. Burlingham, U.S. letter "B," 1932 (n.d.). Dorothy T. Burlingham memorabilia.

235 *"Yesterday we went* ... *restless."* —Mary T. Burlingham to Dorothy T. Burlingham, U.S. letter "A," 1932 (n.d.). Dorothy T. Burlingham memorabilia.

235 *"Daddy* ... *not sick* ..." —Mary T. Burlingham to Dorothy T. Burlingham, U.S. letter "E," 1932 (n.d.). Dorothy T. Burlingham memorabilia.

235 *"He loves us . . . you . . ."* —Mary T. Burlingham to Dorothy T. Burlingham, U.S. letter "B," 1932 (n.d.). Dorothy T. Burlingham memorabilia.

235 *"Bompa . . . as I did."* —Mary T. Burlingham to Dorothy T. Burlingham, U.S. letter "E," 1932 (n.d.). Dorothy T. Burlingham memorabilia.

235 *"absolutely . . . nicest man,"* —Goldschmidt interview, June 2, 1983.

236 *"I like . . . Point*]." —Katrina E. Burlingham to Dorothy T. Burlingham, U.S. letter "F," 1932 (n.d.). Dorothy T. Burlingham memorabilia.

236 *"One thing . . . funny."* —Mary T. Burlingham to Dorothy T. Burlingham, U.S. letter "D," 1932 (n.d.). Dorothy T. Burlingham memorabilia.

236 *"When I played . . . nose."* —Katrina E. Burlingham to Dorothy T. Burlingham, U.S. letter "F," 1932 (n.d.). Dorothy T. Burlingham memorabilia.

236 *"That visit . . . himself."* —Mary T. Burlingham to Dorothy T. Burlingham, U.S. letter "E," 1932 (n.d.). Dorothy T. Burlingham memorabilia.

236 *"My father . . . Principle,"* —Author's interview, July 1978.

237 *"Aunt Com Com . . . years."* —Mary T. Burlingham to Dorothy T. Burlingham, U.S. letter "A," 1932 (n.d.). Dorothy T. Burlingham memorabilia.

237 *"He could do . . . person."* —Valenstein interview, January 30, 1985.

238 *"the Cubists . . . arts,"* —Louis C. Tiffany, "The Quest of Beauty," *Harper's Bazaar,* December 1917.

238 *"Woman . . . in nipples."* —"Iridescent Art," *The New Republic,* April 1, 1916. Quoted in Robert Koch, *Louis C. Tiffany: Rebel in Glass,* p.151.

239 *"There . . . money is unimportant."* —Dorothy T. Burlingham writing (in 1977) on the margin of the filmscript "Tracking the Life of an Artist: Louis Comfort Tiffany," by Michael John Burlingham.

240 *"Bob will leave . . . this."* —Anna Freud to Eva Rosenfeld, August 21, 1933. Ross Collection (Heller translation).

240 *"romantic picnics . . . paths."* —Mary T. Burlingham to Dorothy T. Burlingham, U.S. letter "E," 1932 (n.d.). Dorothy T. Burlingham memorabilia.

240 *"I don't know . . . here."* —Mary T. Burlingham to Dorothy T. Burlingham, August 15, 1933. Dorothy T. Burlingham memorabilia.

240 *"where Nazi bombs . . . buildings."* —"League Is Flouted by German Nazis," by Frederick T. Birchall, *New York Times,* January 22, 1934.

241 *"Mother! . . . Bob today."* —Mary T. Burlingham to Dorothy T. Burlingham, August 25, 1933. Dorothy T. Burlingham memorabilia.

241 *"At last today . . . longer!"* —Mary T. Burlingham to Dorothy T. Burlingham, August 26, 1933. Dorothy T. Burlingham memorabilia.

241 *"You don't know . . . wahr?"* —Mary T. Burlingham to Dorothy T. Burlingham, August 28, 1933. Dorothy T. Burlingham memorabilia.

242 *"lightness, gayness . . . acting."* —Robert Burlingham, Jr., to Dorothy T. Burlingham, October 11, 1933. Dorothy T. Burlingham memorabilia.

242 *"It is good . . . methods."* —Robert Burlingham, Jr., to Dorothy T. Burlingham, October 29, 1933. Dorothy T. Burlingham memorabilia.

242 *"a mockery . . . analysis."* —Robert Burlingham, Jr., to Dorothy T. Burlingham, March 14, 1933. Dorothy T. Burlingham memorabilia.

242 *"The Versailles . . . policy."* —Charles C. Burlingham to Robert Burlingham, Jr., January 22, 1934. Dorothy T. Burlingham memorabilia.

242–43 *"What . . . is there?"* —Ibid.

243 *"Do you think . . . it?"* —Anna Freud to Robert Burlingham, Jr., December 30, 1933. Author's collection.

243 *"Our little bit . . . wall."* —Sigmund Freud to Arnold Zweig, February 25, 1934. Quoted in *Sigmund Freud: His Life in Pictures and Words,* p.263.

244   *"[Bompa . . . of exams."* —Robert Burlingham, Jr., to Dorothy T. Burlingham, July 4, 1934. Dorothy T. Burlingham memorabilia.

244   *"all sunburnt . . . best"* —Ibid.

244   *"How can he . . . cried."* —Mary T. Burlingham to Dorothy T. Burlingham, U.S. letter "A," 1934 (n.d.). Dorothy T. Burlingham memorabilia.

245–46   *"I have had . . . them."* —Charles C. Burlingham to Dorothy T. Burlingham, September 5, 1934. Dorothy T. Burlingham memorabilia.

246   *"Mother . . . at times."* —Robert Burlingham, Jr., to Dorothy T. Burlingham, September 29, 1934. Dorothy T. Burlingham memorabilia.

246   *"so thin . . . do. . . . "* —Robert Burlingham, Jr., to Dorothy T. Burlingham, October 4, 1934. Dorothy T. Burlingham memorabilia.

246   *"not well altogether."* —Robert Burlingham, Jr., to Dorothy T. Burlingham, September 4, 1935. Dorothy T. Burlingham memorabilia.

246   *"Dorothy did not . . . summer."*—Anny Katan to Michael J. Burlingham, May 17, 1983.

247   *"personal welfare . . . me."* —George S. Messersmith to Charles C. Burlingham, April 24, 1934. Schmiderer Collection.

247   *"Mrs. Burlingham . . . returning."* —George S. Messersmith to Charles C. Burlingham, November 7, 1935. CCBP.

247   *"If any man . . . is."* —Quoted in the *United States Law Review,* Volume LXX, Number 2 (February 1936), p.60.

247   *"whether it was . . . effort."* —Harvard Law School Library Exhibit, *Charles C. Burlingham: Twentieth Century Crusader,* catalog essay by Andrew L. Kaufman, p.ii.

248   *"the Madame Pompadour . . . into one. . . . "* —Felix Frankfurter to Charles C. Burlingham, November 17, 1936. CCBP. Quoted in "La Guardia and Burlingham: A Study of Political Friendship and Personal Influence," master's thesis, by Frank Vos, p.3.

248   *"never fell . . . grace."* —According to Judge Edmund L. Palmieri. Quoted in "La Guardia and Burlingham," p.4.

248   *He listened . . . judge."* —"La Guardia and Burlingham," p.75.

248   *"Bompa . . . for me."* —Mary T. Burlingham to Dorothy T. Burlingham, Black Point Letter "E," 1932. Dorothy T. Burlingham memorabilia.

248   *"Washington . . . wish fulfilled . . ."* —Robert Burlingham, Jr., to Dorothy T. Burlingham, November 18, 1935. Dorothy T. Burlingham memorabilia.

248   *"re-Americanization,"* —Charles C. Burlingham, *Harvard College Class of 1879 Bulletin of 1936,* p.6.

248   *"what the Nazis . . . Germany."* —Frank Taussig to Charles C. Burlingham, December 25, 1933. Schmiderer Collection.

248   *another unfinished symphony.* —Robert Burlingham, Jr., to Dorothy T. Burlingham, September 4, 1935. Dorothy T. Burlingham memorabilia.

249   *"alive . . . get sick."* —Robert Burlingham, Jr., to Dorothy T. Burlingham, March 2, 1936. Dorothy T. Burlingham memorabilia.

250   *"A costly . . . analysis."* —Erik Erikson, "Personal Tribute to Anna Freud." *Bulletin of the Hampstead Clinic,* Volume 6, Part 1 (1983), p.53.

250   *"Quod . . . licet bovi"*—See *Reminiscences of a Viennese Psychoanalyst,* p.124.

250   *"turn . . . last stone."* —Robert Burlingham, Jr., to Dorothy T. Burlingham, (n.d.). Dorothy T. Burlingham memorabilia.

251   *But . . . clinical support.*— It now appears that Anna Freud forsaw problems almost from the start. According to Elizabeth Young-Bruehl, in her recent biography of Anna Freud, a second phase (in 1924–1925) to Anna's analysis with her father brought new insight to bear on her altruistic tendencies. Competing with this need to fullfil herself through others, Anna discovered, was a "dependency," a "wanting-to-have-something" for herself, which she recognized as a positive striving. The materialization of the Burlinghams in Vienna directly following this final phase in her analysis, gave Anna the opportunity to realize this need through Dorothy and the Four. But, as early as

February 1926, Anna Freud had begun to appreciate the dangers of this possessiveness to the therapy she was providing to Bob and Mabbie. To Max Eitingon she wrote that she was all too often having "thoughts which go along with my work but do not have a proper place in it. . . . I think sometimes that I want not only to make them healthy but also, at the same time, to have them, or at least have something of them, for myself. Temporarily, of course, this desire is useful for my work, but sometime or another it really will disturb them, and so, on the whole, I really cannot call my need other than stupid." She added that, "Towards the mother of the children it is not very different with me." In retrospect, Anna Freud's need for a family of her own was not "stupid," since it helped balance her life and consequently, notes Bruehl, her work as well. It was, instead, Anna's role as therapist that rapidly became suspect, and which she did not prove herself willing to relinquish until too late. Bruehl's research illuminates a further point: that Anna Freud's pedagogic analysis did in fact allow for a positive transference (though Anna Freud is careful to call it a positive attachment), and this "stood in the way of analytic exploration of aggression and of negative transference." Bruehl writes that Anna Freud's period of preparation for analysis, which was intended to create the positive attachment, like her analytic admixture, "were the most obvious manifestations of her [then] unresolved father-complex," and she gradually modified or withdrew these in favor of analysis of defensive mechanisms. (With regard to the analytic admixture, there is no mention of its modification or withdrawal in the introduction to the first volume of *The Writings of Anna Freud*, published in 1974, during discussion of changes made since the 1926 lectures.) Whatever technical and theoretical advances resulted from Anna Freud's relationship with the Bur-linghams, the children's analyses remained problematic. Bruehl notes that Mabbie, for one, "neither freed herself nor was freed from the fact that Anna Freud was not just her analyst but the person to whom her mother gave unstinting devotion—a figure for deep jealousy—and the beloved person whose houses were in a very elementary way home."

252 *"The enjoyment . . . without it."* —Sigmund Freud, *Civilization and Its Discontents,* S.E., Vol. 21, p.82.

253 *"Early psychoanalytic . . . goal."* —*Anna Freud: A Life Dedicated to Children,* p.104.

253 *"analysis . . . than that."* —Janet Malcolm, *Psychoanalysis: The Impossible Profession,* p.108.

254 *"I find . . . children."* —Felix Deutsch to Helene Deutsch, September 26, 1935. Quoted in Paul Roazen, *Helene Deutsch: A Psychoanalyst's Life,* p.287.

255 *"dreadfully,"* —Dorothy T. Burlingham to Robert Burlingham, Jr., July 4, 1937. Author's collection.

255 *"I guess . . . yourself. . . ."* —Ibid.

255 *"I feel . . . all right."* —Anna Freud to Robert Burlingham, Jr., July 14, 1937.

256 *"something . . . & glowing."* —Dorothy Burlingham to Rigmor S. Burlingham, August 8, 1945. Author's collection.

257 *"Bob's decision."* —Robert Burlingham, Sr., to Charles C. Burlingham, September 22, 1937. Schmiderer Collection.

257 *"from . . . and love."* —Ibid.

257 *"tubercular history."* —According to Elizabeth Young-Bruehl's *Anna Freud: A Biography,* Anna Freud had herself once been infected with this disease.

258 *"1. Mabbie's . . . background."* —Robert Burlingham, Sr., to Charles C. Burlingham, November 14, 1937. Schmiderer Collection.

258 *"I have . . . blessing."* —Robert Burlingham, Jr., to Charles C. Burlingham, November 15, 1937. Schmiderer Collection.

259 *"Austrians! . . . save Austria!"* —Kurt von Schuschnigg, *My Austria.*

259 *"Nazi Germany . . . Austria!"* —Ibid.

260 *"as an empire . . . culture."* —Ibid.

260 "Für *meinen* Führer"—Interview with Marinka Gurewich, January 28, 1984.

260 *"open . . . the Torah."* —Quoted in Ernest Jones, *The Life and Work of Sigmund Freud,* Volume 3, p.221.

261 *"the sedative Veronal . . . tortured."* —Evidently, under the worst circumstances, it was Anna Freud's intention to commit suicide.

261 *"Both Freud . . . Anna."* —Anny Katan to Michael J. Burlingham, January 19, 1987.

261 *"Michael has . . . Technology."* —Robert Burlingham, Sr., to Dorothy, Bob, and Mary Burlingham, March 29, 1938. Dorothy T. Burlingham memorabilia.

XI THE BLITZ

Page 263 *"an udder . . . Italy."* —Anthony Burgess, "On the Fringe of Switzerland," *New York Times,* November 22, 1987, p. 19.

264 *"Please . . . not herself."* —Dorothy T. Burlingham to Edith Jackson, April 13, 1938. EBJP.

264 *"exact . . . of flesh"* —Ernest Jones, *The Life and Work of Sigmund Freud,* Volume 3, p.221.

264 *"It . . . rest somewhere."* —Sigmund Freud to Ernest Freud, May 12, 1938. Quoted in *The Life and Work of Sigmund Freud,* p.225.

264 *"The anti-Jewish . . . want."* —Robert Burlingham, Jr., to Dorothy T. Burlingham, May 5, 1983. Dorothy T. Burlingham memorabilia.

264 *"Tomorrow . . . 10–14 days."* —Robert Burlingham, Jr., to Dorothy T. Burlingham, May 5, 1938. Dorothy T. Burlingham memorabilia.

265 *"the whole story."* —Interview with Helena G. Miller, August 13, 1983.

265 *"a jigsaw . . . pieces."* —Dr. Alexander Tertius Martin to Charles C. Burlingham, May 30, 1938. Schmiderer Collection.

265 *"serious radiance."* —Robert Burlingham, Sr., to Dorothy T. Burlingham, May 18, 1938. Dorothy T. Burlingham memorabilia.

266 *"You will go . . . me."* —Comfort T. Gilder to Dorothy T. Burlingham, May 29, 1938. Dorothy T. Burlingham memorabilia.

266 *"through the shock."* —Freud had written Dorothy on May 29, 1938, "Maybe even the most intimate of friends, whose lives are indissolubly linked with yours, should keep their distance at this time and leave it up to you to take hold of your emotions and memories and to conquer them. But I am beset with worry that you may cause yourself pain, unjustifiably so, by an understandable effort on your part to grant your love (which never died) one last expression. Therefore, someone outside the family should be allowed to remind you of how little guilt, in the ordinary sense, there was in your relationship with your husband, but instead how overpowering was the influence of his illness, which made it impossible to have a satisfactory relationship, and which has to be accepted as yet another of those acts of fate that fall upon us human beings and cannot be changed by any brooding or self-analysis." Quoted in Elizabeth Young-Bruehl's *Anna Freud: A Biography,* p. 238.

266 *"Life is very . . . illness."* —Dorothy T. Burlingham to Edith B. Jackson, June 20, 1938. EBJP.

266 *"I am . . . sorrow."* —Mary B. Schmiderer to Dorothy T. Burlingham, June 6, 1939. Dorothy T. Burlingham memorabilia.

267 *"I am . . . 'Heil Hitler.' "* —Quoted in *The Life and Work of Sigmund Freud,* Volume 3, p.229.

267 *"The house . . . regret it."* —Dorothy T. Burlingham to Edith B. Jackson, June 20, 1938. EBJP.

267 *"Melanie Klein . . . situation."* —Ibid.

268 *"Sometimes . . . for me."* —Dorothy T. Burlingham to Edith B. Jackson, September 20, 1938. EBJP.

268 *"too much."* —Valenstein interview, May 1, 1983.

268 *"the sun . . . Danube."* —Michael Burlingham to Charles C. Burlingham, (n.d.) Dorothy T. Burlingham memorabilia.

268   *"I think . . . time."* —Robert Burlingham, Jr. to Dorothy T. Burlingham, October 8, 1938. Dorothy T. Burlingham memorabilia.

268   *"the sooner . . . the better,"* —Ibid.

269   *"so ideal . . . too perfect,"* —Dorothy T. Burlingham to Edith B. Jackson, October 1, 1938. EBJP.

268   *"so terribly tired."* —Ibid.

269   *"You should . . . them."* —Ibid.

269   *"one foot . . . America,"* —Dorothy T. Burlingham to Edith B. Jackson, October 27, 1938. EBJP.

269   *"if they . . . right."* —Ibid.

269   *"The Society . . . ever."* —Dorothy T. Burlingham to Edith B. Jackson, October 20, 1938. EBJP.

270   *"It is . . . resistances. . . ."* —Quoted in Phyllis Grosskurth, *Melanie Klein: Her World and Her Work,* p.172.

270   *"Who is . . . yourself."* —Ibid., p.179.

270   *"We are guests . . . trouble."* —Quoted in Raymond Dyer, *Her Father's Daughter: The Work of Anna Freud,* p.142.

270   *"wonderful . . . tics."* —Dorothy T. Burlingham to Edith B. Jackson, October 20, 1938. EBJP.

270   *"electrifying tension,"* —*Melanie Klein: Her World and Her Work,* p.243.

270–71   *"but decided . . . way."* —Dorothy T. Burlingham to Edith B. Jackson, December 27, 1938. EBJP.

271   *"inoperable, incurable cancer"* —*The Life and Work of Sigmund Freud,* Vol. 3, p.24.

271   *"Why do you . . . hear?"* —Mary B. Schmiderer to Dorothy T. Burlingham, August 8, 1939. Dorothy T. Burlingham memorabilia.

271   *"Do give Prof. . . . pact."* —Mary B. Schmiderer to Dorothy T. Burlingham, August 9, 1939. Dorothy T. Burlingham memorabilia.

271   *"The Professor . . . worse."* —Dorothy T. Burlingham to Robert Burlingham, Jr., August 14, 1939. Author's collection.

272   *"In New York . . . subject."* —Mary B. Schmiderer to Dorothy T. Burlingham, June 6, 1939. Dorothy T. Burlingham memorabilia.

273   *"Life for us . . . slightest . . . "* —Dorothy T. Burlingham to Robert Burlingham, Jr., May 1, 1940. Author's collection.

273   *"I can only . . . does . . . "* —Dorothy T. Burlingham to Robert Burlingham, Jr., April 19, 1940. Author's collection.

273   *"I am glad . . . me."* —Dorothy T. Burlingham to Robert Burlingham, Jr., June 16, 1940. Author's collection.

273   *"without chick . . . child."* —Ibid.

273   *"three very worthwhile"* —Dorothy T. Burlingham to Robert Burlingham, Jr., May 1, 1940. Author's collection.

273   *"very pleased."* —Ibid.

273   *"I've never . . . to."* —Dorothy T. Burlingham to Robert Burlingham, Jr., April 19, 1940. Author's collection.

273   *"as a way . . . together,"* —Dorothy T. Burlingham to Robert Burlingham, Jr., July 7, 1940. Author's collection.

273   *"unbelievably beautiful"* —Dorothy T. Burlingham to Rigmor S. Burlingham, May 6, 1940. Author's collection.

273   *"I don't . . . enough."* —Ibid.

273   *"normal wildness."* —Dorothy T. Burlingham to Robert Burlingham, Jr., July 7, 1940. Author's collection.

273–74   *"You know . . . world."* —Dorothy T. Burlingham to Robert Burlingham, Jr., June 2, 1940. Author's collection.

274   *"messy"* . . . *"incorrect"* —Wilhelm Salber, *Anna Freud.*

274 "Echt . . . *whole household.*" —Dorothy T. Burlingham to Edith B. Jackson, October 1, 1938. EBJP.

274 *"I love . . . her."* —Dorothy T. Burlingham to Robert and Rigmor Burlingham, July 28, 1940. Author's collection.

274 *"Anna . . . I arrived."* —Dorothy T. Burlingham to Robert Burlingham, Jr., July 7, 1940. Author's collection.

274 *"You must . . . existence."* —William C. Bullitt to Dorothy T. Burlingham, August 23, 1940. Dorothy T. Burlingham memorabilia.

275 *"a tough . . . morsel."* —Quoted in *Melanie Klein: Her World and Her Work,* p.256.

275 *"Neither Anna . . . U.S."* —Dorothy T. Burlingham to Robert and Rigmor Burlingham, July 28, 1940. Author's collection.

275 *"Isn't it . . . in?"* —Dorothy T. Burlingham to Mary B. Schmiderer, August 16, 1940. Author's collection.

275 *"Certainly . . . quite queer."* —Dorothy T. Burlingham to Robert Burlingham, Jr., August 18, 1940. Author's collection.

275 *"show."* —Dorothy T. Burlingham to Robert Burlingham, Jr., September 3, 1940. Author's collection.

276 *"You could . . . nearer . . ."* —Dorothy T. Burlingham to her children, August 25, 1940. Author's collection.

276 *"We always . . . fireworks . . ."* —Dorothy T. Burlingham to Rigmor S. Burlingham, August 31, 1940. Author's collection.

276 *"Search lights . . . night."* —Dorothy T. Burlingham to Robert Burlingham, Jr., September 3, 1940. Author's collection.

276 *"I understand . . . anything,"* —Dorothy T. Burlingham to her children, August 25, 1940. Author's collection.

276 *"weak point"* —Dorothy T. Burlingham to Edith B. Jackson, October 1, 1940. EBJP.

276 *"down in the city . . . destruction."* —Dorothy T. Burlingham to Rigmor S. Burlingham, October 5, 1941. Author's collection.

277 *"It's interesting . . . events."* —Dorothy T. Burlingham to her children, September 12, 1940. Author's collection.

277 *"poor little . . . humanity"* —Dorothy T. Burlingham to Robert and Rigmor Burlingham, January 8, 1941. Author's collection.

277 *"I went off . . . Krippe"* —Dorothy T. Burlingham to Robert Burlingham, Jr., September 3, 1940. Author's collection.

277 *"delighted . . . the possibilities,"* —Ibid.

277 *"We still . . . plans."* —Dorothy T. Burlingham to her children, September 12, 1940. Author's collection.

277 *"some English friends,"* —*The Writings of Anna Freud,* Volume 3, p.xxiii.

277 *"a Swedish Committee"* —Ibid.

277 *"electric energy"* —Dorothy T. Burlingham to Mary B. Schmiderer, November 19, 1940. Author's collection.

277 *"fascinating magnetism,"* —Ibid.

277 *"such fun . . . order."* —Dorothy T. Burlingham to Rigmor S. Burlingham, November 4, 1940.

277 *"Rest Centre"* —First referred to as such: Dorothy T. Burlingham to Robert and Rigmor Burlingham, October 15, 1940. Author's collection.

278 *"the war . . . agent."* —*The Writings of Anna Freud,* Volume 3, p.xviii.

278 *"Today we are . . . delighted."* —Dorothy T. Burlingham to Robert Burlingham, Jr., March 2, 1941. Author's collection.

279 *"Freud's Girl . . . On,"* —*The People.* Quoted in Cynthia Kee, "Daughter of Freud," *Harpers & Queen* (May 1983), London, p.115.

279 *"life was . . . Anna*]." —Dorothy T. Burlingham to Robert Burlingham, Jr., August 6, 1941. Author's collection.

279 *"There were . . . down . . ."* —Dorothy T. Burlingham to Mary B. Schmiderer, November 19, 1940. Author's collection.

279 *"a purely . . . scheme"* —Anna Freud quoted in *Her Father's Daughter,* p.151.

280 *"the dust . . . ages"* —Dorothy T. Burlingham to her children, September 12, 1940. Author's collection.

280 *"One could . . . to."* —Interview with Gertrude Dann, June 22, 1983.

280 *"Quite a task,"* —Dorothy T. Burlingham to Robert Burlingham, Jr. (n.d.). Author's collection.

280 *"Since World War . . . series."* —*The Writings of Anna Freud,* Volume 3, p.xvii.

280–81 *"Children . . . infantile nature."* —Ibid., p.163.

281 *"We were shocked . . . eyes."* —*The Writings of Anna Freud,* Volume 3, p.20.

281 *"exactly . . . its master."* —Ibid., p.37.

281 *"the most . . . work,"* —Dorothy T. Burlingham to Robert Burlingham, Jr., September 17, 1941. Author's collection.

281 *"I don't feel . . . it."* —Dorothy T. Burlingham to Rigmor S. Burlingham, October 5, 1941. Author's collection.

281 *"It really . . . wonderful."* —Dorothy T. Burlingham to Robert Burlingham, Jr., September 17, 1941.

281–282 *"Now . . . great shame."* —Dorothy T. Burlingham to Robert Burlingham, Jr., December 21, 1941. Author's collection.

282 *"In another . . . security."* —Dorothy T. Burlingham to Robert Burlingham, Jr., March 11, 1942. Author's collection.

282 *"unpleasant work"* —Dorothy T. Burlingham to Rigmor S. Burlingham, March 8, 1942. Author's collection.

282 *"the right people."* —Ibid.

282 *"Both Anna . . . started."* —Dorothy T. Burlingham to Robert Burlingham, Jr., April 4, 1942. Author's collection.

282 *"the blitz with Melanie Klein."* —George E. Gifford, Jr. (ed.), *Psychoanalysis, Psychotherapy and the New England Medical Scene, 1894–1944,* p.360.

282 *"into an . . . fury,"* —*Melanie Klein: Her World and Her Work.*

282 *"The psychoanalytic . . . analysis."* —Dorothy T. Burlingham to Rigmor S. Burlingham, January 11, 1942. Author's collection.

283 *"We have . . . be."* —Dorothy T. Burlingham to Robert and Rigmor Burlingham, October 25, 1942. Author's collection.

283 *"We are . . . work."* —Dorothy T. Burlingham to Robert Burlingham, Jr., November 16, 1942. Author's collection.

283 *"put humanity . . . out."* —Ross interview, June 26, 1983.

283–284 *"It seems . . . way."* —Dorothy T. Burlingham to Robert and Rigmor Burlingham, September 20, 1942. Author's collection.

284 *"something small . . . care,"* —Dorothy T. Burlingham to Robert Burlingham, Jr., December 28, 1942. Author's collection.

284 *"twin house"* —Dorothy T. Burlingham to Robert Burlingham, Jr., August 29, 1942. Author's collection.

284 *"always dreamed of,"* —Dorothy T. Burlingham to Robert Burlingham, Jr., December 28, 1942. Author's collection.

284 *"could . . . private lives."* —Dorothy T. Burlingham to Robert Burlingham, Jr., August 29, 1942. Author's collection.

284 *"There . . . be difficult. . . ."* —Ibid.

284 *"It's impossible . . . artificiality."* —Dorothy T. Burlingham to Rigmor S. Burlingham, March 14, 1943. Author's collection.

284 *"Well . . . Anna Freud."* —Dorothy T. Burlingham to Robert Burlingham, Jr., August 29, 1942.

284   *"dropping . . . friends,"* —Dorothy T. Burlingham to Robert and Rigmor Burlingham, September 11, 1943. Author's collection.

285   *"I get . . . you."* —Dorothy T. Burlingham to Robert Burlingham, Jr., August 29, 1942. Author's collection.

285   *"Sometimes . . . quieter again."* —Dorothy T. Burlingham to Robert Burlingham, Jr., November 16, 1942. Author's collection.

285   *"I . . . my grandchildren."* —Dorothy T. Burlingham to Rigmor S. Burlingham, March 14, 1943. Author's collection.

285   *"up the slot"* —Michael Burlingham to Michael J. Burlingham, April 1985. Author's collection.

285   *"quite crazy . . . desire. . . ."* —Dorothy T. Burlingham to Robert Burlingham, Jr., August 6, 1943. Author's collection.

285   *"Such . . . 4 years almost."* —Dorothy T. Burlingham to Robert Burlingham, Jr., August 29, 1943. Author's collection.

286   *"to avoid . . . incendiaries,"* —Dorothy T. Burlingham to Robert and Rigmor Burlingham, February 27, 1944. Author's collection.

286   *"We have . . . again,"* —Ibid.

286   *"Quite sick . . . craving,"* —Dorothy T. Burlingham to Rigmor S. Burlingham, April 23, 1944. Author's collection.

286   *"I think . . . here."* —Dorothy T. Burlingham to Robert Burlingham, Jr., May 28, 1944. Author's collection.

286–87   *"I know . . . about it."* —Dorothy T. Burlingham to Robert and Rigmor Burlingham, June 24, 1944. Author's collection.

287   *"I have . . . of."* —Dorothy T. Burlingham to Robert Burlingham, Jr., August 29, 1942. Author's collection.

287   *power of her will* —It is true that her brush with tuberculosis in childhood would have had a resistance-building effect, as would have had the serious bout in 1938.

287   *"birdcage"* —Dorothy T. Burlingham to Robert Burlingham, Jr., December 15, 1940. Author's collection.

287   *"everything . . . I enjoy."* —Dorothy T. Burlingham to Robert and Rigmor Burlingham, June 24, 1944. Author's collection.

287   *"just like a tire,"* —Dorothy T. Burlingham to Robert Burlingham, Jr., summer 1945 (n.d.). Author's collection.

287   *"ridiculously tired,"* —Dorothy T. Burlingham to Rigmor S. Burlingham, February 16, 1945. Author's collection.

288   *"It's lucky . . . two,"* —Dorothy T. Burlingham to Charles C. Burlingham, May 30, 1945. Schmiderer Collection.

288   *"It's very curious . . . brush."* —Dorothy T. Burlingham to Robert Burlingham, Jr., June 24, 1945. Author's collection.

288   *"That means . . . taxi."* —Dorothy T. Burlingham to Charles C. Burlingham, October 5, 1945. Schmiderer Collection.

288   *"In this . . . here."* —Dorothy T. Burlingham to Charles C. Burlingham, April 5, 1944. Schmiderer Collection.

288   *"I immediately . . . me."* —Dorothy T. Burlingham to Charles C. Burlingham, July 27, 1945. Schmiderer Collection.

XII "I HAVE BEEN VERY LUCKY"

Page 289   *"frighteningly"* —Dorothy T. Burlingham to Charles C. Burlingham, July 16, 1946. Schmiderer Collection.

289   *Sleeping Beauty.* —Interview with Dr. Josephine Stross, June 23, 1983.

289   *"What will . . . austerity?"* —Quoted in Lucy Freeman and Herbert S. Strean, *Freud & Women,* p.79.

290   *"a bungalow . . . old mill."* —Dorothy T. Burlingham to Robert Burlingham, Jr., August 15, 1944. Author's collection.

290   *"wild & glorious"* —Dorothy T. Burlingham to Robert Burlingham, Jr., July 7, 1946. Author's collection.

290   *"through fields . . . colors,"* —Dorothy T. Burlingham to Charles C. Burlingham, July 16, 1946. Schmiderer Collection.

290   *"sitting . . . herons."* —Dorothy T. Burlingham to Robert Burlingham, Jr., July 7, 1946. Author's collection.

290   *"old . . . original houses"* —Ibid.

290–91   *"This is . . . come."* —Ibid.

291   *"calamities."* —Manna Friedman, "Personal Tribute to Anna Freud." *Bulletin of the Hampstead Clinic* (1983), Volume 6, Part 1, p.102.

291   *"the question . . . to know,"* —Ross interview, June 26, 1983.

291   *"The relationship . . . house."* —Dr. Richard F. Sterba to Michael J. Burlingham, January 4, 1984.

292   *"intellectual lesbians,"* —Interview with John Heller, February 24, 1985.

292   *"amazing job"* —Interview with Alice Colonna, May 14, 1983.

292   *"difficult,"* —Ibid.

292   *"bore . . . of Paula."* —Ibid.

292   *"a very . . . embarrassed."* —Simon Schmiderer to Michael J. Burlingham, 1987 (n.d.).

292   *"There was . . . D.B."* —Ibid.

292   *"In . . . second and last."* —Rigmor S. Sheldrick in conversation.

292   *"sad" . . . "subservient"* —Interview with Helena G. Miller, August 13, 1983.

293   *"cold . . . tense."* —Erikson interview, July 31, 1983.

293   *"arrived . . . incongruous here."* —Dorothy T. Burlingham to Charles C. Burlingham, May 30, 1945. Schmiderer Collection.

293   *Comfort and Julia.*— The Tiffany twins had been only one of three sets in their Brearley class, one of which committed suicide returning after World War I from Europe, where they had been engaged in Red Cross work.

293   *"What interests . . . one."* —Dorothy T. Burlingham to Rigmor S. Burlingham, May 26, 1942. Author's collection.

294   *"the Mecca . . . children,"* —Hermann Argelander, "Public Tribute to Anna Freud." *Bulletin of the Hampstead Clinic* (1983), Volume 6, Part 1, p.35.

294   *"during . . . her work."* —Anna Freud, "Contribution Read at the Dorothy Burlingham Memorial Meeting of the Hampstead Clinic." *Bulletin of the Hampstead Clinic* (1980), Volume 3, Part 2, p.75.

295   *"didn't make . . . congresses."* —Interview with Ilse Hellman, June 22, 1983.

295   *"It's so curious . . . day."* —Dorothy T. Burlingham to Robert and Rigmor Burlingham, November 30, 1941. Author's collection.

295   *"She was . . . herself."* —Gurewich interview, January 28, 1984.

295   *"enormous."* —Hellman interview, June 22, 1983.

295   *"the human being . . . teacher."* —Interview with Hansi Kennedy, June 21, 1983.

295–96   *"will be . . . relationships."* —Dorothy T. Burlingham, *Twins,* p.10.

296   *"Many . . . his role."* —Ibid., pp.85–86.

296   *"collective analytic memory."* —Quoted in Raymond Dyer, *Her Father's Daughter: The Work of Anna Freud,* p.197.

296   *"these cases . . . factor."* —Ilse Hellman, "Contribution Read at the Dorothy Burlingham Memorial Meeting of the Hampstead Clinic." *Bulletin of the Hampstead Clinic* (1980), Volume 3, Part 2, p.84.

297 *"Entirely . . . into analysis."* —Anna Freud, "Contribution Read at the Dorothy Burlingham Memorial Meeting of the Hampstead Clinic."

298 *"in the . . . suburbs"* —Dorothy Burlingham, "Analytic Observations of Blind Children," in *Psychoanalytic Studies of the Sighted and the Blind,* p.256.

298 *"The blind . . . right."* —Doris Wills, "Contribution Read at the Dorothy Burlingham Memorial Meeting of the Hampstead Clinic." *Bulletin of the Hampstead Clinic* (1980), Volume 3, Part 2, p.85.

298 *"Where . . . in the field?"* —"Analytic Observations of Blind Children," *Psychoanalytic Studies of the Sighted and the Blind,* p.229.

298 *"double psychic lives."* —Ibid., p.231.

298 *"false self,"* —Ibid.

299 *"phonographic"* —Some Problems of Ego Development in Blind Children," *Psychoanalytic Studies of the Sighted and the Blind,* p.340.

299 *"they remember . . . error."* —Ibid., p.328.

300 *"the mother's . . . perceptions."* —"Some Notes on the Development of the Blind," ibid., p.298.

300 *"When I saw . . . moved."* —Anna Maenchen to Michael J. Burlingham, July 7, 1984.

300 *"the truthfulness . . . clarity"* —Gurewich interview, January 28, 1984.

300 *"social artifice"* —Ibid.

300 *"She was . . . being."* —Ibid.

301 *"a powerful magnet."* —Charles C. Burlingham to Dorothy T. Burlingham, June 11, 1947. Dorothy T. Burlingham memorabilia.

301 *"it is easier . . . day."* —Dorothy T. Burlingham to Robert and Rigmor Burlingham, August 3, 1946. Author's collection.

301–302 *"To see two . . . again."* —Dorothy T. Burlingham to Robert Burlingham, Jr., August 31, 1946.

302 *"How often . . . see."* —Dorothy T. Burlingham to her children, July 18, 1946. Author's collection.

303 *"Will you . . . lovelier."* —Ibid.

303 *"She really . . . think?"* —Dorothy T. Burlingham to Charles C. Burlingham (n.d.). Author's collection.

303 *"darling daughter"* —Charles C. Burlingham to William James, Jr., December 3, 1940. Schmiderer Collection.

303 *"It hurt . . . accusations."* —Interview with Charles Burlingham, Jr., July 27, 1983.

303 *"the monarch . . . surveyed."* —Edmondson interview, July 25, 1983.

304 *"One of . . . as you."* —Dorothy T. Burlingham to Charles C. Burlingham, June 13, 1950. Schmiderer Collection.

304 *"Your grandchildren . . . uncivilized."* —Charles C. Burlingham to Dorothy T. Burlingham, April 29, 1946. Dorothy T. Burlingham memorabilia.

304 *"[Mabbie] . . . business anyway."* —Charles C. Burlingham to Dorothy T. Burlingham, July 14, 1946. Dorothy T. Burlingham memorabilia.

304 *"You ask . . . life."* —Dorothy T. Burlingham to Charles C. Burlingham, June 16, 1946. Schmiderer Collection.

304 *"I appreciate . . . either."* —Charles C. Burlingham to Dorothy T. Burlingham, May 17, 1947. Dorothy T. Burlingham memorabilia.

305 *"the best"* —In conversation with Rigmor S. Sheldrick.

305 *"It is . . . means."* —Dorothy T. Burlingham to Robert Burlingham, Jr., August 24, 1947. Author's collection.

306 *"in fine form . . . himself."* —Charles C. Burlingham to Dorothy T. Burlingham, February 1, 1946. Dorothy T. Burlingham memorabilia.

306   *"Yes, Michael . . . charm."* —Charles C. Burlingham to Dorothy T. Burlingham, November 20, 1946. Dorothy T. Burlingham memorabilia.

306   *"I don't . . . you?"* —Charles C. Burlingham to Dorothy T. Burlingham, February 26, 1947. Dorothy T. Burlingham memorabilia.

306   *"my independence . . . 1938."* —Michael Burlingham to Michael J. Burlingham, July 27, 1988.

307–308   *"I am sure . . . come."* —Anna Freud to Robert Burlingham, Jr., March 9, 1940. Author's collection.

308   *"With Annafreud . . . needed."* —Dorothy T. Burlingham to Michael J. Burlingham, April 3, 1975.

309   *"We . . . concerned."* —Annette Müller Kitt to Michael J. Burlingham, August 3, 1986.

309   *"My request . . . concerned."*—Evidently, it was this request, or demand, that finally led Bob, in the last years of his life, to end his analysis with Anna Freud. He then began with Max Goldblatt, a musically-oriented colleague of Anna's with whom he had played chamber music.

310   *"Yes, Mabbie . . . them."* —Katrina B. Valenstein to Michael J. Burlingham, July 27, 1984.

310   *"When I get . . . heavenly."* —Mary T. Burlingham to Dorothy T. Burlingham, letter to Tegel, "D," 1932. Dorothy T. Burlingham memorabilia.

310–311   *"I am . . . continually."* —Dorothy T. Burlingham to Michael J. Burlingham, August 31, 1974.

311   "realm of pharmacology."—Freud had himself left open this avenue, writing in *An Outline of Psychoanalysis* (1940) that "the future may teach us how to exercise a direct influence, by means of particular chemical substances, upon the amounts of energy and their distribution in the apparatus of the mind."

311   *"even wilder . . . Walberswick."* —Quoted in Wilhelm Salber, *Anna Freud.*

311–12   *"It is . . . should be. . . ."* —Dorothy T. Burlingham to Michael J. Burlingham, July 6, 1971.

312   *"I am glad . . . lucky."* —Dorothy T. Burlingham to Michael J. Burlingham, April 3, 1975.

312   *"an isolated . . . medicine."* —Harold Bloom, "Freud, the Greatest Modern Writer." *New York Times,* March 23, 1986.

312   *"Go tell . . . lie."* —Quoted in W. Ernest Freud, "Funeral Tribute to Anna Freud," *Bulletin of the Hampstead Clinic* (1983), Volume 6, Part 1, p.8.

313   *"Why . . . in him."* —Dorothy T. Burlingham to Michael J. Burlingham, January 29, 1977.

313   *"On the . . . stillness."* —Susan Vas Dias, "Personal Tribute to Anna Freud." *Bulletin of the Hampstead Clinic* (1983), Volume 6, Part 1, p.91.

314   *"a friend . . . Mr. Land,"* —Dorothy T. Burlingham in conversation, October 1979.

314   *"The leaves . . . Bergerac."* —Anna Freud in conversation, October 1979.

314   *("The Song of the Earth")* —This music reached far deeper than the world-weary theme with which Dorothy and Anna identified. It would seem fateful that both Louis Tiffany and Sigmund Freud had had personal dealings with Mahler shortly before his death. The composer had written *The Song of the Earth* in Austria over the summer of 1908, after learning that his heart was giving out. This had not prevented him from returning to New York in the fall to resume his position as conductor of the Metropolitan Opera. It was probably to the following year, after Mahler had joined the newly founded Philharmonic Society of New York, that his widow referred, when she wrote, "Shortly after the founding of Mahler's orchestra we received a card from Louis Tiffany. He wrote that he was afraid of people; could he attend rehearsals unseen? Mahler granted the request and so we were invited to a party at Tiffany's." This was

the affair that Alma Mahler Werfel described as "a dream: Arabian nights in New York." Later, in the summer of 1910, back in Austria, the dying composer spent an afternoon on Freud's couch, during which the Professor unearthed "the infantile pattern behind [his] philosophical facade." What Tiffany and Mahler definitely shared in common was the struggle to reach essentially unattainable ideals of art, and their rejection of everyday, commonplace reality. Mahler, Freud believed, was driven by a Holy Mary complex or mother fixation. And it is possible that Louis's obsession with beauty and passion for flowers may have been interpreted by Dorothy as the parallel expression of an unrealizable, infantile longing for his mother. Thus did "The Farewell of a Friend" reflect not only a source of Dorothy's own childhood sorrows, but also her attempts to overcome them in analyses, the reasons for her children's analyses, and her partnership with Anna Freud; indeed, her entire life.

Bibliography

BOOKS AND ARTICLES

Aaron, Daniel; Hofstadter, Richard; and Miller, William. *The Structure of American History.* Englewood Cliffs, N. J.: Prentice-Hall, 1964.

Aichhorn, August. *Wayward Youth.* New York: Viking Press, [1925] 1935.

Andrews, Wayne. *Architecture in New York.* New York: Harper & Row, 1973.

Baigell, Matthew. *Dictionary of American Art.* London: John Murray, 1979.

Bell, Leland V. *Treating the Mentally Ill: From Colonial Times to the Present.* New York: Praeger, 1980.

Bell, Quentin. *Ruskin.* New York: George Braziller, 1978.

Benson, Richard, and Kirstein, Lincoln. *Lay This Laurel.* New York: Eakins Press, 1973.

Bertin, Celia. *Marie Bonaparte: A Life.* New York: Harcourt Brace Jovanovich, 1982.

Bettelheim, Bruno. *Freud and Man's Soul.* New York: Knopf, 1982.

Bing, Siegfried. *Artistic America, Tiffany Glass, and Art Nouveau.* Cambridge, Mass.: M.I.T. Press, [1895–1903] 1970.

Bingham, Alfred M. "Alf and Annie" (chapter from draft manuscript subsequently published as *Portrait of an Explorer: Hiram Bingham, Discoverer of Macchu Picchu.* Ames, Iowa: Iowa State University Press, 1988).

Black, Mary. *Old New York in Early Photographs.* New York: Dover, 1973.

Blackwell, Elizabeth. *Opening the Medical Profession to Women.* New York: Schocken Books, [1895] 1977.

Brenner, Charles. *An Elementary Textbook of Psychoanalysis.* Garden City, N. Y.: Anchor Books, 1955.

Broderick, Mosette Glaser, and Shopsin, William C. *The Villard Houses: Life Story of a Landmark.* New York: Viking Press, 1980.

———. "Charles Culp Burlingham: Twentieth Century Crusader." Cambridge, Mass.: catalog of Harvard Law School exhibition, 1980.

Burlingham, Dorothy T. *Twins: A Study of Three Pairs of Identical Twins with Thirty Charts.* London: Imago, 1952.

———. *Psychoanalytic Studies of the Sighted and the Blind.* New York: International Universities Press, 1972.

Butterfield, Rodger. *The American Past.* New York: Simon and Schuster, 1947.

Byron, Joseph, and Lancaster, Clay. *New York Interiors at the Turn of the Century.* New York: Dover, 1976.

Cantor, Mindy (ed.). *Around the Square 1830–1890.* New York: New York University Press, 1982.

Caro, Robert A. *The Power Broker: Robert Moses and the Fall of New York.* New York: Vintage Books, [1974] 1975.

Carpenter, Charles Hope. *Tiffany Silver.* New York: Dodd, Mead, 1978.

Chotas, James, and Sturm, James L. *Stained Glass from Medieval Times to the Present.* New York: E.P. Dutton, 1976.

Deák, Gloria-Gilda. *American Views, New York.* Viking Press and the New York Public Library, 1976.

De Forest, Izette. *The Leaven of Love.* New York: Harper & Brothers, 1954.

De Forest, Lockwood. "Indian Domestic Architecture" (unpublished manuscript, undated, but after 1913).

———. "Lockwood de Forest: Painter, Importer, Decorator." Huntington, N. Y.: catalog of Heckscher Museum exhibition, 1976.

[DeKay, Charles.] *The Art Work of Louis C. Tiffany.* Garden City, N. Y.: Doubleday, Page, 1914.

Duncan, Alistair. *Tiffany Windows.* New York: Simon & Schuster, 1980.

Dyer, Raymond. *Her Father's Daughter: The Work of Anna Freud.* New York: Jason Aronson, 1983.

Ehrenreich, Barbara, and English, Deirdre. *Witches, Midwives and Nurses: A History of Women Healers.* Old Westbury, N. Y.: Feminist Press, 1973.

Eliot, Alexander. *Three Hundred Years of American Painting.* New York: Time Inc., 1957.

Engelman, Edmund, and Gay, Peter. *Bergasse 19, Sigmund Freud's House and Offices, Vienna, 1938.* Chicago: University of Chicago Press, 1976.

Freeman, Lucy, and Strean, Herbert S. *Freud and Women.* New York: Frederick Ungar Publishing Co., 1981.

Freud, Anna. *Introduction to Psychoanalysis, Lectures for Child Analysts and Teachers 1922–1935. The Writings of Anna Freud,* Vol. 1. New York: International Universities Press, 1973.

———. *Infants Without Families. Reports on the Hampstead Nurseries. Writings,* Vol. 3. New York: International Universities Press, 1973.

Freud, Ernst; Freud, Lucie; and Grubrich-Simitis, Ilse (eds.). *Sigmund Freud: His Life in Pictures and Words.* New York: Harcourt Brace Jovanovich, [1974] 1978.

Freud, Sigmund. *The Interpretation of Dreams. The Standard Edition of the Complete Psychological Works of Sigmund Freud,* ed. James Strachey, 4 and 5. London: Hogarth Press [1900].

———. *Studies on Hysteria. Standard Edition,* 2 [1895].

———. *Three Essays on the Theory of Sexuality. Standard Edition,* 5 [1905].

———. "The Disposition to Obsessional Neurosis: A Contribution to the Problem of Choice of Neurosis." *Standard Edition,* 12 [1913].

———. "On the History of the Psycho-Analytical Movement." *Standard Edition,* 14 [1914].

———. *Beyond the Pleasure Principle. Standard Edition,* 18 [1920].

———. *The Ego and the Id. Standard Edition,* 19 [1923].

———. *Inhibitions, Symptoms and Anxieties. Standard Edition,* 20 [1926].

———. *The Future of an Illusion. Standard Edition,* 21 [1927].

———. *Civilization and Its Discontents. Standard Edition,* 21 [1930].

———. *Moses and Monotheism: Three Essays. Standard Edition,* 23 [1937–39].

———. *An Outline of Psychoanalysis. Standard Edition,* 23 [1940].

Gardiner, Muriel. *Code Name Mary.* New Haven: Yale University Press, 1983.

Gay, Peter. *Education of the Senses. The Bourgeoise Experience, Vol. 1.* New York: Oxford University Press, 1984.

———. *Freud: A Life for Our Time.* New York: W. W. Norton, 1988.

Gifford, George E., Jr. (ed.). *Psychoanalysis, Psychotherapy and the New England Medical Scene 1894–1944.* New York: Science History, 1970.

Gilder, Rosamond (ed.). *Letters of Richard Watson Gilder.* Boston: Houghton Mifflin, 1916.

Gillon, Edmund V., and Watson, Edward B. *New York Then and Now.* New York: Dover, 1976.

Glaser, Milton, and Weymouth, Lally. *America in 1876: The Way We Were.* New York: Vintage, 1976.

Gody, Lou (ed.). *The W.P.A. Guide to New York.* New York: Pantheon Books, [1939] 1982.

Gosse, Edmund. *Portraits and Sketches.* London: W. E. Heinemann, 1912.

Grosskurth, Phyllis. *Melanie Klein: Her World and Her Work.* New York: Knopf, 1986.

Grunfeld, Frederick V. *Vienna.* New York: Newsweek, 1981.

Heller, John. *Memoirs of a Reluctant Capitalist.* New York: Abaris Books, 1983.

Holder, Alex (ed.). *Bulletin of the Hampstead Clinic,* Vol. 3, Part 2. London: Hampstead Child-Therapy Clinic, 1980.

———. *Bulletin of the Hampstead Clinic,* Vol. 6, Part 1. London: Hampstead Child-Therapy Clinic, 1983.

Howat, John K. *The Hudson River and Its Painters.* New York: Penguin, 1978.

Howe, Helen Huntington. *The Gentle Americans, 1864–1960. Biography of a Breed.* New York: Harper & Row, 1965.

Huntington, David C. *The Landscapes of Frederic Edwin Church: Vision of an American Era.* New York: George Braziller, 1966.

Jones, Ernest. *The Life and Work of Sigmund Freud,* in 3 volumes. New York: Basic Books, 1957.

Kagan, Donald; Ozment, Steven; and Turner, Frank M. (eds.). *The Western Heritage Since 1648.* New York: Macmillan, 1979.

King, Moses. *King's 1893 Handbook of New York.* New York: B. Blom, [1893] 1972.

Koch, Robert. *Louis C. Tiffany: Rebel in Glass.* New York: Crown, 1964.

———. *Louis C. Tiffany's Glass-Bronzes-Lamps: A Complete Collector's Guide.* New York: Crown, 1971.

———. *Louis C. Tiffany's Art Glass.* New York: Crown, 1977.

Kouwenhoven, John A. *The Columbia Historical Portrait of New York.* New York: Harper & Row, 1953.

Lewis, Arnold; McQuillan, Steven; and Turner, James. *The Opulent Interiors of the Gilded Age.* New York: Dover, 1987.

Lewis, W.B. *Edith Wharton: A Biography.* New York: Harper & Row, 1975.

Lieberman, James E. *Act of Will: The Life and Work of Otto Rank.* New York: Free Press, 1985.

McCabe, James D., Jr. *New York by Gaslight.* New York: Greenwich House, [1882] 1984.

McKean, Hugh F. *The "Lost" Treasures of Louis Comfort Tiffany.* Garden City, N. Y.: Doubleday, 1980.

Malcolm, Janet. *Psychoanalysis: The Impossible Profession.* New York: Vintage, [1980] 1982.

———. *In the Freud Archives.* New York: Knopf, 1984.

Manners, William. *Patience and Fortitude: Fiorello La Guardia.* New York: Harcourt Brace Jovanovich, 1976.

Marboe, Ernst. *The Book of Austria.* Vienna: Osterreichische Staatsdruckerei, 1985.

Mosley, Leonard. *The Battle of Britain.* Alexandria, Va.: Time-Life, 1977.

Neustadt, Egon. *The Lamps of Tiffany.* New York: Fairfield Press, 1970.

O'Neil, John P. (ed.). *In Pursuit of Beauty: Americans and the Aesthetic Movement.* New York: Metropolitan Museum of Art and Rizzoli International Publishers, 1986.

Paul, Tessa. *The Art of Louis Comfort Tiffany.* New York: Exeter Books, 1987.

Peters, H.P. *My Sister, My Spouse: A Biography of Lou Andreas-Salomé.* New York: W.W. Norton, 1974.

Peters, Uwe Henrik. *Anna Freud: A Life Dedicated to Children.* New York: Schocken Books, 1985.

Purtell, Joseph. *The Tiffany Touch.* New York: Random House, 1971.

Roazen, Paul. *Helene Deutsch: A Psychoanalyst's Life.* Garden City, N. Y.: Anchor Books, 1985.

Rose, Phyllis. *Parallel Lives: Five Victorian Marriages.* New York: Knopf, 1983.

Rosenfeld, Eva. "Memoirs" (unpublished, 1973).

Rossi, Alice S. (ed.). *The Feminists Papers from Adams to de Beauvoir.* New York: Columbia University Press, 1973.

Salber, Wilhelm. *Anna Freud.* Hamburg: Rowohlt, 1985.

Schorske, Carl. *Fin-de-Siècle Vienna: Politics and Culture.* New York: Vintage Books, [1961] 1981.

Schur, Max. *Freud: Living and Dying.* New York: International Universities Press, 1972.

Silver, Nathan. *Lost New York.* Boston: Houghton Mifflin, 1967.

Smith, Page. *The Rise of Industrial America,* Vol. VI. New York: McGraw-Hill, 1984.

Speenburgh, Gertrude. *The Arts of the Tiffanys.* Chicago: Lightner, 1956.

Sterba, Richard. *Reminiscences of a Viennese Psychoanalyst.* Detroit: Wayne State University Press, 1982.

Sulloway, Frank J. *Freud: Biologist of the Mind.* New York: Basic Books, 1979.

Terry, Ellen. *Ellen Terry's Memoirs.* New York: Benjamin Bloom, [1908] 1969.

Tiffany, Louis Comfort. "American Art Supreme in Colored Glass." *The Forum,* Vol. 15, 1893.

———. "Brittany Diary" (unpublished, 1907).

———. "The Gospel of Good Taste." *Country Life in America,* Vol. 14, No. 2, 1910.

———. "The Tasteful Use of Light and Color in Artificial Illumination." *Scientific American,* Vol. 104, 1911.

———. "What Is the Quest of Beauty?" *The International Studio,* Vol. 58, 1916.

———. "Color and Its Kinship to Sound." *The Art World,* Vol. 2, 1917.

———. "The Quest of Beauty." *Harper's Bazaar,* December 1917.

———. "The Dream Garden." Philadelphia: Curtis Publishing Company, 1915.

———. "Louis Comfort Tiffany: The Paintings." New York: catalog of New York University exhibition, 1979.

Varnedoe, Kirk. *Vienna 1900 Art, Architecture & Design.* New York: Museum of Modern Art, 1986.

Von Schuschnigg, Kurt. *The Brutal Takeover: The Austrian Chancellor's Account of the Anschluss of Austria by Hitler.* New York: Atheneum, 1971.

Vos, Frank. "La Guardia and Burlingham: a Study of Political Friendship and Personal Influence" (master's thesis, 1983).

Weinberg, H. Barbara. *The Decorative Work of John La Farge.* New York: Garland, 1977.

Weisberg, Gabriel P. *Art Nouveau Bing: Paris Style 1900.* New York: Harry N. Abrams, 1986.

Wheeler, Candace. *Yesterdays in a Busy Life.* New York: Harper & Brothers, 1918.

Wilkinson, Burke. *Uncommon Clay: The Life and Work of Augustus Saint Gaudens.* New York: Harcourt Brace Jovanovich, 1985.

Wilson, Angus. *The Strange Ride of Rudyard Kipling.* Middlesex, England: Penguin, 1977.

Wilson, Richard Guy (ed.). *The American Rennaissance 1876–1917.* New York: Brooklyn Museum, 1979.

Wolfe, Gerard R. *New York: A Guide to the Metropolis.* New York: McGraw-Hill, 1975.

Young, Dorothy Weir. *The Life and Letters of J. Alden Weir.* New York: Da Capo Press, [1960] 1971.

Young-Breuhl, Elizabeth. *Anna Freud: A Biography.* New York: Summit Books, 1988.

INTERVIEWS

Bernays, Edward, Cambridge, Mass., July 16, 1983.

Binger, Clarinda Garrison, Little Compton, R. I., August 7, 1983.

Bingham, Alfred M., New York City, May 1983; Salem, Conn., August 31, 1983.

Bingham, Mitchell, New York City, August 1983.

Blos, Peter, New York City, April 20 and June 6, 1983.

Bourne, Charles, phone interview, July 20, 1988.

Burlingham, Charles, Jr., Cambridge, Mass., May 1 and July 27, 1983.

Burlingham, Cora Weir, New York City, March and April 14, 1983.

Burlingham, Dorothy Tiffany, London, June 4, 1978 (conducted and taped by Rodman and Mary Ellen Gilder), July 1978, October 1979.

Colonna, Alice M., phone interview, May 1983; New York City, May 14, 1983.

Dann, Gertrude, London, June 22 and 23 and (with Sophie Dann, West Hoathly, Sussex) 24, 1983.

de Forest, Kellam, phone interview, February 18, 1984.

Edmondson, Rosamond Taylor, Cornish, N. H., July 25, 1983.

Erikson, Erik and Joan, Stockbridge, Mass., July 31, 1983.

Freud, W. Ernest, London, June 21, 1983.

Gilder, Rodman and Mary Ellen, Scarsdale, N. Y., March 1983 and May 6, 1984; New York City, March 17, 1983.

Goldschmidt, Margot, New York City, June 2, 1983; phone interview, June 1983.

Gurewich, Marinka, New York City, January 28 and February 25, 1984.

Hawes, Rosilla Hornblower, Washington, D.C., May 7, 1983.

Heller, John, Scarborough, N. Y., February 24, 1985.

Hellmann, Ilse, London, June 22, 1983.

Kennan, George and Annelisa, Princeton, N. J., May 19, 1983.

Kennedy, Hansi, London, June 21, 1983.

Lord, Comfort Parker, New York City, March and April 24, 1983.

McKean, Hugh F., New York City, May 1983.

Miller, Helena Gilder, Montclair, N. J., August 13, 1983; New York City, November 7, 1983.

Molumphy, Henry, phone interview, July 20, 1988.

Nixon, Elliot, New York City, March 13, 1984.

Nunberg, Margarethe Rie, New York City, January 23, 1984.

Palitz, Lillian Nassau, New York City, May 3, 1983.

Platt, Louise Lusk, Syosset, N.Y., March 1983; January 19 and 20, 1985; and April 19, 1986.

Ross, Victor, London, June 26, 1983.

Ryan, James, Hudson, N. Y., October 21, 1984.

Ryan, Joseph, phone interview, 1985.

Schmiderer, Simon, phone interview, March 19, 1985.

Schmiderer, Timothy and Nancy, New York City, March 1983.

Schuld, Emilie, Staten Island, N. Y., May 11, 1983.

Shedd, Elizabeth Ely, phone interview, 1986.

Sheldrick, Rigmor Sorensen, Princeton, N. J., May 4, 1983; 1985.

Smith, Beatrice Stewart, Concord, Mass., August 5, 1983.

Stross, Josephine, London, June 23, 1983.

Taves, Judy de Forest, Marlborough, N. H., July 26, 1983.

Valenstein, Katrina Burlingham, Cambridge, Mass., April 29 and 30, May 1, and July 14, 1983; January 30 and 31, 1985; phone interviews July 13, 1983, May 20 and 31, 1988.

Voss, Frank, New York City, August 26, 1983.

Wolff, Anna Kris, phone interview, September 1983.

CORRESPONDENTS

Bingham, Alfred M.

Buffum, William P.

Burlingham, Michael

Colonna, Alice B.

Dann, Gertrude

Day, Holly

Edwards, Margaret F.

Fleischmann, Trude

Freud, W. Ernest

Gardiner, Muriel M.

Goldschmidt, Margot

Hawes, Rosilla Hornblower

Heller, Peter

Katan, Anny

Kennan, George F.

Kennedy, Hansi

Kitt, Annette

Kris, Anton O.

LaFarge, Henry A.

Lampl-de Groot, Jeanne

Maenchen, Anna

McKean, Hugh F.

Michaels, Barbara L.

Miller, Helena Gilder

Platt, Louise Lusk

Ross, Victor

Schmiderer, Simon

Silberman, Sara Lee

Smith, Beatrice Stewart

Valenstein, Katrina Burlingham

Index